HARDPRESS.NET
HOME OF HARD-TO-FIND BOOKS

On Nature and Grace. Philosophical Introduction
by William George Ward

2652 e. 40

ON

NATURE AND GRACE.

Book I.

Philosophical Introduction.

BY

WILLIAM GEORGE WARD, D.Ph.

LATE LECTURER IN DOGMATIC THEOLOGY, AT ST. EDMUND'S SEMINARY, HERTS.

Printed for Private Circulation.

1859.

LONDON:
Printed by G. BARCLAY, Castle St. Leicester Sq.

PREFACE.

I AM hoping, if God enables me, to publish a theological treatise, on 'Nature and Grace;' founded on part of my course at St. Edmund's. The general subjects, to be included in this treatise, will be sufficiently understood by a prospectus of the Contents.

Book   I. Philosophical Introduction.
Book II. Theological Prolegomena.
Book III. On Human Action.
Book IV. On Divine Grace.
Book V. On God's Providence and Predestination.

Having now concluded the First Book, I have thought it well at once to have it printed, and to circulate privately a limited number of copies. One principal reason for my doing this, has been the following :—

No one can be surprised, that I feel most deeply the anxious and momentous character of the work which I have undertaken, and the great danger of falling into serious mistakes in its accomplishment. I greatly desire therefore, as I proceed, to obtain the judgment of any theological friends, who may be kind enough to take the trouble of perusing it. Such criticisms as I receive, will be at all events most useful as guides in the future volumes ; as shewing me deficiencies which require to be filled up, and awkwardnesses, whether of style, expression, or arrangement, on which I may hope to improve. But it is abundantly possible of course, that I may be also shewn such serious faults, as may induce me to cancel whole sheets, or even re-write the whole.

I should have felt such anxiety as I have described, in undertaking any theological treatise. But surely there is no part of Theology, on which it is so easy to fall into serious mistakes,—in which it is so difficult to preserve faithfully the true mean,—as in that, with which my succeeding volumes are to be occupied. Let one important instance of this be considered, as a sample of several. On the one hand there is the danger, lest theological doctrine should be so represented, as unduly to alarm those, who sincerely desire and pray for their own sanctification, but who are conscious of indefinite weakness and inconsistency. On the other hand there is the danger, lest any thing should be even accidentally stated, which might confirm in their blind and presumptuous confidence those most misguided men, who have no practical fear in regard to their eternal lot, while yet they are making no efforts at all to discover their latent faults; to remove their affections from objects of this earth; to measure worldly events by the Divine standard; to grow in personal love of their God and Saviour. One hardly knows, which of these two extremes is the more mischievous and dangerous; and it is most difficult, consistently to avoid giving some countenance to one or to the other.

Such being my dread of the task before me, I might well have shrunk from attempting it. And certainly indeed I *should* have so shrunk, had not circumstances of various kinds led me strongly to think, that it is a work which God desires at my hands. In this opinion I have been confirmed, by more than one clerical friend, thoroughly conversant with the state of the case, and on whose judgment I have the greatest reliance.

This belief indeed could afford me no kind of defence, for not taking all reasonable pains to ensure correctness. But if I *do* take such pains, then surely it is a belief of comforting and encouraging tendency. I may reasonably in that case indulge the humble hope, that a work, thus undertaken, may receive God's guidance during its progress, and His blessing as to its results. That my intention, in attempting it, is on the whole pure, I really believe. Well am I aware of the various unworthy motives, which escape one's notice even when most powerfully influential. But I can truly say, that so far as by examination I am able to discover, my main desire in the matter, is to do that which God wishes of me, and to promote His Glory (if indeed I were enabled to promote it) in the sanctification and salvation of souls.

It will be readily understood then, how truly grateful I shall be for any suggestions, in regard to the future conduct of the work; and still more, for any masses or prayers, which kind friends may be disposed to offer in its behalf.

I have retained the form of Lectures throughout, and have addressed my various remarks to an imaginary audience of pupils. One chief reason for this, has been my desire of thereby rendering my style less dull and heavy than it naturally is. The same desire has led me, in various places, to be much more frequent in the use of Italics, than is (I fear) really conducive to the very purpose at which I aimed.

I beg my readers particularly to observe the Appendix to Chapter I., printed at the end of the volume. The propositions, for which I argue in the First Chapter, cannot be understood as I mean them, except by being taken in connection with what I have said in the Appendix.

Northwood Park, Cowes,
Rosary Sunday, Oct. 2, 1859.

TABLE OF CONTENTS TO BOOK I.

CHAPTER I.

ON THE PRINCIPLES OF MORALITY.

Section I.

On Intuitions and the Principle of Certitude.

Section II.

On the Idea of Moral Obligation.

Section III.

On the Relation between God and Moral Obligation.

Section IV.

Catholic Authority on the Statements of the Preceding Section.

Section V.

On the Idea of Moral Worthiness.

Section VI.

On the Extent of the Natural Rule.

Section VII.

On God's Power of Interference with the Natural Rule.

CONTENTS.

SECTION IV.

On Certain other Phenomena of the Will.

SECTION V.

On the Adaptation of our Nature to Virtue.

* By some mistake nn. 149–151 have been *repeated.*

Section VI.

On the Marks of Moral Degradation in our Nature as it now exists.

Section VII.

On Certain Philosophical Terms.

CHAPTER III.

ON SELF-CHARITY.

SECTION I.

On Man's Desire of Felicity.

SECTION II.

On the Claims of Self-Charity.

CHAPTER IV.

ON THE VARIOUS KINDS OF CERTAINTY AND IMPOSSIBILITY.

APPENDIX TO CHAPTER I.

On the Relation between God and Necessary Truth.

BOOK FIRST.

PHILOSOPHICAL INTRODUCTION.

B

BOOK FIRST.

PHILOSOPHICAL INTRODUCTION.

I AM not professing, as you are well aware, to carry you through a regular course of Philosophy. I only wish to give you a full and complete grasp of certain great philosophical principles, which are essential to our subsequent theological course. We are not therefore to be considered here as occupied with Philosophy for its own sake, but simply as an introduction to Dogmatic Theology.

We are met at starting by a great disadvantage, under which many other scientific courses also lie. It would be greatly desirable if the earlier part of our work could be rendered comparatively clear and easy; for by such means an interest might be excited in the study, and an ardour be stimulated for its prosecution, which would greatly animate and encourage you in encountering any unavoidable difficulty which meets us in our path. It happens however most unfortunately, that the chief difficulties occur at the very outset; they occur before you have had any opportunity of tasting the sweets (as I may say) of theological science, and of appreciating, even in a moderate degree, those most beautiful and attractive Objects, which it opens to our contemplation. For we must begin by the establishment of abstract principles; and to master abstract principles, is necessarily among the most laborious and ungrateful tasks in the world. I can only earnestly exhort you, to take that on faith which you have as yet had no means of knowing by experience. I can only exhort you to believe, on the word of others, that whatever amount of discouraging and repulsive labour may meet you at the outset, the prize for which that labour is to be encountered — I mean the mastery of dogmatical truth — is so great and precious a treasure, as most abundantly and superabundantly to recompense you for all preliminary toil.

It will cost you then, I think, much more trouble to master the first chapter of the first book, than to apprehend any subsequent part of the entire study; and it will give you much more trouble to master the first section of that chapter, than any subsequent portion. In regard indeed to the first section, I beg you to pass and repass carefully in your mind the various statements therein contained, so as fully and familiarly to grasp them, before you attempt any study of the subsequent sections.

On my part, I will do all in my power to save you unnecessary trouble; and I will state what I have to say in the clearest and most intelligible language I can command. I heartily wish I had more power than (I know) belongs to me, of putting abstruse and recondite matter into an easy and familiar shape.

CHAPTER I.

ON THE PRINCIPLES OF MORALITY.

SECTION I.

On Intuitions and on the Principle of Certitude.

1. I MUST begin by begging your particular attention
to a distinction, which seems to me vitally important,
between two different classes of intellectual acts. I
will call them respectively *Judgments of Experience*
and *Judgments of Intuition.* And now to explain the
meaning of this distinction.

I form the judgment, that I am this moment suffering the sensation which we call cold. This is simply
a judgment of *experience;* I reflect on the fact, that I
am at this moment affected in a certain way; the
judgment begins there and ends there. Again, I form
the judgment, that I am suffering under that which we
call low spirits; or that I am out of humour; or the
like. These are all judgments of experience; the
mind's reflection on its own present consciousness.

But now suppose I *remember*, that half an hour
ago I was walking in the garden. Here first there is,
or may be, a judgment of experience; I reflect on the
impression which is now in my mind, that the past fact
was so. But there is another judgment of far greater
importance, which I also confidently form, and which we
may call a judgment of *intuition* or an *intuitive judgment.* I judge confidently indeed, that I have *the present
impression* of that past fact having taken place; but
this is not all. I confidently form another judgment

also : viz. that the fact *actually did* take place ; that I actually *was* walking in the garden at that time. Moreover I regard this truth, not as known to me by way of *consequence* or *deduction* from other truths ; but as known to me *immediately* and *in itself.* Such a judgment we may call a judgment of intuition : a judgment, which on the one hand is quite distinct from the mind's reflection on its own present consciousness ; and which on the other hand is quite distinct also, from a judgment arising in my mind in the way of *consequence* from *other* judgments.

As our second illustration of an intuitive judgment, let us take our belief in the validity of reasoning. A well-instructed thinker follows some chain of demonstrative reasoning, and forms the following judgment without the faintest shadow of doubt : ' if the various premisses are true, the various conclusions here deduced from those premisses are most certainly true also.' He does not elicit merely a judgment of *experience :* ' I am *impressed with the idea* that these conclusions are true, if the premisses are true ; I am so constituted that I *cannot help thinking* this to be so.' No ; he forms also an *intuitive* judgment. It is not merely ' I *cannot help feeling* as if the conclusions followed from the premisses,' but ' I see for certain that they *do* so follow.'

As a third instance, let us take mathematical axioms. ' A rectilineal figure of three sides has neither more nor less than three angles.' So soon as I understand the meaning of this proposition — so soon as I can produce in my mind the representation of a three-sided figure and have a moment's leisure for reflection — I see at once that this proposition is quite certainly true. I never think of confining myself to a *subjective* judgment ; ' I am so *constituted* that I cannot *help thinking* the proposition is true :' no ; the judgment which I form is *objective;* ' the proposition *is* true.'

As a fourth instance, let us take our belief in an external world. The great mass of men never think of confining themselves to a mere judgment of experience on this matter; ' I am impressed *as if* there were external objects:' they always form an intuitive judgment, ' there *are* external objects.' It is well known that certain philosophers have existed, who deny that there are *grounds* for any such judgment. But it is no part of our business here to consider the arguments of these philosophers; for we are not here considering how far these intuitive judgments are *true*, but explaining what is *meant* by an intuitive judgment. I say then, the great mass of men (rightly or wrongly) do, as a matter of fact, elicit the intuitive judgment, ' external objects exist.'

Such then are intuitive judgments, in the sense which we shall consistently assign to that word. They are judgments, which I do not hold as being inferred in any way from other judgments, but as *immediately* evident. Yet on the other hand they are totally distinct from what we call judgments of *experience;* or, in other words, from the various reflections made by my mind upon its present consciousness.

2. We must carefully distinguish however these intuitive judgments, from another numerous class which on the surface resemble them. There are very many judgments, which *appear* to be formed immediately; in forming which, the mind does not *reflect* on any premisses from which they result; but which nevertheless *are* in fact formed as conclusions from premisses. For instance. An experienced farmer goes into a corn-field, and says to himself on looking around ' in what excellent condition and how abundant is this corn!' Yet this judgment, though so spontaneously formed, is in fact not elicited as immediately evident, but as a conclusion resulting in part from various judgments which already existed in his mind. These judgments will be such as the following.

(1.) ' I remember a number of fields, in which the corn was in very good condition.'

(2.) ' These fields all agreed in certain characteristic marks.'

(3.) 'If certain marks prove one corn-field to be in a good state, marks precisely similar must prove another to be so.'

To these judgments, with which he was already familiar, one intuitive judgment is added, which he now elicits for the first time. 'There are *in this field* the same marks, which everywhere characterise a good condition of corn.'

All these various propositions go to make up the grounds, for his opinion on the corn-field before him. Most of them indeed are so familiar to him, and they are all formed so readily and inevitably, that he does not *reflect* upon them at all, and is inclined to fancy his judgment to be *immediate*. Yet it is manifest on a moment's consideration, that unless *every one* of the preceding propositions had passed through his mind, he could not by possibility have formed the original judgment which he did form. That judgment was in fact the conclusion resulting from a certain chain of syllogisms; and those syllogisms contained these respective propositions among the premisses on which they rested. Let his belief be shaken in any one of these propositions, his judgment on the healthy state of the corn-field before him must at once fall to the ground.

On the other hand take a really intuitive judgment: —for instance, 'half a minute ago I was standing just where I now am.' It is plain that I hold this, not as the conclusion of any syllogism whatever;—not as depending on *any* proposition, whether reflected on or not;—but in the strictest sense as an immediate conviction.

If our direct theme were Philosophy, it might be desirable to proceed at greater length, in illustrating this distinction; but under our present circumstances, thus to have indicated it will suffice.

I shall take leave to use the verb 'intue,' as corresponding to the substantive 'intuition;' an usage which will be often convenient, for expressing what we may wish to state. And I shall also use the word 'inferential judgment,' to express a judgment which we hold, not immediately, but as a conclusion from premisses which were previously in the mind.

3. When we have sufficiently mastered the distinction between the two kinds of immediate judgments—judgments of experience and judgments of intuition—we shall be able to understand wherein *philosophical scepticism* precisely consists. The thesis which expresses it is this :—' No intuitive judgment can reasonably be held with any confidence.'

A thinker of this class may be imagined, with a certain superficial consistency, to argue as follows :—' There ' can be no possible ground for holding *any* intuitive ' judgments ; and the mass of men, in confidently holding ' them, are simply unreasonable. Take for instance the ' case of memory—what imaginable reason can I have for ' supposing, that those various impressions, which I call ' acts of remembrance, correspond to real facts of my ' past history? How can I know, for instance, that I ' have not been formed by some malignant being, who ' has given me mendacious faculties for the very pur- ' pose of deceiving me? How can I know but that ' this being makes me *fancy* I was reading, *e. g.* or ' walking half an hour ago, when I was really in another ' planet? But this indeed is only one, out of a hundred ' suppositions which might be made ; each one at vari- ' ance with the supposition, that my memory can be ' trusted. Surely I can have no more real ground ' for believing, that I have actually *gone through* those ' various events of which my memory presents the ' *impression*, than a madman has for imagining himself ' to be Cæsar or Alexander the Great.'

4. And the apparent strength of the sceptic's ground will be still more obvious, if we consider the answers which he may make to all the various arguments attempted in refutation. This one unanswerable reply indeed he may make against every one ; viz. that it *is* an argument. How do we believe that reasoning, in its most rigorous form, is really valid? Evidently by an intuitive judgment. ' What can be more illogical,' then

the sceptic may proceed, 'than your whole procedure?
'You profess to *prove* that intuitive judgments may be
'trusted; and in every step of your proof you *assume*
'that they may be trusted: for the very profession of
'*argument* implies that precise assumption.'

So much on the mere fact that arguments are used
against him at all.   Let us next see the answers which
are ready to his hand, in reply to the particular arguments which have been chiefly attempted.   Thus Des
Cartes puts the very hypothesis I have made, that we
may have been formed by some malignant being, who
has implanted mendacious faculties for the very purpose of deceiving us.   Des Cartes meets this difficulty,
by setting himself to prove the existence of a Holy
God; and from this, as from a fundamental truth, he
deduces the proposition, that we may most reasonably
trust those faculties which He has implanted.*   But how
obvious is the sceptic's reply.   'Either you believe in
'God's existence by an immediate judgment of intui-

---

* My authority for this statement is Reid.   His whole passage is worth
considering.
  'Des Cartes certainly made a false step in this matter; for having
suggested this doubt among others—that, whatever evidence he might
have from his consciousness, his senses, his memory, or his reason, yet
possibly some *malignant being had given him those faculties on purpose to
impose upon him;* and, therefore, that they are not to be trusted without
a proper voucher;—to remove this doubt, he endeavours to prove the being
of a Deity who is no deceiver; whence he concludes, that the faculties He
had given him are true and worthy to be trusted.
  'It is strange that so acute a reasoner did not perceive that in this
reasoning there is evidently a begging of the question.
  'For, if our faculties be fallacious, why may they not deceive us in this
reasoning as well as in others? and, if they are to be trusted in this
instance without a voucher, why not in others?
  'Every kind of reasoning for the veracity of our faculties, amounts to
no more than taking their own testimony for their veracity; and this we
must do implicitly, until God gives us new faculties to sit in judgment upon
the old.   And the reason why Des Cartes satisfied himself with so weak an
argument for the truth of his faculties, most probably was, that he never
seriously doubted of it.
  '*If any truth can be said to be prior to all others in the order of nature,
this seems to have the best claim;* because, in every instance of assent,
whether upon intuitive, demonstrative, or probable evidence, the truth of
our faculties is taken for granted, and is, as it were, one of the premisses on
which our assent is grounded.   How then come we to be assured of this
fundamental truth, on which all others rest?   Perhaps evidence, as in many
other respects it resembles light, so in this also—that, as light, which is

' tion, or you believe in it as in a truth deduced from
' a chain of reasoning. In the former case, you take
' for granted the trustworthiness of that intuitive
' judgment; in the latter case you take for granted
' the validity of reasoning. In either case you *assume*
' the precise proposition, which you undertake to
' prove; viz. that there *are* trustworthy judgments of
' intuition.'

Another argument against the sceptic was devised
by the unhappy La Mennais. He says: 'We may
' derive confidence in various intuitive judgments, from
' the fact that all mankind agree, and cannot but agree,
' in forming them.'

But the sceptic's reply here might be in appearance
no less triumphant. 'Unless you *assume* that certain
' intuitive judgments may be trusted, you can have no
' knowledge whatever of the fact that men *do* agree in
' trusting them; you cannot understand the very mean-
' ing of a single sentence which is uttered by your fel-

the discoverer of all visible objects, discovers itself at the same time, so
evidence, which is the voucher of all truth, vouches for itself at the same
time.

'This however is certain, that such is the constitution of the human
mind, that evidence, discerned by us, forces a corresponding degree of assent.
And a man who perfectly understood a just syllogism, without believing
that the conclusion follows from the premisses, would be a greater monster
than a man born without hands or feet.

'We are born under a necessity of trusting to our reasoning and judging
powers; and a real belief of their being fallacious cannot be maintained for
any considerable time by the greatest sceptic, because it is doing violence
to our constitution. It is like a man's walking upon his hands: a feat which
some men, upon occasion, can exhibit; but no man ever made a long
journey in this manner. Cease to admire his dexterity, and he will, like
other men, betake himself to his legs.'—Reid's *Inquiry*, Essay vi. Chap. v.

Gioberti quotes the following passage from Jouffroy, which may also be
cited in illustration.

'Quand une faculté vient à s'appliquer et à nous donner la notion qui
lui est propre, il est évident que nous ne croyons et ne pouvons croire à la
vérité de cette notion, qu'à une première condition; c'est que *nous avons
foi à la véracité native de cette faculté*. . . . . car pour peu que nous en
doutions, il n'y a *plus de vérité, plus de croyance, possible* pour nous. Et
cependant rien ne prouve, rien ne peut prouver, cette véracité native de
nos facultés. . . . . Donc, messieurs, le principe de toute certitude et de
toute croyance est d'abord un acte de *foi aveugle* en la véracité naturelle
de nos facultés.'—*Cours de Droit Naturel.*

I find this passage quoted in M. Alary's French translation of Gioberti's
"Introduction to Philosophy," vol. ii. note 33, p. 362.

' low-men; nay you cannot so much as apprehend its
' external bodily sound.   I say, you cannot so much as
' apprehend the very sound, of which a spoken sen-
' tence is composed, unless you *assume* that certain
' intuitive judgments may be trusted.   You are hear-
' ing at this moment the *last* word of the sentence ; but
' how do you know the *other words* of which it con-
' sists ?   Simply by *remembering* them : either then
' you must trust that kind of intuitive judgment which
' we call an act of memory, or else you cannot appre-
' hend the very sound of which a spoken sentence is
' composed.   And as for the *meaning* of such sentence,
' it is still more manifest that various exercises of me-
' mory are requisite, in order that you may ever so
' distantly guess it.'

5. It is very curious to see how completely a sceptic
overreaches himself, if he set himself thus frankly and
energetically to carry out his principles.   For the
sceptic's argument, above stated, lands us in this conclusion ;—that we cannot begin listening to his objections, we cannot so much as know that there *is* such
a doctrine as scepticism in the world, until we have
first committed ourselves to its denial; until we have
taken for granted that precise thesis, which scepticism
rejects.   Unless I can trust my memory, I don't even
know what the sceptic *says*, much less what he *means*.
But if I *can* trust my memory, then certain intuitive
judgments may with reason be confidently formed ;
which is the very point at issue between him and
myself.

Here too we see the truth of what sound philosophers continually say ; viz. that to attempt *argument*
against scepticism is a simple absurdity.   I cannot know
what the sceptic says, until I have trusted my memory ;
i.e. have trusted *one* intuitive judgment : and I cannot
argue against what he says, until I have trusted *another*.
For to *argue* implies a *belief in the validity of the
reasoning process;* and what can such a belief possibly
be, except an intuitive judgment?

Yet let this be most carefully observed.   While on

the one hand it is a simple absurdity to *argue* against scepticism, on the other hand to *hold* sceptical opinions in their full consistency, is not less than physically impossible. As a first proof of this take the following. I have just said, that until we have committed ourselves to anti-sceptical opinions, we cannot even listen to the arguments brought against them. The converse is equally true. The sceptic complains that men in general most unreasonably trust their intuitive judgments. Now consider this most noteworthy circumstance: he cannot know, or have the most distant idea, that the fact *is* so, until *he* has himself followed their example; until *he* has trusted at least one intuitive judgment of his own, viz. the soundness of his memory. Unless he first trust his memory, he cannot so much as guess at the opinion of his fellow-men on any single particular (see n. 4). Now, I ask, has he really the *physical power* of doubting in many cases what their opinion is?

For another instance, the story told of Pyrrho is well known. He was lecturing to his disciples, it is said, on the inability of our faculties to apprehend truth; when a waggon suddenly came rushing down the hill, and the sceptical philosopher was the first who took to flight. We may ask—had he so much as the *physical power* at that moment, *really* to distrust that faculty of memory, through which alone he had the means of so much as guessing, that he was in any danger at all? evidently not. So in like manner, let any one of us try to regard it as really doubtful whether he was doing a minute ago what his memory declared him to have been doing—let any one try to do this, and he will see readily the truth of my remark that the task is physically impossible. He can no more compel himself really to doubt that he was writing, or reading, or speaking to a friend, as the case may be,—in other words, he can no more prevent himself from holding a certain intuitive judgment with the most undoubting confidence,—than he can raise himself into the air and fly to the top of a tree.

6. Let us call the doctrine, contradictory to philosophical scepticism, by the name 'principle of certitude.' The principle of certitude then will be this proposition: 'there are certain intuitive judgments, which we may 'legitimately hold with confidence:' or in other words, '*our faculties, if rightly directed, are able to inform* '*us with absolute certainty of various truths external* '*to experience.*'

7. In regard to this principle of certitude, the considerations which we have gone through enable us to enunciate these two propositions.

Prop. I. If the principle of certitude were untrue, our knowledge would be less than that of the brutes; it would be strictly confined to the mind's reflection at each instant on its own existing consciousness. We could not compare *e. g.* our present consciousness with our past; for unless we hold the principle of certitude, we cannot even guess what our past consciousness has been. Much less, as is evident, could we even contemplate comparing our own consciousness with that of others.

Prop. II. It is difficult to imagine any principle resting on stronger grounds than this principle of certitude; since it is physically impossible (see end of n. 5) that any human being can consistently call it in question. When any one is found seriously to doubt whether he was doing a minute ago that which his memory testifies, then (and not till then) will there be found a human being, who consistently questions the principle of certitude.

8. It may plausibly then be objected, 'if all men 'thus by absolute necessity hold this principle, where 'is the importance of thus laboriously presenting and 'illustrating it?' I reply, that although no human being can *consistently* question it, many *philosophers* have questioned or denied it *partially and inconsistently*. And as the first instance of my statement, strangely enough I can cite one among the most eminent and most sober English philosophers of the present day — Mr. Mansel.

Take for instance the following passage from his " Prolegomena Logica :"—

" *It may be* indeed, that the conditions of possible thought correspond to conditions of possible being; that what is to us inconceivable is in itself non-existent. *But of this, from the nature of the case, it is impossible to have any evidence.* If man as a thinker is subject to necessary laws, he cannot examine the absolute validity of the laws themselves, except by assuming the whole question at issue; for such examination must itself be conducted in subordination to the same conditions. Whatever weakness, therefore, there may be in the object of criticism, the same must necessarily affect the critical process itself.

" *We may indeed believe, and ought to believe, that the powers which our Creator has bestowed upon us are not given as the instruments of deception.* We may believe, and ought to believe, that, intellectually no less than morally, the present life is a state of discipline and preparation for another; and that the portion of knowledge which our limited faculties are permitted to attain to here, may indeed, in the eyes of a higher Intelligence, be but partial truth, but cannot be absolute falsehood. But in believing thus, we *desert the evidence of Reason to rest on that of Faith; and of the principles on which Reason itself depends it is obviously impossible to have any other guarantee.*

" But such a faith, however well founded, has but a regulative and practical, not a speculative, application. It bids us rest content within the limits which have been assigned to us: it cannot enable us to overleap them, or to exalt to a more absolute character the conclusions obtained by finite thinkers concerning finite objects of thought. For the same condition, which disqualifies us from criticising the laws of thought, must also deprive us of the power of ascertaining how much of the results of those laws is true in itself, and how much *is relative and dependent upon the particular bodily or mental constitution of man during the present life.*"*

Mr. Mansel, in this passage, seems to make the three following statements.

1. Reason by itself can never give us the faintest means even of guessing, whether any of our intuitive judgments are true or false.

2. There is however an informant, wholly distinct from and independent of Reason, which we call *Faith.*

* The italics are *not* Mr. Mansel's.

3. This tells us, not indeed that any of our intuitive judgments are more than partially true, but that they cannot be absolutely and totally false.

Various propositions are implied in the above statements, which every Catholic philosopher must recognise as serious errors. It would lead us however too far to attack in detail those propositions; but I will make one remark, in accordance with the observations I have already put forth. I will apply then the above statements to the case of memory.

Mr. Mansel remembers distinctly at this moment, that a minute or so ago he was sitting at his desk where he is at present. His philosophy leads him however to hold that, unless he lived under a Divine Revelation, he could not guess ever so faintly whether he *were* in fact a minute ago so seated at his desk; or whether on the other hand he were occupied *e. g.* in constructing the Pyramids or visiting the man in the moon.* Since however he does enjoy the light of divine revelation, he knows, not indeed for certain that he *was* at his desk a minute ago, but that this belief of his cannot be absolutely and totally false.

I would ask Mr. Mansel, with most sincere respect and with great admiration of his many high philosophical

---

* "Une autre conséquence également juste" (from that doctrine of scepticism which the author is opposing), "est que nous n'avons *aucune certitude évidente de ce qu'hier il nous arriva on ne nous arriva pas;* et même si nous existions on si nous n'existions pas. Je crois bien être évidemment certain qu'hier j'étais au monde; mais c'est un jugement *qui peut se trouver sujet à erreur, selon les philosophes dont nous parlons.* Car, selon eux, je ne puis avoir d'évidence que par une perception intime qui est toujours actuelle; or, actuellement, j'ai bien *la perception du souvenir* de ce qui m'arriva hier; mais ce souvenir n'est qu'une *perception intime de ce que je pense présentement,* c'est-à-dire d'une pensée actuelle, laquelle n'est pas la même chose que ce qui se passa hier et qui n'est plus aujourd'hui. Par la même raison, je serai encore moins certain si je ne suis par en ce monde depuis deux ou trois mille ans, et si je n'ai point animé le corps d'un crocodile ou d'un moineau. Il est très-évident que je n'en ai aucune mémoire; mais tout cela s'est pu faire, *sans que je m'en souvienne actuellement;* comme il arrive effectivement que chacun de nous est demeuré plusieurs mois dans le sein de sa mère, sans en avoir conservé le moindre souvenir. Ce manque de mémoire n'est donc pas une certitude évidente, contre ce qu'on voudrait supposer de l'ancienneté de mon existence, et des situations différentes ou je me serais trouvé dans le système de la métempsychose."—Buffier, *Œuvres Philosophiques,* chap. iii. s. 20.

gifts—whether in this shape he could himself accept his own theory ?

It is commonly considered that Kant, whose disciple Mr. Mansel would to some extent profess himself to be, advocates the same sceptical notion. I have every reason, from authority, to believe that he does so ; but I cannot claim any such acquaintance with his works, as would enable me to answer the question confidently from my own knowledge.

I will take my second instance from a school of philosophy the most opposed to Mr. Mansel—the so-called philosophy of *experience:* a school of which perhaps Mr. Stuart Mill may be cited as the worthiest English representative. These philosophers claim as their special characteristic, that they build wholly upon *experience;* 'and this,' they proceed to say, 'is the only ' sure basis of philosophy : for once abandon the solid ' ground of experience, each man will at every turn ' mistake his own personal fancies and prepossessions ' for absolute truth.'

I would ask of these philosophers, do they mean by ' experience' the experience of the present moment, or do they include past experience also ? If they say the former, I reply it is obviously false that they *do* in any sense build their philosophy wholly or chiefly on experience. But if they answer (as they most certainly will) that they *do* include past experience as well as present, then again I deny their allegation, that they build their philosophy wholly on experience ; and I proceed thus to argue against them on behalf of my denial.

You make use of your own past experience—you make use of other men's experience—as part of the foundation on which you build. How can you even guess what your past experience has been ? By trusting your memory. But how do you prove that your memory can be trusted ? So far from this being provable by past experience, it must be *assumed* and *taken for granted,* before you can have any cognizance whatever of your past experience.

C

Moreover, from these facts of past and present experience, you deduce argumentative conclusions. In so doing, you *assume* the validity of the reasoning process. It cannot be even superficially or plausibly maintained, that *this* proposition is derivable from experience.

At all events then you are compelled to assume two propositions—and those of the most vital importance — on no ground of experience whatever; viz. that (1) your memory, and (2) also your reasoning faculty, may legitimately be trusted. In making these two tremendous assumptions, why are *you* not also exposed to that danger, which you would fain represent as exclusively besetting your opponents—the danger of mistaking your own personal fancies and ideas for absolute truth? You will reply perhaps, that you assume no more than all mankind necessarily assume. I will give one only of the many replies which might be made to that statement—and I answer thus. You assume these two propositions, before you know or can so much as guess that any other man living assumes them; for it is only by *means* of their assumption, that it is possible to know, or even so much as to guess, what other men's opinions are.

You cannot then rescue yourselves from the common lot of humanity; you can establish no difference of principle between yourselves and other philosophers; you, no less than they, must take certain intuitive judgments for granted. The difference is in no sense of principle, but wholly and solely of detail and of degree; viz. what is the *number* of those legitimate intuitions, or what the *test of their legitimacy*, which are the necessary foundation of all human knowledge.

9. This then brings us to the next matter which we have to consider. The principle of certitude is, as we have seen, the one key to any knowledge worthy of the name. But so soon as the philosophical edifice has been unlocked and entered, then the question which first meets us on the threshold concerns this very matter which we have just mentioned, *the test of legiti-*

mate intuitions.   All reasoning of course must be built upon premisses; and there must therefore of necessity be a certain number of primary premisses, which are known to us not by reasoning but by intuition.   The whole of our knowledge is obtained, and can be obtained, by no other process, than combining and building upon such primary premisses.   If then this be so, how vitally important is the task of distinguishing true intuitions from false!   For once suppose our foundation to be erroneous, then in proportion as we reason the more consistently, the more accurately, the more frankly and energetically, so much the more widely mistaken, and in all probability so much the more mischievous, will our conclusions become.   This all-important preliminary inquiry,—the mode of distinguishing true intuitions from false,—has met (I cannot but think) with very far less attention from philosophers than was its due.   The intellect, as Father Tapparelli incidentally remarks, has two main functions; the intuitive and ratiocinative :* but the former has surely been very far less methodically and systematically treated than the latter.

10. Here however, in order to prevent very probable misconception, I must make two explanatory and qualifying statements.

(1.) I am very far indeed from meaning to imply, that no one can form a legitimate intuition, unless he be himself prepared with some philosophical test to establish its legitimacy.   Far indeed otherwise.   The parallel case of inferential judgments will here precisely illustrate what I mean to convey.

There is no more common phenomenon in the world than the following.   A man of great natural shrewdness but uncultivated intellect, displays the greatest acuteness in deciding, what means will or will not be conducive to some end which he has greatly at heart.   His reasoning will be most sound from first to last ; yet not only he will be quite unable to give

* "La faculta intellettiva, *nelle due funzioni d'intuito e rasiocinio,*" &c-
—*Natural Diritto,* n. 32.

any philosophical test of its validity, but even so much as to state the various premisses on which he proceeds. Now who will be so wild as to maintain, that this man has really no valid *ground* for his conclusions ? that he is taking them up accidentally and at random, and is as likely to be wrong as to be right? No : we shall all recognise, that he is using that power of reasoning, which is one of the highest faculties implanted in his nature, and using it most healthily and legitimately ; nor shall we under ordinary circumstances have any wish at all, that he should draw out with any greater accuracy the process through which his mind has travelled. Yet on the other hand, if we had to do with a man of totally inaccurate mind, who is leading himself or others into serious mischief by his bad reasoning, we should act otherwise ; we *should* aim at persuading him to state methodically his various premisses, in order that he may see how ludicrously inadequate they are to his conclusions. And lastly, in the case of philosophical and systematic writers, of them we *do* most reasonably expect, not merely that they argue correctly, but that they put before us their premisses in sufficient detail ; and not only so, but be prepared also to vindicate the validity of those reasonings which they have built thereon.

The case of intuitions is in every respect similar to this. There are multitudes of men who elicit legitimate intuitions, who would be wholly unable to state any philosophical test which shall establish that legitimacy : yet it would be monstrous to say that such intuitions may not most reasonably be trusted. Again there are multitudes of men (other men or the same) who mistake this or that prejudice of their own for a legitimate intuition ; and in such instances it is most suitable to urge upon their notice, on philosophical grounds, the spuriousness of such a conviction ; the fact of its being utterly destitute of all pretension to be accounted true and genuine. Lastly, we may most fairly call upon those who profess to write scientifically and to instruct us in philosophy, that they lay down some plain and intelligible method, whereby we may distinguish these true primary premisses from spurious counterfeits ; and that they establish moreover to our satisfaction the *reasonableness and sufficiency* of that method.

(2.) Now for my second explanatory statement. There are certain intuitions, so intermingled (if I may so express myself) with the very first springs of thought—such indispensable prerequisites to every intellectual act worthy the name,—that it is simply impossible to apply directly and methodically any test of their legitimacy. Impossible for this reason, that in order to apply any test imaginable, *some* intellectual act must be elicited ; which act implies, in the very process of eliciting it, that those particular intuitions are genuine. Instances of such intuitions will be those already mentioned ; our various intuitions of memory and of reasoning. But then it is these very intuitions, in regard to which each one of us has the strongest possible guarantee for their truth ; viz. the fact that it is not less than physically impossible (see n. 5) to doubt them for one moment.

Again, even as to these most fundamental intuitions, a certain subsequent and negative test of their genuineness may be directly and methodically applied. It is *imaginable*, that my to-day's memory of the events which passed last Sunday, shall be contradictory to my yesterday's memory of those same events ; so that by the fact of trusting my memory, I am led into endless contradiction and confusion. It is *imaginable* again, that the same premisses, if combined in one order, would lead to one conclusion ; if in another, to another and a contradictory conclusion : so that by the fact of trusting my *reasoning faculty* I am brought into endless contradiction and confusion. I need not say that nothing of the sort takes place ; but that on the contrary, the deepest harmony exists between those various propositions, which my memory and my reasoning faculty combine to establish. Here then is a subsequent and a negative test, yet one of a somewhat cogent description, that those two fundamental classes of intuition are genuine.

11. Having so far explained my meaning, I return to my former remark. Philosophers in general have laboured far less, it seems to me, than they ought to have laboured, at the all-important task of providing us with tests, whereby genuine intuitions may be distinguished from spurious. F. Buffier indeed, the well-known Jesuit metaphysician, has applied himself to this work, and deserves no slight praise for seeing its importance and fundamentality; yet no one, I think, can regard his treatment of the question as very subtle or profound. The tests which he suggests are these three:—

(1.) That the judgments, alleged to be first truths, be so clear, that when one undertakes either to prove or to oppose them, one can only do so by the help of propositions, which are manifestly neither clearer nor more certain.

(2.) That they be so universally received among men in every time and place, and by every sort of character, that those who oppose them find themselves, in comparison to the rest of mankind, not more than one in a hundred or even in a thousand.

(3.) That they be so strongly impressed on our minds, that we conform our conduct to them, notwithstanding the refinements of those who imagine contrary opinions; which latter class indeed act, not in conformity with their opinions thus imagined, but with those first truths which are universally received. *

* "Le premier de ces caractères est qu'elles soient si claires, que quand on entreprend de les prouver ou de les attaquer, on ne le puisse faire, que par des propositions qui manifestement ne sont ni plus claires ni plus certaines;

"D'être si universellement reçues parmi les hommes en tout temps, en tous lieux, et par toutes sortes d'esprits, que ceux qui les attaquent se trouvent, dans le genre humain, être manifestement moins d'un contre cent, ou même contre mille;

"D'être si fortement imprimées dans nous, que nous y conformions notre conduit, malgré les raffinements de ceux qui imaginent des opinions contraires, et qui eux-mêmes agissent conformément, non à leurs opinions imaginées, mais aux premières vérités universellement reçues."—Buffier, chap. vii. p. 22.

While admitting that I cannot be satisfied with these three criteria as at all adequate to the occasion, it must not be supposed that I profess in any way to improve upon them. But I would venture to solicit the serious attention of philosophers to the question; as I must think that no edifice of metaphysical science can be considered stable and trustworthy, where the security of its very foundation has been so greatly neglected. Until the question of intuitions has been systematically and fully considered, I must think it truer to affirm that most copious and valuable *materials* for metaphysical science have been brought together, than to affirm that that science itself has been definitively called into existence.

For my own part I can only say that, without attempting any *general* solution of the question, at all events I will not allege any one intuition as legitimate, until I have brought together so many grounds for my statement, as will (I think) satisfy every reflecting man.

12. We have already seen quite enough, to guard us against falling into a fallacy, which need only be stated to be exposed. It happens sometimes, that when we claim intuition in behalf of some important proposition, certain unphilosophical men, who claim to be specially philosophical, regard that claim itself as a confession of argumentative weakness. When we say plainly that we can advance no chain of syllogisms in behalf of our thesis, they regard this as tantamount with a confession, that we do not allege *reason* in its behalf at all; that we cling to it, and admit ourselves to do so, on grounds of fancy, feeling and prepossession, in defiance of reason. But after the various considerations which have occupied us in this Section, it is not necessary to do more than state very briefly the following most obvious truth. We are guiding ourselves fully as much by *reason* when we hold confidently legitimate intuitions, as when we proceed further to draw *inferences* from those intuitions. Nay it may be said in one sense, that we go *more* by reason in the

former case than in the latter; so far as in every case premisses may be said (see *postea*, Chap. IV.) to possess *higher* certainty, than the conclusions which they tend to establish. When men thus thoughtlessly call for *argument* in each particular case, they forget that all argument must depend on certain primary premisses which are not based on argument (see n. 9). If then nothing is reasonable except that for which *argument* is produceable, those primary premisses are *not* reasonable; hence neither are the conclusions based on them reasonable; and hence again, no knowledge of any kind is possible at all.

If indeed no more is meant by such statements, than that we should be very careful *what* intuitions we claim as legitimate—that this must not be left to each man's private fancy, but must proceed on certain fixed and cognizable principles—then no more is meant, than what I not merely admit but have most earnestly maintained. But many men really seem to think (most extravagant as the proposition must appear when formally stated) that *all* intuitions, from the very nature of the case, are and must be the mere offspring of fancy, prejudice, or caprice.

13. Of truths thus legitimately intued, some are intued as *necessarily true*, others not so. When, *e. g.* I intue by memory that five minutes ago I was seated at this table, I am intuing no necessary truth whatever. But when I intue that a rectilineal figure of three sides has three angles, the truth is necessary, and is legitimately intued as such. As no Catholic philosopher (I believe) has doubted the existence of necessary truths, and as my direct purpose is not philosophical disquisition, we need not say much in explanation of this term 'necessary.' Anything, I suppose, is *necessarily* true, when its truth arises from nothing whatever external to itself; when its truth arises simply from what is contained in the subject and in the predicate of that proposition which expresses it. Thus the verity, now intued by me, that I was seated five minutes ago at this table, resulted from the external circumstance that my

will then gave my body the requisite command.   But
the verity, now intued by me, that every three-sided
rectilineal figure has three angles, arises simply from
the *intrinsic* connexion which exists between a three-
sided and a three-angled rectilineal figure.   The truth of
this latter verity, I say, does not result, nor is intued by
me as resulting, from any external circumstance, as for
instance from a Creator commanding that such figures
should have such a property ; but is intued as wholly intrinsic to the objects themselves whereof we are judging.*

* There has been a small school of non-Catholic philosophers, who have
denied the existence of necessary truth altogether, professing that all our
knowledge is derived from experience.   There has been no greater writer
among these than Mr. Stuart Mill, whom I have mentioned in n. 8 ; and I
should be very sorry if I appeared insensible to his rare candour and love
of truth.   But in his treatment of this very subject he has singularly
exemplified the old proverb, "Naturam expellas," &c.   In the very act of
strenuously denying that *mathematical axioms* have any character of
necessity, he has quite unawares allowed the admission to slip in, that the
validity of the reasoning process is a necessary truth.   He cannot so
contend against the clearest intuitions of his intellect as consistently to
deny this ; though I need hardly say that its admission is fatal to his whole
theory.

I observed this myself when first reading his "System of Logic," and I
drew attention to it in a review of that work, which I wrote for the "British
Critic" many years ago.   Since that time Mr. Spencer has hit the same
blot ; and has exposed indeed Mr. Mill's inconsistency, much more powerfully and clearly than I had been able to do.   It will be worth while here
to quote his remarks :—

"But the inconsistency into which Mr. Mill has thus fallen, is most
clearly seen in the second of his two chapters on 'demonstration and
necessary truths.'   He admits, in this, the validity of proof by a *reductio
ad absurdum.*   Now what is a *reductio ad absurdum* unless a reduction to
inconceivableness ?   And why, if inconceivableness be in other cases an
insufficient ground for rejecting a proposition as impossible, is it a sufficient ground in this case ?

"Again, calling in question the necessity commonly ascribed to the
deductive sciences, he says :—

"'The results of these sciences are indeed necessary, in the sense of
'necessarily following from certain first principles, called axioms and
'definitions ; of being certainly true, *if* these axioms and definitions are so.
'But their claim to the character of necessity in any sense beyond this
'. . . . must depend on the previous establishment of such a claim in
'favour of the definitions and axioms themselves.'—Chapter vi.

"Or, as he previously expresses the same view :—

"'The only sense in which necessity can be ascribed to the conclusions
'of any scientific investigation, is that of necessarily following from some
'assumption which, by the conditions of the inquiry, is not to be
'questioned.'—Chapter v.

"Here, and throughout the whole of his argument, Mr. Mill assumes
that there is something more certain in a demonstration, than in anything

This leads the way to a very well-known philosophical discussion. We believe of course most firmly, and believe as a truth which reason by itself can establish, that there exists an All-holy Almighty God, Infinite in every Perfection. Here then a difficulty presents itself; for this Omnipotent God seems limited in power, by the existence of necessary truths. 'It is certain ' that God cannot create a rectilineal figure of three ' sides, which has more than three angles ; or again ' whose three angles, taken together, amount to either

else ; some necessary truth in the steps of our reasoning, which is not possessed by the axioms they start from. How can this assumption be justified ? In each successive syllogism, the dependence of the conclusion upon its premisses is a truth of which we have no other proof than the inconceivability of the negation. Unless our perception of logical truth is *à priori,* which Mr. Mill will not contend, it too, like our perceptions of mathematical truth, has been gained from experience. In the one case, as in the other, we have simply an induction, with which no fact has, to our knowledge, ever conflicted. And if this be an insufficient warrant for asserting the necessity of the one order of truth, it is an insufficient warrant for asserting the necessity of the other.

"How complete is the parallelism may indeed be best proved from Mr. Mill's own admissions. In an earlier chapter he has endeavoured to shew that by analysis of the syllogism we arrive at 'a fundamental prin-' ciple, or rather two principles, *strikingly resembling the axioms of mathe-* ' *matics.* The first, which is the principle of affirmative syllogisms, is, that ' things which coexist with the same thing, coexist with one another. ' The second is the principle of negative syllogisms, and is to this effect : ' that a thing which coexists with another thing, with which other a third ' thing does not coexist, is not coexistent with that third thing.' Elsewhere, if I remember rightly, he points out the remarkable analogy between this logical axiom — things which coexist with the same thing, coexist with one another — and the mathematical axiom — things which are equal to the same thing are equal to one another. Analogous however as they are, and similarly derived as they must be, Mr. Mill claims for the first a necessity which he denies to the last. When, as above, he asserts that the deductive sciences are not necessary, save 'in the sense of *necessarily* '*following* from certain first principles called axioms and definitions ; of ' being *certainly* true *if* those axioms and definitions are so '— he assumes that, whilst the mathematical axioms possess only hypothetical truth, this logical axiom involved in every step of the demonstration possesses absolute truth — that whilst the inconceivability of its negation is an imperfect guarantee for the one, it is a perfect guarantee for the other. Evidently this is an untenable position. Unless it can be shewn that this truth — things which coexist with the same thing coexist with each other — has some higher warrant than the inconceivability of its negation (which cannot be shewn), it must be admitted that axioms and demonstrations stand on the same footing ; that if necessity be denied to the one, it must be denied to the other, and, indeed, to all things whatever."—*Principles of Psychology,* chap. ii. pp. 23–25.

' more or less than two right angles.   How is this not
' a limitation of Omnipotence ? '

The various philosophical schools answer this question in different ways; but it is not necessary for us
here to enter on the discussion at all.   It is admitted
by every Catholic philosopher that there *are* such
necessary truths — truths which are not caused by God's
creative power, but which are intrinsecally such ; and
this is all which concerns the particular purpose before
us.

14.   Having now then sufficiently prepared the way,
for that thesis which I am mainly anxious to prove, I
shall here close the present Section.   The various propositions, which we have (I think) established in the
course of it, are very closely connected with philosophical controversies, which have been at all times
most keenly and earnestly discussed, and never more
so than at the present time.   I have endeavoured however to steer as clear as possible of these controversies,
so far as was consistent with what was absolutely
necessary for my design.   Not that I regard these controversies as unimportant : on the contrary, they appear
to me vitally momentous; and perhaps more so now
than at any former period.   Nor has the reason of my
procedure altogether been, that I am without a decided
opinion upon them; for on some of the matters at issue
I have been led to form a very decided opinion.   But
my direct subject being Theology and not Philosophy,
I have felt all through, that it was very desirable to
confine strictly our philosophical discussions to the
establishment of those truths, which are indispensably
requisite as a foundation for what is to follow.

Section II.

On the Idea of Moral Obligation.

15. LET us begin this Section by stating an extremely simple case of conscience.

A friend of mine, who has loaded me with benefits, entrusts to my keeping a jewel of great value for the sake of its safe custody, while he goes to seek his fortune in other lands. He returns in a state of great distress, and reclaims his jewel. I recognise immediately, and without the faintest shadow of doubt, that I *ought* to restore it; that the refusing to restore it would be *morally evil*. Nor is there any human being, possessed of reason, who under similar circumstances would fail to recognise the same truth. Calling this a moral judgment, I set myself to establish in order these three propositions. First, this moral judgment is intuitive and not inferential. Secondly, it is a *legitimate* intuition ; or in other words the thing intued is true. Thirdly, it is legitimately intued as *necessarily* true (see n. 13).

16. First I say this moral judgment *is* an intuition; it is not one of those cases mentioned in n. 2, where I fancy that to be an *intuition* which is really an *inference*. In those cases we can state various propositions, either already recognised as true or now themselves intued, which lead by way of logical consequence to the judgment in question. The whole distinction between intuitive judgments and inferential, I need hardly say, turns upon this very fact. But it is perfectly impossible to do this in the present case; as any one will find who makes the experiment. Various judgments no doubt are formed, antecedently to the moral judgment which we are now considering; but they are formed,

merely as the *matter* on which the moral judgment is exercised, not as *premisses* whereof the moral judgment is a conclusion. The proof of this statement is obvious : it is perfectly impossible to array these antecedent judgments in any number or order of syllogisms, such that the moral judgment which we are considering can emerge as a conclusion. That idea of moral good or evil, which is the most characteristic element of this moral judgment, is not met with ever so distantly in any of those antecedent judgments to which we refer.

There are some philosophers certainly, who explain this moral judgment in a manner which *would* allow us to admit it as inferential and not intuitive. It is necessary therefore next to consider the statements which these philosophers advance.*

The most plausible theory which they have devised, as to the origination of our moral judgments, is the following. 'In the case above supposed, in refusing ' restoration of the jewel I should have to undergo the ' displeasure and hostility of society, in a very severe ' degree. So ruinous to all social welfare is the habit ' of thus violating confidence, that society in self-defence ' places those under its ban who pursue such a course. ' My moral judgment then, that I am under the obliga- ' tion of restoring the jewel, is nothing else than my ' recognition, that in withholding it I should have to ' encounter that severe infliction, which the hostility of ' society would involve. I may not be aware of the ' fact, but this is really the whole account of my moral ' judgment.'

Now we may fully admit that if this were, as it professes to be, a true analysis of our moral judgments, they *would* be inferential and not intuitive. I am already well acquainted with the proposition, ' society inflicts its severe hostility on those who keep back deposits;' and I am already acquainted with the further proposition, ' the hostility of society would be felt by

* Those who are convinced—as pretty well all Catholics will be at starting—that this *is* a real intuition, may, without inconvenience, save themselves much painful attention by omitting all the rest of this n. 16.

me as a very severe infliction.' But from these two propositions the conclusion follows, 'if I withhold the jewel, I have reason to fear a very severe infliction from society.' If therefore this proposition were a correct analysis of the moral judgment 'I *ought* to restore the jewel,' doubtless that judgment *would* be inferential and not intuitive. But there cannot be a more preposterous statement than to say that this *is* a correct analysis; so preposterous indeed, so perfectly monstrous, that the only difficulty in the whole matter is, to imagine, how men of the least thoughtfulness or reflection could possibly suppose so. We ought not indeed to allege without proof, that there *are* men of sound mind who can put forth such a statement; and I will extract therefore the following passage from Mr. James Mill's "Analysis of the Human Mind." There cannot be a fairer sample of utilitarian argument than Mr. Mill; for he is undoubtedly a writer of very conspicuous ability. The whole of his chapter on the 'Moral Sense' (chap. xxiii.) deserves our careful study; but there is no room for more than the following extract :—

"All men have the daily experience, that their own acts of Justice, and Beneficence, dispose other men to be Beneficent to them; their own acts of injustice and malevolence, dispose other men to bring evil (which in this case they call punishment) upon them; and to abstain from doing them good. This experience is of course followed by the usual association between cause and effect. The man who does acts of Justice and Beneficence, *anticipates the favourable disposition* of mankind, as their natural effect; and *this association* is his belief, or conviction, or sense (he calls it by all those names), of *deserving* the favourable sentiments of mankind. The man on the other hand who performs acts which are unjust and hurtful to others, anticipates the unfavourable and hostile sentiments of mankind, as the natural consequents of his acts; in other words, has the belief, or conviction, or sense (for the association in this case also has these various names), of deserving, not well, but ill, at the hands of other men. . . . .

"*This anticipation of the hostile, or benevolent sentiments of mankind,* as the natural effects of actions of a certain description on our part, *is the foundation* of that remarkable association of which we had very recently occasion to make mention, the association which Dr. Smith has called *the love of Praiseworthi-*

ness, and which is sometimes found to be much more powerful than the love of actual Praise.

"The *Disposition* which corresponds to those *Motives*, or the faculty of forming the associations which constitute them, is the result of habit in this as in all other cases.

"The *Affection*, in this case, *has the name of Moral Appro-bation and Disapprobation*."—Vol. ii. p. 252, 3.

You see, our ' love of praiseworthiness,' according to Mr. Mill, is simply an association of ideas, founded on our ' anticipation of the hostile or benevolent sentiments of mankind.' And now to examine this doctrine.

' I *ought* to restore this jewel;' or ' I am under the *moral obligation* of restoring it;' or 'my refusal to restore it would be *morally evil.*' These various propositions do not state *different* things; they are but different modes of expressing the *same* thing. And whenever I ponder on this thing, various cognate judgments are spontaneously and inevitably elicited. 'I should deserve *blame* if I did not restore the jewel;' 'I should deserve *punishment* if I did not restore it;' 'no amount of personal advantage would justify me in retaining it.' These various propositions will enable us to enter still further into the meaning of this term, ' ought' or ' obligation.' And the more we do so, the more unmistakably shall we see, how utterly different, nay heterogeneous, it is from that other notion, with which these writers attempt to confound it, the anticipation of probable suffering from the resentment of society. I refer this assertion to the one, the only possible, court of appeal on such a question; I mean, the impartial judgment of every reasonable man, who will reflect on what passes in his own mind. Let him first master this proposition; ' I *ought* to restore the jewel:' next let him master the other proposition; ' I expect some severe infliction from society if I retain the jewel:' and thirdly let him compare the two with each other. If there is any man possessed of his senses who, having done so, pronounces the two to be identical or nearly identical in meaning, I give up the whole argument.

Yet we may bring the matter to a somewhat more

clenching issue, by making a very probable supposition.
We may well imagine that this friend of mine himself
lies under the ban of society, in consequence of accu-
sations which I know to be false. In such a case, to
keep back his jewel would be my best way of obtaining
the favour of society ; and my *restoring* it would involve me in its *severe hostility*. Under these circumstances, in our opponents' view, I should at once, and
without the possibility of a moment's hesitation, recognise my *duty* to lie in *keeping it back;* this would be
my whole moral judgment in the matter. According
to *our* view on the contrary, I should not feel my perception of *duty* in the least affected by the circumstance that *society* is on the opposite side : I might find
far greater difficulty in *practising* my duty ; but my
notion of that duty would be just the same as before.
Here then we bring the matter to a crucial experiment.
Can any one, who questions his own consciousness for a
moment, bring himself to doubt which is the true alternative ?

But further, that very displeasure of society against
moral evil, which our opponents make the foundation
of their argument, tells in fact entirely on our side.

No doubt a criminal is a great enemy to society, and
is felt by men in general to be such. But take a man
who, with the best intentions, devises some most mischievous social theory ; is he a less enemy to society
than the criminal? Plainly not. Moreover, it will
commonly happen that a large number of men see fully
through the emptiness of his reasonings, and regard him
with the fullest conviction as a man who is inflicting on
society the deadliest mischief. Yet so long as they
regard his *intentions* to be good, will any one be so
wild as to maintain, that their feelings towards him are
the same, with which they regard the heartless and
unprincipled criminal? How do you account for this
difference? In one obvious way. The wild theorist is
regarded indeed with *hostility and displeasure;* but the
criminal with *moral disapprobation.* It is not chiefly as
an *enemy of society* that the latter is visited with their

displeasure, but as a *violator of moral obligation;* as a committer of acts, which are *morally evil.*

It is most true indeed, that there is a constant tendency in men to attribute bad *motives* to those, whose *opinions* are felt as injurious to the fabric of society ; and it frequently enough happens in this manner, that a well-intentioned man *is* visited with moral disapprobation.   But this very fact is a further argument on my side : it is not *until* they attribute bad motives, or in other words it is not until they regard him as morally culpable, that they feel moral disapprobation to be legitimate.   The mere circumstance of their conduct being injurious to society, is never regarded as in itself a sufficient foundation for moral disapproval.

But our opponents may further reply as follows. ' Even yet you are very far from doing justice to our ' arguments.   You ignore the immense power possessed ' by association of ideas.   When once some idea is ' associated with the thought of any object, the clearest ' conviction that it is mistakenly applied in any par- ' ticular case, will fail to destroy the association.   Not ' only the *imagination* will be constantly haunted with ' this idea, in connexion with the object in question,— but ' the same association again and again will influence ' our *conduct itself,* whenever reason is not in a special ' degree lively and on its guard.   Take, as one instance ' out of a thousand, the case of one who has been con- ' verted to Catholicism from some Puritanical form of ' Protestantism ; and who has learned to believe very ' many things sinful, if done on a Sunday, which to a ' Catholic's eye are most perfectly innocent.   His old ' view of the Sunday long influences his habits and ' haunts his imagination.   His feelings will be impressed ' with the notion of Sunday being a gloomy day.   He ' will instinctively abstain on that day from many ' innocent things, unless his reason be awake on the ' matter ; unless he compel himself to do them, for the ' very sake of delivering himself from his superstitious ' thraldom.   Even while he does so act, the echo of his

D

' past associations will loudly sound in his ears ; his
' past prejudices will cause present repugnance; and he
' will have to act in despite of an inward remonstrance,
' which may very easily be mistaken for the voice of
' conscience. A result entirely analogous is found,
' when once a person has been, *e.g.* thoroughly imbued
' with the conviction, that refusing to restore a deposit
' is one of those offences which society very heavily
' visits. He will have formed very strongly an associ-
' ation of these two ideas; and even though in this
' individual case society were to act on precisely the
' contrary side, yet he could not rid himself of this
' deeply-rooted association.'

Such a reply as this however, though very often
made, proceeds on a total misconception, either of the
phenomenon before us, or of the point at issue. The
point at issue is precisely the following. When I form
the judgment that I am under the moral obligation of
restoring the jewel, what is the true analysis of this
phrase 'I am under the moral obligation?' Our opponents reply that the true analysis is, 'I should be
' exposed to the displeasure of society if I refuse to
' restore it.' This, and no other, is the allegation which
we are confronting.

Now all may very readily be admitted which the
preceding argument will establish, and yet our opponents' cause will not be advanced one step thereby.
No doubt, when I have long connected the thought of
acting dishonestly with that of incurring the displeasure of society, a very powerful association will have
been generated between those two ideas. Though I
may see clearly that in one particular case no such
danger is to be feared, yet, whenever reason is not
awake and lively, there will be a great reluctance to
commit a dishonest action, from the impression made
on my *imagination* by this association. Nay further,
even if I forced myself to do it, there would still be a
nervous dread of some future infliction as likely to result.

But how on earth does this avail our opponents in
the present case? I am not supposing a period when

reason is *not* lively and awake, but on the contrary, when it *is* so in the highest degree. Let us imagine that I am in agonies of fear, at the thought of what I shall suffer from society if I *restore* the deposit to one, whom they regard as their enemy. Let us suppose that my imagination is at this moment keenly impressed with the same prospect ; and that my reason is busily occupied with devising means for averting the storm. So far then from its being true, that my imagination is haunted with the notion of future social suffering through *dishonesty*—reason, passion, imagination, are all actively conspiring in the very opposite direction ; they are all deeply imbued with this one perception, that I incur danger from society through my *honesty*. And yet at the same time I retain my clear conviction, that such honesty is of moral obligation. Certainly therefore, my conviction that restitution is morally obligatory, is utterly different from any conviction, that I should suffer at the hands of society from its evasion.

At last however it may well be doubted, whether the most irrefragable mode of silencing our opponents be not that which is also the simplest; the calling on them to ponder their own statement on the one hand, and to interrogate their own consciousness on the other hand. They allege that in saying ' I am under the moral ' obligation of restoring this jewel,' I simply mean ' I ' am exposed to suffering from society unless I restore ' it.' Let any one master the meaning of this statement, and then examine what passes in his own mind : let him thus see, when it is nakedly stated, whether he is literally *capable* of accepting this truly monstrous allegation.

All this is so very undeniable, that it can be no matter of surprise, if utilitarians shift their ground and argue the question at a step further back. They may admit then that men do recognise moral obligation, as something quite distinct from the impending pressure of society ; but they may ask a further question. They may ask, ' how does this subjective fact prove any objective

' truth? How does man's *recognition* of moral obliga-
' tion establish that there *is* such a rule, possessing
' intrinsic authority over our acts?' In other words,
they may admit that men often enough *elicit* such intuitive judgments, but may question their *legitimacy*.
Our present proposition however, as will be remembered,
is simply that these judgments *are* intuitive and not
inferential. The question of their *legitimacy* is to be
considered immediately afterwards.

It will be by no means necessary to enter at equal
length, on the consideration of *other* theories, which
would represent our moral judgments as inferential
and not intuitive; for none other has even such little
plausibility, as appertains to the one just considered.
Some philosophers declare, that in the judgment 'I
ought to restore the jewel,' I have regard to the
psychological fact, that bad acts engender bad habits;
and to another truth, also founded on experience, that
bad habits are injurious to happiness. They would
fain persuade me, that what really passes through my
mind is a keen desire for my own happiness, and a
prescient augury, that I shall be seriously *injuring*
that happiness if I lay the foundation for a habit of
peculation. It is impossible to refute gravely this
transparent absurdity. If any man, who calmly reflects
on what passes in his mind, can seriously say that he
believes this to be a true account of this moral judgment,—such a man is far beyond the reach of any
argument which I could adduce.

Others lastly say, that the moral judgment rests on
a Revelation of God; and that it is none other than
this: 'God has revealed that He will punish me unless
I restore the jewel.' To this it suffices to reply, that
those who have received no authenticated revelation
from God,—nay those whose imaginary deities are
regarded by them as given up to theft and every
kind of knavery,—will form this moral judgment as
readily and undoubtingly, as will those to whom God
has spoken, and has authenticated His revelation.

17. Having shewn then that this moral judgment

is an intuition, our next statement shall be that it is a *legitimate* intuition. In order to establish this, let us begin by applying F. Buffier's three criteria. (See n. 11.)

(1.) The first of these criteria is, that the judgment intued is so clear, that when we undertake either to prove or to attack it, we can only do so by means of propositions, which are manifestly neither clearer nor more certain. This most undoubtedly holds here. Suppose you set about proving to me my duty of restoring this jewel; what proposition can even be imagined, which could serve you as a premiss? which could strike me as in any· respect clearer or more certain, than the very conclusion at which you would aim? If I don't see my duty at once, it may very safely be said that no imaginable course of argument could make me see it.

(2.) The second criterion is, that the judgment intued shall be one, so universally received among men in all times and places and by every sort of character, that those who attack it shall be plainly, as compared with the rest of mankind, fewer than one to one hundred or to one thousand. The moral judgment before us does more than satisfy this criterion; for among all the men possessed of reason, who ever lived or who ever will live, not one could be found to call it in question.

(3.) The third, and perhaps the most important, criterion suggested by the Jesuit philosopher, is the following; that the judgment shall be so strongly impressed on our minds, that we always conform our conduct to it, notwithstanding the refinements of those who imagine a contrary opinion : which very men indeed themselves act conformably, not to their opinions thus imagined, but to those first truths which are universally received. Now to apply this. Certain ingenious philosophers maintain, that he who keeps back a deposit may legitimately be regarded by us with hatred, such as that with which we regard a foreign invader, as an enemy to the peace and welfare of society. Or again,

they say that he may be regarded by us with pity, as
a man who has calculated wrongly his own chances of
happiness. But they add, that the feeling which we
call that of moral disapprobation—our feeling that he
deserves *blame*, that he deserves punishment, that his
conduct is precisely what we call culpable—that all
this is unfounded and delusive. I ask, in conformity
with F. Buffier, can these philosophers themselves
carry out their principles consistently on one single
occasion? Is it possible for them to hear of conduct
so flagitious, without the judgment spontaneously
arising in their mind, and influencing their whole demeanour to the offender, that it *is* flagitious? I repeat,
not merely that it is injurious to society or injurious to
the agent, but that it is also flagitious? So much on
F. Buffier's criteria.

But again. Suppose we wish to establish, that the
affirmation of some mathematical axiom is a legitimate
intuition : how should we set about the proof? For
instance, 'every rectilineal figure which has three
sides has three angles :' how do we know that our
intuition of this verity is legitimate? I suppose it is a
sufficient answer to say, that every one, who possesses
an intellect sufficiently cultivated to understand the
term of the proposition, by the constitution of his nature
must assent to it. To apprehend precisely what is
meant by a rectilineal figure of three sides, and again
of three angles,—in other words to apprehend what is
meant by the subject and the predicate respectively—
this may require some little mental effort. But so
soon as any one *has* apprehended this, he forms by
necessity that judgment, which recognises that the
subject and predicate agree together. I am not aware
that any further proof than this can be brought, for
the legitimacy of this mathematical intuition.

Now a proof in every respect equivalent is available, to establish the legitimacy of that moral judgment which we have been considering. ' He to
whom a kind and bountiful friend has entrusted a
deposit, *ought* to restore it when reclaimed ; or acts

wickedly if he refuses to do so.' To enter sufficiently into the meaning of this sentence — in other words to master the circumstances of the case — may require some little effort; but any one who is enabled to master it, by the constitution of his nature forms necessarily the above judgment. I may add also, that any one who *finds* himself under similar circumstances, and who by consequence penetrates most thoroughly into the conditions of the case, forms the relevant moral judgment with far greater keenness and promptitude, than that with which he would form any mathematical judgment whatever.

18. Lastly, I maintain that we legitimately intue this moral obligation, not simply as existing, but as *necessarily* existing. And now to illustrate this further statement.

It is admitted by all Catholic philosophers, that mathematical axioms are *necessarily* true. I ask, how they would profess to establish this important statement? For I am convinced that any test, which would be serviceable to their purpose, would quite as fully establish the necessary character of those *moral* axioms, which we are here considering. I suppose, in the case of mathematical axioms, they would put the thing in some such way as the following. When I intue that a rectilineal figure of three sides has three angles, I intue this in the first instance, simply with reference to that *particular* three-sided figure, which I have summoned up in my imagination. Yet a moment's further consideration shews me, that the proposition is not confined exclusively to *this* figure; that it can be predicated with equal truth of *every* three-sided rectilineal figure, which ever did, which ever will, which ever possibly can, exist. The test, whereby we determine that the axiom is legitimately intued as necessary, is precisely this absolute universality of the judgment which we form concerning it.

Now in the moral case before us, this identical test applies in all its fulness. Supposing me to be circumstanced as originally supposed, I intue in the first instance that I am under the moral obligation of restoring the jewel. But a moment's consideration enables me to carry the judgment much further. On reflection I further intue, that this obligation is by no means peculiar to myself, and to this present case; I intue that every one would most certainly be under the same obligation, who in any time or place should be found under the same circumstances.

One explanation only has here to be made. When we say 'under the same circumstances,' we suppose that the *whole* circumstances, which can have any bearing on the morality of the case, are identical in the various instances. I might imagine the case, *e. g.* in which this friend of mine, to my certain knowledge, should require the jewel, for the purpose of committing some great crime. To say the least, I should no longer intue with any clearness that it would be my duty under *such* circumstances to restore it. But I do intue with the greatest clearness, that, so long as the circumstances bearing on the morality of the case remain the same, every rational being, in every time and place, would be under the same obligation with myself.

19. We intue it then as a necessary truth, that under the supposed circumstances the jewel *ought* to be restored; that its retention would be *sinful* or *morally evil*. Nothing of course would be easier, than to mention various other combinations of circumstances, under which also the path of duty would be marked out with extreme clearness. In every such case, the arguments which have been brought forward in this Section retain their entire force; and the same conclusion therefore holds. I say, we legitimately intue it as a necessary truth, that in every such combination of circumstances a certain course '*ought*' to be pursued; or in other words, that there is a '*moral obligation*' of pursuing it; or in other words again, that pursuing any different course would be '*morally evil.*'

Further, this idea 'morally evil' is a simple idea; that is to say, we cannot decompose it into other more elementary notions, from which the idea results. When

I say that any different course would be 'morally evil,' I do not mean that it would 'bring upon me the displeasure of society;' much less do I mean that it would 'injure my own personal happiness;' neither does the phrase stand for any other combination of ideas, each simpler than that which the phrase directly expresses.

Every one, who interrogates his consciousness, knows what is *meant* by the term 'morally evil' as applied to acts, just as he knows what is meant by 'bitter' or 'sour' as applied to natural substances : but it is as impossible to *explain* this meaning by any kind of analysis, in one case as in the other.   That which is morally evil 'deserves blame;'—'deserves punishment.'   These are intuitive judgments, which, as soon as stated, commend themselves as true to all mankind ; and they tend to make us realise, more fully and definitely, what is contained in this idea 'morally evil:' but no one will say, that these judgments contain any *analysis* or *explanation* of the term.

Since then it is a necessary truth, that there are various combinations of circumstances (be they more or fewer) under which a certain line of conduct would be morally evil, one most obvious, yet most important, proposition results.

It is a necessary truth then, that there *is* such an attribute as we denote by the term moral evil; an attribute, which appertains to certain courses of conduct, pursued by certain beings under certain circumstances.

I am not, of course, maintaining it as a necessary truth, that there *are* such beings, or that they are ever *placed* in such circumstances.   But we have shewn it to be a necessary truth, that *if* these beings exist, and *if* they are placed in such circumstances, certain acts done by them would be morally evil.   These acts may be injurious to society — this is one attribute ; injurious to their own happiness — this is another ; forbidden by their Creator — this is a third ; * but they possess neces-

* The meaning of this statement will be more fully developed in the following Section.

sarily another attribute also, totally distinct from any of these, viz. that they are *morally evil*. If they are injurious to society, or opposed to the agent's temporal happiness, this is merely because God has so appointed; because He has so arranged the constitution of society, or so created the individual soul. But that they are *morally evil*, is a *necessary* truth ; a truth not in any way resulting from God's appointment; a truth as simply necessary, as is the truth that the base-angles of an isosceles triangle are equal to each other.

And to this term ' morally evil,' the other term 'moral obligation' is simply correlative. When I say that such an act, under such circumstances, is of ' moral obligation,' I mean neither more nor less, than that to abstain from doing it would be ' morally evil.' When I say that ' the *avoidance* of such an act would be of moral obligation,' I mean that ' the doing it would be morally evil.' Any one, who interrogates his consciousness, will find (I think) that this is a true statement. The term ' moral obligation' then, by no means implies the existence of some other person, who *imposes* the obligation ; it implies no more, than the inherence in certain acts of this quality, ' moral evil.' * The latter quality inheres *necessarily* in the omitting, or in the doing, of certain acts under certain circumstances ; and so also, there exists *necessarily* a moral obligation, under such circumstances, of doing this or avoiding that. The latter of these statements is precisely equivalent to the former.

* " Ceux qui ne veulent pas, que *la connaissance du juste et de l'injuste* suffise pour imposer *une obligation proprement dite*, sont fort embarrassés de trouver le fondement de l'obligation à la loi naturelle."—*Gerdil*, to be quoted at length in Sec. iv.

Section III.

On the Relation between God and Moral Obligation.

20. The proposition, established in the preceding Section, implies one truth in particular, which (in my humble opinion) is of such vital moment both in Philosophy and in Theology, that we must give it our very particular attention. And this we should do the rather, because many good Catholics, from feelings of sincere piety, are greatly averse to it when they first hear it stated.

These excellent persons are in the habit of thinking, that the phrase, 'I ought to do this,' or 'I am under the moral obligation of doing it,' is simply synonymous with the phrase, 'I am commanded by my Creator to do it.' In like manner, they consider the phrase, 'such an act is morally evil,' to be simply equipollent with this other, 'such an act is forbidden by my Creator.' We maintain on the contrary, with the greatest confidence, as one of the most absolutely certain and elementary truths in Philosophy, that these two ideas, 'morally obligatory' and 'commanded by my Creator,' are as perfectly distinct as any one idea can be from any other.

Before putting into shape our reasons for this statement, let us make one preliminary assumption, which will enable us to argue the question more completely at this early stage. Let us assume, what is hereafter to be proved, that the acts, to which the quality of 'moral obligation' attaches, belong to various classes, among which classes justice, veracity, and benevolence may be conspicuously mentioned. Whereas then certain acts of justice, veracity, and benevolence, are intrinsically obligatory, we are now to argue against those who maintain, that to say this is simply synonymous with saying that our Creator commands them.

(1.) Let us draw our first argument, from the distinction which every one will recognise, between a 'tautologous' and a 'real' proposition. A tautologous proposition is one, in which the predicate contains no further idea, than one which the subject has already conveyed clearly to the mind. Suppose, for instance, I define a pentagon to be a rectilineal figure with five sides; and then proceed to enunciate the proposition, 'every pentagon has five sides.' This of course is the same kind of statement, as though I were to say 'a table is a table' or 'a tree is a tree.' All these are tautologous propositions. But suppose I say 'every pentagon has five *angles*,' this is a real proposition : a very obvious and axiomatic one no doubt, but still a real proposition. I may add also, that we are all wearied and disgusted by the solemn enunciation of a tautologous proposition ; and we look upon the individual who *does* thus solemnly enunciate it, as either a stupid puzzle-headed fellow, or else as what is vulgarly called 'a humbug.'

Now take the following proposition: 'I ought to do what my Creator commands ;' or 'it is my duty and obligation to do what my Creator commands.' Will any one call this a *tautologous* proposition ? Will any one say that its solemn enunciation shews either stupidity or the absence of fair dealing ? On the contrary. The proposition might with great edification be the theme of a whole sermon. ' Consider the claims which ' our Creator has on us ; consider the peculiar relation, ' implied in the very idea of creation, of being formed by ' Him out of nothing ; consider His tender Love for the ' works of His hands ; consider His infinite Sanctity — ' can there be a higher and more indispensable duty, than ' that of obeying even the least of His commands ?' These topics, and such as these, might be the theme of a most interesting and impressive discourse ; and certainly the very last thing which any of the audience could imagine would be, that the preacher had been.

merely occupied in enforcing such a truth, as that tables are tables and trees are trees.

Yet on our opponents' view the proposition *is* most simply tautologous; quite as much so, as these two last-named propositions. We can shew this with the greatest ease.

According to our opponents, 'I ought' simply means 'my Creator commands me' to do this or that. Let us then *substitute* this latter phrase, for the other to which it is considered equivalent; and what will be the result?

Original Proposition.

'I ought to do that which my Creator commands me to do.'

But for the phrase 'I ought to do that' my oppo-nents consider that I may substitute, without the least change of meaning, the phrase 'my Creator commands me to do that.' Let us make then this substitution.

Proposition in its new Shape.

'My Creator commands me to do that, which my Creator commands me to do.'

The solemn enunciation of which, would certainly be precisely parallel to the solemn enunciation of those other tautologous propositions, 'a table is a table' 'a tree is a tree.'

Since therefore the original proposition would, on our opponents' theory, be simply tautologous—and since by the consent of all mankind that same pro-position would be admitted as being *very far indeed* from tautologous—it follows, that our opponents' theory issues necessarily in a result, which is repug-nant to the consent of all mankind.

Indeed let any one weigh with any care these two propositions—he must see how totally distinct they are from each other.

Prop. I. 'I ought to do what my Creator com-mands.'

Prop. II. 'My Creator commands what He does command.'

(2.) Our second argument shall be the following.

Perhaps the highest and most vital proposition in all Theology is the following: 'Our Creator is All-holy.' But on our opponents' theory, this proposition is literally destroyed and emptied of all meaning. Now to shew this.

There are various acts recognised by all mankind as morally evil; whether they be offences against justice, veracity, benevolence, or some other virtue. Our opponents maintain, that in calling these morally evil, it is only meant that they are forbidden by the Creator; we on the contrary maintain that they are *intrinsecally* evil, apart from all reference to the Creator's Will.

Our opponents must necessarily, and do in fact, always proceed to say, that when I speak of some man, A or B, as morally good in such or such a degree, I mean no more than this, that in such or such a degree he conforms his conduct to the Creator's wishes. But *we* maintain, that when I speak of A or B as morally good in such or such a degree, I mean that he possesses in such or such a degree those qualities, which are *intrinsecally* virtuous, independently of the Creator's wishes; justice, veracity, benevolence, and the rest. *We* understand by 'holiness,' or 'moral goodness,' the possession of certain qualities intrinsecally virtuous; *they* understand by it, the habit of conformity to the Creator's wishes. The question is now to be decided, whether *their* explanation or *ours* be the true one.

Now let us again enunciate that solemn truth, which is the very foundation of all possible religion—' The Creator is All-holy' or (which is of course synonymous) ' possesses moral goodness in the most perfect possible way.' What can be more satisfactory, than the sense which *we* affix to this proposition? 'The Creator pos-' sesses, in the most perfect possible way, Justice, ' Veracity, Benevolence, and all those other qualities ' which are intrinsecally virtuous.' But what must be our *opponents*' version of this proposition? ' The ' Creator possesses, in the most perfect possible way,

' the habit of *conforming His conduct to His own*
' *wishes.*'   Or to put it otherwise, this most solemn
and fundamental truth, the Creator's Sanctity, becomes
in their mouths no more nor less than this; ' the
Creator does in every respect exactly as He likes.'

Here too again, as in the last argument, let any
one of common sense ponder these two propositions;
what can be more monstrous than to say that they
are equivalent?

Prop. I. ' The Creator possesses moral goodness
in the most perfect possible way.'

Prop. II. ' The Creator always does exactly what
He likes.'

The one strength of our opponents is their view (I
think of course a most mistaken one) of what is due to
piety.   How singularly significant, that their doctrine
issues at once in a conclusion, so frightfully *revolting*
to piety !

And see how precisely *our* interpretation brings the
process which we go through, when we predicate *Sanctity* of God, into precise harmony with that which we go
through, when we predicate of Him any other attribute.
Thus when I first form the judgment, ' our Creator
possesses infinite Power,' what passes in my mind?
I understand already, from human things, what is
meant by that quality which I call ' power;' and I
predicate of our Creator a quality, analogous to this,
as existing in an infinite degree.   Or when I judge
that ' our Creator is omniscient,'— I understand from
human things what is *meant* by ' knowing,' and I
judge that, in some analogous way, our Creator knows
every existing and every possible thing.   On our view,
the process is precisely similar, when I first form the
judgment ' our Creator is All-holy.'   I understand
already what is meant by that quality which we call
' holiness'— how that it includes, for instance, justice,
veracity, and benevolence.   And I predicate of our
Creator a quality analogous to this, as existing in an infinite degree.   I think every one, on reflection, will recognise this as a true account of what has passed in his

mind.   And to repeat once more our statement, just as the judgment 'our Creator is Omnipotent or Omniscient' would be simply unmeaning, until we find out what is *meant* by power or knowledge,—so that other proposition, 'our Creator is All-holy,' must be equally unmeaning, until we find out what is *meant* by 'holiness.'

(3.) In our first argument we urged, that the proposition, 'I ought to do that which my Creator commands me to do,' is no mere tautology, but on the contrary a real and most important statement.   We implied however, in addition, that it is a statement which we very readily recognise by our intuition, in proportion as the character of that Creator is unfolded to our view. Here however it is important to insist on a correlative proposition.   In order that this statement be recognised as true, it is necessary that the character of our Creator *should* be more and more unfolded to our view.   Our opponents maintain that the proposition 'I *ought* to do this' merely means '*my Creator commands me* to do this.'   Now we have already urged, that the proposition '.I ought to do what my Creator commands' is no mere *truism*, no mere piece of tautology; but let us now proceed a step further.   If by this proposition it be meant, that so soon as I recognise a being for my creator, the obligation forthwith arises of obeying him,—then the proposition is not only no *truism*, it is not even a *truth*.   Of course it is *most* true (to doubt it were the foulest blasphemy) that 'I ought at every moment to do that which the All-holy Being Who created me commands.'   But I say, this is not simply *because* He is my Creator, but because He is also a HOLY Creator. Let us first vindicate this proposition; then further let us shew its application to the present argument.

It is perfectly imaginable, that some wicked demon might possess the power of calling into existence rational creatures.   We are all of course very well aware, that such a hypothesis is *intrinsecally impossible;* but many a thing is imaginable, though it *be* intrinsecally impossible.   Take as an instance of this, any one of

Euclid's 'reductiones ad absurdum.' Take *e. g.* the case, where he is wishing to prove it as an *intrinsecally necessary* truth, that if the angle A B C is equal to the angle A C B, the straight line A B is equal to the straight line A C. (Book I. Prop. 6.) He says, 'for if not, let us suppose, if possible, that the straight 'line A B is greater than the straight line A C.' He is calling on us to *imagine* that very thing, which he is going to prove *intrinsecally impossible*. And so here; that an evil being can have creative power, is *intrinsecally impossible;* but it is readily enough *imaginable.*

Let us imagine then that certain rational beings had been created by some demon, who commands them to cultivate diligently the dispositions of pride, vindictiveness, mendacity, and impurity; threatening them with the extremity of his anger if they refused to obey. Do we hold that in such a case compliance would be a duty?—that they would be under the strict obligation of practising mendacity, injustice, and impurity accordingly?—of hating each other with all their hearts?—in one word, of seeking by every possible means to please this detestable demon? Yet all this would be so, if the proposition were really true, that so soon as I recognise any being for my creator, the obligation forthwith arises of obeying him.

It appears then that the command of a creator, as such, in no way suffices to generate moral obligation; it must be the command of a *Holy* Creator. And now let us see the bearing of this conclusion on our general argument. It is impossible to put in a stronger light than this the untenableness of our opponents' theory. They say that the proposition 'I ought to do what my Creator commands' is a *truism;* but we have seen that, until we know that that Creator is Holy, it is not even a *truth.*

Our opponents may reply, that this is merely an accidental omission; that they had in their minds of course, not any imaginable creator, but that All-holy Being who *did* create us; that Being who alone possesses, or can possibly possess, the power of creating.

E

They will beg leave therefore to amend their statement accordingly ; and declare, more distinctly than before, that 'I ought' signifies 'my *Holy* Creator commands me.' But to this I reply very readily. What do I mean by a *Holy* Creator? Certainly I cannot mean by this phrase 'a Creator who does whatever He wishes' (see our second argument) : for no one will say that our Creator claims our allegiance, simply because He does whatever He wishes. What then do I mean by the phrase? Among other things, I mean a Being, Who possesses those qualities which are intrinsecally virtuous; Who is incapable of doing or commanding any of those acts which are intrinsecally evil. In using then the very word 'Holy,' our opponents are obliged to abandon their case ; they are obliged to admit that very proposition which they have denied, viz. that there *are* acts, evil *independently;* evil apart from God's prohibition.

(4.) My fourth argument is perfectly distinct from any one of the previous three. How am I enabled to arrive at the knowledge, that my Creator *does* in fact command me to cultivate the dispositions, *e. g.* of justice, veracity, and benevolence? or that He Himself possesses those qualities? I must arrive at this knowledge, either by Reason or by Revelation.

If you suppose this knowledge to be obtained by Reason, I ask by what process of reason? I never heard of any process except this. I first recognise by reason (whether intuitively or inferentially) that our Creator is a Being Infinite in all Perfections. I then accept, as another truth declared by reason, that *sanctity* is a perfection, and that sanctity *includes* these qualities of justice, benevolence, and the rest. Hence I conclude that our Creator possesses these qualities. But there is no process of reason imaginable, which can shew that there is a perfection called sanctity, except that which shews that certain things are in themselves morally evil, apart from God's prohibition. This has been shewn under our second argument. You see then (1) I must recognise by reason that there is a perfection called sanctity, before I can infer that my Creator possesses these qualities ; and (2) I must know that certain things are morally evil apart from God's prohibition, before I can recognise by reason that there is a perfection called sanctity.   I *must* know therefore that these things are independently evil, before I can discover by reason that God prohibits them.

Let us pass then to the other supposition, that it is by *Revelation alone* that we know of God's commanding justice, benevolence, and the rest.   No Catholic of course would venture to take this alternative ; but it is well nevertheless to consider it on grounds of reason.   We ask then at once, by what imaginable means of information can we know of any such revelation, as coming from our Creator?   You will say perhaps, that the revelation might be attested by miracles ; but I rejoin at once, that no amount of miracles, by themselves, can tend to make an alleged revelation even remotely probable.   Most certainly not ; and all Catholic theologians are here in accordance.   On what principle do we accept of miracles, as evidencing the Christian religion ?   On this principle, that we previously recognise our Creator as essentially Veracious.   Suppose *per impossibile* that a being, *not* essentially veracious, had created us, it is obvious at once that he might have multiplied miracles to an indefinite extent, for the express purpose of deluding us.   It is absolutely necessary therefore, that we shall establish God's *Veracity* on grounds of *Reason*, before there is so much as an opening for the entrance of *Revelation*.   And (as was just now observed) no way has ever been so much as suggested, for proving that God is Veracious, which does not assume as a premiss that veracity is of independent obligation.   If then you admit that veracity *is* of independent obligation,—*is* obligatory apart from God's commands,—you totally give up your principle, that those commands are the source of all moral obligation.   But if you do *not* admit that veracity is of independent obligation, you have no means of establishing by Reason that God is Veracious;

nor any reasonable ground therefore whatever, for believing either His Sanctity or any other doctrine, on the
authority of His Revelation.

This then is my fourth argument. If you hold that
God's commands are the foundation of morality, you
have no reasonable ground whatever for believing that
God *does* in fact command justice, veracity, and the
rest: neither the ground of pure Reason, nor the ground
of Revelation.

(5.) Our fifth reason again, for the thesis we are
defending, is perfectly distinct in character from the
other four, being based on the admitted Catholic doctrine ' de Deo;' a doctrine which Reason, no less than
Revelation, conclusively establishes.

In Catholic Theology we ascribe to God every possible perfection, excepting only those which are intrinsecally incompatible with some higher perfection. Thus
it would be a very great perfection, if God possessed
the attribute of clearly and infallibly seeing every future
thing *as* future ; yet we never ascribe to Him that perfection, but on the contrary deny that He possesses it.
Why is this ? Of course, because it is intrinsecally
incompatible with a still higher perfection ; viz. the
existing extra tempus altogether, and viewing alike, as
immutably *present*, what *we* regard as past, present,
and future.

Let us proceed to apply this undoubted doctrine.
We all agree in this, that we deny to God the intrinsic
power of acting in violation of justice, veracity, and
benevolence. In denying Him the power of acting in
every *possible* direction, we plainly deny to Him a certain perfection. Such denial then, as we have seen,
can only be defended, by maintaining that the perfection, which we deny Him, is intrinsecally incompatible with some still higher perfection. This proposition, according to *our* thesis, is manifest enough.
Since the violation of justice veracity and benevolence
is independently sinful, it is an indispensable part of
God's perfections,—it goes in fact to constitute that very
perfection which we call Sanctity,—that He is neces-

sitated by His nature to abstain from any such violation.   But our opponents maintain, that there is nothing
independently evil in the violation of justice veracity or
benevolence; that such violation is only evil at all, because God has forbidden it.   On this theory then, His
inability to act inconsistently with these three qualities
can only be a direct imperfection.   A conclusion, I
need hardly say, absolutely fatal to that premiss, of
which it is the legitimate result.

21. No more surely need be said in favour of our
thesis.   But in proportion as it seems to rest on incontrovertible grounds, you will all certainly be led
to make this obvious enquiry — 'How does it happen
' that a truth, at once so important and so certain, can
' ever have been called in question?'   The one difficulty, I think, which has led any Theist to doubt it
— the one objection, (in other words) which can be
raised in reply to the above quintuple array of argument — is this.   'How can it be otherwise than a great
' imperfection in God, how can it be consistent with
' due reverence towards Him to maintain, that His
' will is thus shackled and limited by a constrain-
' ing bond ? how can He be the Almighty — how
' can He be the One Necessary Self-existent Being —
' if He is thus subjected (as it were) to an external
' necessity ?'

I am very far from wishing to undervalue this difficulty; I only say, that it is not one which we can
be called to answer, in arguing with *Catholics*.   Let
any Catholic philosopher be produced, who denies
that *mathematical* truth is necessary, — *he* would have
most perfect liberty to press the above objection.   But
in truth, not only no Catholic philosopher, hardly any
one possessed of the most ordinary common sense can
be found, who will gravely maintain, that God has the
power of creating a rectilineal figure, which shall have
three sides and four angles; or of so putting together
two straight lines, as that they shall enclose a space.
And if mathematical *axioms* possess this attribute of
necessity, so that God Himself has no power of con-

travening them,—the same attribute beyond all possible question applies to those *further* truths, which result by rigorous *deduction* from these axioms. It is impossible for God to create a triangle, whose three angles taken together shall be greater than two right angles; or to inscribe in a circle any hexagon, except one of such a form that the three intersections of its opposite sides are in the same straight line.*

Now consider the vast extent, I might almost say the unlimited extent, of mathematical truth; the fresh deductions which we are always able to make, from every freshly-discovered conclusion. Remember that this whole domain of truth, by the confession of all Catholic philosophers, is absolutely necessary; and that God has not the physical power of creation, except in complete accordance with it. Remember this, and you will see how utterly extravagant is the reasoning of one, who shall admit indeed the necessity of *mathematical* truth, but shall urge the objection already recited against the necessity of *moral* truth. If it be no derogation from God's Omnipotence (as all Catholics admit it is not) to say that He cannot create a triangle whose three angles shall be greater than two right angles—how can it be any derogation to say, that neither can He create a person, whose obligation it shall be to cultivate the dispositions of pride vindictiveness and impurity?

Indeed, whatever philosophical resource be adopted to reconcile the necessity of *mathematical* truth with God's Omnipotence, will most certainly be equally available for the purposes of *moral* truth. Thus the following statement is often adopted. 'A triangle, with ' three angles greater than two right angles, is no ' *thing* at all; it is a mere chimera. To say that God ' cannot create such a triangle, is not limiting in any ' way His creative power. He can create any *thing* ' which He pleases; but of course He cannot create a ' self-contradictory chimera.'

* I take this mathematical proposition from De Morgan's " Formal Logic," p. 45.

Now all this applies word for word equally to the case before us. ' An imaginary person, whose duty it
' shall be to cultivate the above-named odious disposi-
' tions, is no *person* at all; he is a mere chimera.   To
' say that God cannot create such a person, is not
' limiting in any way His creative power.   He can
' create any person He pleases; but of course He can-
' not create a self-contradictory chimera.'   I am not
at all considering how far this solution is satisfactory;
I am only saying, that if it *be* satisfactory in the case
of mathematical truth, it is evidently to the full *as*
satisfactory in the case of moral truth.

22. Certain writers consider that they avoid the
difficulties of either extreme, by adopting a middle
course.   They say that acts or dispositions, which are
intrinsecally evil, are so, simply because God is necessitated by His nature to detest them.   And thus
they hope to escape the monstrous supposition that
morality is God's free appointment ; while yet they
relieve themselves from the difficulty of supposing,
that anything *can* be in any sense necessary except
God Himself.

Now this statement may have two different meanings ; and in the first of these two meanings, it has
undoubtedly the strongest claim on our attentive consideration.

The following theory then is held by some Catholic
philosophers.   Whenever I intue the necessary, whether it be in the region of morals or mathematics or
any other, I am really intuing the One Necessary Ens:
though in this, as in so many other cases, I may be
very far from recognising the full extent of the Object
which I contemplate.   Hence it follows (according to
these philosophers) that the necessity of all necessary
truth is, in some way wholly incomprehensible to us,
indissolubly bound up with the necessity of God's
existence.   Hence He is restrained by no *extrinsic*
necessity whatever, but wholly by the intrinsic necessity
of His own nature.   It is true indeed that He is
physically unable to reveal a falsehood, or to com-

mand pride and vindictiveness, or to create a triangle
whose angles are greater than two right angles.   But
this fact no more arises from any *extrinsic* necessity,
than does the fact that He is physically unable to
destroy His own existence.

If the statement which I am considering be put
forth in this sense, I have no one adverse remark to
make; it is the very theory to which I myself most
strongly incline, on the relation between God and necessary truth. All for which I am contending is, that moral
truth *is* necessary.   I say it is a *necessary* proposition,
that there is such a quality as moral badness, which
attaches to certain actions in certain circumstances.   I
say it is a *necessary* proposition, that various acts of
injustice mendacity and malevolence are among the acts
to which this quality applies. And so on with the
rest.   I say that the truth of these propositions no
more arises from God's appointment, than the truth
that He is essentially indestructible arises from His
own appointment; or the truth that He exists eter-
nally in Three Persons; or the truth that the base-
angles of an isosceles triangle are equal to each other.
I say that God's detestation of such acts is *founded* on
that intrinsic turpitude, which thus necessarily inheres
in them.   Let this be conceded, all is conceded which
I have wished to establish.

But some writers perhaps do *not* mean this, when
they make the statement which we are considering;
when they say that our obligation to act rightly arises
from the circumstance of God being necessitated by His
nature to detest, *e. g.* pride, vindictiveness, and impurity.   They mean perhaps, that our obligation of
avoiding these dispositions arises from the *mere fact*
that our Creator's nature *happens* (as it were) to necessitate His detesting them.   They deny perhaps, that
there is any *intrinsic turpitude* in those dispositions, on
which turpitude God's detestation of them is founded.
They hold perhaps this doctrine.   ' So soon as I know
' that a certain being created me, and that the nature of
' this being necessitates him to detest certain acts, the

' obligation of avoiding those acts immediately arises.
' This obligation would *as* truly exist, if I believed this
' being to detest, by the necessity of his nature, bene-
' volence, veracity, and purity.'   In other words, they
deny that we legitimately intue the *necessary* obligation
which exists, of shunning the vices opposite to these,
because of their intrinsic turpitude.

If it be their intention to deny this latter proposition, every argument brought against my original
opponents, except perhaps the first, (see n. 20 throughout,) will tell with precisely equal force against these
new adversaries : or rather indeed these thinkers are
hardly other than our old adversaries, appearing in a
new shape.   And I will add one further argument in
addition.   How low and degrading an idea they give
of the Infinite Creator, when they say that His Will
is necessarily determined to one class of acts, while
they deny any intrinsic difference between this class
and the rest !   Every one will see this in an undis-
puted case.   God imposed on the Church, before Christ,
the obligation of circumcision and other rites ; but
when the Holy Spirit came, He removed that obligation.   I would beg you to imagine what your feelings
would be, if you were told that God did not possess the
physical power, either on the one hand of commanding
circumcision, or on the other hand of removing that
command.   The Supreme Lord of the Universe is at
once degraded to a low and subordinate place in His
own creation.   Why on the other hand does no feeling of the kind arise in your minds, when you are told
that He has not the physical power of revealing false
doctrine or of commanding pride and vindictiveness?
Evidently and undeniably, because you *do* possess the
inextinguishable intuition (however energetically men
may labour by sophisms to blind you to its existence)
that there *is* an intrinsic difference of character between the two commands.   Because you intue that
the practising or not practising circumcision, is a thing
intrinsecally indifferent ; but that the cultivating pride
or vindictiveness is a thing intrinsecally detestable—

intrinsecally incapable of being commanded or permitted by a Holy Creator.

We may consider then our thesis as now sufficiently
established.   I hope to shew hereafter, that there can
be no proposition of more vital and universal importance; but I hope I have already shewn, that there can
be none which rests on more incontrovertible grounds
of reason and argument.

23. Before proceeding to our next step, it will be
necessary to explain a distinction, always recognised
in theological treatises ' de Deo.'   There are certain
things, which God cannot do ' de potentiâ absolutâ;'
certain other things, which He can do indeed ' de
potentiâ absolutâ,' but not ' de potentiâ ordinatâ.'   And
now to explain this distinction.

God can do anything ' de potentiâ absolutâ,' which
is not either intrinsecally impossible, or contradictory
to His Attributes.   God cannot ' de potentiâ absolutâ'
create a triangle, whose angles shall be greater than
two right angles ; or command His creature to cultivate pride and vindictiveness.   But short of these
extreme cases, short of cases which involve self-con-
tradiction or contradiction to His essential attributes,
' de potentiâ absolutâ ' He can do everything.

Yet there are many things which, though they do
not involve this absolute contradiction, are manifestly
incongruous and unworthy of Him.   For instance, He
might have infused into the soul of Christ a less degree
of Habitual Grace, than He infuses into you and me at
Baptism. There is nothing here either self-contradictory
or contradictory to His attributes : yet the supposed act
would be so manifestly incongruous and unworthy of
Him, that we might have been quite certain He would
never so have acted.   In all such cases, theologians
say that God cannot so act ' de potentiâ ordinatâ :'
in other words, He cannot *congruously* so act.

24. Let us now proceed with our general subject.
We have seen that there are certain combinations of
circumstances, under which certain acts are of independent obligation.   Let us call the assemblage of

these obligations, by a name not unfrequently given to it; let us call it for the present the Natural Rule of morals (*regula morum*) or the Natural Rule of life.

Now in what relation does God, our All-holy Creator, stand to this Natural Rule? Two things follow, from the principles already laid down. First, He was perfectly free to call into existence creatures, or not to do so ; to call into existence *rational* creatures, or not to do so. Secondly, since He *does* resolve to call rational and free creatures into existence, He is *not* free to appoint, that they shall be exempt from the intrinsic obligatoriness of the Natural Rule. But now further I ask thirdly ; is He necessitated to add a further *distinct command of His own*, in *corroboration* of that Natural Rule? Let us consider for a moment this somewhat important question.

It is very plain that ' de potentiâ ordinatâ ' He could not have acted otherwise. Strange and incongruous indeed it would have been, that an All-holy Being should have created free persons, without commanding them to practise virtue and flee from vice. And that He *has* in fact so acted, no Theist ever doubted. But Suarez goes further than this ; and I think that every Theist, on reflection, will follow him in his further step. He considers that ' de potentiâ absolutâ' God *could* not have abstained from imposing this command ; so that, from the very fact of knowing that He is a Holy Being, we know also that He commands us to fulfil those duties, which are of independent obligation. Suarez's reasoning is as follows. When I know by reason that God is Holy, I know also that what is independently good pleases Him, and what is independently evil dis- pleases ; for otherwise He would *not* be Holy. Now a Holy God, by the very fact of creating us, takes on Himself the office of governing us ; and He who holily governs us, cannot *but* forbid us to do those things, which are independently bad, and therefore intrinse- cally displeasing to Himself.* On a matter where all

* " Quidquid *contra rationem rectam fit, displicet Deo*, et contrarium illi placet ; quia cùm voluntas Dei sit summè justa, *non potest illi non displicere*

Catholics will be probably agreed, it is unnecessary to say more.

Here then we arrive at the idea, implied in that well-known phrase ' the Natural Law.' It is simply this : the command given us by God, and which a Holy Creator

quod turpe est, nec non placere honestum, quia voluntas Dei *non potest esse irrationabilis*, ut dixit Ans. lib. i. Cur Deus homo, c. 8. Ergo ratio naturalis, quæ indicat quid sit per se malum vel bonum homini, *consequenter indicat, esse secundùm divinam voluntatem*, ut unum fiat et aliud vitetur.

" Dices : ex voluntate *complacentiæ aut displicentiæ* in Deo, non sequitur ; quòd sit voluntas obligans *per modum præcepti :* tum quia hâc ratione non tenemur conformari omni divinæ voluntati, quæ est per simplicem affectum ; imo nec omni voluntati beneplaciti seu efficaci ; sed illi tantum, quâ vult nos obligare ; ut suppono ex. 1, 2. q. 19. Unde hâc ratione, licet opera consiliorum placeant Deo, non inde infertur voluntas præcipiens ; tum etiam quia homini justo vel beato displicet quidquid a me contra rationem fit, et tamen nihilominus illa voluntas non est præceptiva. Respondeo primùm, non esse sermonem de *quâcumque voluntate complacentiæ*, sed de illâ, quâ ita placet aliquid ut bonum, ut contrarium vel privativè oppositum per omissionem *displiceat tanquam malum :* opera autem consiliorum non placent hoc modo, sed ita placent, ut in oppositis omissionibus non displiceat aliqua malitia : et ideò illa complacentia vocatur simplex voluntas ; prior autem, quâ ita unum placet ut aliud simpliciter displiceat, censetur magis absoluta. Deinde dico, talem voluntatem spectandam esse in Deo *ut in Supremo Gubernatore*, et non ut inveniri potest in personâ privatâ justâ, sive beatâ sive viatrice : Deus enim, habens illam absolutam displicentiam aut complacentiam, *vult absolutè illud opus fieri vel non fieri*, quantùm ad munus Justi Gubernatoris spectat ; ergo est talis voluntas, ut per illam velit *subditos obligare, ut id faciant vel non faciant*. Non enim potest esse voluntas efficax, ut opus absolutè fiat, vel non fiat ; alias nunquam opus aliter fieret quàm Deus vellet ; quod tamen non ita est, ut constat. Neque id pertinet ad munus Gubernatoris, ad quem spectat ita velle bona, ut permittat mala, et sinat causas secundas liberas suâ libertate uti expeditè et sine impedimento ; ergo oportet, ut sit *voluntas obligans :* nam hoc modo providet subditis in hoc genere, quantùm ad rectam, et prudentem providentiam spectat. * * * *

" Dico igitur ex Cajet. dicto a 8 divinam voluntatem, licet simpliciter libera sit ad extra, tamen ex *suppositione unius actus liberi posse necessitari ad alium ;* ut si vult promittere absolutè, necessitatur ad implendum promissum ; et si vult loqui aut revelare, necessario debet revelare verum. Et cum eâdem proportione, *si vult creare mundum, et illum conservare 'in ordine ad talem finem, non potest non habere providentiam illius ;* et suppositâ providendi voluntate, non potest non habere providentiam perfectam, et consentaneam Suæ Bonitati et Sapientiæ : ideòque *suppositâ voluntate creandi naturam rationalem cum sufficienti cognitione ad operandum bonum et malum, et cum sufficienti concursu ex parte Dei ad utrumque, non potuisse Deum non velle prohibere tali creaturæ actus intrinsecè malos, vel nolle præcipere honestos necessarios.* Quia sicut non potest Deus mentiri, ita *non potest insipienter vel injustè gubernare ;* esset autem *providentia valdè aliena a Divinâ Sapientiâ, et Bonitate, non prohibere vel præcipere suis subditis, quæ talia sunt.* Sic ergo ad argumentum distinguitur minor : nam absolutè posset Deus nihil præcipere vel prohibere : tamen ex *suppositione, quòd voluit habere subditos ratione utentes, non potuit non esse*

could not but give, to perform those acts which in themselves are of independent obligation, and to abstain from those other acts which in themselves are independently evil. Or more briefly — it is God's command, necessarily imposed upon us, to observe the Natural Rule.* Now it is a most undoubtedly legitimate intuition, that disobedience to the commands of an Infinitely Holy Creator is most deeply sinful. Hence it follows, in regard at least to all those who have the means of knowing this command imposed by God, that, in violating the Natural Law, they incur, not merely that sinfulness which is independently intrinsic to the act, but another totally distinct ; viz. disobedience to the Infinite God.† How far it is possible that there may be men possessed of reason, who have *no* sufficient means of knowing God's sanction of the Natural Rule, is a question of some importance ; and it shall be considered in our theological course. A condemned proposition on Philosophical Sin, which we are to treat in the next Section, goes so appalling a length, as to maintain that we cannot gravely offend God, unless we are *distinctly thinking of Him* when we commit a sin. It is difficult to imagine, how any one can have seriously maintained so astounding a paradox.

Legislator eorum, saltem in his quæ ad honestatem naturalem morum necessaria sunt. Item ratio supra insinuata est satis probabilis, quia non potest Deus non odisse malum rectæ rationi contrarium : habet autem hoc odium, non tantum ut privata persona, sed etiam ut Supremus Gubernator : ergo ratione hujus odii, vult obligare subditos ne illud committant."— SUAREZ, *De Legibus,* lib. 2, cap. 6, n. 8, 9, and 23.

* I have taken this definition almost literally from Suarez, though he does not give it *as* a definition. In explaining what is meant by the Natural Law, he says, ' Deus habet perfectam providentiam hominum ; ergo ad Illum, ut ad *Supremum Gubernatorem naturæ,* spectat *vetare mala* et præcipere bona : ergo quamvis ratio naturalis *indicet quid sit bonum vel malum rationali naturæ ;* nihilominus Deus, ut Auctor et Gubernator talis naturæ, *præcipit id facere vel vetare, quod ratio dictat esse faciendum vel vetandum.'—De Legibus,* lib. 2, c. 6, n. 8.

There is a definition of the Natural Law, often ascribed to St. Thomas, precisely equivalent to that which I have given. " Participatio legis æternæ in rationali creaturâ, dictans et præscribens illud esse agendum quod est intrinsecè bonum, et illud fugiendum quod est intrinsecè malum."—See *e. g.* " Philosophia Lugdunensis." But I cannot find it in St. Thomas.

† We shall shew, in our theological course, that this sinfulness is not only totally distinct, but also immeasurably greater.

25. It need hardly be said, that the commands of a Holy Creator claim unswerving obedience at our hands, whether the thing commanded be of independent obligation or not. Hence, when God commanded the Jews to circumcise their children, it was their bounden duty so to do ; when He commands us to obey the laws of the Church, we violate a most solemn duty in refusing obedience.

Here we see the distinction, between the Divine Positive Law and the Natural Law. By the latter, God commands that, which is in itself of independent obligation ; by the former, He commands that, which carries with it no obligation whatever *except* His command.

And here too we see the distinction, which continually meets us in Theology, between 'prohibita quia mala,' and, 'mala quia prohibita.' Pride, vindictiveness, impurity, are 'prohibita quia mala;' prohibited by God, because they are independently evil. To remain separate from the Catholic Church, is 'malum quia prohibitum ;' it is evil, simply because under the Gospel our Holy Creator has forbidden such separation. Again, to eat flesh on Friday, to do servile work on Sunday, to omit confession at Easter, are 'mala quia prohibita ;' evil because they are forbidden by the Church, to which God has given the power of enacting such laws.

Section IV.

*Catholic Authority on the Statements of the preceding
Section.*

26. Since the truths established in the last Section
are so absolutely fundamental,—and since (as I observed) certain Catholics, on first hearing them stated,
recoil with some little surprise,—it will be well, before
going further, to shew how completely they are held
by Catholic writers of the very highest authority.

I am here then to shew, that so considerable a
number of the greatest Catholic writers hold the very
doctrines which we have been advocating, that at all
events any Catholic, who thinks them agreeable to
reason, has the fullest liberty of maintaining them.

27. I will begin with the Church's condemnation of
two propositions ; they are the 48th and 49th of those
condemned by Innocent XI. in 1679. (See Denzinger,
pp. 328, 329.)

" Tam clarum videtur fornicationem *secundùm*
" *se nullam involvere malitiam,* et solùm esse *malam*
" *quia interdicta,* ut contrarium omninò rationi
" dissonum videatur."

" Mollities jure naturæ prohibita non est.
" Unde, si Deus eam non interdixisset, sæpe esset
" bona, et aliquando obligatoria sub mortali."

I will not go the length of saying, that it is impossible to accept this condemnation in any imaginable
sense, without admitting our proposition : yet the
general bearing of the condemnation is none the less
obvious. Caramuel is condemned for maintaining, that
the two sins here mentioned are only 'mala quia prohibita;' in other words, for not admitting that they are

intrinsecally evil, apart from God's prohibition.   But if, apart from God's prohibition, they are independently evil, then, apart from God's prohibition, we are under the independent obligation of avoiding them.

28. Of individual writers, the first whom I cite shall be Cardinal Gerdil; than whom, on these Theologico-philosophical questions, no writer possesses greater authority, if indeed any one possesses so great.   It will be seen that he advocates, not merely the same doctrine, but that doctrine in the same shape in which we ourselves expressed it.   His direct thesis is, that moral truth is necessary, in *the very same sense in which mathematical truth is so.*   It will be further observed, that he notices the denial of this statement in terms of extreme severity; as simply a Protestant error.   In one respect he goes even further than myself: for he uses the phrase 'Natural Law' to express this assemblage of intrinsic obligations; a term which, following (as we shall see) the example of Suarez, I have forborne from adopting.   The length of the quotation must be excused, in regard to its extreme importance; indeed it will be perhaps in many respects useful for you, to see the same principles treated from a somewhat different point of view.

" *I. Principe.*

" Il y a entre le juste et l'injuste, l'honnête et le déshonnête, une différence immuable et nécessaire; en sorte qu'il est autant impossible que le juste devienne injuste, ou que l'honnête devienne déshonnête, qu'il est impossible *que la partie devienne plus grande que le tout, ou que deux choses égales à une troisième ne soient pas égales entr'elles.*

"*Explication.*

" Il est juste et honnête, de préférer l'amour de Dieu à l'amour de la créature; il est injuste et déshonnête, de préférer l'amour de la créature à l'amour de Dieu.   Il est juste et honnête de conserver sa patrie, quand on le peut; il est injuste et deshonnête de la trahir.   Or je dis, que le préférence de Dieu à la créature porte avec soi un caractère de justice et d'honnêteté *immuable et nécessaire;* qu'au contraire, la préférence de la créature à Dieu porte avec soi un caractère d'injustice et de turpitude immuable et nécessaire; que les efforts qu'on fait pour conserver sa patrie portent aussi avec eux ce caractère de justice et d'honnêteté; et qu'au contraire la trahison de sa patrie porte avec soi un caractère immuable et nécessaire d'injustice et de turpitude.

"Preuve.

" *Les rapports de perfection sont autant immuables, que les rapports de quantité:* or est-il que c'est un rapport de perfection, qu'un être plus parfait est préférable à un être moins parfait ; parceque le plus de réalité et de perfection dans l'être plus parfait, est préférable à la privation ou négation de ce plus de réalité et de perfection dans l'être moins parfait ; et cela à cause que l'être est préférable au néant.　Donc ce rapport de perfection fait, que Dieu est *immuablement et nécessairement* préférable à la créature, que la conservation de la patrie est préférable à sa destruction.　D'un autre côté il y a rapport de convenance entre la préférence et ce qui est préférable, et un rapport de disconvenance entre la préférence et ce qui n'est pas préférable : donc le juste et l'honnête étant fondé sur ses rapports immuables de perfection et de convenance, il *est autant impossible que le juste et l'honnête devienne injuste et déshonnête, qu'il est impossible que la partie devienne plus grande que le tout,* &c.

" De là il suit, que comme nous concevons clairement *qu'il ne dépend pas d'une institution libre de la volonté de Dieu de faire que le tout soit plus grand que sa partie,* ou au contraire, parce que Dieu contenant éminemment toutes les réalités des quantités et leurs rapports, ce rapport *se trouve fondé dans l'essence immuable et nécessaire de Dieu même;* de même nous concevons clairement, qu'il ne dépend pas d'une institution libre de Dieu, d'imposer à une créature raisonnable l'obligation de préférer ce qui est préférable à ce qui ne l'est pas, ou au contraire ; parce que Dieu contenant tous les rapports de perfection, par lesquels chaque chose est d'autant plus préférable à l'autre qu'elle participe plus de la plénitude de l'être, et Dieu s'aimant lui-même invinciblement, et chaque chose à proportion qu'elle a plus de rapport à lui de qui seul vient tout l'être, et par conséquent toute l'amabilité,—ces rapports de perfection sont fondés dans l'essence même de Dieu ; et la préférence qu'on doit à ce qui est préférable, est fondée sur la sainteté même de Dieu, qui consiste en ce que Dieu aime, et veut que chaque chose soit aimée ou préférée, à proportion qu'elle est aimable et préférable. Or cet ordre, dans lequel Dieu connoit et aime tout chose à proportion qu'elle est plus ou moins aimable, est ce qu'on appelle la loi éternelle, qui n'est autre que Sa Sagesse, et Sa Sainteté. En un mot Dieu connoit nécessairement et immuablement tout l'ordre, et tous les dégrés de perfection: Son Amour, ou Sa Volonté

F

suit nécessairement l'ordre de Ses connoissances; donc il y a un certain ordre que la Volonté de Dieu suit nécessairement et immuablement: et c'est cet ordre qu'on appelle la loi éternelle. Et c'est en ce sens que David, parlant à Dieu, dit: *Lex tua Veritas.* Votre Loi est vérité: les rapports de perfection, *qui ne sont pas moins vérités immuables que les rapports ou vérités mathématiques,* sont Votre Loi; parce que Votre Amour suit nécessairement l'ordre de Votre Connoissance, et que l'ordre de Votre Connoissance *est exactement conforme à l'ordre des choses elles-mêmes.*

"De là il suit, que c'est pour n'avoir pas assez bien médité cette matière, ni assez bien médité par conséquent le fondement du Droit Naturel, que Pufendorff (*Droit de la Nature, et des gens,* lib. i. ch. 2. § 6) ne craint pas d'avancer, qu'il lui semble, que ' ceux qui admettent pour fondement de la moralité des actions ' humaines je ne sais quelle règle éternelle, *independante de l'insti-* ' *tution Divine,* associent à Dieu manifestement un principe extérieur ' coéternel, qu'il a du suivre nécessairement dans la détermination ' des qualités essentielles et distinctives de chaque chose. D'ailleurs ' on convient généralement, que Dieu a créé l'homme, comme tout ' le reste du monde, avec une Volonté souverainement libre; d'où ' il s'ensuit, qu'il dependoit absolument de son bon plaisir de donner ' à l'homme, en le créant, telle nature qu'il jugeroit à propos. ' Comment donc les actions humaines pourroient-elles avoir quelque ' propriété qui resultat d'une nécéssité interne et absolue, indé- ' pendemment de l'institution Divine, et du bon plaisir de cet être ' souverain?'

"On voit premièrement, que quoique nous disions, que Dieu a du suivre nécessairement l'ordre et la Loi Eternelle, cette loi éternelle n'est pas un principe extérieur qu'on associe à Dieu; cette Loi Eternelle resulte de la perfection même de l'Etre Divin, qui connoit les choses *telles qu'elles sont,* et dont l'Amour est *essentiellement conforme à l'ordre de Ses Connoissances.* Et certaine- ment, sans cette loi éternelle, *comment pourroit-on assurer, que Dieu ne peut mentir, qu'il ne peut tromper les hommes?* S. Paul et l'Ecriture associent donc à Dieu un principe extérieur, en assurant que Dieu ne peut mentir?*

"On voit en second lieu, que la raison que l'auteur apporte pour soutenir son opinion, vient aussi de ce qu'il n'avoit pas assez bien médité les raisonnements métaphysiques. Il est vrai, qu'on

* "Devoirs," &c. liv. i. chap. ii. sec. 8, note I. Dieu lui-même, qui n'a besoin de nous, est sujet à la glorieuse nécessité de ne pouvoir rien préscrire contre les règles inviolables de l'ordre, qui ne sont autre chose qu'une émanation de Ses Perfections Infinies, une suite de la nature des choses dont il est lui-même l'Auteur, de sorte qu'Il Se dementiroit, s'Il agissoit autrement. (Author's note.)

convient généralement, que Dieu a créé l'homme, comme tout
le reste du monde, avec une volonté souverainement libre ; mais
aussi on convient généralement, que supposé que Dieu se soit
librement déterminé à créer le monde, *il ne lui a pas été libre de
la créer d'une manière indigne de Soi*, ou qui ne fut pas conforme
à cet ordre, ou à cette Loi Éternelle fondée sur Sa Sagesse, et sur
Sa Sainteté.   Ce que l'auteur ajoute, est encore plus frivole,
qu'il dependoit du bon plaisir de Dieu de donner à l'homme en le
créant telle nature qu'il jugeroit à propos.   Je crois que l'auteur
a voulu dire, que Dieu, au lieu de créer un homme, pouvoit créer
un oiseau, ou un animal de toute autre nature, à qui on auroit
donné le nom d'homme ; et alors ce qu'il dit est tout-à-fait hors
de propos.   Mais suppose, que Dieu ait voulu créer librement
une nature telle que celle que nous appellons homme ; il n'a pas
certainement pu lui donner une autre nature, ni lui donner par
une institution libre une autre loi naturelle.   *Il ne pouvoit faire
que l'homme connut avec évidence, que la partie fut plus grande que
le tout, ou que la créature fut préférable au Créateur ; et par conséquent il ne pouvoit faire que l'homme jugeat de devoir préférer la
créature au Créateur, et que sa préférence ensuite de ce jugement fut
juste et honnête.*

"De là il suit, que c'est une bien misérable objection que
celle que l'auteur et plusieurs autres tirent du physique des
actions humaines pour prouver qu'elles sont de leur nature
indifférentes, et que les bêtes les font sans péché.   Je ne crois
pas qu'il y aie jamais en au monde un homme si peu sensé qui
voulut que le mouvement physique, ou l'acte extérieur par lequel
on tue un homme, ou qu'on lui vole son bien, fut un péché.
Quand on dit que les actions de l'homme sont souvent honnêtes
ou déshonnêtes par elles-mêmes, on l'entend du consentement de
la volonté, et de la préférence qu'elle donne à un motif plutôt
qu'à un autre.   Or on eut raison d'assurer, que certains consente-
ments ou préférences de la volonté sont dereglées de leur nature,
comme quand elle préfère la créature au Créateur, &c.   C'est
donc bien mal à propos, que Pufendorff reprend Grotius (ibid.
p. 32) pour avoir mis au rang ' des choses, *auxquelles la Puis-
sance Divine ne s'étend point,* à cause qu'elles impliquent contradiction, *la malice de certaines actions humaines ;* qui sont essentiellement mauvaises, en sorte *qu'il n'est pas au pouvoir de Dieu
même de faire qu'elles ne soient pas telles.*'

"II. Principe.

"On peut appeller Loi Naturelle la connoissance qu'on a de la
différence du juste et de l'injuste, de l'honnête et du déshonnête.

"*Explication.*

" La même lumière, qui nous fait connoître qu'une action est juste ou injuste, honnête ou déshonnête, *nous fait aussi connoître que nous devons faire* ce qui est juste, et nous abstenir de ce qui est injuste ; c'est-à-dire, que dès que nous connoissons qu'une préférence est juste ou injuste, nous ne pouvons ignorer *notre devoir* par rapport à cette préférence. Donc cette connoissance de la différence du juste et de l'injuste, peut et doit servir de règle aux actions humaines ; on peut donc lui donner le nom de loi. Or cette loi est assurement naturelle,* et non positive, parce qu'elle ne dépend pas de l'institution libre et positive d'un législateur ; *mais qu'elle est fondée sur la connoissance de certains rapports naturels ou essentiels des choses mêmes. On pourroit disputer si on doit donner le nom de loi à une règle, quand on ne sait pas qu'elle ait été donnée par un législateur légitime ; mais ce seroit une dispute de nom ; il suffit que cette règle puisse imposer une véritable obligation de la suivre :* or la connoissance du juste et de l'injuste impose à tous les hommes une vraie obligation de faire ce qui est juste, et de s'abstenir de ce qui est injuste, *sans attendre la connoissance explicite de la volonté d'un législateur.* Ceux qui ne veulent pas que la connoissance du juste et de l'injuste suffise pour imposer *une obligation proprement dite,* sont fort embarrassés de trouver le fondement de l'obligation où sont les hommes d'obéir à la loi naturelle."

* * * * * *

" J'ai dit que la connoissance des vérités fondées sur les rapports de perfection impose *un véritable devoir, et par conséquent une obligation* de s'y conformer. Pour éclaircir cette question qui regarde le fondement de l'obligation, et qui est fort subtile et fort délicate, il faut dire deux mots du sentiment opposé. Plusieurs célèbres auteurs *entre les Protestants,* outre Pufendorff et Barbeyrac, prétendent qu'il n'y a point de véritable obligation de faire ou d'omettre une action, *sans la volonté ou la loi d'un législateur légitime,* qui la commande ou qui la défende. Or pour faire une loi parfaite qui impose une obligation parfaite, ils veulent que cette loi ait deux parties, l'une qui enseigne ce que l'on doit faire, l'autre qui menace de la peine qu'on encourra si on ose la violer.

---

* C'est ainsi que Ciceron définit la loi naturelle : ' Lex est ratio insita in naturâ, quæ jubet ea quæ facienda sunt, prohibetque contraria.' Fausse est par conséquent la maxime de M. Hobbes ('Fond de la Politiq.' ch. 12, ar. 1) conçuë en ces termes : 'Mais entre les opinions qui disposent à la ' sedition, l'une des principalles est celle-ci, qu'il appartient à chaque par- ' ticulier de juger ou de ce qui est bien, ou de ce qui est mal,' &c. Voyez le reste de l'article. La confutation en est aisée. (Author's note.)

" 1. De là il s'ensuivroit, qu'on ne seroit obligé d'obéir à la loi que par la crainte des peines; puisque sans cette crainte qui répond à la partie coactive de la loi, ou sans la partie coactive dont l'action ne rend qu'à inspirer la crainte, il n'y a point de loi parfaite.

" 2. Je dois remarquer une contradiction, dans laquelle ils tombent à ce sujet.   Ils avouent qu'un Prince dépouillé de son autorité peut faire une loi qui oblige: cependant la loi d'un tel Prince ne peut contenir que la partie directive; car dans cette supposition la partie coactive ne sauroit avoir d'effet.

" 3. Mais si la loi d'un Prince dépouillé de son autorité, qui ne conserve que la partie directive, ne laisse pas que d'imposer une véritable obligation; si les gens de bien, indépendemment de la crainte, se croient obligés de s'y soumettre,—sur quoi est fondée cette obligation, si non sur les lumières naturelles de la raison, qui font voir le rapport de convenance qu'il y a eu ce qu'un sujet obéisse à son supérieur ?

" D'ailleurs dans la société civile il peut arriver, qu'un homme aime mieux subir la peine infligée par la loi, une amende pécuniaire par exemple, que d'observer cette loi; il peut même quelquefois, comme il arrive aux contrebandiers, si bien prendre ses mesures, qu'il ne sera pas découvert, ou qu'il ne craindra aucunement d'être pris.   Alors la partie coactive de la loi n'a aucune force par rapport à cet homme.   Est-il donc absous de l'obligation de s'y soumettre?   C'est ce qu'on n'oseroit dire. C'est donc en virtu de la partie directive; c'est donc parce qu'il juge qu'il est juste de se soumettre à une loi légitime, même sans y être forcé; et il juge que cela est juste, à cause de ce rapport de convenance qu'il y découvre, c'est-à-dire en d'autres termes, à cause de la conformité de cet acte avec les lumières de sa raison.   Puis donc que cette conformité, &c., est la règle, ou le fondement de l'obligation où l'on se reconnoit d'obéir à un supérieur, on ne sauroit douter que cette conformité ne soit le premier fondement de toute obligation; car il est clair, que ce n'est qu'en virtu *de l'obligation générale de se conformer aux lumières de la droite raison*, qu'on vient à connoître l'obligation particulière d'obéir à un supérieur.   Car la connoissance de cette obligation particulière suppose nécessairement ces deux connoissances plus générales : l'une, que c'est une chose conforme à la droite raison et convenable, de se soumettre à un supérieur; l'autre, *qu'on doit faire ce qu'on connoit conforme à la droite raison.* Ces deux connoissances sont comme les deux premisses d'un syllogisme, dont la connoissance de l'obligation de se soumettre à la loi d'un supérieur est une conséquence nécessaire.

" Un sujet obéit à son Prince légitime dépouillé de son autorité, qui ne sauroit lui faire du mal.   Un autre obéit à un brigand, entre les mains de qu'il est tombé, par la crainte des supplices, quoique ce brigand n'ait aucune supériorité légitime sur lui. Dans le premier cas il y a une obligation d'obéir; dans le second il n'y en a point, des qu'on peut désobéir en cachette, pour ne pas s'exposer à la mort. Qu'on en donne d'autre raison que celle que nous avons dit. Cela fait voir, que l'autorité d'infliger des peines n'accompagne pas toujours la supériorité légitime. Ce sont donc les lumières de la raison, qui font connoître la supériorité légitime, et l'obligation de s'y soumettre.

" Quand on connoit une vérité fondé sur les rapports de perfection, par ex., que la vie de son ami est préférable à celle d'une bête, ou connoit aussi le rapport de convenance qu'il y a à préférer la vie de cet ami à celle de la bête. Or ce rapport de convenance est aussi une vérité, qu'on exprime en ces termes : 'il convient, on *il faut* préférer la vie d'un ami à celle d'une bête; quand on voit un ami prêt à être décliné par une bête qui s'est jetée sur lui, *il ne faut pas* balancer à conserver la vie de cet ami au dépens de celle de la bête, si on peut la tuer.' *La connoissance de cette vérité fait donc naître dans l'ésprit un jugement aussi certain de ce qu'il faut faire en cette occasion, que la connoissance d'une vérité de géométrie fait naître un jugement certain de ce qu'il faut affirmer ou nier.* Or comme le jugement certain en fait de spéculation est la règle de ce qu'on doit affirmer ou nier, le jugement certain en fait d'action, c'est-à-dire de ce qu'il faut faire ou ne pas faire, est la règle de ces mêmes actions. Or comme on appelle vérité ou fausseté, ce qui est conforme ou contraire à la règle en fait de spéculation,—on appelle bon ou mauvais, ce qui est conforme ou oppose à la règle des actions; la lumière la plus simple de la vérité fait connoître, que chaque chose, pour être dans l'ordre et n'être pas fautive, doit être conforme à sa règle. L'esprit ne peut donc connoître la règle de ses actions, sans connoître aussi qu'il doit les y conformer. ' Est autem vitium primum animæ rationalis voluntas ea faciendi, quæ vetat summa et intima veritas,' dit S. Augustin. (*Lib. de vera Relig.*, cap. 19.) Ce fondement de l'obligation est si naturel, que les païens mêmes, qui avoient aussi bien que les modernes l'idée de l'obligation (puisque *tout le monde sait ce que c'est que l'obligation,* quoique tout le monde ne connoisse peut être pas les fondements), n'en ont pas pensé autrement. Quoiqu'un crime put être éternellement caché aux dieux et aux hommes, on ne devroit pas le commettre, disoient-ils ; car en évitant tout autre châtiment, on ne pourroit éviter les reproches de la conscience. Or *ce reproche de la conscience ne consiste qu'en ce que l'esprit connoît qu'il manque à ce qu'il doit,* lorsqu'il agit contre ce qu'il connoit être la règle de ses actions. C'est donc sur la conformité à cette règle qu'est fondée l'obligation. C'est en ce sens, que S. Paul dit (Ep.

ad Rom. xi. xii.): ' Qui sine lege peccaverunt, sine lege peribunt.'
Comment donc le Traducteur de Pufendorff a-t-il pu prétendre,
pour excuser en quelque manière l'erreur que nous avons combattu
ci-dessus, que quoique *indépendamment de la Volonté de Dieu* il
ne soit pas aussi beau * de manquer à sa parole, que de la tenir
&c., cela ne suffit pas pour imposer une obligation proprement aussi
nommée ?

" III. Principe.

" La connoissance du juste et de l'injuste ne dépend pas d'une
connoissance explicite de la volonté de Dieu: en sorte qu'on ne
puisse juger qu'une chose est juste et honnête, que parce qu'on
sait que Dieu la commande ; et qu'au contraire elle n'est injuste
et déshonnête, que parce qu'on sait que Dieu la défend.

" Explication.

" Le Traducteur de Pufendorff (lib. ii. c. 2, § 6, n. 1) avoue
qu'il y a des actes qui par eux-mêmes ne conviennent à Dieu en
aucune manière ; c'est-à-dire, dont Il ne sauroit être susceptible
sans déroger à Ses Perfections, et sans se contredire lui-même ; et
je crois que c'est une vérité, dont on ne sauroit douter, pour peu
qu'on ait de bon sens et de religion. Or ce qui nous porte à
ne pas attribuer à Dieu ces sortes d'actes, c'est *par ce que nous
les connoissons manifestement contraires aux notions communes que
nous avons de la bonté, et de la justice, &c., que nous savons être des
attributs de la Divinité.* Donc il y a des choses que nous connoissons *par elles-mêmes honnêtes et déshonnêtes, justes et injustes,
indépendamment d'une connoissance explicite de la volonté de Dieu.*
C'est ce que S. Paul explique clairement. (Ep. ad Rom. cap. ii.):
' Quum enim gentes quæ legem non habent, naturaliter ea quæ
legis sunt faciunt, ejusmodi legem non habentes, ipsi sibi sunt
lex ; qui ostendunt opus legis scriptum in cordibus suis; testimonium reddente illis conscientiâ ipsorum, et inter se invicem
cogitationibus accusantibus et defendentibus.' De là suit le

" IV. Principe.

" Au contraire, sans une expresse révélation, *on ne peut connoître, qu'une telle action soit commandée ou défendue par Dieu,
que parce qu'on sait qu'elle est de soi bonne, ou mauvaise.*

---

* Pufendorff (" Devoirs," &c. liv. i. chap ii. § 1) dit : " L'ordre et la beauté
de la société humaine demandoit nécessairement, qu'il y eut quelque règle,
à laquelle on fut tenu de se conformer." Lors donc, qu'on connoit une
règle qui dirige les actions d'une manière conforme à cet ordre, et à cette
beauté, pourquoi cette règle ne sera-t-elle pas une loi, comme l'auteur la
nomme même au § 2 ? (Author's note.)

"*Explication.*

"Le Traducteur de Pufendorff, qui malgré le passage de l'Apôtre que nous avons cité ci-dessus *ne reconnoit pour fonde-ment de l'obligation que la volonté de Dieu ;* dit, que cette volonté se découvre à nous par la convenance de telles ou telles actions avec la nature humaine. Mais comme il n'explique point en quoi il fait consister cette convenance, on est en droit de lui répondre, que ce qu'il avance, ne signifie rien. Il ne sauroit simplement entendre, par cette convenance, les actions qui peuvent tourner à l'avantage et au bonheur de l'homme ; puisque son auteur avoue qu'il y en a plusieurs qui ne sont pas moralement bonnes, comme on peut le prouver par la connoissance des arts, qui n'est pas moralement bonne (car on n'est pas d'autant plus honnête homme qu'on est grand géométre) et qui pourtant contribue infiniment à l'avantage de la société. Qu'est ce donc que c'est cette convenance avec la nature humaine ? On ne peut l'expliquer autrement, si non que la nature humaine étant une nature raisonnable, elle connoit, entre les choses qui se présentent, entre les fins qu'elle se peut proposer en agissant, entre les motifs qui la meuvent, certains rapports de perfection, par lesquels elle connoit qu'une telle action est préférable à une autre action, et qu'il y a un rapport de convenance à préférer ce qui est préférable. Mais alors c'est l'idée de l'ordre qui est la règle de nos actions, et qui suffit pour *obliger même à agir ceux que l'on suppose n'avoir aucune idée de Dieu.* Nous avons donc une idée du juste et de l'injuste, de l'honnête et du déshonnête, *indépendamment de la connoissance explicite de la volonté de Dieu.* Ce n'est que par cette idée, que nous jugeons, que c'est la volonté de Dieu qu'on fasse du bien à ceux qui nous en font ; sans cette idée, comment les païens, qui n'avoient aucune expresse révélation de la volonté de Dieu, auroient-ils pu donner de si beaux préceptes de morale, distinguer l'utile de l'honnête, enseigner qu'on doit 'omnem cruciatum perferre, intolerabili dolore lacerari, potius quam officium prodere, aut fidem ;' et reconnoître que cela étoit conforme à la volonté de l'Etre souverain, essentiellement Juste, Bon, et Saint ? Il faut donc convenir qu'il y a des choses, qui sont ' malæ, quia prohibitæ ;' et qu'il y en a d'autres, qui sont ' prohibitæ, quia malæ.'"—*Morale Chrétienne de Card. Gerdil,* pp. 44–49, 51–57, vol. ii. of the Roman edition of his works.

29. Next let us proceed to the great post-Tridentine scholastics; who will be found, in treating the subject, to cite no small amount of anterior testimony also. And first for Suarez. This great theologian treats the question very fully in his "De Legibus;" which is

usually considered his greatest and most authoritative
work. The chapters in which this treatment is to be
found, are the fifth and sixth chapters of the second
book. I will first give various extracts from these
chapters, and then an analysis of their contents.

Let us commence with certain statements, put
forth by him as arguments for a certain doctrine of
Vasquez, which he (Suarez) opposes. These statements themselves are certainly true in Suarez's judgment, because he immediately subjoins these words :
‘ In hâc [Vasquezii] sententiâ, *veram esse existimo doc-*
‘ *trinam* quam in fundamento supponit, *de intrinsecâ*
‘ *honestate vel malitiâ* actuum, quæ sub Legem Natu-
‘ ralem cadunt.’ (lib. ii. c. v. n. 5.) What his difference
from Vasquez *is*, we shall see when we analyse the
chapter : but he at once states that he has *no* difference with that theologian on the question immediately
before us ; on the intrinsic virtue or vice of those acts,
which fall under the Natural Law.

What then are those statements, which may be
supposed as put forth by Vasquez, and to which
Suarez expresses his complete assent ? Such as the
following :—

 “ Sunt aliquæ actiones ita intrinsecè malæ *ex naturâ suâ,* ut
nullo modo pendeant in malitiâ ex *prohibitione extrinsecâ* nec *ex
Judicio vel Voluntate Divinâ* . . . . Quod suppono *ex communi sententiâ theologorum* . . . . Ratio est, quia actus morales habent *suas
intrinsecas naturas et essentias immutabiles*, quæ non pendent *a
causâ vel voluntate extrinsecâ*, magìs quàm *aliæ rerum essentiæ, quæ
per se non implicant contradictionem.*”—(Ibid. n. 2.)

 Again :—

 “ Sicut essentiæ rerum, quatenùs non implicant contradictionem, sunt tales vel tales in esse essentiæ, *ex se et ante omnem
causalitatem Dei et quasi independenter ab Ipso*—ita honestas veri-
tatis et turpitudo mendacii talis *est ex se et secundum æternam
veritatem.*”—(n. 4.)

So much, where stating his agreement with Vasquez. In the next chapter, while stating his own doctrine, he is equally clear :—

 “ Dictamina rationis naturalis, in quibus hæc lex consistit, sunt *intrinsecè necessaria* et independentia ab omni voluntate *etiam Divinâ;* . . . . ut 'Deus est colendus,' 'parentes honorandi,' 'mendacium est pravum et cavendum,' et similia."—(c. vi. n. 1.)

" Etiam in Deo, ad Voluntatem antecedit, secundùm rationem, Judicium mentis indicans *mentiri esse malum,* servare promissum esse omninò rectum et necessarium."—(c. vi. n. 6.)

Again, having explained that the Natural Law refers properly to God's Command, and not to the intrinsic rectitude or pravity of acts, he proceeds :—

" Hæc Dei Voluntas, Prohibitio aut Præceptio, *non est tota ratio bonitatis et malitiæ* quæ est in observatione vel transgressione Legis Naturalis, sed *supponit in ipsis actibus necessariam quamdam* honestatem vel turpitudinem; et *illis adjungit* specialem Legis Divinæ obligationem.   Hæc assertio . . . . colligitur *ex illo communi axiomate theologorum,* quædam mala esse prohibita quia mala; si enim prohibentur quia mala, non possunt primam rationem malitiæ accipere à prohibitione." (c. vi. n. 11.) . . . . " Secundùm ordinem rationis [mendacium] priùs est actus malus quàm prohibitus per propriam legem."—(c. vi. n. 14.)

Lastly :—

" Respondeo, in actu humano esse aliquam bonitatem vel malitiam, *ex vi objecti præcise spectati* ut est consonum vel dissonum *rationi rectæ;* et secundùm eam posse denominari *et malum, et peccatum, et culpabilem,* secundùm illos respectus, seclusâ habitudine ad propriam legem.   Præter hanc verò, habet actus humanus *specialem* rationem boni et mali *in ordine ad Deum,* additâ *Divinâ Lege prohibente vel præcipiente."* —(c. vi. n. 17.)

Let us now proceed to our promised analysis of the two chapters.

' It is said that the Natural Law is nothing else ' than the rational nature.   But this may be held in ' two senses :—

' First, it may be held that the Natural Law is ' nothing else than the rational nature, according to ' that sense of the latter phrase, in which we say that ' things intrinsecally good are conformable to the ra-' tional nature, and things intrinsecally evil repugnant ' to it.

' In another sense it may be said that the Natural ' Law is our rational nature, meaning thereby that the ' *discernment of duty,* which appertains to the rational

' nature, is the very promulgation of the natural law.
' (c. 5, n. 1.)

' Vasquez holds the proposition in the former sense;
' and though he quotes no authorities in behalf of his
' statement, something may be said in its behalf on
' grounds of reason.   First, as theologians commonly
' admit, certain acts are intrinsecally right or intrinse-
' cally wrong.   Yet they must be right from conformity
' with *some* law or other, and not from mere conformity
' with our judgment.   But they are right from con-
' formity with .our *rational nature ;* hence our rational
' nature is a real *law.*   But if it be *any* law, then
' plainly it is the Natural Law.

' Secondly, these acts are right, *antecedently* to any
' judgment formed concerning them by God : hence
' the obligation to perform them, that is the Natural
' Law, cannot come from God : what else therefore can
' it be, except our rational nature ? (nn. 2–4.) *

' Now I quite agree with Vasquez in all that he
' says about the intrinsic obligation of acts; yet I can-
' not agree with his conclusion.

' First, theologians and philosophers do not in
' general so express themselves.   Secondly, a law
' should give command, light, and direction ; but the
' rational nature (in Vasquez' sense) does not give
' command, light, or direction.   Thirdly, there can be
' no law, properly so called, without the *will* of some
' one giving command. (n. 5.)

' In the third reason I anticipate, c. 6, n. 1, 'Lex
' enim propria et præceptiva non est, sine voluntate
' alicujus præcipientis.'   To proceed however with our
' analysis :

' Besides, see what consequences would follow.   It
' would follow in the first place, that God is no less
' subject to the Natural Law than we are : for in God
' also, as well as in man, to act viciously would be to
' act against His nature.   If therefore this fact suffices
' in *our* case to constitute our nature as a law to us, it

---

* I have omitted as irrelevant the third reason suggested by Suarez in
Vasquez' behalf.

' would no less constitute God's Nature as a law to
' Him. And it would follow in the second place, that
' to *us* the Natural Law would not be a *Divine* law at
' all. (nn. 7, 8.)

' The common doctrine of theologians therefore is,
' that our rational nature in the *second* sense is the Natu-
' ral Law' (he means, is the promulgation to us of the
Natural Law); 'for by our rational nature, in this sense,
' the human will receives command or prohibition, as to
' 'quod agendum est ex naturali jure.' (c. 5, n. 9.)
' This view may be supported by Scripture, Fathers,
' and Reason. (nn. 10–15.)

' But here we come to a great difficulty. For
' those things which the light of reason thus dictates,
' as 'Deus est colendus,' 'parentes sunt honorandi,'
' and the like, are *truths independent even of the
' Divine Will.* If then the mere light of reason be
' the promulgation of the Natural Law, how can that
' Law be in any strict sense a law at all? for the light
' of reason does not make known to us (it may be
' said) the command of any *superior*, but only the
' intrinsic virtuousness or viciousness of certain acts.
' (c. 6, nn. 1, 2.)

' Some theologians have accepted this conse-
' quence; they have said that the Natural Law is
' *not* in strictness a law, is not the command of any
' superior, but only an inherent light, teaching us
' what is intrinsically good. It is a 'lex indicans,'
' but not a 'lex præcipiens.'' (n. 3.)

It would seem, though Suarez does not advert to
it, that this is precisely Vasquez' view. Gerdil also
plainly speaks in this way; for throughout he calls
our perception of the intrinsic goodness and badness
of acts, our recognition of the Natural Law. To
proceed however with the Doctor Eximius.

' An extremely opposite view has been taken by
' some other theologians; who maintain that the Natural
' Law is simply a collection of commands, imposed by
' God as the Author and Governor of our nature.

' These theologians say, that the whole distinction

' between good and evil turns on the will of God; and
' that God does not command a thing because it is in-
' trinsecally good, but on the contrary it is intrinse-
' cally good because He commands it.' (n. 4.) *

Pray observe, that this is the precise doctrine
against which I argued throughout the previous Section.   Let us now see how completely our author dis-
claims it:—

' I am satisfied with neither opinion; and therefore
' judge that a middle course should be held, which I
' think is the *opinion of St. Thomas and the common*
' *one of theologians.*†

' I say then *first* [against the first opinion] the (pro-
' mulgation of the) Natural Law is not merely a pointing
' out of the intrinsic good and evil contained in actions,
' but contains an express command of good and pro-
' hibition of evil on God's part. (n. 5.)

' This I prove by two arguments.   First, *à pos-*
' *teriori*, otherwise the Natural Law would not pro-
' perly *be* a law.   Secondly, *à priori*, because reason
' itself, in recognising a Holy God, recognises *e. g.*
' His prohibition of things intrinsecally evil.' (nn. 6–10.)

We have developed this latter reason in n. 24.

' I say secondly [against the second opinion] this
' prohibition or command of God, given in the Natural
' Law, *supposes* a certain *necessary* virtuousness or base-
' ness in the acts themselves; and *adds to those acts the*
' *special obligation of a Divine Law.*‡ (n. 11.)

' The former part of this statement (viz. that the
' acts themselves have intrinsic virtuousness or baseness
' necessarily inhering) is implied in that axiom of theo-
' logians, that some evils are ' prohibita *quia* mala;' and
' is quite evident indeed from the arguments suggested
' in behalf of Vasquez' doctrine.   The second part of

---

* 'Qui etiam addunt totam rationem boni et mali, in rebus ad legem
naturæ pertinentibus, positam esse in Voluntate Dei ; et non in judicio
rationis, etiam Ipsius Dei, neque in rebus ipsis, quæ per talem legem
vetantur aut præcipiuntur.'

† 'Mihi vero neutra sententia satisfacit ; et ideò mediam viam tenen-
dam censeo, quam existimo esse sententiam D. Thomæ et communem
theologorum.' (n. 5.)

‡ See quotation already given in note to n. 24.

' this statement (viz. that the Natural Law adds a *special*
' obligation in addition to this intrinsic virtuousness or
' baseness) follows upon what has already been said.   I
' have shewn that the Natural Law is a real Divine Law;
' therefore it *must* add *some* obligation.   Nor is there
' any imaginable repugnance in the idea, that a new
' obligation may be added where one already exists.
' (nn. 11, 12.)

   ' I say therefore thirdly (recapitulating what has
' preceded) that the Natural Law is a true law, God being
' Legislator.   Yet it supposes a *judgment* in God, that
' the acts commanded by the Natural Law are conform-
' able, and the acts forbidden by it are repugnant, to
' our rational nature : to which judgment of God, this
' Natural Law *adds an act of His Will*, obliging men to
' observe that which right reason dictates.* (n. 13.)

   ' Now to consider the arguments in favour of the
' two opinions which I reject.   Their consideration will
' turn entirely on this hypothetical statement; " even
' though God did not prohibit or command those things
' which belong to the Natural Law, nevertheless to lie is
' evil, and to honour parents good and obligatory."   In
' regard to which hypothetical statement, I must consider
' two things : First, what would follow from such a
' hypothesis ?   Secondly, is the hypothesis a possible
' one?' (n. 14.)

   We omit his statements of other opinions in nn.
15 and 16, and come to his own in n. 17.   ' As to the
' first question, I make this answer.   In a human action
' there is a certain goodness or badness from the object
' considered precisely; and according to this (badness)
' it may be called an *evil*, a *sin*, culpable, without *any*

---

* ' Unde probandum non est, quod doctores posteriori loco allegati
dicunt, Voluntatem Divinam, quâ lex naturalis sancitur, non supponere
dictamen divinæ rationis dictantis, hoc esse honestum vel turpe ; neque
Voluntatem illam Dei [non] supponere in objecto *intrinsecam convenientiam
vel disconvenientiam ad naturam rationalem*, ratione cujus vult unum fieri et
aliud vetari : constat, enim, ex dictis in secundâ conclusione, hoc *falsum
esse et contra rationem Legis Naturalis.*   Quamvis ergò obligatio illa quam
addit lex naturalis, ut propriè præceptiva est, sit ex Voluntate Divinâ,
tamen illa voluntas *supponit judicium de malitiâ*, verbi gratiâ, mendacii et
similia : tamen, quia ex vi solius judicii non inducitur *propria prohibitio*,
vel obligatio *præcepti*, quia hoc sine voluntate intelligi non potest, ideo
adjungitur Voluntas prohibendi illud, quia malum est.' (cap. 6, n. 13.)

' *relation to a law properly so called.** Besides this
' badness, a human act has a *special* quality of good or
' bad *in relation to God*, from the Divine Law being
' added which commands or prohibits it. (nn. 17–19.)

' As to the second question—whether the hypothesis
' is a possible one (that God should *not* prohibit or com-
' mand those things which are in themselves evil or
' obligatory respectively)—there are two opinions. First,
' that it is impossible ' de Dei potentiâ ordinatâ,' but not
' ' absolutâ ;' secondly, that it is impossible even ' de Dei
' potentiâ absolutâ.' This latter is plainly St. Thomas's
' opinion, and I follow it. It would be contrary to the
' very Attributes of a Holy and Wise Creator, if He did
' not impose such an obligation on His rational creatures.
' You may object, that God's will is free in all external
' actions ; but I reply with Cajetan, not altogether so.
' He is free *e. g.* to make or not to make a promise ; but
' if He *does* make one, He is necessitated to keep it : He
' is free to make or not to make a revelation ; but if He
' *do* make one, He is necessitated to reveal *truth*. And
' in a way precisely similar, He is free to create or not
' to create rational persons; but if He *do* create them,
' He is necessitated to impose on them the obligations of
' the Natural Law. (nn. 21, 23.) †

' A second objection may be made ; viz. that *promul-*
' *gation* is essential to a law properly so called. Now
' God is certainly free, it may be said, as to whether
' He will or will not *promulgate* His command, that
' men shall act conformably with reason; and there-
' fore it still remains, that He is free whether He shall
' or shall not impose the Natural Law. But I reply,
' that He *is* necessitated to promulgate such a law ; for
' if He be necessitated to enact it, He must be necessi-
' tated to promulgate it. And He has in fact promul-
' gated it, by the fact already mentioned, that reason
' alone suffices to shew us His will in this particular.' ‡

* 'Malum, peccatum culpabile, *seclusâ* habitudine ad propriam *legem.*'
† See quotation already given in the note to n. 24, " Dico igitur ex
Cajetano," &c.
‡ Hac de causâ per lumen naturale cognoscitur, Deum offendi peccatis
quæ contra Legem Naturalem fiunt, et ad Ipsum pertinere illorum punitionem

I would beg you to read carefully over these two
chapters of Suarez; and see whether I have not represented him with the most perfect faithfulness.*

It is quite impossible then to doubt his meaning.
His immediate subject is not morality but *law ;* and it
is a very important matter therefore, from his point of
view, to oppose Vasquez's notion, that there can be a
law, strictly so called, without a lawgiver.   Yet with
all his earnest opposition to Vasquez, never for a moment does he lose sight of the great truth, that the
acts prohibited by the Natural Law are also independently wrong; and would be ' mala, peccata, culpabilia,'
(c. 6, n. 17), even though that Law did not exist.

30. Vasquez, as is evident from what has preceded,
will be found even more emphatic than Suarez himself, in declaring that the intrinsic wickedness of vice
does not arise from God's Prohibition; but that on the
contrary God's Prohibition of it arises from its intrinsic
wickedness.   One citation then will suffice, from that
chapter of his which Suarez quotes :—

" Si verò sermo sit de Lege Naturali, quæ suâpte naturâ
constare dicitur *non autem placito aut alicujus voluntate,* aliter
dicendum est.   Cùm enim lex aut jus sit regula cui æquari
debent actiones ut justæ sint, *naturalis* lex aut *naturale* jus erit
regula *naturalis,* quæ *nullâ voluntate sed suâpte naturâ* constat.
Porrò talem esse aliquam legem aut jus, quod nullâ *voluntate etiam
Dei constitutum sit,* illud maximè confirmat quod superius diximus (disp. 97, c. 3); nempe quædam ita *ex se* mala et peccata esse,
ut *ex nullâ voluntate etiam Dei eorum prohibitio pendeat:* id quod à
nobis supérque probatum est.   Nec solùm hoc ita esse ostendimus,
verùm etiam monstravimus, multa ita esse ex se mala, ut *eorum
malitia præcedat,* secundùm rationem, *omne judicium Divini Intellectûs ;* hoc est, non ideò sint mala quia mala judicantur à Deo,

etjudicium. Ergò ipsum naturale lumen est de se sufficiens promulgatio Legis
Naturalis : *non solùm* quia manifestat *intrinsecam* disconvenientiam vel
convenientiam actuum, quam lumen Dei increatum ostendit ; sed etiam
quia intimat homini, contrarias actiones *displicere Auctori naturæ,* tanquam
Supremo Domino, et Curatori, ac Gubernatori, ejusdem naturæ. (cap. 6,
n. 24.)

* Suarez' " De Legibus " is a book so commonly met with, and I have
been obliged, as it is, to make so many extracts from it, that I have not
thought it necessary to swell the bulk of my volume by copying the
entire chapters.

quin potiùs *ideo talia judicentur quia ex se talia sint.* Ex quo illud efficitur, ut ante omnem Dei Voluntatem et Imperium, imò etiam ante omne Judicium, aliqua ex se sint bona opera vel mala; ut ibidem monstratum est. Cùmque omne bonum vel malum per ordinem *ad regulam aliquam* dicatur bonum vel malum, justum vel injustum, consequens fit, ut ante omne imperium, ante omnem voluntatem, imò ante omne judicium, *est regula quædam harum actionum, quæ suâpte naturâ constet,* sicut res omnes suâpte naturâ contradictionem non implicant. Hæc autem non potest alia esse, quàm ipsamet rationalis natura ex se non implicans contradictionem; cui, tanquam regulæ et juri naturali, bonæ actiones conveniunt et æquantur, malæ autem dissonant et inæquales sunt; quamobrem et illæ bonæ, hæ autem malæ, dicuntur" (in 1ᵐ 2ᵐ d. 150, nn. 22, 23).

31. Lessius is equally clear with Suarez and Vasquez. We are not here concerned with the conclusion which he is labouring to prove; on which however I shall speak before we close the Section. What we are here concerned with however, are the principles which he assumes as undoubted, in order to *establish* his conclusion. He assumes two principles. First, that sin cannot become mortal, *i.e.* cannot deserve an *Eternity* of punishment, unless so far as it is against the commandment of God. Secondly, he assumes— and this it is with which we are here concerned—that even if, 'per impossibile,' there were no Divine Law, nay and no God, yet that there would remain intrinsic morality; and that offences against that morality would be sins, though not mortal ones.

Thus:—

" Ex quibus sequitur, primò, Si nullus esset Deus, nullum fore peccatum verè et propriè mortiferum, sed omnia fore venialia: quia carebunt illâ malitiâ, quæ spectatur in ordine ad Deum."—*De Perfectionibus Divinis,* lib. xiii. n. 186.

You see offences would still be ' peccata,' but ' venialia.'

Again:—

" Sequitur secundò, Nullum etiam fore peccatum mortiferum, si Deus peccata non prohibuisset, saltem per Legem Naturæ mentibus hominum insculptam: quod intellige de peccatis, quæ per se non continent Dei contemptum. Si enim peccata non essent à Deo itâ prohibita, ut homines intuitu Dei seu reverentiæ Divinæ

G

tenerentur illa vitare, non censerentur Deum contemnere, vel
injuriam irrogare, patrando peccata; sed solùm naturam suam
dedecorare et contra rectam rationem agere.   Verum sicut *impossibile est, ut actus liber rectæ rationi repugnans non sit prohibitus à
Deo*, ita etiam impossibile est ut non sit peccatum mortiferum, si
sit in re gravi ab homine Deum aliquo modo cognoscente. Dices:
‘ Furtum, adulterium, perjurium, et similia, quæ sunt contra
‘ Legem Naturæ, non ideò mala sunt quia prohibita Lege Naturæ,
‘ sed ideò sunt prohibita quia mala: ideò enim ratio naturalis et
‘ Lex Æterna dictat illa esse fugienda, quia in se mala sunt. Unde
‘ prius est illa esse mala quàm esse prohibita, et malitia prævenit
‘ Prohibitionem: ergo etiam si fingamus non esse prohibita, retine-
‘ bunt tamen suam malitiam.’   Respondeo, *ante omnem Prohibitionem* considerari in illis quamdam malitiam objectivam et
materialem, quatenùs isti actus sunt dissoni naturæ rationali, ita
ut non possint rectè appeti, nec rectè fieri, ab eo qui ratione utitur.
Potest etiam in illis considerari quædam *malitia formalis, quatenùs
fiunt ab aliquo liberè contra regulam rectæ rationis*: hæc tamen per
se *non est mortifera*, ut ostensum est. Unde non potest in istis actibus considerari *malitia mortifera, nisi sint contra Legem Divinam*;
ita ut Divina Auctoritas per illa censeatur contemni, et homo à
Deo averti: quo fit ut prius sit actum esse prohibitum Lege
Divinâ quàm esse formaliter peccatum *mortale; cùm peccatum
mortale* constituatur per Legis Divinæ contemptum.”—*Ibid.* n. **187.**

32. I next turn to Lugo:—

“ Præceptum diligendi Deum est omnino de *Jure Naturæ;* et
obligaret, secluso quovis Dei Decreto; ut omnes concedunt.”—*De
Penitentiâ*, d. 7, n. 250.

Lugo considers it, you see, as conceded by all, that
a Precept of the Natural Law *obliges*, apart from any
Decree or Command of God whatever.

Next, I will put before you his remarks, on a
subject similar to that which Lessius was treating.
And here again we are not concerned with the conclusion which he is advocating, but with the principles
which he takes for granted as tending to that conclusion. Lugo is considering this question. Suppose
(per possibile vel impossibile) that a man committed
murder, or did any other act which he should know to
be contrary to right reason; but in regard to which
he should be invincibly ignorant or inadvertent, that
it is prohibited by Almighty God. Lugo is inquiring
whether, in such a case, the sin would be mortal, *i. e.* de-

serve eternal punishment; and whether it would be such, that no mere man could pay for it condign satisfaction. He makes the following incidental remarks, in treating this subject:—

"De hoc dubio in hoc sensu theologi antiqui non satìs distinctè loquuntur. Ex recentioribus vero aliqui illud tetigerunt, inter quos P. Salas, tom. ii. in 1, 2, tract. 13, disp. 16, sect. 22, refert sententiam recentiorum, qui dicunt, eo casu illud homicidium non fore peccatum mortale. Ipse verò in hanc sententiam acriter invehitur, appellans eam parùm tutam et valdè perniciosam; quia ex eâ sequitur, de facto plurima homicidia, adulteria, et alia ejusmodi, esse solùm peccata venialia, quia fiunt cum ignorantiâ, vel saltem inadvertentiâ actuali, inculpabili Legis Divinæ; nec enim homo quoties peccat, recordatur Dei aut Divinæ Legis.

"Hanc sententiam Patris Salas ejus auctoritate ducti docuerunt (ut dixi) aliqui recentiores, et pro eâ adducunt plures ex antiquioribus et recentioribus; sed sine sufficienti fundamento. Nam ii solùm dicunt, illud homicidium adhuc in eo casu fore *malum moraliter, et peccatum;* quod quidem *verissimum est, cùm adhuc in eo casu haberet malitiam moralem per oppositionem cum regulâ rationis.* Nunc autem non quærimus an esset *peccatum,* sed an absque malitiâ formali offensæ Divinæ, quam tunc non haberet, adhuc haberet *illam gravitatem,* ratione cujus nunc theologi tribuunt illi infinitatem quandam et incompensabilitatem."—*De Incarnatione,* disp. 5, nn. 71, 72.

Lugo speaks of it, you see, as most true (verissimum), and testified by a great number of theologians, that the mere opposition to 'regula rationis,' with invincible forgetfulness of God's Law, would fully suffice to constitute 'malitia moralis' and 'peccatum.'

He proceeds in the following words to quote with agreement Gregory of Ariminum and Gabriel; 'quatenùs dicunt, quòd si per impossibile *non esset Deus,* adhuc homo peccare posset:' adding however his own opinion that such sin would not be *mortal.*

In another place he takes for granted the same doctrine, as perfectly unquestioned:—

"Mendacium est *intrinsecè malum,* et ex iis, quæ non sunt mala quia prohibita sed *prohibita quia mala;* ut suppono ex

S. Thom. et aliis infra quest. 110, art. 3, adeò ut *nec Deus possit in eo dispensare.*"—*De Fide,* disp. 4, n. 23.*

33. I shall next adduce Coninck, a scholastic of great name; who is thus quoted textually by Lugo, in the same disputation of the "De Incarnatione," from which I have already quoted Lugo's own opinion :—

"Si enim furtum v. c. nullo modo à Deo prohiberetur Eive displiceret quantùmvis pergeret, *non minùs quàm modò repugnaret justitiæ ;* tamen nullo modo mereretur pœnam æternam, et consequenter non contraheret *omnem malitiam quam modò contrahit.*"—*Lugo de Incarnatione,* disp. 5, n. 76.

If theft were not prohibited by God, it would not contract *all* the badness which it now contracts : therefore in Coninck's opinion it would contract *some.*

34. Bellarmine is also sufficiently plain :—

"Actiones quædam ità sunt per se atque intrinsecè malæ, ut deformitas ab eis sit omnino inseparabilis; et prohibita sint quia malæ, non malæ quia prohibitæ; ac denique nullo modo benè fieri possint: quales sunt, mentiri, odisse Deum, et alia id genus."—*De Amiss. Grat.* lib. ii. c. 18, n. 5.

Again,—

"Si fingamus Deum non esse in rerum naturâ ; qui leges justas violabunt, *peccabunt quidem in conscientiâ ;* sed nec Deum offendent, nec ad inferos damnabuntur."—*De Summo Pontifice,* l. iv. c. 20, n. 7.

35. I will next cite theologians from other schools; that you may not imagine this to be any doctrine peculiar to the Jesuit Theology. And first for Billuart, the well-known Thomist :—

"Suppono *ut certum,* Legem Naturalem non posse propriè mutari ab intrinseco, quia non est lata ad tempus: neque potest fieri de justâ injusta; cum nihil præcipiat quod non sit *intrinsecè et ex naturâ rei bonum,* neque aliquid prohibeat quod non sit *intrinsecè et ex naturâ rei malum,* proindeque *immutabiliter :* naturæ enim seu essentiæ rerum sunt immutabiles."—*De Legibus,* dissert. ii. art. 4.

---

* I may add in a note a quotation from St. Anselm, adduced by Lugo, ibid. n. 22. 'Non sequitur, justum est mentiri, si Deus vult mentiri ; sed potius *Deum illum non esse.* Nam nequaquam potest velle mentiri voluntas, nisi in quâ corrupta est veritas ; imò quæ deserendo veritatem corrupta est.' In other words, lying is intrinsecally evil ; and a being who would lie could not *be* that God Whom we worship.

" Hi actus enumerati, et similes prohibiti Lege Naturali, sunt *intrinsecè* et ex naturâ suâ, *independenter à voluntate Dei*, turpes, mali, et rationi dissoni."—*Ibid.*

Of these two quotations, the first is near the commencement of the article ; the second about three quarters through the body of it.   Very shortly before the ' solvuntur objectiones,' we find another most clear statement.   He is speaking of certain most frightful sins, and says,—

" Deus non potest dispensare in [illis], quia suppositâ dispensatione adhuc sui horrorem ingerunt, tum propter horribilem indecentiam, tum propter omnimodam naturæ subversionem, tum etiam quia *nullo fine cohonestari possunt.*   Porro non aliâ ratione adhuc horrorem ingerunt, suppositâ dispensatione, nisi quià ex intrinsecis suis, *independenter à Dei Voluntate*, sunt turpia et mala ; et ideò, non obstante dispensatione, retinent indecentiam, subvertunt naturam, et nullo fine cohonestari possunt.   Atqui etiam homicidium, furtum, adulterium, fornicatio, pollutio, sunt ex suis intrinsecis mala et turpia *independenter à Voluntate Dei.*" —P. 425.

Lastly, in the first article,—

" Neque refert quòd si Deus mentiretur peccaret ; quia in hâc hypothesi *non esset Deus*, cùm *implicet* quod is sit Deus, cui non repugnat mentiri : tenetur ergo Deus non mentiri, non vi alicujus legis id ei prohibentis, sed ratione repugnantiæ et impossibilitatis."—P. 408.

36. On Billuart's judgment then there can ˙be no doubt : let us proceed to another Thomist, Sylvius,—

" Stuprum, adulterium, et alia hujusmodi, *præveniendo omnem Dei Voluntatem*, essent quidem *peccata ;* utpote secundùm se *rectæ rationi contraria* et dissentanea . . . . . Nihilominùs non essent hìc et nunc peccata *in ordine ad Deum*, non enim Deum offenderent, posito quòd Deus ea non prohiberet.   Addendum porrò, quod sicut *impossibile est illa*, stuprum, adulterium, et hujusmodi, esse bona, ita impossibile quòd Deus ea per Legem Naturæ non prohibeat."—*Sylv.* in 1, 2, art. 1, ad. 2.

Again, a little earlier,—

" Si quæras utrùm Deus Legem Naturæ ferat *liberè ;* sive an Lex Naturæ sic à liberâ Dei voluntate pendeat, ut posset eam non ferre.— Resp. Deum Legem eam ferre liberè, *in quantùm liberè producit creaturam rationalem* quam potest non producere.   Supposito autem quòd eam producere velit, *non liberè fert Legem*

Naturalem, sed necessariò necessitate ex hypothesi; posito enim quòd angelum vel hominem creare velit, eique rationis usum dare, *non potest non velle* dare ipsi lumen ac dictamen rectæ rationis; neque *potest velle* quòd non teneatur illud sequi."

٭ 37. Let us now turn to the Augustinians, and take Berti as their representative. One passage will amply suffice to shew his judgment:—

" Quidquid prohibet Lex Naturæ, est naturâ suâ et intrinsecè malum, et quidquid præcipit est naturâ suâ et intrinsecè bonum: quod sanè ipsa Naturalis Legis notio manifesta declarat. At Deus non potest imperare quod suâpte naturâ malum est, ut odium, mendacium, blasphemiam: neque potest prohibere quod intrinsecè suâque naturâ bonum est, ut justitiam, pietatem, religionem. Si enim illa præcipere, hæc prohibere posset, posset etiam agere quæ cum summâ Æquitate ac Sapientiâ, atque cum essentiâ creaturæ rationalis repugnant; atque ità poterit mentiri, poterit ad peccatum impellere."—*De Theologicis Disciplinis*, lib. xx. c. 5, prop. 3.

38. Lastly, we will take a specimen from the Scotists. Frassen treats the subject as follows :—

" Dices secundo: ' Lex Naturalis non facit obligationem, sed ' supponit: Ergo obligatio non est ejus effectus. Antecedens patet ' ex dictis; nam Lex Naturalis in hoc à Lege Positivâ distinguitur, ' quòd illa prohibet aliquid, quia malum est; hæc verò prohibet ' aliquid, quod sit malum quia est prohibitum. Et idem est cum ' proportione de imperio et præcepto faciendi bonum quia bonum ' est.'

" Respondeo, cum Suarez, lib. ii. cap. 9, hanc objectionem nostræ assertionis esse confirmativam: nam, inquit, si Lex hæc prohibet aliquid quia malum, propriam et specialem necessitatem inducit vitandi illud; quia hoc intrinsecum est prohibitioni, ut vitetur quod prohibitum est. Probat etiam hæc objectio, aliquid hanc Legem supponere, quod pertinet ad *intrinsecum debitum naturæ;* siquidem unaquæque res quodammodo sibi debet, ut nihil faciat suæ naturæ dissentaneum. *Ultra verò hoc debitum* etiam Lex Naturalis addit *specialem obligationem* moralem, quam jurisperiti obligationem naturalem appellant."—*De Legibus,* disp. 2, art. 2, q. 2, concl. prima.

You see he expressly holds, with Suarez, that things commanded by the Natural Law are intrinsecally due (debita) independently of the Natural Law; and that to this debitum, the Natural Law adds a special obligation of its own. He states however distinctly that these things are of real *obligation*, quite *independently* of the Natural Law. These are his words :—

"Deus in Lege Naturali aliquam *obligationem* ex parte rerum *supponit,* quæ videtur *essentialis ipsis rebus,* quia honestæ sunt et bonæ *ex naturâ rei;* nam, ut supra diximus, hoc est discrimen inter Legem Naturalem et Positivam, quod Lex Naturalis præcipit ea, *quæ per se honesta sunt* et bona ; prohibet autem, *quæ per se mala sunt."*—*Ibid.* 4. art. 3. q. 1.

39. We have now therefore collected, sufficiently for our purpose, the judgment of theologians belonging to all the great schools of Theology ; though we might most easily have continued them indefinitely. Certainly (to say the very least) it is most permissible that any Catholic may hold a doctrine, which has such extremely strong testimony in its favour.

It will have been observed however, that the quotations from Lessius, and the chief of those from Lugo, occur in arguments, put forth by those writers under somewhat questionable circumstances. For they are directed towards a conclusion, which bears some considerable resemblance to the proposition, condemned by Alexander VIII. after their time, on the subject of Philosophical Sin. And still more, in looking at that proposition itself, it might be at first sight supposed by unwary readers, that the principle of intrinsic morality is therein censured. I will treat the matter *directly,* in reference to the proposition itself; and will introduce *incidentally* what it is necessary to say, on Lessius and Lugo.

The condemned proposition is the following :—

"Peccatum philosophicum seu morale est actus humanus disconveniens naturæ rationali et rectæ rationi : theologicum verò et mortale est transgressio libera divinæ legis. Philosophicum, quantùmvis grave, in illo, qui Deum vel ignorat, vel de Deo actu non cogitat, est grave peccatum, sed non est offensa Dei, neque æternâ pœnâ dignum."—*Denzinger,* p. 344.

Now there is no fact more undoubtedly certain in

all Theology, than that the first sentence of this proposition, which defines the term 'Philosophical Sin,'
was never imagined by any one to fall under the
Church's censure.   Nothing is more common, in the
case of condemned propositions, than such a procedure
as the following.   A statement is selected from some
unsound theologian, which contains the recital of an
undoubted premiss; and also of some false conclusion,
which he sophistically endeavours to build upon that
premiss.   The Church condemns the whole statement,
prout jacet: not meaning of course to throw the slightest
discredit on the undoubted premiss; but intending to
brand (firstly) the conclusion itself, and (secondly) the
allegation, that such a conclusion can *follow* from such
a premiss.   I repeat, there is no fact more certain in all
Theology, than that this is the case here.   Indeed there
is a special reason in this instance, for inserting the
first sentence as well as the *second ;* viz. that unless it
be so inserted, the very meaning of the second sentence
is wholly unintelligible.   Now then to shew the truth
of what I have stated; to shew that this first sentence,
which declares that the mere repugnancy to right
reason suffices to constitute a sin, was never thought
by any one to fall under the Pope's condemnation.

One consideration strikes us on the very surface.
It was but a short time before this censure, that the
Church condemned those other two propositions, which
were cited at the beginning of this Section.   Those
were then censured, who *refused* to admit that certain
definite offences are sinful *intrinsecally, apart from the
Divine Prohibition.*   It would be strange indeed, if
only eleven years afterwards, the whole notion, that
anything whatever *could* be sinful intrinsecally apart
from the Divine Prohibition, had been condemned in
one sweeping decree.   In addition to the inherent
impossibility of such a supposition, we will adduce
three arguments; any one of which will amply suffice
to shew, that the case is very far otherwise.

(1.) The Pontiff, Alexander VIII. expressly declares
in his decree, that the proposition before us was a *new*

proposition.* Now no one (I believe) of any opinions whatever has so much as suggested the notion, that the intrinsic 'malitia' of immorality, irrespectively of God's will, was a *new* doctrine in the time of Alexander VIII. We have seen on the other hand that Suarez considers it as St. Thomas's, and as the common sentiment of theologians. And Dmowski tells us, that those Protestants who object to it, are so far from calling it *new*, that they clamour against it as an invention of the Catholic scholastics.†

(2.) There was at one time a great controversy raised against the Jesuits, by many who maintained, that certain Jesuit doctrines lead by necessary consequence to this condemned proposition. Against *which* of the Jesuit doctrines was this charge adduced? Against the doctrine, that morality is intrinsecally obligatory apart from God's commandment? So far was this from being the case, that on the contrary the independent existence of morality was for the most part admitted on *both sides* as a *first principle in the dispute.* The Jesuit propositions attacked had reference to the *kind or degree of advertence required in mortal sin.* Every one knows this well, who is at all acquainted with the controversies of that time; but one quotation will put it beyond doubt. No one will doubt that F. Buffier, whom we have seen so earnestly contending for first truths, regarded the first principles of morality as contained in the class. Now this same F. Buffier was accused of holding, by implication at least, the error of Philosophical Sin. In regard to which statement of his was this charge made? in regard to any statement concerning the intrinsic character of morality? Nothing of the kind: the statements to which exception was taken, referred without exception to the advertence

---

* Viva, vol. iv. p. 3. 'Sanctissimus D. N. Alexander Papa Octavus non sine magno animi sui mœrore audivit duas theses seu propositiones, unam denuo et in majorem fidelium perniciem suscitari, alteram *de novo erumpere.*' It is this second which concerns Philosophical Sin.

† 'Pufendorfius . . . . . . *tanquam inventum scholasticorum* respuit differentiam istam moralium actionum, scilicet : . . . quasdam esse prohibitas quia malæ et quasdam malas quia prohibitæ.'

required for mortal sin. The following is his **disavowal** of the charge, as related by Serry in his history of the congregation " De Auxiliis:"—

" Secundum hæc nuperrimè pronunciavit Illustrissimus Rothomagensium Archiepiscopus, dum P. Buffierum Jesuitam, à quo *idem ille Peccati Philosophici insanus error* sparso per Normanniam libello *recusus fuerat,* solenni decreto damnavit; jussitque ut scripto publico hisce duabus propositionibus, inter multas alias, subscriberet, in obsequentis ac pœnitentis animi fidem. 1. *Quod spectat ad Peccatum Philosophicum,* damno quod Summus Pontifex Alexander VIII. Decreto suo damnavit 24 Augusti 1690. Ipse autem privatim agnosco (*ut Jesuitæ jam publicè agnoverunt* in sententiâ suâ publicè scripto editâ *super Peccato Philosophico*) non esse necessarium *actu attendere animum ad malitiam actionis,* ut peccato imputetur. 2. Obcæcati et indurati peccatores, qui cædes, adulteria et alia scelera, sine ullo conscientiæ stimulo perpetrant, ne *minimè quidem cogitantes* hujusmodi sceleribus offendi à se Deum, aut hæc contraria esse Legi Naturali, nihilominùs merentur pœnas inferorum : nec quòd *actu non attendant* ad malitiam actionis, ideò peccati mortalis rei non sunt " (lib. iii. c. 48).

You see, the whole matter turns on this question of advertence as on a hinge.

(3.) Thirdly, consider how absolutely atrocious is the statement contained in the condemned proposition. The condemned writer by no means confines his statement to *invincible* ignorance or *invincible* inadvertence. No: according to him, any sinner in the world, whose will is so utterly alienated from his True End, that in committing the greatest enormities he forgets his Creator altogether—such a sinner is *ipso facto* exempt from the guilt and from the penalties of mortal sin. Can any one credit, that the Pontiff, having so frightful a proposition to censure, not content with smiting it, should travel out of his way to pronounce a judgment on a question most totally distinct ; a question which no one on either side of the existing controversy had (I believe) so much as raised?

Lugo and Lessius were very far indeed from holding so extreme a position. At the same time I must frankly profess, that I *do* regard the doctrine on advertence, held by them and by some few other Jesuits, as leading *by necessary consequence* to this condemned proposition.* I hope, therefore, to argue against that doctrine, on this very ground as well as on others, in the appropriate part of our theological course.

Serry, in the passage immediately preceding that already quoted, confirms what I have said in the amplest manner; declaring that the whole doctrine of Philosophical Sin, both in its first inventor and his followers, turned *wholly* on the question of *advertence* as on a hinge.

"Nemo quippe est qui non videat, errorem hunc ab Alexandro proscriptum, *eo ut monui principio veluti cardine niti*, quo largi illi ac liberales Gratiarum Sufficientium distributores fabulantur, nullum re ipsâ veri nominis peccatum admitti, nullamque Deo offensam inferri æternâ pœnâ plectendam, nisi *præviâ illustratione animus perfundatur*, internâque excitatione pulsetur humana voluntas. Immò *non alio illum argumento muniebat*, in dictatis scriptis, Professor Theologus Divionensis, à quo in publicam Thesium lucem editus est; nec alio principio nitebantur illi ipsi, quos assertionis suæ magistros ac duces proferebat."

Finally, the only commentators on condemned propositions with whom I am acquainted, are these three; Van Ranst, Milante, Viva. Now all these agree in either implying or expressly declaring, that our doctrine of independent morality is not in any way affected by this condemnation.

Thus Van Ranst:—

"Hâc in propositione *duo* expendenda sunt. *Primò* supponit illa, *dari posse ignorantiam Dei invincibilem*, proindeque a peccato excusantem. *Secundò* requirit ad theologicè peccandum *actualem de Deo cogitationem*. Primum liquet ex verbis istis, 'philosophicum, quantumvis grave in illo, qui Deum ignorat:' alterum in sequentibus, 'vel de Deo actu non cogitat.'

"Dari non posse ignorantiam invincibilem Dei, asserit hæc stupenda moles universi, certatim prædicans, Dei notitiam homini esse insitam, ingenitam, implantatam, inseminatam. Hæc est vis veræ Divinitatis, inquit Doctorum Aquila (tr. 106 in Joan.), ut creaturæ rationali, jam ratione utenti, non omninò ac penitùs possit abscondi. Adeoque nequit dari ignorantia Dei invincibilis, et consequenter inculpabilis. Hinc dicitur Ps. lxxviii. 'Effunde

* Which was condemned, however, after their death.

iram tuam in Gentes, quæ te non noverunt;' et tamen cognoscere potuerunt. Ruit igitur Peccatum Philosophicum, *quod in præfatâ potissimùm ignorantia fundabatur.*

" Cæterùm fuerunt nonnulli, qui ipsum Doctorem Angelicum, hujus erroris (ut vidimus) prædebellatorem, in illius patronum vocare non sunt veriti; ob illa, quæ habet 2, 2, q. 20, art. 3, in corp. ' Si posset esse conversio ad bonum commutabile sine aversione à Deo, quamvis esset inordinata, non esset peccatum mortale.' Sed quis hìc non videat, D. Thomam (ut alia ad textum loci oportuna præteream) loqui hypothetice? in hypothesi scilicet, quòd detur ignorantia Dei invincibilis? *In tali enim suppositione, peccatum non esset theologicum* (cùm ignorantia invincibilis a peccato excuset) *sed merè philosophicum.*

" ' Benè est,' inquiebant Peccati Philosophici defensores : ' theo-
' logi nostri defendunt hanc propositionem dumtaxat de Peccato
' Philosophico, si, vel quando, existentia Dei invincibiliter ignora-
' retur, adeoque in hypothesi jam allegatâ ; proinde nos Alexan-
' drina non involvit condemnatio.'

" Sed quantus hic error, et cæcitas ! Certè Alexander VIII. non feriit propositionem conditionatam, sed absolutam ; non feriit phantasma, sed rem ipsam. Sic et fulmen Apostolicum non fuit vibratum in phantasma Jansenii (ut filii iniquitatis volebant), sed in hæresim Jansenianam reverà talem. En verba Alexandri VIII. ' Peccatum Philosophicum, quantumvis grave, in illo qui Deum vel ignorat' (ecce ignorantia absoluta non conditionata) ' vel de eo actu non cogitat, est grave peccatum, sed non est offensa Dei,' &c.

" Superest consideranda actualis de Deo cogitatio ; quam famosi istius Peccati Philosophici assertores ad theologicè peccandum requiri sustinebant.

" Sanè illam non requiri, sed *verè, formaliter, et theologicè peccare eum, qui de Deo actu non cogitat,* luce meridianâ clariùs ex Sacris patet Oraculis. ' Exacerbavit Dominum peccator,' Ps. ix. Sed cur exacerbavit? Fuitne semper in illo actualis de Deo cogitatio? Semperne fuit Deus in conspectu ejus, *alioquin non peccaturi?* Minime vero : imò *hoc ipsum ei jure merito exprobratur,* et peccato vertitur, *quòd de Deo non cogitârit,* seu Deum oculis suis non præfixerit. 'Non est Deus in conspectu ejus.' Eodem Ps. v. 26.

" Deinde : si ad theologicè peccandum semper actualis de Deo, aut de peccati, quod Deum infinitè offendit, malitiâ cogitatio requireretur, *nonne innumeri* Athei, Machiavellopolitici, et consuetudinarii, *in criminum voraginem, sine ullâ Dei vel malitiæ consideratione, se præcipitantes, à peccatis eximerentur?*

" Solida docet Theologia, ad peccatum *requiri et sufficere, quòd quis potuerit et debuerit de Deo cogitare,* vel reflectere ad Deum, aut ad gravitatem peccati infinitam involventis malitiam : quòdque ad illa omnia non reflexerit.

" Sed ecce errorem, quasi suis exortum temporibus, formalissimè damnatum ab Angelico 1, 2, q. 74, a. 7, ad. 2. ' Ratio superior,' inquit, seu mens ' dicitur consentire in peccatum, sive cogitet de Lege Æternâ' (quæ Deus est) 'sive non.'"

In like manner Milante :—

" *Ex tam infami confixo dogmate*, à theologicâ culpâ eximitur, qui, *actu non cogitans de Deo*, Ejus præcepta conculcat. Quapropter dubio procul nemo feliciùs faciliùsque Veneri et sensui indulget, qùam perditissimus quisque homo, qui, assuetus peccata peccatis addere, certè nec de Deo actu cogitat, nec Deum pertimescit, cùm peccat obduratus in malo. . . . .

" *Quæstio igitur est in præsenti de solâ ignorantiâ* Juris Naturæ, præsertim de ignorantiâ Dei ; an *hæc possibilis sit in facto?* an, cùm possibilis sit, *sit quoque invincibilis dicenda?* et iterùm an peccans cum hâc ignorantiâ de Deo, vel Deum non advertens Ejusque injuriam non respiciens in actu pravo, committat peccatum philosophicum *ità sejunctum à theologico*, ut ex illius, non verò ex istius, deformitate reus sit judicandus ?   Quo ex momento, dum ejus peccatum ex præfato modo operandi est duntaxat philosophicum, qui illud committit non est dignus æternâ pœnâ, quia Deum suo actu peccaminoso non offendit.   *In hoc quidem*, ut nuper indigitavi, *cardo difficultatis est situs.*"

Next, let us see Viva's statement :—

"Quod vero attinet ad doctorum sententias de Peccato Philosophico ; certum in primis est, Alexandrum VIII. in hâc thesi *noluisse damnare, quæ in antiquis, et gravibus theologis de hoc peccato scripta legimus;* aliter non diceret, thesim hanc de novo erupisse.   Docuerunt autem plurimi primæ notæ scriptores . . . . . absolutè esse simpliciter impossibile (sive metaphysicè, sive saltem moraliter), peccatum purè philosophicum. Addendo tamen, veluti hypotheticè ac speculativè, quòd si per impossibile quis haberet invincibilem Dei ignorantiam, aut *de Deo actu invincibiliter nullatenus, ne implicitè quidem, cogitaret*, dum advertit furtum *v. g.* esse *rationi dissonum*, in tali casu *peccatum* non foret Dei offensa, nec peccatum theologicum, sed purè *philosophicum;* eò quòd impossibile sit Deum offendi, nisi aliquo modo cognoscatur. . . . . . . Et in hoc duntaxat sensu hypothetico, nonnulli Societatis Professores, vestigiis tantorum virorum inhærentes, idipsum in suis thesibus propugnârunt; rejiciendo semper absolutè, cum iisdem auctoribus, saltem moralem possibilitatem Peccati Philosophici." — *Viva*, n. 3.

Viva tells us, you see, that, according to ' plurimi primæ notæ scriptores,' if a man could be invincibly ignorant or inadvertent of God's Prohibition, he might nevertheless advert to the fact that theft, *e. g.* is contrary to reason; and that, committing theft with such advertence, he would really sin: yet that such sin would be philosophical and not theological. And Viva further says, 'It is *certain* that Alexander VIII. never intended to condemn' this opinion.

40. This leads me to Viva's own statement, on the relation between God and moral obligation. It is quite different from Suarez's, and will be understood by the following extracts from his work on the "Theses Damnatæ:"—

" Diversimodè est dissonum mendacium Deo, et homini; esto in utroque sit moraliter malum, per difformitatem cum Divinâ Voluntate, quæ est prima regula morum. Etenim Deo ita est dissonum, ut etiam sit metaphysicè impossibile; quia Deus à propriâ naturâ, quæ essentialiter est cumulus omnium perfectionum, determinatur, sicut ad amandum Semetipsum, ita ad odio habendum quod est intrinsecè malum, seu quod argueret imperfectionem in Divinâ Voluntate, si ab illâ amaretur; ut est mendacium, odium Dei, perjurium, et similia: et idcirco, ut hæc sint illicita Deo, non debent a lege superiore ipsi vetari, sed sufficit, qùod essentialiter sint contra ipsius Dei voluntatem, metaphysicè determinatam ad bonum."—*De Peccato Philosophico*, n. 11.

" Quamvis cognitio explicitè attingens peccatum ut dissonum naturæ rationali, non eatenùs attingat explicitè illud ut transgressivum Divinæ Legis,—nihilominus repugnat, quòd peccatum sub illo priori conceptu attingatur, quin simul attingatur *implicitè* sub hoc secundo, quantùm satìs est ad quemdam contemptum Divinæ Legis, atque adeò ad offensam Dei. Ergo metaphysicè repugnat peccatum mortale purè philosophicum, quod Divinam Amicitiam non dissolvat, nec sit Dei offensa. Antecedens probatur, quia præcisè per hoc quòd peccatum attingatur explicitè ut disconveniens naturæ rationali et rectæ rationi, attingitur implicitè ut illicitum, atque adeo ut prohibitum, et nullatenùs patrandum. Ergo etiam attingitur implicitè ut oppositum Divinæ Voluntati illud prohibenti; atque adeò ut contemptivum Divinæ Prohibitionis, et ut Dei offensa. Probatur hæc consequentia, quia quoties peccatum apparet ut prohibitum ità ut nullatenùs liceat, apparet ut prohibitum ab eâ voluntate, quæ unicè potest illud prohibere; *atqui sola Dei Lex et Voluntas potest peccatum prohibere, ità ut nullatenùs liceat, quibuscumque creaturis illud suadentibus aut præcipientibus;* ergo quoties peccatum apparet ut omnino prohibitum, apparet etiam oppositum Divinæ Voluntati illud prohibenti, atque adeò contemptivum Divinæ Legis. Quòd autem confusa ista et implicita advertentia ad Divinam Prohibitionem sufficiat ad contrahendum reatum odii Divini, atque adeò dissolvendam Divinam Amicitiam,— ex eo patet, quia sicut, in omnium sententiâ, qui invincibiliter in sylvis enutritus nunquam audivit de pœnæ æternitate, aut ad illum non advertit dum peccat, si verè advertit ad Dei offensam, adhuc sit reus pœnæ æternæ, per hoc precisè quòd consentiendo in culpam implicitè consentiat in pœnam illi annexam naturâ suâ, etiamsi non habeat claram notitiam de æternitate pœnæ debità : ita qui in sylvis enutritus invincibiliter nunquam audivit de Dei Existentiâ, aut ad illum non advertit dum peccat, si verè advertit ad dissonantiam culpæ cum naturâ rationali et cum rationis dictamine, atque adeò ad prohibitionem sibi factam ab aliquo Superiore ita ut nullatenus possit ea operatio sibi licere quibuscumque creaturis ad illam impellentibus, adhuc fit reus odii Divini ; per hoc præcisè, quòd consentiendo in operationem illam sibi interdictam, implicitè consentiat in violationem Legis prohibentis, atque adeo in contemptum talis Voluntatis ; etiamsi careat clarâ notitiâ, quòd Lex seu Voluntas illam prohibens sit Voluntas Divina, unde Deus contemnatur : et consequenter metaphysicè repugnat peccatum purè philosophicum, quod non sit Dei offensa, nec Ejus Amicitiam rescindat."—*Ibid.* n. 9.

Viva, I should add, expressly states (as indeed we have seen already) that this view of his is only *one* out of those held in the Catholic Schools ; and that the other view also is maintained by ' plurimi primæ notæ scriptores.'—(See nn. 3 and 12.)

" Illud solùm ad quæstionem speculativam spectat : num ea, quæ sunt *mala ab intrinseco*, formaliter habeant rationem peccati, seu mali moraliter ac inhonesti, per oppositionem cum Lege prohibente, an verò per disconvenientiam cum naturâ rationali? Quâ in re communiùs docent, per disconvenientiam cum naturâ rationali esse tantùm *fundamentaliter* peccata, et habere solam *prohibenditatem, seu exigentiam ut prohibeantur;* formalem verò peccati rationem habere, per violationem Legis prohibentis : ut proinde *carerent malitiâ formali, si non prohiberentur,* sive possibile sit ea positivè non prohiberi à Deo, sive impossibile ; quod verius censeo cum Suar. lib. ii. de Leg. c. 6, contra Okanum, et alios. Quinimmo arbitrior esse metaphysicè, nedum moraliter, impossibile, quòd homo Deum, saltem ut Supremum Legislatorem, ignoret, aut de Illo actu non cogitet, dum ponit operationem, quam advertit esse naturæ rationali disconvenientem."—*In Props.* 48 *et* 49 *Innocent XI.,* n. 1.

You will see from these extracts that, according to Viva, the source of moral obligation is simply God's necessary Command. In other words (to take his own instances), we are *morally obliged* to avoid lying and perjury, for this reason and for no other whatever; viz. that God by the necessity of His Nature forbids such acts. Of late years several Catholic philosophers seem to have adopted this view. In regard to the theologians known by Viva himself, there are only two (I think) whom he quotes by name as favourable to his doctrine, viz. Curiel and Zumel; neither of them certainly being very eminent names: and this, though Viva himself is about the latest in date of the great scholastic writers. At the same time he calls his own the *most common* opinion;* while frankly admitting that the other doctrine (which I have followed throughout) is held by 'plurimi primæ notæ scriptores.'†

This doctrine of Viva's must not be confounded with another, which at first sight greatly resembles it, and which I have mentioned in n. 22. According to that other doctrine, the moral obligation of avoiding mendacity, *e. g.* and perjury, arises from the fact that God is necessitated by His Nature to detest those vices. But, according to Viva, His *Detestation* of them does not *suffice* for imposing on us any moral obligation; there must be a direct *Command* prohibiting them. In regard to the former doctrine (you may remember) I said that it may be taken in two very different senses; and that, taken in one of those senses, I most strongly incline to it as true. But of Viva's statement I can imagine no such favourable interpretation; it seems to me absolutely intolerable, absolutely self-contradictory, in any imaginable sense which it can possibly bear. In behalf of this adverse criticism, I thus argue.

God is necessitated to prohibit lying and perjury; or in other words, He is not free to withhold that prohibition. So far Viva agrees with Suarez and the great body of theologians. *Why* is God not free to with-

---

* "De Peccato Philosophico," n. 8. This statement however comes to very little; it is so very common a tendency of theologians, to regard their own opinion as the most common.
† Ibid. n. 3.

hold that Prohibition?   Of course 'because to do so would be repugnant to His essential sanctity.'   *Why* would it be thus repugnant?   'Because lying and perjury are intrinsecally evil.'   But *why* are lying and perjury intrinsecally evil?   If you say 'simply *because God has prohibited them*,' then Viva's argument comes to this; 'God is not *free* to *withhold* the Prohibition ' of such acts, simply because He has *in fact* prohibited ' them:' than which a more absurd statement cannot be imagined.   Viva then must admit, that lying and perjury are intrinsecally evil, for some reason *wholly distinct* from God's Prohibition; but then this is precisely the logical contradictory to his original assertion. Whatever is intrinsecally evil, we are morally obliged on that ground to avoid.   If then lying and perjury are *intrinsecally evil*, for reasons wholly independent of God's Prohibition;—then we are *morally obliged to avoid them*, for reasons wholly independent of God's Prohibition.   And this is the thesis which Viva expressly denies.

Indeed, if we examine his language with any care, we shall soon see how false is his position.   No abler or subtler theologian can easily be found, among the whole body of scholastics; and yet see how vaguely and confusedly he speaks.   Does he, or does he not, hold that lying and perjury are intrinsecally evil, apart from God's Prohibition?   No consistent answer can possibly be given.   In the last extract, he says that they are not *formally* evil; 'carerent *malitiâ formali*, si non prohiberentur:' yet in that very passage he calls them ' mala ab intrinseco;' and he says in the first of the three extracts, that they are 'intrinsecè mala.'   What distinction of *ideas* can possibly be imagined, answering to this distinction of *words*, between 'formaliter mala' on the one hand, and ' intrinsecè mala' on the other hand?   He says that, apart from God's Prohibition, such acts are so intrinsecally evil, that they are 'illicita Deo;' and that the not detesting them would be repugnant to His Sanctity. (First Extract.)   If they

H

are ' unlawful to *God*,' I suppose they are unlawful
to *us ;* if the not detesting them would be repugnant
to sanctity in the Creator, so would it also be in the
creature.   If then certain acts, apart altogether from
God's Prohibition, are ' unlawful to us,' and ' repugnant
to sanctity,' what imaginable sense can there be in
denying that they are ' formaliter mali?'

Then, Viva's second extract simply takes for
granted the whole question at issue.   He *assumes* that
nothing can be morally evil, until it is prohibited ;
and then *proves* (easily enough) that, on such an
hypothesis, the Prohibitor must be of Infinite Authority.
' Quoties,' he says, ' peccatum apparet ità prohibitum
' ut nullatenùs liceat, apparet prohibitum ab Eâ Vo-
' luntate, Quæ unicè potest illud prohibere.'   But his
opponents maintain, that many things are so *morally
evil* ' ut nullatenùs liceant,' without reference to any
prohibition whatever : to this allegation, which alone
concerns him, he does not, throughout the extract, so
much as allude.

All the arguments of the previous Section have
in fact been arguments against Viva's doctrine.   We
have been opposing ourselves to the proposition, that
God's Will is the source of morality ; and all our
reasoning applies to His necessary, no less than to
His free, Will.   Yet it seemed worth while also, to
give some *special* consideration, to this *special* phase
of the view antagonistic to ours.

Viva, you see, holds quite decidedly the intrinsic
necessity of moral truth ; and is so far adducible in our
favour.   You will ask perhaps, this being so, why I have
been so eager and peremptory in repudiating his statement.   I reply, because, though he *does* hold this great
doctrine, he holds it inconsistently : because he gives
an opening to its enemies, of which they will not be
slow to take advantage : because his doctrine leads, by
necessary consequence, to that very proposition which
he would himself abhor ; viz. that God's *free* Command
is at last the source and the measure of all morality.

No one has a more grateful sense than myself, of the most important services conferred by Viva on Theology; no one more highly appreciates his rare mental gifts. But it will happen now and then to the best theologians, that they incautiously admit some statement, the full bearing and consequences of which they have by no means duly considered.

It may be questioned, at first sight, whether Gerdil does not hold the opinion maintained by Viva, that the obligation of morality depends on God's *necessary* Will. For in one or two places he lays stress on the statement, that it does *not* depend on His *free* Will: 'why,' it may be asked, 'does he add the word *free*, except to contradistinguish it from *necessary?*' It is quite clear however, on careful consideration, that he does *not* hold this. For first indeed, he says so in as many words; he expressly states, that the mere *knowledge* of the just and unjust suffices to establish *obligation*.* And secondly, the one thesis which he labours throughout to establish is, that moral truth is necessary, in the very same sense in which mathematical truth is so. Now no one ever imagined, that *mathematical* truth originates in the *necessary* Will of God, any more than in His free will.

Every other theologian whom we have cited, with one exception, says expressly, that the obligation of avoiding what is intrinsecally wrong is ' independens à Dei Voluntate,' or words to that effect; not ' Voluntate *necessariâ*,' but ' Voluntate' simply. This may be seen at once, by looking back at their statements. The one exception is Berti, who does not seem to have considered this precise question.

With Viva I close my extracts from theological writers; which I could have indefinitely increased indeed, but that there seemed no reason for doing so. Further quotations however will be made from them in a later Section, on the question of dispensation from the Natural Law; quotations which will place their meaning (if possible) in even a clearer light.

* See the passage quoted in note to n. 19, p. 42.

All these theological quotations indeed appertain, in strict propriety, to our theological course, rather than to our philosophical. But it seemed important at once to shew, how very strong is the theological authority on which we rest, in this most important and fundamental doctrine.

41. I will now give specimens of the treatment which this question receives, in the philosophical compendia, or other school treatises, now in use among Catholics. Of these, no one enjoys a higher reputation, than the " Prælectiones Philosophicæ" used at S. Sulpice. Nothing can be clearer or more convincing than the statements which we here find :—

" Thesis Secunda—*Discrimen boni et mali à Voluntate Dei, sive liberâ sive necessariâ, non est repetendum.*

" Prob. prima pars, nempe discrimen istud à *liberâ* Dei Voluntate repeti non posse.—Vel enim bonum est Deo aliquid ut bonum jubenti obtemperare, malum verò illi resistere; vel non. Si prius : ergo *ante Dei liberum decretum* boni et mali discrimen instituens, jam *bonum et malum existebat;* quod adversariorum hypothesi prorsus opponitur. Si posterius : ergo *bonum et malum etiam nunc nullatenùs discriminantur.* Posito enim quod malum non sit decreto divino resistere, *malum igitur non erit agere quod prohibet* ut malum ; porro quod sine malo effici potest, malum dici nequit. Ergo, &c.

" Prob. secunda pars, nempe discrimen boni et mali à Voluntate Dei *necessariâ* desumi non posse.—Etenim Voluntas Dei necessaria nihil efficit, nisi juxta Lumen Idearum Divinarum. Non potuit igitur Deus boni et mali discrimen statuere per suam Voluntatem necessariam, nisi *illud discrimen jam in suis ideis intellexisset.* Porro quidquid Deus intelligit, *eo ipso realitatem habet;* alioquin *veritate carerent Conceptus Divini.* Ergo Actus Voluntatis necessariæ, quo Deus discrimen boni et mali determinavisse diceretur, hoc discrimen *jam existens supponeret.* Ergo," &c.*—N. 1492, pp. 75, 76 of vol. iii.

42. The present professor of Moral Philosophy at the Roman College, is Solimani; whose authority is very highly thought of. No words can be clearer, no arguments more forcible, than those which he adduces on this matter :—

---

* This argument will be found enforced in the Appendix to Chap. I., ' On the Relation between God and Necessary Truth,' which is printed at the end of this book.

" Extare aliquod principium, ex quo in hominem obligatio descendat, ita facile demonstratur : si nullum est principium, ex quo in hominem obligatio derivetur, homo plenam habet libertatem moralem. Atqui hoc dici nequit. Etenim si homo plenâ polleret libertate morali, nullum existeret inter actiones humanas morale discrimen ; nullus esset moralis ordo in humanis actionibus ex rationis præscripto servandus ; quamobrem, quidquid homo ageret, nunquam esset laudandus, nunquam culpandus, nunquam præmio, nunquam poenâ, dignus censendus. Jam verò id communi hominum sensui plane repugnat. Omnes enim inter humanas actiones morale agnoscunt discrimen ; omnes contendunt esse ordinem quemdam moralem in iisdem servandum. Nemo est, vel inter eos qui cupiditatibus indulgere solent, qui non maximè *laudet* hominem corpori animum præferentem, pravis animi motibus fræna injicientem, animo excolendo ac perficiendo intendentem, modum denique atque ordinem in dictis factisque suis omnibus perpetuo servantem ; qui non culpet eum, qui contrariam huic vivendi rationem tenet. Atque hæc quidem laudare aut culpare homines consueverunt, non modo in aliis, sed etiam in seipsis licet inviti ; *internâ saltem illâ naturæ voce,* quam nullus compescere penitùs posset.

" Conjice, inquit Genevensis philosophus, conjice oculos in omnes latè populos, versa omnes historias. In tam ingenti religionum planè crudelium atque absurdarum multitudine, in tantâ morum atque ingeniorum varietate, easdem ubique justitiæ atque honestatis ideas, eadem ubique morum principia, easdem ubique boni et mali notiones, sine dubio deprehendes. Vana Ethnicorum superstitio infandos peperit Deos, qui, scelestorum more, meritam apud nos subituri fuissent poenam, quique in exemplum supremæ cujusdam felicitatis non aliud præ se ferebant, quàm flagitia omnigena admittenda, pravasque omnes cupiditates explendas. At vitium, sacrâ licet instructum auctoritate, ex æternis coeli sedibus nequaquam ad nos descendebat ; nam instructus quidam moralis illud ab humanis pectoribus usque repulsabat. Homines eo ipso tempore, quo effrænatam Jovis libidinem celebrabant, *præclaram Xenocratis pudicitiam admirabantur.* Sancta naturæ vox, *ipso Deorum exemplo validior,* hominum obsequia in terris sibi vindicabat, culpamque, una cum iis qui illa inficiebantur, in supernas coeli regiones relegâsse quodammodo videbatur. *Est igitur in intimis animi nostri recessibus innata quædam justitiæ ac virtutis norma,* ex quâ, contra ipsa, quibus imbuti sumus, præjudicia, tum nostras, tum aliorum actiones, rectas vel pravas esse decernimus.

" Cùm igitur inter humanas actiones aliquod agnoscendum sit morale discrimen, atque homines plenâ careant libertate morali, agnoscendum quoque est aliquod principium, ex quo ad eos profluit obligatio.

"Hujusmodi principium, spectato naturæ ordine, quemlibet Volun-tatis Divinæ præcipientis actum antecedit. Id vero hâc ratione ostendi posse arbitramur : principium obligationis non est aliud, quàm *norma quædam, obligandi vi prædita.* At verò *admittenda est hujusmodi norma, quæ quovis Voluntatis Divinæ præcipientis actu prior sit.* Etenim quædam sunt *suâpte naturâ* moraliter bona ; quædam verò ita moraliter mala, ut bona fieri nullo modo possint. Atqui *rerum naturæ* quovis Rationis ac Voluntatis Divinæ actu priores sunt. Neque enim *res ideò tales sunt, quia Deus cognoscit ac vult eas tales esse ;* sed contrà Deus ideò cognoscit ac vult res esse tales, *quia tales suâpte naturâ sunt.* Ita *circulus* non ideò radios habet inter se æquales, *quia Deus cognoscit* ac vult in circulo eam radiorum æqualitatem ; sed contrà Deus ideò cognoscit ac vult illam circuli proprietatem, quia *in intimâ circuli naturâ* necessariò illa continetur. Hinc est quòd Deus rebus quidem *existentiam dare aut recusare pro arbitrio potest ; intimam autem naturam mutare nequit.* Quæ igitur, in genere morum, bona sunt vel mala, *suâpte naturâ* ea talia sunt, *ante quemlibet Rationis ac Voluntatis Divinæ actum.* Jam verò nihil est bonum aut malum in genere morum, nisi comparatè ad aliquam *normam, quæ obligandi virtute sit prædita.* Nam bonum morale positum est in conformitate cum normâ quâdam verè obligante, malum autem morale in discrepantiâ ab eâdem. Normam, inquam, *verè obligantem :* siquidem quæcumque alia norma, quantumvis sapiens atque honesta, bonum malumve morale metiri nequit. Neque enim ideò benè agimus, quia consilium hominis pruden-tissimi sequimur ; neque, si non sequimur, idcircò in aliquam incidimus culpam. Nullum igitur bonum aut malum morale concipi animo potest, quin simul concipiatur *norma obligandi vi prædita,* ad quam illud necessario refertur. Atqui nos facile apprehendimus bonum malumque in genere morum suâpte naturâ tale, ante quemcumque Rationis ac Voluntatis Divinæ actum. Ergo admittenda est *aliqua norma virtute obligandi instructa,* quæ *omnem Voluntatis Divinæ præcipientis actum re ipsâ præcedat.*

" Et sanè antequam Deus quidquam homini præcipiat, plenum profecto habet ac perfectum præcipiendi jus : hujusmodi enim jus in ipso Creatoris Providentissimi Attributo intimè continetur ; ratio autem Creatoris quocumque præcipiendi actu naturâ prior est. Atqui pleno illi ac perfecto præcipiendi juri, quo pollet Deus, plenum æque ac perfectum obtemperandi officium neces-sariò respondet in homine. Hæc enim duo, scilicet jus præci-piendi atque obtemperandi officium, inter se coæquantur, atque ita sunt invicem connexa, ut alterum sine altero intelligi nullo pacto possit. Igitur non modò illud Dei jus, sed etiam *hoc hominis officium, quocumque Divino Præcepto naturâ prius est.* Re-vera quemadmodum jus illud in Attributo Creatoris, ita *officium hoc in ipsâ creaturæ conditione,* quæ quovis Dei Præcepto per se anterior est, intimè continetur. Porrò hoc officium, quo omnes homines ad parendum Deo perfectè obstringuntur, quid quæso aliud est, quam *vera quædam ac propriè dicta obligatio?* Igitur ante quodvis Dei Præceptum, *vera concipitur esse obligatio, ac proinde aliqua etiam veræ obligationis effectrix norma. Sane si antequam Deus quidpiam nobis præciperet, verâ nos obligatione, ad Ejus Præcepta implenda, minimè teneremur, omnem Illi obedientiam jure optimo recusare possemus; quemadmodum omnem homini cuilibet obedientiam abnuere meritò possumus, si, antequam is aliquid jubeat, verâ nos obligatione ad jussa ejus facessenda nequaquam obstringimur."*—Vol. i. pp. 175–178.

43. Dmowski is another Roman writer, and one who enjoys a great name. His remarks on the question before us shall here follow :—

" Inter antiquos, Epicurei cæterique, de quibus Tullius, omnia voluptate vel utilitate dimetientes, boni et mali moralis, honesti et inhonesti, naturale discrimen sustulerunt. Eorum vestigia premunt plerique recentiores impii ; inter quos Spinosa, et Hobbesius, (tam in libro de Cive quam in Leviathan,) ab opinionibus arbitrariis hominum, vel ab arbitrariâ legum civilium constitutione, hoc discrimen repetit. Pufendorfius, quem sequuntur Coccejus et ex parte Heineccius, arbitratur discrimen hoc *à liberâ Dei Voluntate et Lege Positivâ pendere;* ità ut *tanquam inventum scholasticorum* respuat differentiam istam moralium actionum, scilicet, quasdam esse *præceptas quia sunt bonæ,* quasdam verò bonas quia præceptæ ; et item, quasdam esse *prohibitas quia malæ,* quasdam vero malas quia prohibitæ. Adversus hos omnes generatim probabimus, dari *intrinsecum discrimen* inter bonum et malum morale ; quasdam morales actiones esse bonas et honestas, alias malas et turpes, citra omnem reflexionem ad ullam legem humanam, vel etiam *Positivam Divinam a liberâ Dei Voluntate manantem.*

" Ad pleniorem quæstionis intelligentiam advertendum est, hypothesim istam, in quâ statuitur, *aliquas actiones esse ità moraliter bonas, aliquas ità malas, ut etiamsi per impossibile Deus illas non præciperet has non vetaret, adhuc remanerent tales,* convenientes scilicet vel repugnantes naturali rationi,—esse abstractionem mentalem, *præscindentem à Deo,* minimè âutem excludentem eum, supponentemque rationalem naturam sicuti est, conformatam. Cùm absurdum prorsus videatur, exclusâ omni absolutâ ac immutabili realitate et ordine ejusque fundamento, velle adhuc disputare de convenientiâ et discrepantiâ aliquarum realitatum et ordinis, easque admittere ; præsertim quòd nec concipi valeant humani actus ut proprie morales, ante ipsam quoque *rationem* spectatam velut *naturalem eorum normam.*

" Assertio, sic explicata, pluribus evincitur argumentis. Primò, ex suppositâ doctorum distinctione, inter actiones prohibitas quia malæ, et malas quia prohibitæ; quæ distinctio communi sensu probatur, cùm *etiamsi Divinam aut humanam legem cogitatione removeamus,* adhuc unicuique *turpe ac malum videri debeat, à rationis regulâ rectoque ordine declinare,* honestum ac bonum utrique suas actiones conformare; bonum enim est unicuique enti, juxta exigentiam suæ naturæ agere; et in homine omnia ordinantur sub ratione, tanquam sub naturali et nobiliori eorum principio discernente. 2°. Sublato omni intrinseco discrimine inter bonum et malum morale, *tollitur fundamentum legis* humanæ vel *Positivæ Divinæ.* Quid enim? Estue ex se bonum iisdem legibus subjici et malum reluctari, vel neutrum eorum? Si primum, ergo *ante conceptum harum legum* datur *aliquid ex se bonum et malum;* si alterum, ergo leges illæ, utpote indifferentes, nullam speciem boni vel mali moralis determinabunt. 3°. Plura sunt practica rationis principia, *e.g.* ' Deus est amandus,' ' nemo lædendus,' &c. *quæ ex sui naturâ animum ad assensum cogunt,* vimque rationalitati inferunt; non secus ac illa theoretica, *e. g.* ' idem nequit simul esse et non esse,' ' *totum est majus suâ parte,'* &c.; ergo sicut ex his, ante omnem conventionem et pactionem, quædam *naturaliter vera* dimanant judicia, ita ex illis quædam actiones *naturaliter ac per se bonæ et honestæ,* iisdemque oppositæ malæ et inhonestæ. 4°. Ut arguit S. Thomas, secundùm naturalem ordinem, corpus hominis est propter animam, et inferiores virtutes animæ propter rationem; est igitur naturaliter rectum quòd sic procuretur ab homine corpus et inferiores vires animæ, ut ex hoc et actus rationis et bonum ipsius minimè impediatur, si autem secus accideret, erit naturaliter peccatum; vinolentiæ igitur comessationes et alia inordinata, quæ liberum judicium rationis esse non sinunt, sunt naturaliter mala. Deinde, cùm homo naturaliter ordinetur in Deum sicut in finem, hinc ea, quæ ducunt in cognitionem et amorem Dei, *sunt naturaliter recta,* quæ vero e contrario se habent, *sunt naturaliter homini mala.* Patet igitur, quod bonum et malum in humanis actibus *non solùm sunt secundum legis positionem, sed etiam secundùm* naturalem *ordinem.* 5°. Denique, si omne discrimen boni moralis a malo penderet a solâ positivâ divinâ voluntate et lege, potuisset Deus facere ut cuncta quæ nunc sunt moraliter bona essent mala, et vicissim; ideoque potuisset efficere ut bonum esset Ipsum odio habere, proximum lædere, &c., malum verò Ipsum diligere, proximo benefacere, &c.; quod evidentissimam involvit absurditatem, redditque impossibile medium cognoscendi (exceptâ divinâ revelatione), quid Deus revera naturaliter præcepit et quid prohibuit."—Vol. iii. pp. 67, 8, 9.

This passage, at first reading, might appear somewhat in favour of that opinion, which makes God's *necessary Will* the source of all moral obligation. But a careful study of it will quite destroy this impression. For instance, in the first italicized passage of the second paragraph, he declares that certain evil actions would remain evil, even though 'per impossibile' God did not forbid them. In the first italicized passage of the third paragraph he adds, that though in thought we remove from the matter all *law* whether Divine or human, it still should appear to every one *base and evil* to depart from the rule of reason and from right order.

44. I next come to the Lyons course of philosophy. The following passage seems to shew, that in this work also an intrinsic obligation is attributed to morality, over and above that obligation, which results from God's necessary Command of it. The words are as follows :—

"Obligatio nascitur, *tùm* à Voluntate Divinâ summè Perfectâ, Cui voluntas humana, admodùm imperfecta et debilis, omnem debet subjectionem exhibere: *tùm à naturâ ordinis*, qui cùm sit *intrinsecè bonus* utpotè necessarius entibus, ab omni intelligentiâ *debet amari; tùm* etiam," &c.—*Ethica Generalis*, dissert. v. vol. iii. p. 48.

The Divine Command, you see, is given as part, but only part, of the source from which moral obligation springs. Even without reference to this Divine Command, every intelligence (or intelligent being) *ought* to love (or is under the obligation of loving) what is intrinsecally good.

45. Noget-Lacoudre, like Dmowski, professedly only opposes the opinion, that the obligation of morality springs from God's *free* Will. But he also, as Dmowski, in fact extends his statements to God's necessary Will also :—

"Discrimen inter bonum et malum morale repetendum non est à Voluntate Positivâ et Liberâ Dei tantummodò.

"Probatur. Illa enim regula moralis rejicienda est, quæ 1°. contradicit notioni quam habemus boni et mali moralis; 2°. quæ nullam obligationem potest parere : atqui talis est regula, quæ discrimen inter bonum et malum morale repetit ex Voluntate Positivâ et Liberâ Dei tantùm; *nullo autem modo ex essentiâ rerum.*

"1°. quidem regula hæc contradicit notioni quam habemus boni et mali moralis; quisque enim existimat plurimos actus, quos agnoscunt tanquam bonos et malos moraliter, *tales esse ex essentiâ rerum;* eorumdem actuum bonitatem aut malitiam *ab omni voluntate liberâ esse independentem* ideòque immutabilem.   Sic existimant quicumque recto animi sensui vim non inferunt, bonum esse suum cuique tribuere; animum beneficiorum memorem servare; &c.; nec *unquam hos actus malos fieri posse.*   Ergo, &c.

"2°. Regula hæc *nullam obligationem parere potest.*   Si enim tollitur discrimen ex essentiâ rerum profluens, tunc Deo jubenti parere non teneor quia bona est res quam ille imperat; sed tantummodò quia Deus vult: atqui *sola voluntas Dei non potest parere obligationem.*   Nulla enim adesse potest obligatio, quin adsit officium implendum : atqui tunc nullum adest officium implendum: omne enim officium implicat ideam actus boni, seu rectæ rationi consentanei; *non verò solummodò imperium voluntatis, quamtumvis potentis.*   Si enim non adest nisi imperium voluntatis summè potentis, nulla verò notio recti;—sanè *prudentiæ* non erit non parere jubenti; *securitatique et utilitati suæ non sapienter consulet* qui imperium voluntatis istius summè potentis detrectabit : at si *imprudentiæ* reus ille meritò dicitur, nunquàm tamen *recti et æqui violator erit.*   Nullum jus sola violentia parere potest.   Ergo 2°, &c."—Vol. iii. p. 112, 113.   Thesis 6.

One sentence in this passage is very remarkable and important; ' Sola voluntas Dei non potest parere obligationem.'   To unfold more fully its meaning, take this conclusion : ' I am bound to obey the Pope in spirituals, because God commands it.'   The premisses stated in full are as follows :—

Major. I am bound to obey whatever God commands.

Minor. God commands me to obey the Pope.

Conclusion. I am bound to obey the Pope.

The major premiss is very far from a mere *truism,* or mere *tautologous* proposition. (See n. 20.)   It is a *real* proposition, and a most important one ; intued however with extreme clearness, so soon as the idea of a Holy Creator is unfolded before my mind.   Now it is plain, that the minor premiss, *by itself,* would not suffice to establish the conclusion ; or, in other words, no obligation could result from the *mere fact of God giving me a Command,* unless my reason at once supplied the major premiss as above expressed.

What I am here however concerned to point out, is that this statement of Lacoudre applies to God's *necessary* Will, no less than to His free will.

That Lacoudre indeed does not attribute the origin of moral obligation to God's Will in *any* sense, is equally clear from the title which he gives to his next thesis : 'Discrimen inter bonum et malum morale repetendum est *ex essentiâ rerum.*' Not from God's Will, you see, but from the essence of things.

46. But the one writer of the present day, who has entered most fully upon the subject of all whom I know, is F. Chastel, S.J. His statements and arguments are as follow :—

"Le bien et le mal sont fondés sur la nature, sur l'essence immuable des choses; et Dieu, loin de décider arbitrairement le bien et le mal, est au contraire *nécessité par sa perfection même à défendre l'un et à vouloir l'autre.* Par conséquent, il n'est pas besoin d'une révélation pour connaître la Volonté de Dieu sur ce point, ni pour savoir ce qui est bien et ce qui est mal en vertu de la Loi Naturelle. Cette loi primordiale, gravée dans le cœur de chacun de nous, est promulguée par la voix de la raison et de la conscience. Tel a été dans tous les temps l'enseignement Chrétien. Saint Paul (Rom. ii.) affirme que les païens eux-mêmes portent cette loi écrite dans le cœur, et qu'un tribunal irrécusable est élevé dans leur conscience. 'Comment donc les Gentils,' demande Saint Jean Chrysostome, 'peuvent-ils dire : Nous n'avons point de loi posée par elle-même dans la conscience, et Dieu ne l'a pas gravée dans notre cœur? C'est de cette loi que les premiers hommes ont tiré leurs lois, qu'ils ont inventé les arts et les autres choses.' (Homil. ad Pop. Antioch. 12, c. 4.) 'Cette loi,' dit Saint Ambrose, 'ne nous est point enseignée du dehors, elle est née en nous-mêmes ; nous ne la tirons point des livres ; chacun de nous la puise dans la source fécond de la nature.'—*Apud Suarez,* ibid. c. 5.

"Dans la Loi Naturelle, telle que la manifestent la conscience et la raison, il faut distinguer deux choses : 1°. le caractère du bien et du mal, c'est-à-dire, ce qui est *conforme ou contraire à la nature des êtres et à leurs rapports essentiels ;* 2°. l'intervention *nécessaire* du Maître de la nature, qui *veut le bien et défend le mal. D'abord l'exigence de la nature, ensuite le Précepte Divin ;* deux choses *distinctes,* dont *l'une est logiquement antérieure à l'autre.* Pour que Dieu ordonne ou défende, il faut concevoir quelque chose à ordonner et à défendre. Le bien n'est pas tel parce qu'il plait à Dieu, mais *il plait à Dieu parce qu'il est bien ;* de même le mal n'est défendu de Dieu, que parce qu'il est mal.

" *A part le Précepte Divin, il y a donc toujours bien et mal essentiels, il y a l'exigence de la nature.* Or on demande si, *abstraction faite de Dieu et de Sa Volonté,* la seule exigence de la nature suffit pour créer un devoir, pour *constituer une obligation* morale : en d'autres termes, *s'il y a une loi morale indépendamment de toute Loi Divine ;* ou encore jusqu'à quel point la morale est indépendante de la religion. Cette question délicate a été trop souvent et trop vivement soulevée, pour n'avoir pas besoin d'une solution complète.

" Avouons d'abord, que ce qui fait la principale force de la Loi Naturelle, est sans contredit l'intervention de Dieu. La majesté de la Volonté Divine s'imposant à la conscience, et montrant à l'homme une sanction inévitable et clairement determinée, agira toujours bien plus fortement sur nous que la simple considération de la nature. Néanmoins il faut voir si cette seule considération de la nature n'impose point par elle-même une obligation quelconque.

" Voici la réponse de Suarez . . . . . . *Antérieurement à la Prescription et à la Volonté Divine, il y a bien et mal moral ; il y a donc obligation morale,* non aussi forte mais réelle, de faire ce qui est bien et d'éviter ce qui est mal. Cela est si vrai, *que cette loi est la raison même de notre soumission à la Volonté Divine.* Car enfin, si Dieu ordonne ou défende, il faut qu'il y ait en nous *une raison antérieure d'accepter Sa Volonté* et de la suivre.

" On demandera, quelle est la force de cette obligation et quelle est sa sanction ? La raison nous dit, que tout être, ou du moins tout être raisonnable, doit agir conformément à sa nature et aux rapports essentiels qui le lient aux autres êtres ; sous peine, en allant contre sa nature, de marcher à la contradiction, au désordre, à la destruction ; voilà la loi. Or qui va à la destruction et à la souffrance, doit la trouver : voilà la sanction. ✻

" Maintenant, cette obligation morale, simple resultat de la nature des êtres, *l'appellerez-vous une loi,* ou lui refuserez-vous

---

✻ " Quelques lecteurs bienveillants ont paru craindre que nous ne soyons tombé ici dans l'erreur du Péché Philosophique : nous devons les rassurer. La doctrine condamnée du Péché Philosophique consistait à dire, que l'on pouvait pécher contre la nature et contre la raison, sans offenser Dieu en même temps et sans violer son commandement (voir la 2ᵉ prop. condamnée par Alex. VIII., Août, 1690). Or, nous ne disons et ne pensons rien de semblable. L'obligation fondée sur la nature ou la raison, et celle que fonde la Loi Divine, sont deux obligations *distinctes ;* elles ne sont pas *séparées.*

" D'autres auraient préféré du moins que nous eussions évité cette difficile question, qui n'était pas nécessaire à notre thèse. Ces personnes n'ont pas lu, sans doute, tout ce que les rationalistes et les traditionalistes ont écrit depuis vingt ans sur les rapports de la morale et de la religion, et *les excès déplorables ou l'on s'est porté* des deux côtés. Or, notre thèse était de resoudre le plus complétement possible cette importante question, et de montrer la vérité *entre ces erreurs opposées.*" (Author's note.)

ce nom, sous prétexte que toute loi émane d'un supérieur?
Peu importe. Suarez vous dira qu'elle n'est pas une loi proprement dite; *bien que d'autres théologiens lui donnent ce nom,* en
distinguant deux espèces de loi, celle qui *indique,* qui *détermine*
le devoir, et celle qui *l'impose comme expression d'une volonté*
supérieure (Suarez, ibid. n. 3). Mais cette dispute *de mots*
n'empêche pas qu'il y ait toujours *obligation morale, devoir réel,*
quand on ferait abstraction de Dieu et de la religion. Cette
vérité n'a point échappé au puissant génie de Leibnitz. ' Il est
très-vrai,' dit-il, 'que Dieu est par sa nature supérieur de tous
les hommes. Cependant, cette pensée que tout droit naît de
la Volonté d'un Supérieur *ne laisse pas de choquer et d'être*
fausse, quelque adoucissement qu'on apporte pour l'excuser. Car
Grotius a judicieusement remarqué, qu'il y aurait quelque obligation naturelle, *quand même on accorderait,* ce qui ne se peut,
qu'il n'y a point de Divinité, ou en faisant abstraction pour un
moment de son existence.' —*Pensées,* t. xi. p. 306.

" Dieu, a t'on dit, est la source de la morale; donc elle
répose sur lui. Oui, Dieu est la source de tous les êtres, de
toutes les vérités, *des vérités morales comme des vérités mathé-*
matiques ; cependant, ne peut-on prouver les vérités mathématiques,
sans recourir au dogme de l'Existence de Dieu?"—Pp. 40-45.

47. The quotations which I have now brought together, are most abundantly sufficient, as every one must
admit, for the purpose for which I have made them.
They are most abundantly sufficient to shew, that any
Catholic has the fullest liberty of holding the conclusion, which I advocated in the preceding Section,
if it be the one which appears to him borne out by
reason and argument. These writers may differ from
each other, in some instances, on their *positive* doctrine,
as to the source and measure of morality; but they
agree absolutely in this *negative* proposition, that it is
wholly independent of any Act, whether free or necessary, of the Divine Intellect or Will. They all
agree (1) that things forbidden by the Natural Law
possess *intrinsecally* the formal character of moral evil;
and (2) that God's Detestation and Prohibition of them
are based *on* that character.

That another class of Catholic writers consider the
obligations of morality to flow from the Will of God,
I have readily admitted; but these writers regard the

Will of God as *necessarily* determined by the Perfection of His Nature, to *issue* those Commands and
Prohibitions, which appertain to the Natural Law.   I
have given my reasons for thinking, that this doctrine
is logically self-contradictory; that it leads by necessary
consequence to its own denial.   (See n. 40.)   Still we
must never forget, that, according to these writers no less
than according to the former, the distinction between
right and wrong *is* intrinsic and necessary.

As to the extreme and (I will take leave to call it)
the appalling proposition, that morality flows from
God's *free* Will,—it comes in other words to the following : ' He might well have commanded us to cultivate
' the dispositions of pride, vindictiveness, and impurity ;
' and the distinction between these and the opposite
' virtues consists merely in the *fact*, that He *has* com-
' manded the latter.'   On this doctrine, a very few
concluding words will suffice.

Suarez quotes some of the mediæval nominalists, as
advocating it ; but I have not been able to meet with a
single Catholic author of the present day, who attempts
to do so.   If such an opinion could be found in any
school of philosophy, it would be among the tradi-
tionalists.   But I have before me a most vigorous
assault on F. Chastel by F. Ventura, in which the
writer (as I understand him) expressly declines to carry
his opposition any such monstrous length.   These are
his words :—

"' Dieu,' dit cet auteur semi-rationaliste (Chastel), 'loin de
décider arbitrairement le bien et le mal, est au contraire *nécessité*
par Sa Perfection* à défendre l'un et à vouloir l'autre.'   *Cela est très-
vrai.*"— *Le Semi-Rationalisme Dévoilé.*   Par le Père Ventura de
Raulica, p. 82.   Ed. 1856.

In fact, there is no contemporary Catholic work,
either philosophical or theological, so far as I have been
able to find, alluding to this doctrine *at all*, which gives
any verdict but one upon it.   All Catholic writers, I
say, treat it as a *most grievous error;* which certain
Protestant schools have indeed admitted, but which
every Catholic is bound to reject, as opposed to the

most fundamental truths of natural religion. Billuart expressly says, that in his days this opinion had entirely disappeared from among Catholics :—

"Okam, Gerson, Petrus de Alliaco, et pauci quidam antiqui, opinati sunt Deum posse absolutè dispensare in omnibus præceptis Legis Naturæ, imò totam illam Legem abrogare; ità ut etiam odium Dei non esset peccatum. Sed hæc opinio meritò rejicitur ab aliis theologis, *et nunc inolevit.*"

Perrone observes as follows :—

"Hùc demum, ut plura alia ejusdem generis silentio prætereamus, recidit doctrina illa, cui tot *Protestantes* juris naturæ scriptores firmissime adhæserunt, nullum intrinsecum inter bonum ac malum morale dari discrimen, sed illud *à Liberâ tantum ac Positivâ Dei Voluntate* totum esse repetendum; unde consequitur, ipsum ex positivâ duntaxat Dei revelatione posse innotescere."

And he appends the following note :—

"Hæc fuit palmaris doctrina Pufendorfii, quam ipse *à parente suo Luthero hausit.* Eum sequuti sunt Cocceijus, ac saltem ex parte Heineccius, Thomasius, *aliique è Protestantibus.* Ità etiam Seldenus à positivâ Dei revelatione totum jus naturale repetit. Hinc omnes isti Protestantes juristæ doctores *scholasticos vehementer irrident ac exagitant,* eò quòd *intrinsecum boni ac mali moralis discrimen in ipsis rerum essentiis ac naturâ fundatum tuentur,* ac Legem Æternam in Deo, à Liberâ Dei Voluntate independentem, vindicant. Haud ergo satis mirari possumus, quomodo philosophus Scotus, magni inter recentiores nominis, Dugald Stewart, in præfatione quam præmisit volumini primo Supplementi Britannicæ Encyclopediæ, hanc Melanchthoni tribuere gloriam potuerit, quòd nempe primus omnium docuerit distinctionem inter bonum ac malum morale, non à revelatione, sed *ab intrinsecâ rerum naturâ* dimanantem; sic, ut (ipse subdit) Catholici posthac ex Protestantibus doctrinam hanc sint mutuali. Num hæc ipsa doctrina non omnibus fere jam antea scholasticis communis erat, si Occamum Nominalium parentem, excipias; *qui tamen statim ac contrarium docuit, ceteros pene omnes scholasticos sibi adversos habuit,* et à pluribus, quos inter à Jo. Duns Scoto, invictè refutatus est? Num scholastici ob hoc ipsum tot à Protestantibus, quos commemoravimus, injurias pati non debuerant? Num contraria sententia, quæ morales distinctiones omnino tollit, non fuit *à Luthero ejusque sectatoribus prædicata?* Adeo præjudicia protestantismi philosopho, cæteroqui commendabili, Stewarto, fucum facere potuerint!"—PERRONE *de Locis Theologicis,* pars 3, n. 9.

These two last Sections have treated ' On the Relation between God and Moral Obligation.' The conclusion, at which we have hitherto arrived, has been rather negative than positive. It has been, that moral obligation is in itself altogether independent of any Divine Act ; that *moral* truth is no more the product of God's Will, than is *mathematical.*

I have thought it better however on the whole, not to leave the question there. I have added therefore an Appendix to this Chapter, ' On the Relation between God and Necessary Truth,' in which a more positive statement is put forward. This Appendix is printed at the end of the first book. It will not be *fully* intelligible, till you have studied the three next Sections: but if you feel perplexed at our present negative position, and desirous of further light, there is no reason why you should not at once apply yourselves to its perusal.

SECTION V.

On the Idea of Moral Worthiness.

48. I pointed out in the second Section, that there is a considerable number of intuitions, readily elicited by all who have attained the use of reason, which include the idea of 'ought' or 'moral obligation.' I will now direct your attention to *another* considerable class; containing another idea closely allied to the former, which we may call ' moral worthiness.' Let us give one or two illustrations.

A. and B. are two men of my acquaintance. A. devotes the main current of his life—devotes his labour, his time, his wealth,—to instructing the ignorant, relieving the distressed, promoting the cause of virtue. B. on the other hand, without grossly neglecting any of his immediate duties, leads on the whole a life of great comfort and enjoyment. I am very far from intuing, as an obvious truth, that B.'s course of life is *wrong ;* but supposing I believe A.'s motives to be pure and simple, I intue it as most undeniable, that A.'s course of conduct is *morally better*, more *worthy of praise*, or (to use the phrase which we may consistently adopt) more *morally worthy.*

Or let us proceed, from general courses of conduct, to individual acts ; let us revert to our old hypothesis of the deposited jewel. Suppose I am surrounded with enjoyments, while he to whom I owe them is in penury. By restoring that jewel which is his, and which will enable him to procure all necessaries, I satisfy the requisitions of moral obligation. But if, from the pure motive of gratitude, I give him plentifully from what is mine, I act in a manner *more* morally worthy. If from

I

the same motive (and supposing no other claim to
interfere) I share with him my whole substance, my
act is more morally worthy still.

49. Now after what has been said at length in the
second and third Sections, it will not be necessary to
spend many words on a further step.   When we say
that act H, *e. g.* is more *morally worthy* than act K,
this idea 'moral worthiness' is not capable of being
decomposed or analysed into other more simple ideas.
We do not mean, *e. g.* that act H is more *beneficial to
society* than act K ; nor that it is more *conducive to
the agent's happiness.*   It is far more probable indeed,
that the more virtuous act *is* more beneficial to society,
and more conducive to the agent's (even temporal)
happiness.   But to make either of these two latter
statements is one thing ; and to make the original
statement, viz. that H is *morally worthier* than K, this
is quite another thing.   It does follow on the other
hand, by the strictest necessity, that if H is more *morally
worthy* than K, it is more *deserving of praise*, more
deserving of reward, and the like.

Further, and very importantly ; when we say that
act H is more morally worthy than K, we do not at all
mean that H is more *pleasing to our Creator* than K.
The very opposite is true ; H is more pleasing to our
Creator than K, *because* it is intrinsecally better.   Let
us make a supposition, which is intrinsecally impossible,
yet is perfectly imaginable (see n. 20, arg. 3, pp. 48, 9).
Let us suppose we had been created by a being, who
should be necessitated indeed to avoid what is intrinsecally wrong, and to forbid it in his creatures ; but who
should be in no way necessitated to *prefer* that which is
intrinscally more *morally worthy.*   Let us suppose a
being, who should be *less* pleased with the conduct of
one who labours earnestly to avoid every deliberate
imperfection, than with that of another who is totally
indifferent on the subject.   It is quite plain that such
a being would not *be* holy, in that sense in which we
ascribe that Attribute to our own dearest Creator—
the Infinitely Holy—the one Fountain and Source of

holiness.   When Reason declares to us that our Creator is the Cumulus of all Perfections, it inclusively declares that He possesses Sanctity.   And when it declares that He possesses Sanctity, it declares, among other things, that, by the very necessity of His Nature, He prefers that which is intrinsecally *more* morally worthy to that which is intrinsecally *less* so.*

50. It is very plain, that there is some close connection between the idea of *moral obligation* and the more general idea of moral worthiness.   Let us next therefore consider precisely *what* that connection is. We have already seen its essential nature ; for we have seen that the being *morally obliged* to do this or that act, means simply that the failing to do it would be *morally evil* or morally *unworthy*.†   We may suppose then a graduated scale, as of a thermometer, including all moral worthiness and unworthiness; and moral *obligation* will be at the *zero point* of moral worthiness.   Whatever may be the circumstances of the moment, if I simply comply with my obligation and do no more, I keep clear indeed of *moral evil ;* but that is all which can be said.   I am at zero point; removed, and only just removed, above the region of moral evil.   In proportion as I rise above that zero point, I perform acts more and more morally worthy. If I fall below that point, I fall from the region of moral worthiness altogether; and in proportion to the *degree* in which I sink below it, my acts become more and more sinful.

Let us illustrate this, by reverting to our old case of the jewel.   If I share my whole fortune with my friend, this is more morally worthy than if I merely give him even a large gift in addition to his jewel. Another act, still less worthy, will be illustrated, if I give him but a *small* gift in addition to his jewel; and the lowest, consistent *with avoiding evil,* if I simply restore the jewel.   It is plain I cannot fall below *this*

---

* This statement will be further explained, and (in some sense) qualified, in the last Section of this Chapter.
+ See n. 19, p. 42.

act in moral worthiness, without actual sin : hence
this act, the restoration of the jewel, is of strict obligation.

51. Here then are two different classes of moral
judgments: (1) this or that act is good, is obligatory,
is morally evil; (2) this act is *more* morally worthy
than that. And take the two classes together, so far
from its being at all a rare or exceptional thing to
elicit such judgments, it will perhaps be found on consideration, that there are no kind of judgments whatever, more *frequent* with the great mass of mankind.
' How wrongly A. behaved on such an occasion !' ' How
admirably B. encountered that trial !' 'How far preferable is C.'s conduct to D.'s !' Such judgments as
these, surely succeed each other quite rapidly in the
mind throughout the day. We need not at all, and
we cannot, maintain, that the moral judgments of men
in general are commonly *correct ;* but we *do* say that
they·are very *frequent.* In other words, there is no
one idea more constantly familiar to the mind of every
man, than the idea of moral worthiness considered in
itself. Men may make great *mistakes*, as to those acts
or persons whom they praise or blame ; but praise
and blame, for supposed merit or demerit, are among
the very commonest thoughts in their mind.

Much might be said, were this the appropriate
place for saying it, on the religious inferences derivable from this fact. Our Creator, it seems, is quite
in a special degree solicitous, to ensure our remembrance of this moral Rule which has claim over all our
actions. He has therefore so constituted our nature,
that even those who are most engrossed with temporal objects, who live most undividedly for wealth,
or honour, or comfort, bear constant witness against
themselves, in this unceasing reference to the ideas of
moral obligation and moral worthiness. But all such
considerations rather belong to a later part of our
work ; and here I need only say, that you will find it
(I expect) a most edifying and almost surprising
study, as you find one particular after another evolved,

of those which shew how *singularly* He has formed our nature for the practise of virtue.

52. It will be now advisable, to extend the sense in which we use that important phrase the 'Natural Rule.' We have hitherto used it as synonymous with the 'rule of independent obligation' (see n. 24). Let us now use it more extensively, as synonymous with the 'rule of independent virtuousness.' According to its former acceptation, it signified the sum of all those obligations, which bind us independently of God's commands.* According to its new acceptation, let it include also the sum of all those cases, in which one act is *more morally worthy* than another, independently of any special intervention exercised by God.

53. Here then we are led to a further very important enquiry; how far does this Natural Rule extend. And this general enquiry subdivides itself into three. First, we may ask how far *in fact* does this Natural Rule extend. Secondly, how far is *reason in the abstract* capable of discovering it. Thirdly, as to reason *in the concrete*,— exercised under those circumstances in which mankind are placed,—we may ask how great progress is reason *in this sense* able to make, towards discovering the Natural Rule.

Our meaning may be illustrated by a parallel case. There is an indefinite number of properties impressed by God on matter, which, by their various combinations, account for all the physical phenomena of the universe. He who should know all these properties, and all their combinations, would be a master of all physical truth. Now (1) nothing is more probable, than that there may be many of these properties, which Reason is absolutely unable to approach; it may either not possess the data, or the intrinsic power, which would enable it even to advance *towards* their dis-

---

* So Vasquez, already quoted n. 30: '*Regula Naturalis*, quæ nullâ voluntate sed suâpte naturâ constat.' 'Ante omne Imperium, ante omnem Voluntatem, immò ante omne Judicium [Dei, est] *regula quædam harum actionum*, quæ suâpte naturâ constat.'

covery.   And yet we might in other ways, as, *e. g.* by
Revelation, be enabled to acquire a full knowledge of
such properties.   But (2) there will be a considerable
number of other properties, whose discovery *is* quite
within the domain of Reason: Reason, exercising its intrinsic power on those data which are within its grasp,
may be fully competent to attain them.   And yet (3)
there may be multitudes of these latter properties
which are so circumstanced, that the reason of man
here below never *will* in fact, nor indeed can, arrive
at their knowledge.   The process, required for that
purpose, may need such constant and prolonged exercise of Reason, or so very wide a collection of data,
that *in fact*, circumstanced as we are in this visible
world, we are utterly unable to accomplish the task.

Just so, as to the Natural Rule.   One question is,
how far it does in fact actually extend; another, how
far Reason in the abstract is able to attain it; a third,
how far *our* reason, in our existing circumstances,
enables us to proceed.   The following Section will
be devoted to a consideration of these three most
important questions.

Section VI.

On the Extent of the Natural Rule.

54. Various intuitive judgments, which are most certainly legitimate, and which are common to all mankind, enable us to state with confidence one very important proposition. Justice, Veracity, and Benevolence, are intrinsecally good ends of action. The phrase 'good' or virtuous 'ends of action,' I use in somewhat of a technical sense ; which will be fully explained as we proceed. On the other hand, when we speak of *three* ends, we are not speaking with very strict accuracy ; for Veracity should by rights be included under Justice. I mention Veracity however separately, because of its special importance ; since (as already implied) it is only by proving the intrinsic virtuousness of Veracity, that our acceptance of a revelation becomes possible. However, even if the above statement in itself could be considered as ambiguous in any particular, the course of our remarks will amply explain and define it.

I intue that it is wrong, not to give my friend back his jewel : why ? because it is contrary to *Justice.* I intue that it is wrong, if a governor punishes his subjects, for that which they have no real power to avoid : why? because it is contrary to *Justice.* I intue that it is wrong, if a traveller comes home, and tells me all kind of falsehoods about the countries which he has visited : why ? because it is contrary to *Veracity.* Suppose any one has the power most readily to do a great deal, in the way of lessening some terrible mass of evil which surrounds him ; to save numbers, *e. g.* from imminent danger of death ; and suppose nevertheless he does not move a finger in the matter : I intue that such conduct is morally culpable ; why ? because it is contrary to *Benevolence.*

Here are cases, where Justice, Veracity, and Benevolence, are intued as obligatory : now for others,
where, putting aside the question of obligation, they
are intued as virtuous ends of action.   A governor is
aggrieved by some great public evil; but on preparing
to punish the offenders, he finds that they have really
not had the full power of acting otherwise.   Though
greatly provoked at the evil which has ensued, and
though the punishing of these men would be very expedient as a piece of state policy, he refuses to do so,
because it would be unjust.   I intue that this act,
wherein his will is thus powerfully affected towards the
virtuousness of Justice, is a very virtuous act.   A
traveller returns from abroad; and, though he might
obtain great *éclat* and make himself a very interesting
object by romancing on what he has seen, he confines
himself to strict and sober truth.   I intue that these
acts, wherein his will is thus powerfully affected towards
the virtuousness of veracity, are very virtuous acts.
A landlord devotes his energy, his time, his money,
to redress the misery which exists among his tenants or
their labourers.   I intue that, if he does all this because
his will is so powerfully affected to the virtuousness of
Benevolence, these various acts are extremely virtuous.
   Nor are these principles confined to external acts:
they apply fully as much to acts purely internal ; to
acts which are consummated in the will, nay, and to acts
which do not in any way contemplate even *future* action.
If I earnestly *wish* that A. B., who has laboured in the
service of the state, may receive his just reward—
though I do not contemplate my own agency as tending in any way (now or hereafter) to obtain it for him —
yet such *wish* alone is virtuous, under the head of
Justice.   If I rejoice in the thought, that some invention
has greatly mitigated human suffering,—that mere act of
complacence is virtuous under the head of Benevolence.
Still more keenly do I intue, that to rejoice in the
sufferings of any of my fellow - creatures, simply as
such, is among the most detestable sins I can commit ;
one which, more than almost any other, has earned the
title of diabolical.   I intue that this is most fully the

case, even though I should not contemplate *adding to those sufferings by my own acts* in the slightest degree.

It is implied in what we have said—but it needs to be explicitly stated—that there is nothing like this on the opposite side. No one ever thought another virtuous for *this* precise reason, viz. because his will was so powerfully affected towards injustice, mendacity, and cruelty. The meaning and force of this remark will be made clearer, by supposing an objection.

'Surely,' then it will be urged, 'there are number-
'less cases, where unjust, mendacious, and cruel acts
'are applauded. We invade an enemy's country; and
'think it no kind of sin to deprive the poor inhabitants
'of that harvest, on which they have been expending a
'year's toil: yet what can be more unjust? Again,
'multitudes of men think a lie most allowable, if there
'be no other means of defending a friend's life or
'honour. Lastly, men often think it lawful to inflict
'very considerable suffering—*e. g.* all the horrors of
'war—simply for the sake of national honour or terri-
'torial aggrandisement. Here then is a large number
'of intuitions, wherein injustice, mendacity, and cruelty
'are held as virtuous.'

The answer to this is extremely simple. But before giving it, ' ex abundanti cautelâ' it may be as well to make one most obvious remark. The question through-out is not what men *do*, but what they *approve;* not what course they in fact *follow*, but what they *believe* to be the path of virtue. And now to the objection.

Certainly men often think it lawful to inflict suffer-ing, for very inadequate reason. They think it lawful, under many circumstances, to say what is false. But why? Not because of any supposed virtuousness *in mendacity or cruelty as such ;* on the contrary, they probably enough recognize the intrinsic claims of Veracity and Benevolence, at the very moment of acting in opposition to those virtues. Their judgment is of the following kind. 'Undeniable as is the claim
'of Veracity where there is no reason to the contrary,
'my friend's claim on me, to save his life or honour, is
'superior and should prevail.' And the very same

account may be given of the other cases specified.   It
is not *mendacity*, that is recognized as having a counter
claim to Veracity ; but a *friend's life or honour*, which
is thought to possess such a counter claim.   A great
multitude of acts are recognized as morally good, simply
because they are motived by the virtuousness of truth-
telling as such :—when was one ever regarded as good,
simply   because   it   was   motived   by   the   (supposed)
virtuousness of *lying* as such ?

This will appear even more clearly, if we contrast
any of those instances, in which (I fully admit) men *do*
elicit false intuitions, in regard to virtuous ends of
action.   Many, *e. g.* think it morally culpable, if they
leave a stinging injury unrevenged.   They will therefore go through great labour and self-denial, for the
purpose of vengeance ; for the sake of fulfilling the
(supposed) obligation of vindictive retribution.   And
many, who witness this conduct, will admire them for
so acting.   Vindictive retribution then is regarded by
many, I admit it, as a virtuous end of action.   But
who can say that injustice, mendacity, or cruelty, has
ever been regarded as such?   Who ever thought it
his duty to do *any one thing*, for the sake of fulfilling
any supposed obligation to practise injustice, mendacity,
or cruelty, simply as such, and for its own sake? or
who ever admired another *because* he so acted ?

The various intuitions, which have been assumed as
legitimate in the preceding argument, are proved to be
so, on precisely the same grounds, which have been
already (we suppose) admitted as satisfactory.   Let
any one look back at our reasons for maintaining that
the intuition of moral obligation is itself legitimate (see
n. 17, pp. 37, 8); he will see that they apply in their
full force to the intuitions which we have here been
considering.   We infer therefore, that Justice, Veracity,
and Benevolence, are legitimately intued as virtuous
ends of action.

55. Before proceeding with our research for *other*
virtuous ends, let us consider various important truths,
which are implied in the very fact of certain ends *being*
virtuous.   Such truths, as soon as established, will hold

at once in regard to Justice, Veracity, and Benevolence; and they will also of course hold in regard to any *other* ends, which we may afterwards prove to *be* virtuous.

(1.) We have already seen, that in recognizing any virtuous end of action, it is implied that we never regard, as lawful, the contravening such an end purely for the sake of pleasure or caprice. We may often indeed consider that, in this or that particular case, some *other* virtuous end, which happens for the moment to conflict, has a preponderating claim ; that Veracity, *e. g.* may be sacrificed to the claims of Justice or Benevolence. But where no conflicting claim can be put forward, we universally admit the authority of any one virtuous end to be paramount and indefeasible. We never think it lawful, *e. g.* to inflict cruelty, except to satisfy the claims of Justice or of some other virtuous end.

56. (2.) Suppose I confer various benefits on my fellow-men, yet not at all because of the *virtuousness* of Benevolence, but for some different end altogether : for instance, suppose I so act in order that I may keep a promise made to my dying father. Such an act may be virtuous under the head of *Fidelity* (*i. e.* observance of promises); or under the head of *Filial piety :* but in no sense under the head of *Benevolence.* Or suppose I so act, for the simple purpose of obtaining the affection of those whom I benefit, with the sole view of reaping some temporal advantage by their help. *Such* an act will have no virtue whatever; since it is wholly motived by a desire of temporal gain. Both these statements are obvious as soon as made ; from them, and from an indefinite number of propositions precisely similar and intued with equal clearness, we derive a very important generalization.

No act is virtuous, unless it be directed to the virtuousness of some end recognized as virtuous ('nisi fiat propter honestatem boni cujusdam honesti'). Nor is it virtuous at all, except so far as regards that end, or those ends, to the virtuousness of which it has been directed.

There is no philosophical proposition, more constantly used in Theology than this ; I must beg you
therefore most carefully to consider its meaning and
its proof, and remember it for future use.

57. (3.) We are now able easily to understand the
distinction, so frequently expressed by philosophers,
between *objective* and *subjective* morality.   To confer
great benefits on a multitude of men, is *objectively* most
virtuous ; but if I do so merely for the sake of temporal gain, my act is *subjectively* immoral.   In objective morality, we consider merely the thing done or
resolved on ; but in subjective morality, we consider
the *frame of mind* in which, the *circumstances* under
which, above all *the end* for which, the agent does
it or resolves on it.   Nothing is more common, than
for acts to be objectively virtuous, but subjectively
sinful.

On the other hand, it must always be subjectively
sinful, to do that which I recognize as objectively wrong.
It is a contradiction in terms to say, that *any* circumstances can make me right, in doing that which I know
to be under *all* circumstances wrong.

But I may *often* be subjectively virtuous in doing
what is objectively wrong, supposing that I do *not*
know it so to be.   What those circumstances are,—
or in other words when and how far ignorance excuses
from sin,—is a further consideration.   You will find
hereafter, when we arrive at the subject, that there
is hardly a more difficult question in all Theology.

The same distinction applies to *relative degrees* of
moral worthiness.   Let me assume, what every Catholic holds, that the life of Obedience, Poverty, and
Celibacy, objectively speaking, is intrinsically more
morally worthy than the life of an ordinary Christian.
Yet if I have no vocation to that life,—in other words,
if God's gifts to me, whether of nature or grace, are
such that I promote my own sanctification better by
the more ordinary course,—then *subjectively*, in my own
case, that ordinary course is the more morally worthy
of the two.   Or again, if in any way God were to

express His preference that I should pursue the more
ordinary course—wishing, *e. g.* so to employ me in some
providential work—then also this course would be subjectively the better.   But on this latter instance, God's
expression of a preference, we will here say no more, as
we shall treat of it expressly in the next Section.

58. (4.) A. restores his kind friend's deposit under
circumstances of great trial : by doing so, he brings
himself into the necessity of labouring for his daily
bread.   B. restores the deposit, without thereby incurring any serious inconvenience.   Objectively speaking, A.'s act is more virtuous than B.'s ; for the just
and obligatory act is performed under circumstances
of greater difficulty.

But is A.'s act also *subjectively* better ?   On the
surface, we should reply ' certainly yes ;' but a little
consideration will shew that something more has to
be said.   Why are we inclined to think A.'s act the
better ? Because, by the very circumstance of resisting
such great temptation to dishonesty, he displays a *will
firmly and efficaciously adhering to the virtuousness of
justice.*   But it is abundantly possible, that B.'s will
may *in fact* adhere quite as efficaciously to that virtuousness ; only that he has no opportunity for *dis-
playing* that fact.   If therefore we knew (*e. g.* by
Revelation) that such was in truth the case, we should
have no hesitation in considering that B.'s act was
subjectively as virtuous as A.'s.   Here by generalisa-
tion we arrive at another proposition, which is of
extreme importance both to Theology and Philosophy.

My act, cæteris paribus, becomes subjectively more
virtuous, in proportion as my will adheres more
firmly and efficaciously to the virtuousness of the
virtuous end or ends.

59. (5.) We are now able to arrive at our general
idea of a perfectly holy being.   And first we will
suppose that being to be finite.

The intuitions, on which our argument has hitherto
rested, apply not to men only, but to all rational
creatures ; as will be evident to any one who re-

Him because of His Greatness,' 'to obey Him because of His just Authority,' 'to aim at His approbation as being our moral Governor,' 'to conform our Will to His because of His Sanctity :'—all these intuitions, I say, are most obviously legitimate.   They are not indeed so universally elicited by all mankind, as are those on which I have been hitherto insisting ; simply because the mass of men either know so little, or think so little, *about* God. But no one can apprehend the terms of the various propositions just recited, without intuing the truth of these propositions.   They apply also, as is most evident, not to men only but to all rational creatures.

62. But there are other virtues which, in the Christian's eye, have quite as great intrinsic excellence, as Justice, Veracity, and Benevolence. I mean such as the following : Humility, Forgivingness, Chastity.   Revelation indeed declares that they are intrinsecally virtuous, and we can accept that truth of course on God's authority.   Yet it is a question of great interest and of some importance, to see how far, by Reason alone, we can arrive at the same conclusion.   I am confident that we can, to the fullest extent ; and I proceed to lay down two important principles, which will greatly help us in the enquiry.

63. The first of these we may call the 'production of the arc' principle.   It will often happen, that if we see only a very small portion of the arc of a circle, we cannot distinguish it from a straight line : produce it, and its real nature is apparent.   Something altogether analogous takes place in reference to moral conduct. If act A be virtuous under circumstances C, since morality is *necessary*, a *similar* act will be virtuous *whenever* similar circumstances recur.   We have therefore to judge, not on an isolated case, but on a whole class of cases ; we have to consider, not simply whether *one* act A is virtuous, but whether *all* these acts A are virtuous.   And it will frequently happen, that the multitude of men might have been unable to form any confident opinion on the former question, who may yet decide with the most perfect clearness on the latter. For instance, 'is it lawful for a man harassed by poverty

' (I am not supposing actual danger to life) to take
' something from his rich neighbour ? the latter would
' hardly so much as be aware of the loss, while to the
' former it would be an inestimable benefit.'   There
are perhaps many, who could not at all events see
very clearly that this is wrong.   But put the case
universally—produce the arc—there will be no doubt
as to the decision.   No one will fail to see, how monstrous would be the supposition, that *every one*, who
considers himself harassed by poverty, may plunder his
rich neighbour.   To mention no other consequence—
the rich neighbour would soon become as poor as they.

On this ground alone, were there no other, special
weight would be due to the moral judgments of a *good*
man.   He acts *consistently* on his moral rules, hour
after hour, day after day ; and by consequence he has
unconsciously ' produced the arc.'   His moral rules
have been applied to a large number of parallel cases,
and have been proved able to bear the weight of sustained and consistent moral action.

64. But the second principle to which I have
alluded (n. 62), goes far more nearly into the heart of
the matter than the first ; and indeed (in my humble
opinion) gives us far more light on the real trustworthiness of moral judgments, than anything which
has hitherto been said throughout this Section.   It will
require therefore to be treated, at a length somewhat
proportioned to its importance ; and it will necessitate
some little psychological investigation.   The latter circumstance is a matter for regret ; as it would have been
undoubtedly more convenient, if we could have reserved
all our psychology for the next Chapter.

I assume then, from what will be said more at
length in the next Chapter, that the soul is a *simple*
substance.   When therefore we speak of dividing it
into intellect, will, and the like, we are not speaking of
any *real* division ; the intellect and will are not two
different parts of the soul, as fore and aft are two different parts of a ship.   When the soul puts forth acts
of cognition, it is convenient that those acts be referred

K

to the intellect ; when acts of volition, to the will : and the intellect and will respectively are but abstract terms used accordingly.

To this remark we here add another.   Just as we divide the *soul* into intellect, will, and the like, so we *subdivide* the *intellect* into its different faculties.   In this case, as in the former, nothing can be further from our thoughts than the idea of any *real* division ; we are but saying, that, for convenience of arrangement, some intellectual operations of the soul are referred to this faculty and some to that.   Our various acts of *memory* we refer to the *remembering* faculty ; our various acts of *inference* to the *reasoning* faculty ; and so on with the rest.

On what principle do we ordinarily decide, as to the *number* of *distinct* faculties which we shall enumerate ? I think on the following.   Let us suppose that there is a number of intellectual operations, so similar to each other, that whoever performs *one* of these well ordinarily performs *the others* so, and whatever discipline will increase his power of performing *one*, will equally increase his power of performing the *rest ;* — in such a case, we refer these operations to *the same faculty.*   Operations on the other hand, which are *not* so similar, we refer to *distinct* faculties.

Let us take our illustrations from one of the *most* important classes of operation, and from one of the *least* important; the operations of *remembering* and the operations of *observing distances at sea.*   The operations of remembering are connected closely with each other in the mode just described : he who remembers *one* thing very well, probably remembers *other* things also very well, which have been with equal frequency in his thoughts ; whatever discipline will improve his power of remembering *one* thing, will improve his power of remembering *other* things also.   The various operations of observing distances at sea are likewise mutually connected in the same way.

On the other hand, there is no probability whatever, that he who *remembers* well will be clever in *judging rightly on marine distance;* nor will the discipline which assists the *memory*, give any material benefit on the latter undertaking. Hence we refer our various acts of *remembering* to one faculty, and our various acts of *observing marine distances* to one faculty ; but we count these *two* faculties as *distinct* from each other. There is one faculty, and not more, of remembering ; one, and not more, of observing marine distances : but it is to *two* faculties, and *not* to one, that we ascribe the respective operations, 1st of remembering, 2nd of observing distances at sea.

In like manner, I suppose there is a distinct faculty of judging on pictures, and another distinct faculty of judging on music. And so we might proceed; but that enough has been said to explain our meaning.

I conceive that the faculty of *reasoning* is one, and not more. In other words, he who reasons well on one matter, will reason equally well on any other with which he is equally conversant; and the same discipline which will make him reason better on one subject, will also make him reason better on any other with which (as before) he is equally conversant. This is by no means a self-evident fact ; yet on the other hand, as it does not bear on our argument, it will be better not to be led away into those various statements, which would be necessary for the purpose of establishing it. Let it suffice then thus to have stated my own humble opinion.＊

＊ It may, perhaps, be worth while to point out in a note, that those who excel in logical deduction, excel equally in logical *induction*. The latter (I need hardly say) is wholly different from physical or Baconian induction ; and appertains as simply to Formal Logic, as does deduction itself. Its type is such as the following : 'Every right-angled triangle has this property ; every obtuse-angled triangle has it ; every acute-angled triangle has it. But these three classes make up all triangles whatever ; hence all triangles whatever have it.' As the deductive reasoning goes from generals to particulars, so inductive from particulars to generals. I think this inductive reasoning is far more common than we are sometimes apt to fancy. At all events I may take this opportunity of remarking, that it has often occurred in the preceding pages. Thus for instance in this very Section (n. 56) I draw attention to a particular intuition ; I state that there is a countless number of similar intuitions ; and by logical induction I make a generalization.

It may be thought perhaps at first sight, that the acts of observing distances at sea (to take the illustration which I have suggested) are not *intuitive* but *inferential* judgments ; after the type of those mentioned in n. 2. Take the following judgment—'We are now three miles from land,' and no doubt this *is* an inferential judgment. It may arise, *e. g.* from such

Now of all these various faculties three things may be remarked :—

(1.) Some men are by nature far less gifted with this or that faculty than are other men.

(2.) Putting aside exceptional cases, in every man every faculty admits of being indefinitely improved.

(3.) The one mode, by which that improvement takes place, is *practice;* exercise of the faculty in putting it to that purpose, which it was evidently intended to subserve. We learn to *remember* better and better, in proportion as we apply ourselves to *learning things by heart.* We learn to intue more accurately the mutual relations of marine distances, in proportion as we give our attention to the task of comparing them. We improve our judgment in music, by accustoming ourselves to hear it. We grow in good taste for pictures, in proportion as we give exercise to such taste as we have.

65. Our foundation having thus been laid, I proceed to state what appears to me the real process, whereby our moral judgments increase in accuracy. I will first state it and *assume* it to be true. When we have seen the various results to which it leads, I will *then* beg your attention to the various arguments in its behalf. I will merely premise, that, in considering the whole matter, we must put out of sight the fact of Revelation; because our question regards the power of *unaided reason* to discover moral truth.

I lay down then the following two theses :—

(1.) As there is one faculty whereby we remember, and another whereby we observe distances at sea; a third whereby we judge rightly on the excellence of music, a fourth on pictures ;—so, and in precisely the

reasoning as this : 'The present distance is just three-quarters of the distance which I observed last week ; and which I knew aliunde to be four miles.' But it must be observed that the *first* part of this sentence, ' *this* is three-quarters of *that*,' is undeniably an *intuitive* judgment ; and a judgment, which will be probably true or false, accordingly as the faculty of observing distances at sea is in a sound or unsound state. A mere landsman will probably be altogether mistaken in forming such a judgment. This whole remark is applicable to an indefinite number of cases, where it might be thought that the elicited judgment is inferential and not intuitive.

same sense, there is another faculty, whereby we intue moral truth. Let us call this the Moral Faculty.

(2.) As our other faculties improve by *being put to that purpose for which they are intended*, so also does the Moral Faculty.

66. To see the full bearing of this second thesis, let us first consider *what* is the 'purpose' for which the Moral Faculty is 'intended.' Evidently, that it should be *the one guide of our life*. If there *be* such a quality as moral evil attaching to certain actions, we cannot tell how many,—it becomes a most indispensable duty, to take good heed that *none* of those daily actions which we are in the habit of performing, may come under the number. It becomes, I say, a most indispensable duty, to pass under review from time to time our course of life, that we may carefully consider how far we have means of knowing that any part of it is wrong. He who recognizes that there *is* such a thing as moral obligation *at all*, is self-condemned, unless he aims at enthroning it in the place of absolute and despotic authority over his whole life.

The same thing may be more accurately and profitably stated, if we here assume a proposition which is undeniably true. When once men begin seriously to lay to heart moral obligation, they will at once recognize the Existence of a Holy Creator. By what process this recognition takes place — whether, *e.g.* by inference, or intuition, or in what other way,—this is a most important philosophical inquiry, yet here we need not consider it. It could not by possibility be discussed satisfactorily, without occupying very considerable space, and leading us through a number of very difficult questions; while our course of argument is not affected by it one way or the other. I will only here explain how far 1 am from meaning, that *in fact* men first arrive by means of reason at a knowledge of God. On the contrary, I believe that *in fact* the first announcement of God's existence ever comes through the agency of Revelation ; there being no country so barbarous or so isolated, as that some remains at least of the Primitive

Revelation do not remain among them, imparting a real light from Heaven. At the same time, to say that the first *announcement* is in fact due to Revelation, is of course most fully consistent with saying, as I do say, that reason is superabundantly able to establish and substantiate this fundamental truth.

Reverting then to the course of our argument, and interweaving with it this proposition of God's Existence, I assert that those only put their Moral Faculty to that purpose for which it is intended, who are in the habit of striving earnestly and perseveringly to please their Creator. In other words, those only do so, who are in the habit of (1) frequently passing under review every detail of their conduct, for the purpose of considering how far it will be approved by the Omniscient God; and (2) of labouring earnestly, that the current of their lives may be really in harmony with that which they have discovered to be God's Will. That such a course is utterly impossible without Prayer and Grace, I am indeed well aware; and we shall see this truth most fully established, when we come to Theology. Still *reason* alone would shew the importance and obligation of Prayer; while *experience* would testify to its most efficacious results. We are able therefore to make the supposition that men *do* so act with reasonable consistency, without introducing the hypothesis of a special and authenticated Revelation.

Our second thesis comes then to this: that in proportion as we carefully pursue the course just described, our Moral Faculty will acquire a constantly increasing refinement of intuition, enabling it to form 'moral judgments' with constantly increasing fineness and accuracy.* To understand therefore fully the said

---

* This is held by Gioberti; though I cannot but think that he is far from laying such stress upon it, as its extreme importance deserves. Surely all must confess, that *if* a truth, it is a *more important* one than most others. The following is M. Alary's translation of Gioberti's words:

"L'inclination et la propension affectueuse de la volonté . . . tournent au profit de la connaissance elle-même; l'accroissent, la fortifient, la perfectionnent. Voilà pourquoi les amis des vérités intellectives ont de celles-ci

thesis, one final question must be answered ;—'*what* is precisely meant by a *moral judgment?*'

By a 'moral judgment,' we understand a judgment, of which the idea of 'moral worthiness,' in one or other of its various shapes, stands as predicate. Moral judgments therefore will be always reducible to such types as the following : 'A is virtuous,' 'B is of obligation,' 'C is morally evil,' 'D is morally worthier than E,' &c. &c. Thus that humility is virtuous, is a moral judgment ; but that such or such a mental discipline will *conduce* to humility, this is not a 'moral' but a psychological judgment. This latter judgment, I say, does not predicate moral goodness, or badness, or preferableness, of any act or person ; but simply states that a certain relation exists between two certain mental phenomena. Now it is 'moral judgments,' and not psychological nor any other, which (I maintain) will be more accurately elicited, in proportion as the Moral Faculty is improved through moral discipline.

66. Do we mean therefore, that as our Moral Faculty thus grows, we are able for certain to judge more clearly, under every combination of circumstances, what is right or wrong, and what is morally preferable? By no means. The Moral Faculty is able indeed to judge more accurately on the *cases brought before it ;* but the *wrong case* may be brought before it. This very mode of expression suggests an obvious analogy. When we wish to obtain a lawyer's opinion,—so to draw up our case as fully and accurately to represent the circumstances, is often a very difficult task. If we perform this task badly, though the lawyer were the best in all England, his opinion could be of no real service. It might be an excellent opinion on the *case ;* but not on the *real circumstances :* the fault would be, not that the opinion is *legally erroneous,* but that the circumstances are *erroneously represented.* Take another illustration from a pair of scales. They may be so

une intuition *beaucoup plus vive et plus prononcée*, que ceux dont l'âme est *enveloppée et endurcie dans l'affection vicieuse des choses sensuelles,*" &c. —Introduction, vol. iii. p. 40.

exquisitely made, so nicely adjusted, as to be impressed by a feather's weight; and yet what will be
the value of their decision, if the *wrong parcel* is
put in?

To apply these illustrations. Our moral judgments,
as we have seen, are of the following kinds. 'Under
'the circumstances as I conceive them, A is morally
'evil, B is lawful, C is morally better than D.' But
that the circumstances as I *conceive them*, shall be in
fact the circumstances *as they are*,—in other words that
I shall have *accurately represented* the circumstances
to my mind—*this* requires a *different* kind of judgment
altogether. This latter kind of judgment is one, which
it is often most difficult to form correctly; but its
correctness in no way depends on the good condition of
my Moral Faculty. And we shall see this still more
strongly, if we consider the production of the arc (see
n. 63). For the question, on which I have to pronounce
a moral judgment, is not whether in *this particular case*
the act is lawful or preferable, but whether in *every
parallel case* a parallel act is so to be considered. It
is necessary therefore, before the requisite judgment
can be pronounced, that I shall suppose such acts,
as universally done under parallel circumstances;—that
I shall follow out with sufficient accuracy and completeness the various results which would thus ensue;—
that I shall follow out with equal accuracy and completeness the results which would ensue on the opposite
hypothesis;—and then, having thus brought up the
whole case (and no mere fragment of it) for judgment,
that I shall finally pronounce. Plainly it will happen
again and again, that the real difficulty is far more in
the preparatory, than in the final, process; far more
in the process which depends on other intellectual
operations, than on that which specially appertains to
the Moral Faculty.

You will say perhaps, that if this be the only
method of arriving at a sound ethical conclusion, the
cases must be comparatively few, in which reason will
enable us with any confidence to hold such a conclu-

sion.   If this *be* your inference, you are only anticipating what I shall have earnestly to advocate in a
later part of the Section.   Here we are only considering
what the true process is.

A particular instance may perhaps make clearer our
meaning.   The question has sometimes been raised,
whether it is morally preferable to give, or to refuse,
money to a beggar who asks alms, into whose circumstances I have no means of inquiring.   For the moment,
we have nothing to do with decisions of the Church,
texts of Scripture, and the rest, because we are supposed to be investigating the case on pure grounds of
reason.   But, apart from these, as a mere matter of intuition, numbers of excellent persons will in a moment
pronounce, that it is very decidedly *better* to give than to
withhold.   Yet a little consideration will shew, that they
are not really pronouncing on the alternative intended.
Their 'scales' may be in a very good state, but wrong
'parcels' have been put into them.   They understand
the question to be, ' which of these two is morally pre-
' ferable — the giving to an accidental beggar, or the
' retaining for our own enjoyment.'   This however is
not at all what is meant, but rather the following.   ' A
' certain sum of money, a certain amount of self-abne-
' gation, being *fixed*, as that from which the poor are
' to be relieved — is it preferable that this sum should
' be partly given to those of whom we know nothing,
' or that it should be wholly devoted to persons into
' whose circumstances we can fully inquire?'   Now I
suppose the 'moral judgment,' which all would pronounce, as soon as the case proposed is really understood, is of the following kind : ' our answer must de-
' pend on the question, *which* of the two courses is more
' conducive to the *spiritual and temporal benefit* of the
' poor as a class? that course is *morally preferable*,
' which is the more *conducive to such welfare*.'   This
is the only judgment in the case, whereof ' lawful,' or
' wrong,' or ' morally preferable,' stands as predicate;
and this therefore is the only one which is properly a
' moral judgment.'   Thus the real difficulty here does

not lie with the action of the 'scales,' but with the *preliminary* action, of getting together the right 'parcels' which are to be weighed.   The really doubtful part of the question, I say, does not lie within the sphere, within reach, of the *Moral Faculty* at all; even a Saint might judge quite mistakenly upon it : it has to be solved, as best it may, by a careful use of our other intellectual faculties. *

67. So far then I have frankly admitted the insufficiency of the Moral Faculty, for the determination of moral truth.   But there are other instances, and those *far more really important*, in which the growth of this Faculty *is* our one safe and sufficient means of arriving at such truth.   I allude particularly to the question, what are virtuous ends of action (see nn. 54 and 62); and I say that *this* question is at last *far* more practically important than any other.   We have seen that *he* is subjectively *the best* man, whose will is ordinarily fixed, with the greatest degree of firmness and efficacity, on the various good ends of action whatever they may be. (See nn. 58, 59.)   *Our own personal progress in goodness* then, depends on our knowledge, *what* these virtuous ends really are; and it does *not* depend on our knowledge *of any other moral truths whatever*.   Suppose a man could direct his conduct consistently to the (supposed) virtuousness of pride or vindictiveness, he would become, not the better but the worse man, in actual proportion to the steadiness and perseverance of his moral action : it becomes therefore inappreciably important, to shew that such a result is utterly *impossible ;* that it is absolutely and totally repugnant to the constitution of our nature.   But let us assume that he made bonâ fide ever such great mistakes, as to what is the morally preferable way of relieving the poor; or what is the degree of violence which he may innocently use in self-defence; or in what cases he may lawfully receive

* I give this as an illustration of what is meant by my principle.   I should be very sorry if it were thought that I myself disapprove the habit of giving, under various circumstances, to unknown beggars.

interest for his money; or on a thousand other such questions. Well—I am not in the least wishing to understate the serious mischief of this; but evidently such mischief is different, not in degree merely but in *kind*, from the tremendous evil which must ensue, on the *preceding* hypothesis; on the hypothesis of a continued mistake in regard to the truly virtuous ends of action.

Now as to these virtuous ends of action, three in particular (n. 62) remained for consideration; Humility, Forgivingness, Purity. Let us take them in this order.

68. As to pride, it is very certain that its sinfulness is no matter of *universal* intuition. It is plain enough indeed, that to pride myself on what I know to be morally wrong—on the success of my knavery or of my lawless violence,—cannot but itself be morally evil and detestable. Again, to pride myself on my ancient birth or extreme wealth—no one (I suppose) will think *this* virtuous; though as to the *degree* of its viciousness, there will be great difference of opinion.

But suppose I pride myself on what I believe to be good and virtuous. There are multitudes of men, who are just, benevolent, grateful, in their external conduct, mainly and principally for this reason; that they would be ashamed of themselves if they acted differently. This was particularly the case, with those heathens who are popularly called virtuous.* Cato is punctiliously just in his dealings; for it would greatly lower the illustrious Cato in his own eyes, if he were not so. He fulfils the various duties of a just man and a good citizen, so far as he understands those duties, from the same motive. Month after month and year after year, he inhales the sweet incense of his own

---

* I am very far from meaning that heathens perform no really virtuous acts at all. In the theological portion of our work, we shall have again and again to consider the very important condemnation of Baius's proposition, 'Omnia opera infidelium sunt peccata,' and of his follower's, 'Necesse est infidelem in omni opere peccare.' On the other hand we shall also have to consider the Church's singularly emphatic enunciation, 'Fortitudinem gentilium mundana cupiditas . . . facit.' — *Conc. Arausicanum*, canon 17.

esteem; and he is thus ever increasing that intense appreciation, wherewith he regards his own dignity. At length, it seems the one obviously virtuous course, that he shall *stab* himself, rather than that so exalted a character should undergo the ignominy of falling into his enemy's power. Such is heathenism; and there have been many Protestants in various ages, hardly better than heathens, who have loudly applauded his conduct.* This habit, of priding ourselves on our supposed virtue, requires such careful and frequent consideration in Theology, that it should have a distinct name of its own. I will consistently therefore call it ' *moral* pride.' And I ask, can it be shewn by reason, against these heathens and heathenish Protestants, that their intuitions on the virtuousness of moral pride are totally mistaken?

---

* " The celebrated Roman patriot, Cato, stabbed himself when besieged at Utica, rather than fall into the hands of Cæsar. He thought this a very great action, and so have many others besides. In like manner Saul, in Scripture, fell on his sword when defeated in battle ; and there have been those who reproached Napoleon for not having blown out his brains on the field of Waterloo. Now, if these advocates of suicide had been asked why they thought such conduct, under such circumstances, noble, perhaps they would have returned the querist no answer ; as if it were too plain to talk about, or from contempt of him, as if he were a person without any sense of honour, any feeling of what becomes a gentleman, of what a soldier or hero owes to himself. That is, they would not bring out their first principle, from the very circumstance that they felt its power so intensely ; *that first principle being, that there is no evil so great in the whole universe, visible and invisible, in time and eternity, as humiliation* . . . .
" In the instance I have mentioned, the folly and the offence, in the eyes of the Romans, was proselytizing ; but let us fancy this got over, would the Christian system itself have pleased the countrymen of Cato at all better ? On the contrary, they would have started with his first principle, that humiliation was immoral, as an axiom ; they would not have attempted to prove it ; they would have considered it as much a fact as the sun in heaven ; they would not have enunciated it ; they would have merely implied it. Fancy a really candid philosopher, who had been struck with the heroic deaths of the martyrs, turning with a feeling of good-will to consider the Christian ethics ; what repugnance would he not feel towards them ! *to crouch, to turn the cheek, not to resist, to love to be lowest !* Who ever heard of such a teaching ? It was the religion of slaves ; *it was unworthy of a man ;* much more of a Roman. Yet that odious religion in the event became the creed of countless millions ; what philosophers so spontaneously and instinctively condemned, has been professed by the profoundest and the noblest of men, through eighteen centuries. So possible is it for our first principles to be but the opinion of a multitude, not truths.'—*Newman on Catholicism in England,* pp. 268, 269, and 275, 276.

Our thesis on the growth of the Moral Faculty affords us a ready means for doing so. If there be certain acts intrinsecally evil, and before examination a man cannot tell how many there may be,—there is an *objective rule, indefinite in extent,* external to himself, which legitimately *claims his abject deference and submission ;* a rule, which possesses over him nothing less than a paramount authority, from which there is no appeal and no escape. Reason, I say, summons him to exhibit this deference and submission; and yet this pseudo-virtuous heathen has totally failed in doing so. He has pursued his darling pleasure self-esteem, with the very same keen, impetuous, unreserved, eagerness, with which the ambitious man pursues honour, or the money-getter wealth. He has no more checked and restrained himself in the violent pursuit of *his* characteristic pleasure, than *they* in the pursuit of *theirs.* The main difference between him and them is simply this; that whereas he derives his favourite enjoyment from the thought of his own virtuousness, *such imagination of virtuousness is continually in his mind.* But as for anything like subjection to an external, authoritative, paramount, rule, you will find no more trace of it in his conduct than in theirs.

Indeed let us consider on what ground we should justly blame those other characters, the ambitious and money-getting ; for whatever argument can be found available against them, will tell no less forcibly against Cato himself. We should say that they are culpable for this cause—because, having fullest means of knowing this Supreme Rule, in their conduct they have ignored it; they have turned a deaf ear to the Moral Voice within them; and instead of carefully measuring their acts, one after another, by this paramount authority, they have recklessly and unrestrainedly pursued the bent of their various inclinations. All the essential part of this may be said, with equal truth, against the morally proud. He, like they, has recklessly and unreservedly pursued the bent of his dominant inclination ; in him, no more than in them, will be found any traces of abject and slavish submission to a superior authority. His Moral Faculty then is simply in its infancy; it has received no real growth whatever; his moral intuitions deserve neither respect nor even consideration.

Now surely it needs no very careful observation of human nature to see, that if he once began that course of life to which reason summons him, his moral judgments would begin to undergo a total revolution. In proportion as he should even *aim* at pursuing the path of humble deference to this supreme authority, however feeble and vacillating his progress *along* that path, he would see that his former course contained in itself hardly any element of virtue; he would see that virtue consists, and can consist, in nothing else, than in this submission and prostration of the will. In other words, in proportion as his Moral Faculty should receive any kind of cultivation, he would recognize pride as sinful, and humility in its place as the virtuous end of action.

It is very certain indeed, that the Authority whose absolute and peremptory claims he will thus learn to recognize, is no mere abstract *Rule*, but a Personal Being.* I have already said, that from the first moment when we begin seriously thinking of moral obligation, we shall begin to recognize the Existence of an All-holy Creator. And here I may add to this, that nothing will more tend to increase the strength, earnestness, rootedness, of this recognition, than firm and consistent moral action.† It is true that, as I have avoided

* See Appendix to this Chapter.
† "What is the main guide of the soul, given to the whole race of Adam, outside the true fold of Christ as well as within it, given from the first dawn of reason, given to it in spite of that grievous penalty of ignorance, which is one of the chief miseries of our fallen state? It is *the light of conscience*; the 'True Light,' as the same Evangelist says in the same passage, 'which enlighteneth every man that cometh into this world.' Whether a man be born in Pagan darkness, or in some corruption of revealed religion,— whether he has heard the name of the Saviour of the world or not,—whether he be the slave of some superstition,—or is in possession of some portions of Scripture, and treats the inspired word as a sort of philosophical book, which he interprets for himself, and comes to certain conclusions about its teaching,—in any case, he has within his breast a certain *commanding dictate*; not a mere sentiment, not a mere opinion, or impression, or view of things, but a law, *an authoritative voice,*

entering on the philosophical proof of God's Existence, I am not entitled to make use of it in my reasoning : but I have *not* made use of it; as the following summary of my argument will prove.

I have shewn then (1) that the very existence of moral obligation implies the obligatoriness of a certain course of conduct; the course of abject deference to an external rule : and (2) that every human being, in proportion as he sincerely tries to pursue that course, intues, with ever-increasing distinctness, that moral pride is intrinsecally sinful. On these two grounds I base my conclusion, that this intuition is legitimate. And a fully sufficient ground is afforded for this inference, by the second thesis of n. 65; even as that thesis would stand, without any reference to the Existence of a Holy Creator. But if it be further true (as it is) that, by beginning the same course of conduct, we come at once

bidding him do certain things and avoid others. I do not say that its particular injunctions are always clear, or that they are always consistent with each other ; but what I am insisting on here is this, that it *commands*, that it praises, it blames, it promises, it threatens, it implies a future, and it witnesses of the unseen. It is more than a man's own self. The man himself has not power over it, or only with extreme difficulty. He did not make it ; he cannot destroy it. He may silence it in particular cases or directions ; he may distort its enunciations ; but he cannot, or it is quite the exception if he can, he cannot emancipate himself from it. *He can disobey it ; he may refuse to use it; but it remains.*

"This is conscience; and, from the nature of the case, its very existence carries on our minds to a Being *Exterior* to ourselves, for else whence did it come ? and to a Being *Superior* to ourselves, else whence its strange, troublesome peremptoriness ? I say, without going on to the question *what* it says, and whether its particular dictates are always as clear and consistent as they might be, its very existence throws us out of ourselves, and beyond ourselves, to go and seek for Him in the height and depth, whose Voice it is. As the sunshine implies that the sun is in the heavens, *though we see it not ;* as a knocking at our doors at night implies the presence of one outside in the dark who asks for admittance ;—so this Word within us, not only instructs us up to a certain point, but necessarily raises our minds to the idea of a Teacher, an unseen Teacher ; and in *proportion as we listen to that Word and use it,* not only do we learn more from it, not only do *its dictates become clearer and its lessons broader and its principles more consistent,* but its very tone is louder and more authoritative and constraining. And thus it is, that to those who use what they have, more is given ; for, *beginning with obedience, they go on to the intimate perception and belief of One God. His Voice within them witnesses to Him, and they believe His own witness about Himself.* They believe in His Existence, not because others say it, not on the word of man merely, but with a personal apprehension of its truth."—*Newman's Occasional Sermons,* pp. 72–75.

to the clear knowledge of an All-holy Being, in Whose comparison we are but as worms or the very dust of the earth,—it does but follow that the force of our conclusion is increased a thousand-fold. That a reasonable person shall recognize a Holy and an Infinite Creator, and yet in his daily conduct (instead of striving to grow in humble obedience to that Creator) shall deliberately aim at the promotion of his own dignity and aggrandizement—this is a spectacle, the utter and monstrous unreasonableness of which must strike the most casual thinker, who has given any real cultivation to his Moral Faculty. I speak, as my argument leads me, of its monstrous unreasonableness; on its moral odiousness, it is not necessary that I should speak.

We have added then Humility to our catalogue of virtuous ends.

69. We next come to Vindictiveness. There are various men, who regard this as an eminently virtuous end of action; who consider that when I have received a serious affront or injury, a kind of obligation rests upon me to requite it; that until I have done so, I am in a low and contemptible position. What is to be said, on our principles, in opposition to such a view?

First, such an opinion is very far from being so general as at first sight appears. Again and again the wrong *case* is presented to the Moral Faculty for its judgment (see n. 66); for it is supposed by multitudes, as a matter of course, that the forgiving an injury proceeds from cowardice. Here then they are wrong as to the *matter of fact*, but not as to the moral *principle;* for it *is* a thing worthy of blame, that I should so give way to fear, as to be held back by it from conduct which I recognize as right. The real question then must be put in some such way as the following :— Suppose that by great deeds of bravery, or in whatever way, I had shewn most plainly, that fear of danger *could* be to me no restraint upon action; and suppose, having so exhibited myself, I freely forgive the most stinging injuries, on the expressed ground that vindictiveness is sinful. The question is, how great is the number of men, who in *that* case would regard such forgivingness as censurable?

Those who do so, would proceed on one, and one only, ground. They would assume, as a first principle, the great obligation incumbent on each man, of cherishing a sense of his own dignity; and they would regard forgivingness as censurable, precisely because any one, who receives an affront without resenting it, must lower himself in his own eyes, and be deficient in that spirit of self-exaltation which is so great a duty. The supposed virtuousness of revenge is entirely built on the supposed virtuousness of self-exaltation. Their judgment then is not intuitive, but inferential; being based on the premiss above mentioned. But this premiss has been overthrown (I think) in the preceding number; we have shewn that there is no kind of virtuousness in self-exaltation: and the premiss failing, the conclusion also fails. Indeed whoever will attend at all carefully to the phenomena of the human mind, will see quite clearly the following fact. In proportion as I live more and more in subjection to an external rule, which I recognize as possessing over me a paramount claim—immeasurably more, in proportion as I regard that paramount authority to be no mere abstract rule, but the Personal and Living God — in that proportion the following result will ensue. I shall recognize more and more clearly and unmistakably, that there is no baseness whatever in the spirit of forgivingness, no virtuousness whatever in revenge as such. We cannot indeed claim this judgment as *intuitive*, for the reason already given; but it is an *inference* which will be more and more certainly drawn, in proportion as my *intuitive* judgment on the virtuousness of humility becomes more emphatically elicited.

We have already remarked (n. 54), that on the one hand all mankind regard various acts as *virtuous* simply *because* they are *benevolent;* whereas no one ever regarded an act as virtuous simply *because* it was *cruel.* To this we are now able further to add, that neither can any act of aggression on others be truly regarded as

L

virtuous, simply *because* it was done in revenge for some injury, which had been previously received at their hands.

You may object, that I have not proved vindictiveness to be *wrong*, but merely not to be of *obligation*. Why may it not be *lawful* to requite an insult or injury, simply for the sake of that vindictive pleasure which we derive from so doing? I reply readily. We have seen (n. 55) that it is undoubtedly wrong to contravene any virtuous end, except for the sake of some other obligation, which we may regard as justly preponderating. Now Benevolence is most undoubtedly one of these virtuous ends. Hence it is undoubtedly wrong to contravene Benevolence—*i. e.* to inflict an injury on our fellow-men—except for the sake of some other obligation. Now we have just proved, that there is no kind of *obligation* to requite an injury vindictively; hence, neither is it *lawful* so to do.

70. What then will be the various motives, which can justify infliction of pain on our fellow-men? They are reducible perhaps to three heads:—

(1.) Self-defence. If a burglar attacks me with every species of violence, no other way is probably open of repelling his aggression, except repaying him in kind. Or, passing from the mere physical infliction of pain, it will often happen that I cannot vindicate my just rights, without being the cause (contrary to my wish) of much suffering to others. Yet the motives, which lead me to such vindication, may most rightly preponderate over those which would dissuade me from it. This again is one principal end, designed by the civil society in her infliction of punishments. Violent and unruly men would literally tear her asunder, were they not restrained by a salutary fear of her severe penalties.

(2.) Moral improvement of the offender. Thus parents punish their children to wean them from bad habits. This also is one motive (though subordinate to the former) which leads society to enact penalties against transgressors.

(3.) Just retribution for moral evil. It has been the fashion of late years, to deny in theory that the state can legitimately act on this motive. To discuss this question as it deserves, would carry us a great deal too far; I will content myself therefore with protesting most earnestly against any such notion. Indeed if the legislator attempted really to put it in practice—if he attempted, in his apportionment of punishments, wholly to neglect the relative turpitude of the various offences, and consider exclusively their relative injuriousness to the state—I am confident he would be met by an universal cry of horror and indignation.

However, whatever may be the functions of the *state*, no Theist will deny that *God* acts on this principle; that the very idea of a Just moral Governor includes the notion of punishing sin, no less than of rewarding virtue.

And generally, all God's direct inflictions on man may be classed perhaps under one or other of the three foregoing heads.

(1.) Thus He punishes, not indeed exactly for the purpose of Self-defence, but for the purpose of defending and sanctioning His Laws. The punishments which He inflicts on us here, and very much more those which He threatens hereafter, are among the most effectual means whereby He retains mankind in obedience.

(2.) He punishes in this life from the motive of paternal tenderness; for the sake of awakening men to a sense of their faults, and giving them an occasion for self-discipline and merit: 'for whom the Lord loveth 'He chastiseth, and scourgeth every son whom He 'receiveth.'

(3.) Those awful inflictions, which He will inflict on wicked men hereafter, are but the just retribution of the fearful 'malitia' contained in mortal sin. The heinous character of this 'malitia' will be considered in our theological course.

71. We shall be returning more nearly to our immediate subject, if we here consider another question. 'Is Forgivingness a separate and special virtuous end of

' action? or is it only reducible to the more general head
' of Benevolence?'

One thing is plain at starting. Suppose I have
received some most galling injury or affront, and yet
proceed at once to confer some great kindness on the
aggressor; my will must be directed to the virtuousness
of Benevolence with a singular degree of firmness and
efficacity. But then my will *may* be directed with the
same degree of efficacity (see n. 58), when I am benefiting some one who has *not* injured me. The acting
rightly under temptation, *shews* greater virtuousness
than could otherwise be *shewn;* but it does not prove
that greater virtuousness *exists,* than might otherwise
exist.

Now for the question started: it is not very important, but its true answer appears to me the following. In the case of us men — whose wills are so weak,
and who are so constantly offending our Creator —
Forgivingness is a special virtue, when based on the
remembrance that we ourselves so deeply need forgiveness. But in rational creatures who should not be thus
full of sin — or in ourselves when our forgiveness of
others is not based on remembrance of our own sinfulness — then I can see nothing to distinguish an act of
forgivingness, from any other act (internal or external)
of benevolence.

72. Lastly we come to the virtue of Purity. In one
very important respect, this virtue should rather be
classed with those of Justice, Veracity, and Benevolence,
which we first considered, than with those of Humility
and Forgivingness, which have been lately occupying our
attention. For just as no one ever considered an act
as virtuous, simply *because* it was cruel or mendacious;
— so neither did any one ever consider an act virtuous,
simply *because* it was impure. No doubt there are
many most frightful sins under this head, which multitudes of men do not regard as sinful at all; yet no one
thinks them virtuous, *on the ground of* the great sensuality which is involved in their commission. Take then
the worst and most depraved man alive. There are

certain of the more atrocious impurities, which even he regards as censurable; and if I avoid these atrocities simply because of the virtuousness of Purity, I should receive (so far) his praise.   Just then as in the case of Justice and Benevolence, so here.   There are certain acts which are considered good, because directed, under certain circumstances, to the virtuousness of Purity as such ; there are *no* acts which are considered good, because of being directed to any supposed virtuousness inherent in *impurity* as such.   By the consent of all mankind then, Purity is a virtuous end of action.

But in *another* respect, Purity should rather be ranked with Humility and Forgivingness; for there is no virtue, in which we see with more unmistakable clearness, the *increase of discernment* which the Moral Faculty acquires by means of exercise.   Let any man act up to his light in this matter, so far as he has the moral power of so doing, and by help of constant prayer,— and contemplate the certain result.   It is truly amazing, how rapidly his moral perception will expand; and how soon he will see foulness and pollution in a multitude of acts, which he has hitherto regarded as indifferent.

73. We have established then on grounds of reason —and it is difficult adequately to estimate the importance of our conclusion—that virtuous ends of action are such as the following : (1) Love of God; (2) Obedience to God; (3) Reverence for God; (4) Justice ; (5) Veracity ; (6) Benevolence ; (7) Humility ; (8) Forgivingness ; (9) Purity. We become morally better, in proportion as our will adheres to these various ends with greater firmness and efficacity.   Moreover, as will be evident on referring to what has been said, the whole of our reasoning applies, not to mankind only, but to every possible creature possessing reason and liberty. There are but two exceptions to this statement: viz. first in regard to Purity; and secondly in regard to that special *motive* for Forgivingness, which results from human sinfulness.

74. Is there any probable inference which we may

now draw, as to the *extent* of the Natural Rule? If we take the term according to that full sense suggested in n. 52, we shall find reason to think it most widely extensive. Nay, we shall find reason to think that it reaches over almost every act of our daily life: that every such act has by necessity its own independent worthiness, both objective and subjective; intrinsically better than this, intrinsically less good than that. Let A and B be two different acts, either of them at this moment in my power to do, and which seem on the surface of equal moral value. I soon find some good consequence, which I had not thought of before, which would probably result, if act A were universally elicited under such circumstances; or some bad consequence which would ensue, if act B were thus elicited. Every fresh discovery of this kind affects the relative position of A and B in the moral scale. Then suppose that when I have exhausted all such discoveries, the two acts seem yet equally balanced—it still remains very probable, that in proportion as my Moral Faculty increases by exercise in keenness of perception, it will detect some difference where now none is apparent.

But if it appears from reason highly probable, that the Natural Rule, as discoverable by *reason in the abstract*, is thus widely extensive;—it is absolutely certain on the other hand, that our *actual and practical power* of exploring it by reason is trifling indeed. How utterly insignificant is our power of tracing consequences with any accuracy! how miserably small is the degree, in which we have cultivated our Moral Faculty by the practice of virtue!

The disproportion then is enormous, between the *extent* of the Natural Rule on the one hand, and the *practical power of unaided reason to discover it* on the other hand. This is true of the Natural Rule, in that wider sense which we have given to the phrase, as the 'rule of independent virtuousness' (see n. 52); and it is no less true in its narrower sense the 'rule of independent obligation.' Nothing is more probable, than that there may be a large number of acts, objectively sinful in their own intrinsic nature, which man's unaided reason would never have guessed to be such. Their sinfulness, indeed, is in *the abstract* discoverable by reason. Their sinfulness, I say, could be recognized by any man, who should (1) possess preternatural powers of observation; and (2) should have given perfect cultivation to his Moral Faculty, through a course of obedience unsullied by venial sin or imperfection. But as none of us *are* such, the sinfulness of such acts is not (I repeat) discoverable by *us;* we owe our knowledge of it to Revelation, and to Revelation alone.

Now see how precisely this conclusion harmonizes with the dicta of theologians, as to the extent of the Natural Rule in this its narrower sense. According to Suarez, it is an ' axioma theologorum ' that under Christianity there are no *Positive* Divine Precepts (see n. 25) except only under the head of Faith and of the Sacraments; and he quotes a very strong passage from St. Thomas, to that precise effect.*

Now without here proceeding to enquire, as Suarez does, how far even these should strictly be called *Positive* precepts (on which question I hope to touch in the next Section), see how large an idea this gives us as to the extent of the Natural Rule. Every single thing then, forbidden under the Gospel,—except under these two heads of Faith and the Sacraments,—is forbidden by the Natural Rule; is intrinsecally evil, apart from any Divine Prohibition. All that we find in our Moral Theology treatises under the *first* commandment, as to love of God and our neighbour; all that we find under the *sixth*, as to thoughts or acts of impurity; or under the *fifth*, as to forgiving injuries; or under the *seventh*,

---

* " Intelligitur ex dictis, quomodo verum sit *axioma theologorum* dicentium, in Novâ Lege *nulla esse Divina Præcepta* [Positiva], nisi fidei et sacramentorum ; ut loquitur Soto in 4, d. 40, a. 4, et sequuntur alii moderni, et Covar. in 4 Decr. c. 6, § 10, in princ. qui id sumpserunt ex D. Th. in dictâ q. 108 a. 1, ad. 2, ubi non tam expressè id affirmat ; in Quodlibet autem 4, a. 13, dicit, Legem Novam esse *contentam* [1] præceptis moralibus Naturalis Legis, et [2] articulis Fidei, et [3] Sacramentis Gratiæ." — *De Legibus*, lib. 10, c. 2, n. 20.

"Christus *non tradidit* Præcepta moralia *Positiva*, sed *Naturalia illa magis explicavit*."—*Ibid.* lib. 2, c. 15, n. 9.

as to the duty of restitution ; all this, and much else
which might most easily be added, is an integral part of
the Natural Rule : all the duties therein prescribed are
of independent obligation, apart from God's Commandment altogether.   It was most perfectly free to God not
to create men at all, or not to place them under such
circumstances ; it was not free to Him, *having* so
created or so placed them, to abstain from giving the
sanction of His command to these duties, over and
above their intrinsic and independent obligation.

75. But here it may seem that an objection, which
has already been answered in the abstract, derives fresh
force and deserves fresh notice.   ' If the region of
' necessary moral truth,' it may be said, ' is so singularly
' wide and extensive, you seem to exclude God from in-
' fluence in His own creation, to an absolutely intolerable
' extent.'   Repeating to a great extent what has already
been said, I will give three replies to this objection.   I
will only premise, that I am arguing for no private fancy
of my own, but for what Suarez calls an ' axioma theologorum.'

(1.) First, then, I reply, that the mere *extent* of
necessary truth cannot justly cause any increased difficulty to the *reason*, though it may startle the *imagination*.   Let it be but admitted that there *is* such a
thing as necessary truth,—*e. g.*, that God has not the
power of creating an equilateral triangle, which shall
not be equiangular ; or that He has not the power of
creating a person whose obligation it shall be to hate the
Holy Creator ;—let this be admitted, and everything is
conceded which can give the *reason* any real difficulty.
If there be *one* necessary truth, there may be thousands
such ; the difficulty to the reason is no greater in the
latter than in the former case.

(2.) It will be seen in the following Section, that
God does possess very considerable power, in interfering
with the Natural Rule.   It will be seen that this can be
recognized as undeniably the case, without infringing in
the slightest degree on the various principles which we
have been laying down.

(3.) I appeal as I did before (n. 21) to the parallel instance of mathematical truth. Will you maintain that the axioms of geometry are true, because of God's appointment? Will you maintain that the reasoning process is valid, because of God's appointment? If you will maintain neither of these things, you must admit, that the whole assemblage of mathematical truth, built *by means* of reasoning *upon* these axioms, is also true, independently altogether of God's appointment. But how immeasurably vast is this great assemblage of truth! to which indeed it is difficult to imagine that there can be any possible limit. If then necessary *mathematical* truth possesses most undeniably so vast an extent, why should it be thought a difficulty that necessary *moral* truth also is most widely extended? *

Another objection of quite a different kind may be made to our conclusion. It may be objected, that our Blessed Saviour, in various parts of the Gospel, *contrasts* Christian morality with all others; and thereby implies, that it *does* in many important respects add to the Natural Law. These declarations deserve, and shall receive, our most careful attention; but the suitable place for their consideration will obviously be our theological course. In the next Book then, I hope to enter on the whole Scriptural bearing of our doctrine, with sufficient accuracy and completeness.

76. The principles laid down in this Section, as they seem certainly conformable to reason, so also add not inconsiderably to the motives of credibility on behalf of the Catholic religion. It appears (as we have seen) from Reason alone, in the highest degree probable, that the Natural Law extends over a wide circle of human acts; while it is certain that our *unassisted* reason cannot carry us beyond a most insignificant distance, in exploring its various details. With these conclusions, the voice of the Church is singularly in harmony. For theologians declare with almost complete unanimity, on the one hand, that the Natural Law *is* thus widely extensive; on

* See a more direct treatment of this whole difficulty in the Appendix to this Chapter.

the other hand, that one of the most important functions performed by the Church, one of the most important ends for which God has founded it, is to declare and testify moral truth. Reason alone, it is constantly urged by Catholic writers, would ever be leading us astray in matters of morality, were it not for the Church's infallible guidance correcting such aberrations.

Further, Reason, as we have seen, determines that Humility, Forgivingness, and Purity are virtuous ends of action, while their opposites can never be so. Yet of what Protestant body can it be said, that they are to any reasonable extent in possession of these truths? On the other hand, who has realized and practised them comparably in degree to the Saints of the Church? And is not this very fact,—their being so penetrated, so pervaded, by those principles,—the main cause why a Protestant ever so despises these illustrious servants of God; why he regards them as fanatical, narrow-minded men, totally wanting in self-respect and manly feeling? But on all this we shall have to speak at length in our theological course.

77. Such then finally is the answer we give to that wide and general enquiry, which was laid down (n. 53) as our subject in the present Section. I must not conclude however, without putting before you our grounds for *holding* that view of the Moral Faculty, which we have so largely used in the later part of the Section. What then is our reason for thinking, that the Moral Faculty increases in accuracy and precision of judgment, through the means of virtuous action? In answering this question, be it observed, I must avoid various most cogent considerations, founded on the Attributes of God; I must avoid these, I say, because in the present Chapter we have declined entering on the formal proof of His existence.

(1.) The analogy of our other faculties suggests one clear argument to our purpose; for every one of them is capable of indefinite improvement, and yet by no other method than this one of constant exercise.

To this argument one ingenious objection may be

suggested. 'Our other intellectual faculties improve
'by means of *intellectual* acts, and in no other way:
'viz. our memory by the practice of remembering;
'our reasoning faculty by the practice of argument;
'and so with the rest. But you represent the *Moral*
'*Faculty* as moving towards perfection, by means
'of acts, which appertain *not* to the intellect but the
'Will; not through practice in intellectual *discrimi-*
'*nation* between good and evil, but through prac-
'tice in *acting* virtuously. The analogy of the other
'faculties therefore, very far from being in your favour,
'is directly against you.'

I reply firstly, that our whole reasoning, throughout this Section, would stand in every respect, though
we *did* place the Moral Faculty in every respect on
the very same footing with all others. There is no
such phenomenon to be found, as men who exercise
themselves carefully through the day, in discrimination
between good and evil, between the greater and the
less good,—for any other purpose except this one;
the purpose, namely, of *acting in accordance* with such
discrimination. Those therefore who most *practise* the
Moral Faculty are precisely those who *act most consistently on its dictates*. This must be taken as my direct
reply to the objection, and it is amply sufficient.

I cannot but think however myself, and that very
strongly, that the *practice* of virtue *has* a direct and
powerful effect on refining the Moral Faculty. And by
introducing the thought of a Holy Creator, we can give
a very good reason of congruity for this. Every other
intellectual faculty attains the full end for which it was
given, in proportion as we perform certain intellectual
acts: the *memory, e. g.* in proportion as we more accurately remember the past; the *reasoning faculty* in
proportion as we more bring our various opinions into
consistency with each other, and carry them forward to
their full results. The Moral Faculty is the one exception; and for this simple reason, that it is the one which
directly and immediately dictates to the will. Neither
memory nor reasoning faculty elicit the judgment 'my

will *ought* to do this rather than that;' whereas this *is* precisely the kind of judgment elicited by the Moral Faculty.   So far therefore as the will fails to act in harmony with this judgment, the *faculty fails of its due results.*   The Moral Faculty I say, does not attain the end for which God gave it, except in proportion, not as we *know* our duty, but as we *practise* it.   And it is evidently in the highest degree conformable to our natural ideas of God's Moral Government, that He should so act as our theory supposes; that he should reward those who act up to the light they have, by imparting more light.

"It would certainly involve great disadvantages," argues a very thoughtful writer, " if moral knowledge was gained by mere intellectual processes.   Uneducated people would be more unable than ever to judge themselves between right and wrong: and those who were most capable of guiding them, would not necessarily be inclined to guide them right; nay, by that very knowledge would be enabled more easily to guide them wrong.   Much knowledge of good would be wasted on men who did not wish to profit by it; and clever persons, without much energy of character, would be overwhelmed, by seeing at once the extent of that change of nature which they had to effect in themselves, if they were to conform themselves to what was really right.

"Now so far as moral discrimination is acquired by practice, and not by reasoning, these imperfections are avoided.   Viewed as a means of improvement for ourselves, knowledge is given where it will be used; of power over others, where it will not be misused;—viewed as a blessing, it is given to the deserving; —viewed as a trial, it is accommodated to the infirmity of the weak.

"And on the other hand, who are they who require the brand of ignorance to mark them in the sight of their fellow-creatures, who deserve to be left without knowledge of anything beyond their own miserable desires, but those who have refused to obey such knowledge?   What wiser, and what juster, and what more really merciful law, than that man shall not be able to receive into his head, what he will not receive into his heart also?   What less to be wondered at, than the sentence, dreadful as it is, that if man hardens his will, God will harden his intellect against truth?   Surely the true difficulty in the world, if we are to find one, is not that such a law exists, but that it does not exist more exclusively.   Surely it is only the unwarrantable value which is set on intellect in this particular age, which prevents us from seeing how very strange it would be if knowledge of this kind were given only, or even chiefly, to the wise in this world, to the sharp, clear-headed, and argumentative, and not to the humble and conscientious lover of goodness.   What business would *they* have with such advantages?"*

However, as already remarked, our direct and (as it were) formal proof of the proposition before us, must not assume God's Existence.   In meeting therefore the objection which has been raised, it is only the former part of my reply on which I can logically insist; but this former part, as I observed, is amply sufficient.

(2.) I proceed now to the second argument in behalf of our proposition; an argument which (equally with the first) prescinds from the Existence of God altogether.   We have proved incontestably, that there are various genuine intuitions on moral truth: viz. all those on which all mankind are agreed; and especially that fundamental one, that there *is* such a thing as moral obligation, quite apart from the Will of our Creator.   Yet on the other hand, on most matters, the diversity of men's moral judgments is extreme.   Are we to say that in *all* these matters *all* men's intuitions are spurious? or (which is almost as strange) that on all these matters it is quite impossible to distinguish the genuine *from* the spurious?   Surely, if in regard to the great bulk of human conduct, reason were wholly destitute of all intrinsic power to distinguish right from wrong, the better from the less good, a great presumption would arise, that its power of deciding in the few matters of universal agreement is but a delusion.   The reasonableness of this statement is made more evident from the fact, that it is admitted by all mankind. Utilitarians and others, who deny intrinsic morality, have ever built their chief objections on this one fact, the diversity of men's moral judgments; while their opponents, so far from denying the relevancy of this fact, have expended all their skill and ingenuity in denying or extenuating it.   Here then is the first

* From a most able article on " Utilitarian Moral Philosophy," *British Critic*, 1841, pp. 35 and 36.

premiss of my second argument.   If reason have really the intrinsic power in certain cases of perceiving moral truth (and I have shewn 'satis superque' that it has this power) — it is in the very highest degree probable, that this power extends, far beyond those comparatively few cases on which all men are agreed.   In other words, it is in the highest degree probable, that there is some means of distinguishing genuine from spurious intuitions, over and above that obvious one of men's unanimous testimony.

My second premiss is, that according to the principle for which I am arguing — the principle that our Moral Faculty is developed by exercise — two things may be undoubtedly maintained.   First, Reason *in the abstract* has the intrinsic power of advancing without limit, towards the discrimination of true moral intuitions from false, on every single detail of human conduct.   Secondly, Reason *in the concrete*, Reason I mean as it *may* be exercised and *is frequently* exercised by men under their existing circumstances, can take a very important step in the same direction.   For certainly no one can call it an *unimportant* proposition, that Humility and Forgivingness are virtuous ends of action, while their opposites are not so.   And *this* proposition is held with the most complete unanimity and the strongest conviction, by every human being who has given himself to the task of consistently practising virtue; practising it, I mean, according to the extent of his knowledge. *Mankind in general* are not more unanimous in recognizing that *cruelty and ingratitude* are evil, than *these* men are unanimous in denouncing *pride and unforgivingness*.

My third premiss for this second argument is, that no other principles (so far as I know) have ever been laid down, on which there would *be* this approach to unanimity.   Certainly, so far as this last-named moral truth is concerned, *reasoning* has no such tendency to produce unanimity.   No one will say that all *good reasoners* have agreed, in deducing, from the first principles of morality, the sinfulness of pride and unforgivingness.   No one can say this, or anything ever so distantly approaching it.

On these three premisses I build my second argument.   Firstly, it is in the highest degree probable, that there *is* some method, whereby reason may tend towards harmonizing the diversity of men's moral judgments; secondly, the principles of this Section afford such a method; and thirdly, no others which have been suggested hold out any such promise.   Hence it is in the highest degree probable, that these principles are true.

(3.) Yet at last the two arguments just given, are in their nature quite inadequate to the *kind* of conclusion, for which they are adduced.   The real means, whereby the genuineness of an intuition is brought home to my conviction, *must* at last be some *intrinsic* quality, inherent in the intuition itself; and not some merely extrinsic fact, such as the general agreement of mankind.   Of what nature that quality is, and how it may be securely recognized, is a question which seems to have been most unduly neglected by philosophers (see n. 9); but of the fact just stated there can be no doubt.   In regard to two of our faculties indeed, those of remembering and of reasoning, it has already been shewn (n. 10, p. 21) that we are actually *compelled* to trust them, before we can so much as guess that there *is* any agreement of mankind on the matter.   But take other instances also; take the truth, *e. g.* that a pentagon must have five angles, or that I am bound to restore my friend's jewel: surely it is quite plain, that my conviction of these truths is absolute and ineradicable, before I have so much as *considered the question* whether *other men agree with me* or not.

And indeed this intrinsic difference of quality, in a *genuine* as distinguished from a *spurious* intuition, undeniably exists; however difficult it may be to analyse or explain it.   Dreams, *e. g.* abound in spurious intuitions.   I believe myself to see what I do not see, and to remember what never took place; nor does a doubt cross my mind, on the reality of the whole scene.   I wake; and I begin *really* to see, really to remember.   I intue with the most unmistakable distinctness, not merely that my waking impressions correspond to truth, but that my sleeping impressions have not so corresponded.

A distinction, exactly similar in kind though less in degree, may be found in every case, accordingly as any individual faculty has or has not been duly exercised. A novice in music pronounces, with perfect confidence, that a light air of Donizetti's is preferable to a symphony of Beethoven. He gives himself for years to the study, and at the end of that time hears again the same two compositions. It is not merely true that his present intuition is opposed to his first; he recognizes most unmistakably a *difference of quality between these two intuitions.* I repeat; it is not merely that, when thinking of the *music*, he elicits an intuition opposite to that which he remembers to have elicited several years ago : a further phenomenon also takes place. *When thinking of that first intuition*, he plainly discerns in it a faulty and untrustworthy character. As a matter of fact, the case is most undoubtedly the same with moral judgments. A man of the world holds, with the utmost confidence, that self-exaltation is a virtuous end of action, and that he would rightly lower himself in his own eyes, by allowing an insult to go unrequited : he holds with no less confidence, that it is simply absurd, to regard the more ordinary sins of impurity as lessening a man's title to respect and admiration. He happily yields himself to the grace of God, and for years makes it his chief business to adjust his moral conduct, so far as possible, in every particular to his ideas of moral rectitude. At the end of that time, he recognizes the virtuousness of humility, the viciousness of impure thoughts, with a degree of clearness which it is impossible to exceed. It is really no exaggeration at all to say, that *he has no more the physical power of calling in question the truth of these intuitions, than he has of distrusting his memory or his reasoning faculty.*

Indeed the difference is much greater, between

the judgments which proceed from the *trained* Moral Faculty on the one hand and the *untrained* on the other,—than in the case of any other faculty whatever. And it is very easy to see the reason; viz. that the difference in the *degree* of training is greater in the case of this faculty than of any other.   Take the musical faculty for instance.   He who cultivates it most assiduously, will give to it a certain number of hours in each day; while he who cultivates it *least*, hears probably one or other piece of music in every month. In the Moral Faculty on the contrary, the Saint, in almost every waking minute of every day, is pursuing that course which tends to its refinement and perfection; while the careless liver, ' who remembers not God, neither is God in all his thoughts,' floats unresistingly along the current of his inclinations, and never from the motive of duty denies himself one gratification.

A theological difficulty here however may be raised, of the following kind.   ' Faith is the one means of ' merit; but if the saint thus clearly *intues* moral truth, ' how can he accept it on *faith?*   In proportion, there- 'fore, as a man becomes saintly, there is a constantly 'increasing proportion of his acts in which he cannot 'merit.   A more monstrous conclusion cannot well be 'imagined.'   I mention this difficulty, merely to shew that I have not overlooked it.   It cannot be treated of course, until we have methodically considered the exact instrumentality of faith towards justification and merit.   But when this *has* been clearly understood, it will be found that the above difficulty disappears of itself.

78. One concluding question will be asked, in regard to the statements here put forward : how far do they accord with those usually recognized by Catholic theologians and philosophers?   I proceed to answer this question.

(1.) These writers always admit the existence of moral intuitions, which serve as premisses, from which

M

the more remote truths of morality are to be deduced. Thus we have seen that Suarez speaks of these two truths as dictamina rationis, ' Deus est colendus,' 'parentes sunt honorandi.' Now man's perception of these truths is simply a moral intuition in *our* sense of the word. The idea of deserving honour is not *included* in the term ' our parents;' all which is *meant* by that *term* is, ' those two human beings who have been God's instruments in bringing me into the world.' When therefore I recognize as a ' dictate of reason' (and I do, according to Suarez, so recognize it) that these human beings justly claim my honour, I am simply eliciting a real intuitive judgment.

(2.) Yet these writers do not (I think) in general distinctly state, that my correctness in forming such judgments will increase, in proportion as I more consistently practise the duties which I know. On the contrary, in regard to those moral truths which are not recognized by all mankind, these writers seem to regard such truths as known to us mainly in quite a different way ; viz. by *logical deduction* from those moral truths which are universally admitted. In laying stress therefore on the increased power of discernment, accruing (as we maintain) to the Moral Faculty from moral practice, we lay stress on a principle, which has not been inculcated at all prominently by Catholic theologians or philosophers. At the same time Gioberti, as we have seen (n. 66, note), does distinctly state it ; and for my own part (as has been said) I cannot but regard it as altogether conformable to reason.

(3.) Moreover there is a very great analogy, between this principle, and the doctrine laid down by all theologians, as to the means of arriving at faith. For all say that in proportion as men, by the help of grace, act up to their *existing* light, God rewards them by imparting *further* knowledge.

(4.) But indeed the common instinct of Catholics, in regard to Saints, implies (I cannot but think) the whole principle which we have maintained. We Catholics are in the habit of regarding the dicta of Saints, as singularly authoritative in matters of morality and piety; and this, not with reference to their greater or less degree of learning or ability, but to the simple fact of their *being* Saints. What does this mean, except that their moral perceptions have become in a special degree elevated and refined, by their consistent virtue? Yet, on the other hand, suppose that through defect of their other intellectual faculties they are unable rightly to apprehend any particular case submitted to them, this is always considered pro tanto to derogate from the authority of their judgment. Our principle then, in both its leading features, seems to be sanctioned by Catholic instinct.

(5.) I cannot but think, that the explicit and distinct admission of our principle would make the vindication of Catholic doctrine far more satisfactory, in one or two important particulars : specially as regards the various virtues under the head of purity. Take, as an instance, the offences mentioned in those two condemned propositions, which we have already more than once considered. (See n. 27, p. 63.) We are required by the condemnation of those propositions, to hold that such offences are in all possible cases intrinsecally evil, apart from all Divine Prohibition. Now whether we turn to Viva, Milante, or Van Ranst, surely the reasons, adduced in behalf of this conclusion, seem painfully inadequate, to sustain the weight which is rested upon them. And the reason of the fact is obvious. These theologians consider themselves bound to prove, that the moral theses, for which they argue, are inferrible, by way of *logical deduction*, from those moral theses which are universally admitted. Now this, to say the least, is an allegation which it is very difficult to maintain. On the other hand, it is most intelligible, and most consistent with phenomena, to say, that in proportion as any man grows in his obedience,—his Moral Faculty, becoming more and more enlightened, will come to elicit, more and more keenly, a legitimate intuition of

such inherent pravity.   Reason shews at least that the
fact very probably *may* be so ; the Church's decision
might complete all that was wanting in the way of certainty, and assure us that the fact *is* so.

And thus at length I bring this arduous Section to
a close.

Section VII.

On God's Power of Interference with the Natural Rule.

79. By *interference* may be meant either *addition* to the Natural Rule or *subtraction* from it. I do not mention of course *change ;* for this is merely *subtraction* of one thing and *addition* of another.

80. In regard to addition, it must first be remarked, that in a very true sense, God's free Will alone is the cause, that this Natural Rule exists at all; for it arises wholly from His good pleasure, that free and rational creatures have been called into existence. Accordingly, every fresh combination of circumstances, in which He places such creatures, may cause in a very true sense an addition to the Natural Rule; for a certain moral obligation may be thereby binding on a rational creature, which otherwise would *not* be binding on any such creature.

The chief matter, which deserves our attention under this head, is the great increase accruing to the Natural Rule, from the Christian Revelation. To give instances of this. It was perfectly free to God, either that He should, or should not, place before men a Revelation of Divine Truth. But when He *has* done so, it becomes *independently* obligatory, on all who have means of knowing this revelation, firmly to believe the truths therein contained. Again, as it was perfectly free to Him that the Second Person should be Incarnate, so it was also free to Him that this most august truth should be communicated to men. But when once it *has* been communicated, there arises an *independent* obligation to *adore* the Incarnate Saviour *with divine worship*. It was free to Him whether He would work, and also whether He would reveal, the miracle of

Transubstantiation; but when He *has* wrought and revealed it, men are under the *independent* obligation of paying divine homage to that God, Who lies hid under the Sacramental species.*

81. A far more difficult and more important ques-

---

* " Eo ipso quòd mysteria fidei *sufficienter proponantur, intrinsecè et ex naturâ rei* sequitur obligatio credendi quæ proposita sunt . . . . .

"Sed instabis ; ' quia in Lege Novâ non tantum est præceptum cre-
' dendi hæc mysteria, *quasi ex suppositione revelationis* et propositionis
' rerum credendarum, sed etiam est *absolutum præceptum* ea audiendi et
' sciendi, et consequenter credendi ; quod est præceptum longè diversum, et
' *simpliciter positivum :* ergò quoad hoc negavi non potest, quin Lex Nova in
' materiâ fidei addiderit positiva præcepta. Assumptum declaratur, quia
' hoc præceptum fidei, secundum ordinariam legem, applicatur hominibus
' per auditum ; teste Paulo ad Roman. 10 : ergò ut homines possint obligari ad
' credendum, necesse est ut obligentur ad *audiendum ;* ergò per aliquod præ-
' ceptum, quod sub nullâ consideratione potest dici naturale, sed positivum.
' Et declaratur ampliùs : nam fideles tenentur nunc explicitè credere mys-
' terium verb. grat. Trinitatis, vel Incarnationis, ex Jure Divino, quia talis fides
' est nunc medium necessarium ad salutem (ut suppono) ; hæc autem neces-
' sitas involvit præceptum divinum, quod non potest esse, nisi absolutum et
' *positivum :* nam illud prius, quasi conditionatum, credendi ea quæ reve-
' lantur, non sufficeret ad dictam necessitatem : nam sine violatione hujus
' præcepti hypothetici, ut sic dicam, posset quis nunquam credere explicitè
' Trinitatem, aut Christum ; ergò, *ut ad hoc obligentur fideles,* necessarium
' est speciale præceptum *positivum* et absolutum. Item in Pastoribus Eccle-
' siæ est obligatio prædicandi et docendi hanc fidem, ex præcepto Christi ;
' "Docete omnes gentes, et prædicate Evangelium ;" undè est illud Pauli 1.
' ad Corinth. 9. "Necessitas enim mihi incumbit, væ enim mihi est, si non
' evangelizavero :" hoc autem præceptum *positivum* etiam est."

"Incipiendo ab hoc ultimo, majoris claritatis gratiâ, respondeo, præceptum illud prædicandi vel docendi, datum pastoribus Ecclesiæ, in radice,
id est in institutione, esse positivum ; *in se autem et formaliter esse naturale.*
Munus enim episcopale seu pastorale est in Ecclesiâ ex positivâ institutione
Christi, ut ut per se constat : *supposito autem tali munere, obligatio docendi
aut prædicandi Evangelium de Jure Divino Naturali est.* pertinens ad obligationem justitiæ et fidelitatis, *quæ intrinsecè ex tali munere nascitur ;* quod
significavit Paulus suprà dicens, "Dispensatio mihi credita est." Ad
primum ergò in primis respondeo, cum proportione, *non esse necessarium,*
ut ex parte audientium præcedat *speciale præceptum positivum* audiendi
doctrinam, vel prædicationem fidei. Nam si sit sermo de hominibus nondum
credentibus in Christum, illi non sunt capaces obligationis provenientis
ex præcepto supernaturali, donec illis sufficienter proponatur fides ; quia
propositio supponit auditum : ergò antea non potest præcedere obligatio
audiendi, proveniens ex supernaturali præcepto. Igitur nulla obligatio
præcedit ex parte *audientium,* sed tantum ex parte *prædicantium.* Quæ
moraliter reputari potest sufficiens ; quia si ex parte evangelizantium sit
zelus et solicitudo, non deerunt qui de facto audiant ; ad quod magis
trahendi sunt, suavi inductione invitando illos, quàm rigorosâ obligatione.
Vel certè quando hæc obligatio incipit, magis est ex ratione naturali,
quam ex lege supernaturali. Quia homo *naturaliter tenetur veram Dei
cognitionem : veramque felicitatem quærere :* unde quomodocunque, vel per
vocem prædicationis, vel per famam, vel per proprium discursum, inceperit

tion, is God's power of *subtracting* from the Natural Rule. In treating this, I shall follow the doctrine, laid down by the immense majority of Catholic theologians and philosophers ; and I will sufficiently shew

dubitare de suâ lege vel statu, tenebitur eis attendere, qui viam salutis docere profitentur : ergo respectu infidelium, non est necessarium ponere hoc speciale præceptum positivum. Neque enim respectu jam credentium in Christum ; tum quia illi jam obligantur præcepto charitatis infusæ ergà se ipsos, ad propriam salutem spiritualem quærendam, et consequenter *ad audiendum Dei verbum, quando ad suam salutem fuerit necessarium :* neque enim ex Jure Divino majorem habent obligationem. Et simili modo teneri poterunt *ad audiendam doctrinam fidei, quando fuerit necessarium ad credendum quantùm oportet ;* tunc autem obligatio nascitur ex ipsomet præcepto fidei, de quo dicendum superest.

"Ad alteram ergò partem respondeo, admittendo, in Lege Novâ esse specialem necessitatem fidei explicitæ, tàm ad justitiam, quàm ad salutem æternam consequendam : concedendo item, hanc necessitatem provenire ex peculiari institutione Christi Domini ; quæ positiva sine dubio est, cùm non fuerit simpliciter necessaria. Unde fit etiam consequens, præceptum talis fidei, prout est proprium Legis Novæ, et Divinum Positivum censeri posse, saltem ratione institutionis. *Positâ autem institutione* respectu illius et statûs Legis Gratiæ, tale præceptum merito existimari potest connaturale illi. Primò, quia præceptum recognoscendi Auctorem Legis et obediendi Illi, est valdè connaturale cuicunque legi ; ad hoc autem necessaria est expressa, et distincta cognitio Ejus : cum ergò Christus sit Auctor hujus Legis, valde connaturale est illi præceptum credendi in Christum. Cum hoc autem conjunctum est præceptum cognoscendi Trinitatem, ut nunc suppono ; quia cùm Christus sit Secunda Trinitatis Persona, non potest haberi fides de Illo sufficienter explicita sine fide explicitâ Trinitatis. Secundò, quia fides præcipitur, non solùm tanquam speculativa cognitio, sed etiam tanquam practica et operativa ; ad usum autem sacramentorum hujus Legis, necessaria est fides explicita Trinitatis, quam oportet in Baptismo profiteri, et fides explicita Christi, Quem oportet in Eucharistiâ recipere et Patri in sacrificium offerre ; ergo suppositâ institutione maximè consentaneâ perfectioni hujus statûs, etiam talis fides, et præceptum ejus, merito dici potest esse de Jure Divino connaturali gratiæ, ut existenti in tali statu, in quo gratia tam perfecto modo communicatur.

"Atque hinc facile respondetur ad secundam partem, de præcepto spei : fatemur enim, usum spei multò perfectiorem postulari in lege Evangelii, quàm antea ; tùm quoad modum sperandi gloriam, tùm quoad multa media supernaturalia. Nunc enim sperare tenemur remissionem peccatorum per Baptismum, et per Absolutionem sacerdotis ; et augmentum justitiæ per alia sacramenta : tum etiam quoad modum sperandi per Christum, et per speciales promissiones per Ipsum factas. Non est autem necesse, ut propter has et similes perfectiones data fuerint in hâc lege specialia *præcepta positiva circa materiam spei,* quia tota hæc perfectio et obligatio *ad illam ex naturâ rei sequitur, suppositâ perfectione fidei circa Christum, et redemptionem Ejus,* et suppositâ tali sacramentorum institutione. Sicut etiam, *suppositâ fide Incarnationis et institutione Eucharistiæ ac fide ejus, nascitur in hâc Lege obligatio adorandi cultu latriæ Christum, tàm in Se, quàm in Eucharistiâ :* et nihilominus illa obligatio *non oritur ex Præcepto Positivo* Divino, sed *ex Jure Divino naturali,* et connaturali talibus mysteriis : ita ergò de spe dicendum est."—SUAREZ *De Legibus,* lib. 10, c. 2, n. 6, 7, 8, 9, 10.

that the fact is so, by the quotations which I hope to subjoin.

It is most manifest then, from the principles of Section III., that this subtraction can never be in the way of *dispensation*. God, having created free persons, cannot (as we have seen) even ' de potentiâ absolutâ' abstain from adding the sanction of His command, to the intrinsic obligation of the Natural Rule. *Much less* therefore, can He remove this *latter obligation itself;* much less can He *remove* by His will that intrinsic character of evil, which inhered in this or that act independently of His will altogether.

But yet that in some sense God *can* subtract from this Natural Rule, is very certain. Scripture records, that He commanded Abraham to slay Isaac, and the Israelites to spoil the Egyptians. And even if Scripture were silent, it does seem indeed a monstrous statement, that the Lord of life cannot impart a commission to take away life ; or that the Lord of the whole earth cannot transfer property from one man to another.

Now this very statement of the difficulty, precisely implies the solution. Reason declares, that it is a sinful act to take away my fellow-man's life, without any necessity in the way of self-defence, and at the same time without express authority. True: but if God commissions me to take away life, I *no longer* do so without express authority; by the very fact of giving me that commission, He totally *changes the case on which reason has to pronounce.* In like manner, reason pronounces that it is sinful, under ordinary circumstances, to keep back a jewel from its rightful proprietor. But God is at last the *Supreme* Proprietor of all the universe; and if He transfers the property in this jewel from my friend to myself, at once and ipso facto I *become* its rightful proprietor.

Under such circumstances as these then, there arises what theologians call a ' mutatio materiæ;' a change of that object-*matter*, whereon a moral judgment has to be formed. By means of that ' mutatio materiæ,' a certain external act, which *was* intrinsecally wrong, *ceases* to be so and becomes lawful. Then the Command of God supervening is a kind of *positive* Command (see n. 25); and I owe to it obedience, on the same principle which obliges me to obey any *other* Positive Precept, imposed by my Holy Creator.

In the above cases, the ' mutatio materiæ' is wrought by God, not as Legislator, but as Supreme Proprietor and Lord of the Universe. It is often said by theologians, that such ' mutationes materiæ,' when they take place, are *always* wrought by Him in that capacity; that they are *always* wrought by Him as Supreme Lord, and *never* as Legislator. But with very great deference to their authority, I venture on this single particular to question their statements. In order the better to explain the kind of instance to which I allude, I will begin with an illustration of a purely human kind; a case, where there is no interference of God whatever.

I am living at home, with my wife and family, quite free from any laborious occupation. Under these circumstances, certain acts of kindness, towards those thus closely connected, are intrinsecally of actual obligation; nay, in many easily supposable cases, are obligatory under mortal sin. But war breaks out and my country requires my services; a command is issued by my sovereign, requiring me to join the army; and I obey that command. Here is a real ' mutatio materiæ.' Those services to my wife and children, which were before obligatory, cease altogether from being so; my sovereign's just command has superseded them.

Now if my temporal superior has thus the power to subtract duties from the Natural Rule, how far more must God possess that power! A real command may reach me, not from my earthly sovereign but from God, requiring me to give such service as I am capable of giving, towards some holy enterprise in progress. In such a case God works a real ' mutatio materiæ;' and in consequence of His command, certain duties, which *were* of intrinsic and independent obligation, cease from being so. Yet surely He works this 'mutatio materiæ,' not as Lord of the Universe, but as Legislator; *i. e.* as being that Holy Creator, who has a rightful authority to command. On this principle He might (as Suarez observes) forbid me, *e. g.* during some given period, from occupying any time in direct meditation on His attributes, or in special and explicit prayer. He might forbid this directly; or He might forbid it indirectly, by strictly commanding a *different* mode of employing each successive moment. You will object, that unless I devote time to special and explicit prayer, I have no moral power to avoid mortal sin. True, 'in præsenti providentiâ;' but of course it would be implied in God's giving such a command, that He would so far *change* His Providence, as that He would furnish me with amply sufficient grace, *without* my giving myself to such pious practices.

82. It is abundantly evident then, that through this 'mutatio materiæ' God has full power to subtract, from the Natural Rule, *far* the greater number of its external precepts.* Such subtraction, I need not say, has been most rare and exceptional in the history of the world; but God has the full power to exercise this prerogative, as His Infinite Wisdom may dictate. One important remark however must here be made, in final explanation. It is impossible that we can have any knowledge of such Divine subtraction, except by means of direct Revelation; whether mediate or immediate. Wherever no such revelation reaches us, there is *no* 'mutatio materiæ;' in all such cases therefore — in all cases where we receive no direct revelation to the contrary — Reason itself (as we have already seen) declares, that God adds the sanction of His Command to the intrinsic obligation of the Natural Rule.

The assemblage of such Commands may be called the 'mutable' part of the Natural Law. They *belong* to the Natural Law; for they are Divine Precepts, commanding that which, in itself and apart from such Command, is of independent obligation. And they make

---

* What is meant here by 'external' will be explained clearly in the following number.

up the *mutable* part of that Law; because (as was supposed) they are those Precepts, which admit of being subtracted by God from the Natural Law through ' mutatio materiæ,' as above explained.

Theologians here proceed to treat, on these principles, the various instances found in Scripture of God's subtraction from the Natural Law. The appropriate place however for this question, is our theological course; and as there is no reason of convenience (but rather the contrary) for anticipating its treatment, I postpone it for the present. Here I will only observe, that objections are brought from Scripture, by two most opposite parties, for two most opposite purposes. They are brought by certain Protestants, who reverence the authority of Scripture, for the purpose of proving that morality is not independent; and they are brought by certain infidels, who hold that morality *is* independent, for the purpose of disparaging the Bible. By the help of the principles which we have now considered, we are able to meet both classes of opposition with the most perfect confidence and security. We are able at once to hold, in the fullest extent, that morality is independent;—and also to hold, in the fullest extent, the perfect consistency of this doctrine with the statements of Scripture.

83. But as there is a mutable part of the Natural Law, so also there is an *im*mutable: and we should fall into the most frightful misconceptions, if we did not carefully master this truth. We need not attempt (what perhaps is impossible) to make an exhaustive catalogue, of those Precepts which cannot be subtracted: the following will suffice. The first two particulars in the enumeration, are of an importance which it is impossible to exaggerate.

(1.) *Virtuous ends of action must ever and in all circumstances remain what they are.* An *external* precept may be *reversed* ; but as regards the *movement of our will*, all that God can possibly call on us to do, is to act towards *one* virtuous end rather than towards *another*. Let us illustrate this, in the often-repeated instance of my friend's jewel. Put the ordinary case, that God does not specially interfere; I am under the obligation of restoring my friend his jewel, *because of the virtuousness inherent in Justice.* But now we will suppose that God does specially interfere, and commands me to retain it. What then results? Does He command me to regard, as the *motive* of such retention, any supposed virtuousness inherent in *injustice?* A monstrous supposition indeed! It *was* my duty to *restore* it because of the virtuousness inherent in *Justice;* it *is* my duty to *retain* it, because of the virtuousness inherent in *Obedience to my Holy Creator.*

It must ever then, and in all circumstances, remain true, that we are morally better, holier, more acceptable to God, in proportion as our will adheres, with greater firmness and efficacity, to those ends of action enumerated in the last Section. God is *not* free, by means of any possible interference, to touch or affect in any way this essential and necessary truth. Those virtuous ends, as we have seen, are such as the following: viz. Justice, Veracity, Benevolence, Love of God, Obedience to God, Reverence for God, Humility, Forgivingness, Purity. God, in virtue of His Sanctity, is under the glorious inability of proposing any ends of action at variance with these.

(2.) 'Negative' precepts, which regard 'internal' acts, are absolutely immutable. Here there are two terms requiring explanation; 'negative' precepts and 'internal' acts.

'Affirmative' precepts command the performance of a duty; 'negative' precepts forbid the commission of a sin. Negative precepts therefore bind, as theologians say, 'semper et pro semper;' for *at every moment* we are forbidden to commit any sin: but nothing like this is true in regard to 'affirmative' precepts. It is an *affirmative* precept, that we love God; *i. e.* that we elicit certain acts of love to Him: it is a *negative* precept that we *prefer no creature to Him;* still more that we do not *hate Him.* We are not *always* bound to be eliciting acts of love to Him; but we *are* always bound, to abstain from anything *contrary* to that Love which is His due: from preferring, *e.g.* to Him any creature whatever. The negative precept binds at every instant of our waking lives; the affirmative precept binds only on certain fixed and definite occasions.

Now it is very clear, how much more *conceivable* it is, that *affirmative* precepts be subtracted from the Natural Law than *negative*. God may command us *not to meditate* on His attributes for a certain given period; but He can*not* command us to hold those Attributes in contempt or hatred. He *may* command us to elicit no formal acts of *love* to our brethren; but He *cannot* command us to elicit formal acts of hatred in their regard. We have shewn in n. 81, that the former class of commands are possible, at least ' de potentiâ absolutâ;' that He can prohibit us from direct acts of love, to Himself or to our brethren. On the other hand it is evident, as soon as stated, that the latter class of commands are absolutely *im*possible; that under no possible circumstances *can* it be lawful to despise God or to hate our brethren.

Next as to ' internal ' acts. In our theological course we shall have to enter more at length on the force of this term : here it will suffice to say, that ' internal ' acts are those consummated in the will itself; ' external ' are free acts consummated *externally* to the will. That I restore my friend his jewel, this is an ' external ' act; that I *resolve* on so doing, this is an ' internal.'

Now it is quite plain, from what has been said, that as regards *external* acts, even negative precepts may be subtracted. It is a *negative* precept of the Natural Law, that I shall not retain a jewel, deposited with me by a friend, when that friend requires and seeks it for his own reasonable wants. And yet God has the full power of reversing this precept, by ' mutatio materiæ.' It is a negative precept of the Natural Law, that we shall not treat our children harshly; and yet God commanded Abraham actually to *slay* his son.

You will object perhaps, that if the *external* act may be reversed in character, so also may be the *in-*

ternal; if my *retaining* the jewel, *e. g.* may become lawful, so also may my *resolving* to retain it. By considering this objection, we shall throw considerable light on the statement above made. Put again the ordinary case, that God does not specially interfere: what is that *internal* act, concerning the jewel, which is strictly forbidden by the Natural Law? This: 'I resolve to ' retain unjustly the deposited jewel, because of the ' personal or other advantage which I shall derive from ' its retention.' But this internal act can *never* be made lawful by any 'mutatio materiæ' imaginable. When God commands me to retain the jewel, the *internal* act which he requires me to elicit is totally different; viz. this: ' I resolve to retain that jewel, ' which has now become mine, because of the virtuous- ' ness inherent in Obedience to God's Command.' You see, the *external* act may be reversed in character by a Holy God; from unlawful it may become even obligatory: but no such reversal of character can possibly take place, in regard to that *internal* act, which is consummated in the will itself.

(3.) The following statement is not to be found (so far as I know) explicitly made by theologians; yet it is fully implied, in their whole doctrine concerning God's Providence. God cannot 'de potentiâ absolutâ' impose a Precept, which would place its recipients in circumstances of moral inability to avoid mortal sin. What is precisely understood by moral inability, is to be explained in our fourth Chapter; but you have already, no doubt, a sufficient general knowledge of its meaning. And as an instance of what I intend by my statement, take the following. Suppose I had been familiar with deeds of cruelty; and suppose God commanded me to kill, with every circumstance of protracted torture, a man, who had inflicted on me some deadly injury. It is plain that, with no more than ordinary grace, I should, in fulfilling such a command, be morally unable to avoid mortal sin under the head of vindictiveness. Even then if on other grounds it were possible for God to give such a command, He would at least be necessitated by

His Sanctity to give me most abundant help, that I might have full power of avoiding mortal sin.

(4.) Certain more enormous sins against the sixth commandment must always remain such; no 'mutatio materiæ' can possibly affect their intrinsic pravity.

(5.) It is agreed by all theologians without exception, that a lie must ever remain intrinsecally evil, and that its prohibition can in no possible way be subtracted from the Natural Rule. As this statement is but very indirectly connected with our general subject, and as its elucidation would require considerable space,—let it suffice thus to enunciate this universally received principle.

84. The doctrines, expressed in this Section, follow most obviously from those of Section III. Having therefore in Sect. IV. shewn at such great length the amount of theological authority for those earlier doctrines, it will not be necessary to give more than a *sample*, in regard to this their further development.

From Suarez however, I will take a chapter almost entire; because he not only states his own judgment, but gives also a very clear account of the other opinions, which have been maintained in the Church:—

" *UTRÙM DEUS DISPENSARE POSSIT IN LEGE NATURALI ETIAM DE ABSOLUTA POTESTATE.*

" Ratio dubitandi est, quia omnis legislator potest in suâ lege dispensare; quod, in humano legislatore, tam generaliter et sine exceptione verum habet, ut etiam si absque causâ dispensat, factum teneat; ergò multò magìs in Deo: ergò cùm Ipse sit Auctor Naturalis Legis, poterit in eâ dispensare. Confirmatur, quia ita fecisse videtur, dispensando cum Abrahamo, in quinto præcepto Decalogi, Genes. 22; et cum Osea in sexto, quando illi præcipit accipere; mulierem fornicariam, Oseæ 2; et cum filiis Israel in septimo, quando ex Dei facultate spoliaverunt Ægyptios, Exod. 12.

" Distinguimus tres ordines præceptorum naturalium. Quædam sunt universalissima principia, ut 'malum, faciendum non est,' et 'bonum est prosequendum:' quædam verò sunt conclusiones immediatæ, et omninò intrinsecè conjunctæ dictis principiis; ut præcepta Decalogi: in tertio ordine sunt alia præcepta, quæ multò magìs sunt remota a primis principiis, imò et ab ipsis Decalogi præceptis; de quibus postea exempla ponemus. De primis non est controversia inter auctores: nam certum est, in ea non cadere dispensationem, respectu hominis liberè et moraliter operantis. Nam si Deus *faciat ut homo careat omni operatione morali*, liberum usum rationis et voluntatis impediendo, excusaretur homo ab omni Lege Naturali, quia nec benè, nec malè moraliter operari posset: tamen illa non esset *dispensatio* in Lege Naturæ, sed esset *impedire subjectum ne esset capax obligationis illius;* sicut nunc infans non obligatur propriè Lege Naturali.   At verò si homo relinquitur capax liberæ operationis, absolvi non potest ab omnibus illis principiis legis naturæ: quia *positâ quâcumque dispensatione,* necesse est ut illa principia sint regula honestè operandi : vel enim dispensatio facit operationem vel carentiam ejus licitam, vel non facit: si non facit, nulla est dispensatio ; si vero facit, necesse est ut ratio judicet, hìc et nunc operationem esse licitam : ergò dispensatio non potest cadere in illud principium, 'bonum est prosequendum:' quod ampliùs ex dicendis constabit.   Controversia ergò est de aliis duobus ordinibus præceptorum ; et præsertim tractatur à doctoribus de secundo : nam de tertio pauca dicunt, et ideò in fine breviter illam expediemus.

   " Est ergò prima sententia, generaliter affirmans posse Deum dispensare in omnibus Præceptis Decalogi.   Quæ consequenter ait, non solùm posse Deum dispensare, sed etiam *abrogare totam illam Legem,* auferendo omninò ejus obligationem, vel prohibitionem.   Quo facto, inquit hæc opinio *futura fuisse licita omnia, quæ Lex Naturæ prohibet, quantùmvis mala nunc esse videantur.* Ex quo tandem concludit, non solùm posse Deum hæc non prohibere, sed etiam *præcipere ut fiant :* quia si mala non sunt sed licita, cur non poterit illa præcipere?   Hæc fuit sententia Ocham in 2, q. 19, ad. 3, dubium; quem sequitur Petrus de Aliaco in 1., dict. 7, et Andr. de Castr. Novo in 1, d. 48, quæst. 1, Artic. 1, et inclinat Gerson. Alphabet. 61, lit. E. & F. Almain etiam 3, Moral. capit. 15, ut probabilem tractat hanc opinionem: posteà verò illam rejicit.   Fundantur præcipuè, quia omnia, quæ cadunt sub Legem Naturæ, *non sunt mala, nisi quia prohibentur à Deo ;* et Ipse liberè ipsa prohibet, cùm sit Supremus Dominus et Gubernator.   Item quia oppositum non implicat contradictionem: ablatâ enim prohibitione, reliqua omnia facile consequuntur.

   "Hæc verò sententia, tanquam falsa et absurda, à reliquis theologis rejicitur: et à priori improbanda est ex dictis suprà cap. 6. ubi ostendimus Legem Naturalem (licèt, ut est propriè Lex Divina, Præcepta et Prohibitionem Dei includat, nihilominùs) *supponere* in suâ materiâ *intrinsecam honestatem vel malitiam, ab eâ prorsùs inseparabilem :* et prætereà ibi ostendimus, suppositâ Divinâ Providentiâ, *non posse Deum non* prohibere mala illa, quæ ratio naturalis ostendit esse mala.   Sed licet fingamus, Prohibitionem *additam* per Voluntatem Dei posse auferri, nihilominùs *prorsùs repugnat,* ad id, quod per se et intrinsecè malum est, *desinere esse malum;* quia *rei natura non potest mutari:* unde non potest talis actus liberè fieri, quin *malum sit et dissonum naturæ rationali:* ut ex Aristot. et aliis ibi ostendimus. Et videtur per se notum: quî enim fieri potest, ut odium Dei, vel mendacium, liberè facta, non sint prava? *Fundamentum ergò hujus sententiæ, scilicet, quòd omnis malitia humanorum actuum proveniat ex Prohibitione extrinsecâ, omninò falsum est.* Ideòque ne in æquivoco laboremus, separanda est quæstio de *Prohibitione extrinsecâ Dei,* an possit ab Ipso non fieri, vel respectu omnium, vel respectu alicujus. Nam de hâc Prohibitione esse potest res magìs dubia, ut in dicto cap. 6. dixi; *probabilius tamen esse ostendi, esse à Divinâ Providentiâ inseparabilem:* illâ verò quæstione omissâ, hìc absolutè inquirimus, an fieri possit à Deo, ut actiones illæ, quæ per legem Decalogi prohibentur, malæ non sint ullo modo; ità ut nec *per legem ostensivam naturalis rationis vetentur,* ut malæ: et in hoc sensu dicimus, *esse falsam sententiam Ochami et aliorum.*

"Unde à fortiori constat, multò majus absurdum esse dicere, posse Deum homini præcipere, ut Ipsummet Deum odio habeat; quod planè sequitur ex illà sententiâ. Nam si potest illum actum non prohibere, et ablatâ Prohibitione non est malus;—ergò potest illum præcipere. Consequens autem esse absurdum patet; quia non potest Deus facere, ut Ipsemet sit odio dignus; nam repugnat ejus Bonitati: neque etiam potest facere, ut sit rectum et ordinatum, *habere odio rem amore dignam.* Item esset ibi quædam contradictio: nam obedire Deo, est quidam virtualis amor Ejus, et obligatio ad obediendum præsertim nascitur ex amore: ergo repugnat *obligari ex Præcepto* ad Ipsummet Deum odio habendum. Idem argumentum fieri potest de mendacio: nam si Deus illud posset præcipere, etiàm *posset Ipse mendacium dicere; quod erroneum est: sic enim tota certitudo fidei periret.* Atque hæc etiam ratio probat de dispensatione: nam si potest Deus dispensare in omnibus, ergò in mendacio; non tantùm officioso, sed etiam pernicioso, et in quâcumque materiâ: multò ergò magìs poterit (ut ita dicam) Secum Ipse Dispensare, vel potiùs sine dispensatione mentiri: quia respectu Illius nulla est prohibitio, et aliàs dicitur actum *secundùm se malum non esse.*

"Secunda sententia est Scoti in 3 distinction. 37 quæstion. unicâ, quem ibi sequitur Gabriel quæstione primâ articulo secundo, et refert etiam ibidem Almain. Distinguitque inter præcepta primæ et secundæ tabulæ. Primæ tabulæ dicuntur, tria Præcepta Decalogi, quæ versantur *circa Deum:* de quibus sentit, duo prima, quæ negativa sunt, esse indispensabilia; tertium autem, quatenùs involvit circumstantiam Sabbati, et dispensabile et abrogabile fuisse (quod est manifestum apud omnes, quia quoad

N

id non fuit Naturale, sed Positivum) quatenùs verò absolutè con-
tinet affirmativum præceptum cultûs divini, dubitat an dispensabile
sit; et de totâ hâc parte hujus opinionis infrà dicam. Præcepta
secundæ tabulæ, dicuntur reliqua septem ; et in universum omnia,
quæ *circa proximos vel creaturas versantur;* de quibus omnibus
sentit Scotus dispensabilia esse . . . .

"Tertia opinio est Durandi in 1 distinct. 47 quæstione quartâ,
et Majoris in 2 dist. 37 quæst. 10, qui distinguunt inter
præcepta *negativa et affirmativa;* quamvis non omninò inter se
conveniant. Nam Major dicit, negativa esse indispensabilia,
excepto quinto præcepto, ' Non occides.' Durand. vero eandem
regulam constituens de exceptione, dixit, si verbum, ' Non occides '
generaliter sumatur pro quâcumque hominis occisione, sic dispensabile esse: si verò sumatur pro occisione hominis, prout eam
prohibet ratio naturalis, sic etiam illud indispensabile esse. Sed
profectò distinctio non erat necessaria ; quia priori modo occisio
non cadit sub Prohibitione Legis Naturæ, quia dicit quid commune, abstrahens ab occisione justâ et injustâ ; de quâ constat,
ut sic, non prohiberi Lege Naturæ. Igitur, loquendo propriè de
Quinto Præcepto, sine causâ fit exceptio, ut patebit; et eodem modo
possent isti auctores excipere Septimum Præceptum, vel in illo distinguere ; quia etiam acceptio rei alienæ potest interdùm justè fieri.

" De affirmativis autem præceptis, Major absolutè dicit, omnia
esse dispensabilia. Et probat primò, quia potest Deus non con-
currere cum homine ad quemcumque actum præceptum. Sed
hoc impertinens est; quia hoc non est dispensare, sed tollere
potestatem operandi. Quis enim dicat, unum hominem dispensare
cum alio nè audiat missam, violenter illum detinendo, aut ità
graviter vulnerando ut illam audire non possit? Probat deinde,
quia pro quocumque tempore signato potest Deus præbere facul-
tatem non exercendi actum præceptum, vel etiam *præcipere facere
aliud;* ergò hoc modo poterit pro toto tempore vitæ dispensare.
Sed neque hoc urget: si consideremus, *præceptum affirmativum
non obligare pro semper;* et stando in purâ Lege Naturæ, non
habere aliud tempus pro quo determinatè obliget, nisi illud, quod
necessaria occasio vel opportunitas definierit. Unde, quamvis
contingat *totum vitæ tempus* transigi sine tali occasione vel opportunitate, et ideò *numquam occurrere obligationem Præcepti,* non
proptereà interveniat *dispensatio;* nam hoc etiam naturaliter et
sine miraculo contingere potest. Ratio ergò illa ad summum
probat, posse Deum facere, ut, in singulis temporibus, Præcepti
necessitas non occurrat; vel quia *urget aliud Præceptum magis,*
vel quia rerum circumstantiæ mutantur. Quòd si Major velit,
*stantibus eisdem circumstantiis cum quibus obligat Naturale Præcep-
tum,* posse Deum dare licentiam ne impleatur,—illud non probat,
sed assumit tantùm.

" Durandus autem distinguit inter *præceptum primæ; et secundæ tabulæ, et prius dicit esse indispensabile, posterius autem dispensari posse.* Probat hâc ratione, quia omnis materia, à quâ potest auferri ratio debiti, dispensabilis est; illa verò quæ habet debitum inseparabile, est indispensabilis: sed materia illorum præceptorum ita se habet: ergo. Minorem probat hâc analogiâ: quia dependentia à Deo est inseparabilis ab homine; dependentia verò unius hominis ab alio est separabilis à quocumque: sic ergò à cultu Dei est *inseparabile* debitum; ab honore autem parentum *reparari potest :* unde non potest Deus facere quin illi credendum sit, et reverentia exhibenda: potest autem facere, ne parentes honorentur. Sed quoad neutram partem videtur mihi ratio efficax, nec distinctio constans. Primum probo, quia longè aliud est de dependentiâ à Deo *in esse;* hæc enim essentialis est, quia sine illâ non potest homo subsistere: *sine actione autem morali ergà Deum potest existere;* imò et benè operari circà alia objecta. Item quamvis potuerit Deus facere, ut Petrus v. g. non habuerit esse à suis parentibus, tamen hoc non esset dispensare in Præcepto de honorandis parentibus: supposito autem quòd ab illis habuit esse, jam intervenit dependentia, à quâ inseparabile est debitum honorandi parentes; sicut à dependentia à Deo inseparabile est debitum colendi Ipsum. Et hinc patet secunda pars; nam si sit sermo de debito, æquè inseparabile est sumptum cum proportione, seu suppositâ emanatione à tali causâ: si verò sit sermo de actibus, quibus solvitur hoc debitum,—sicut potest Deus facere, ut homo sine peccato nunquam in totâ vitâ exerceat actum honoris circa parentes, ita *potest etiam facere, ut numquam exerceat actum cultûs divini ;* ergò vel neutra est dispensatio, vel in utroque Præcepto dispensari potest.

" Est igitur quarta opinio, quæ absolutè et simpliciter docet, *hæc præcepta Decalogi esse indispensabilia etiam per potentiam Dei absolutam.* Tenet D. Th. q. 100, Artic. 8, et ibi Cajetan. et alii ; Sotus lib. 2, de just. q. 3, Articul. 8 ; Victor. relect. de homicid ; Viguer. in Instit. Theolog. cap. 15, § 1, versu 7 ; Vincent. in Speculo Moral. lib. 1, par. 2, distinct. 6 ; Altisiodor. in Summâ, lib. 3, tract. 7, cap. 1, qu. 5 ; Richard. in 3, distinct. 37, articul. 1, quæstion. 5, et ibi Paludan. Bassolis, et alii ; Abulen. in 20 caput Exodi, q. 35, et Molin. tom. 6, tractat. 5, disputat. 57, num. 6. Fundamentum D. Thomæ est, quia ea quæ continent intrinsecam rationem justitiæ et debiti, indispensabilia sunt; sed hujusmodi sunt præcepta Decalogi; ergò. Major patet, quia implicat contradictionem, esse debitum et non esse debitum ; quod autem dispensatur, eo ipso fit indebitum; si autem habet debitum inseparabile, necessario illud retinet; ergò repugnat dispensare quod hujusmodi est. Et ideò ait Divus Thomas, nec Deum dispensare posse, quia *non potest agere contra Suam Jus-*

titiam; quod tamen ageret, si licentiam daret faciendi id, quod *per se et intrinsecè injustum est.*

" Hanc verò rationem impugnant auctores aliarum opinionum, quia vel petit principium, vel æquè procedit in omni præcepto et dispensatione ejus. Probatur, quia si sit sensus, stante et manente debito, non posse dispensationem habere locum, hoc in omni lege locum habet ; quia repugnat dispensare, ut manente debito legis liceat agere contrà legem ; nam ratio dispensationis *consistit* in hoc, *ut auferat debitum legis,* et ideò in illis terminis contradictio involvitur : vel est sensus, hoc debitum non posse auferri in præceptis naturalibus ; et hoc probandum est ; cùm hoc ergò assumitur, principium petitur.

" Respondetur, duplex esse debitum. Aliud procedens ab ipsâ lege, tanquam effectus ejus ; et de hoc procedit apertè objectio: tamen Divus Thomas in dictâ ratione non loquitur de hoc debito. Aliud est debitum, proveniens ex intrinsecâ proportione inter objectum et actum comparatum ad rectam rationem, seu naturam rationalem ; et de hoc debito procedit ratio Div. Thomæ. Nam (ut sæpè dictum est) Lex Naturalis prohibet ea, quæ secundùm se mala sunt, quatenùs talia sunt ; et ideò *supponit in ipsis objectis* seu actibus intrinsecum debitum, ut non amentur seu non fiant ; et è contrario præcipit bona, quatenùs intrinsecam connexionem et necessitatem habent cum naturâ rationali. Hoc autem debitum inseparabile est, non quia non sit dispensabile (sic enim peteretur principium), sed quia *intrinsecè supponitur in ipsis rebus, ante omnem legem extrinsecam ;* et ideò, stantibus eisdem rebus auferri non potest, quià non pendet ex extrinsecâ voluntate, neque est res aliqua distincta, sed quasi modus omninò intrinsecus, seu quasi relatio, quæ impediri non potest, posito fundamento et termino: et hanc rationem confirmant, quæ circa alias opiniones dicta sunt, et quæ in cap. 6, diximus.

"*Hæc igitur sententia, formaliter et propriè loquendo, vera est.* Quia verò negare non possumus, *Deum aliquando efficere, ut actus illi materiales liceant, qui aliàs, non interveniente Deo Ipso et Ejus Potestate, licitè fieri non possint,* ideò (ut intelligatur quomodo hoc fiat, et cur illa non sit, nec appelletur, dispensatio,) oportet distinguere in Deo varias rationes. *Est enim Supremus Legislator ;* unde habet, ut possit nova et varia præcepta imponere : *est etiam Supremus Dominus,* quia potest dominia mutare vel concedere : est item *Supremus Judex,* Qui potest punire, vel unicuique reddere quòd ei debetur. *Dispensatio* ergò propriè pertinet ad Deum *sub primâ consideratione ;* quia ejusdem potestatis est, tollere et condere legem : itaque ut intelligatur Deus *dispensare,* oportet ut utendo *solâ illâ jurisdictione,* et non adjungendo potestatem dominativam per quam res ipsas immutet, licere faciat, quòd anteà non licebat. Nam si per *Dominium Suum* mutet humanum [officium ?], hoc non erit dispensare, sed tollere materiam Legis ; ut ex superioribus constat. Quoties ergò Deus facit licitum actum, qui Jure Naturæ videbatur prohibitus, nunquam id facit ut purus Legislator, sed utendo aliâ potestate : et ideò non dispensat.

"Hoc videre licet in exemplis positis. Quando enim Deus præcepit Abrahæ interficere filium, id fecit tanquam Dominus vitæ et mortis : si enim Deus Ipse per Seipsum voluisset interficere Isaac,—non indiguisset dispensatione, sed ex Suo Dominio id facere posset ; eodem ergo modo potuit uti Abrahamo ut instrumento : et Quintum Præceptum *non prohibet esse instrumentum Dei in occisione*, si Ipse præceperit. Idem sentit Divus Thomas de facto Oseæ in assumendâ muliere fornicariâ ; ut patet dicto art. 8, ad 4, et 2, 2, quæst. 154. Potest enim Deus transferre in virum dominium mulieris sine consensu ejus, et ita efficere vinculum inter illos, ratione cujus illa copula jam fornicaria non sit. Sed licet hoc sit verum de potentiâ absolutâ, locus Oseæ non cogit ad hanc interpretationem : jussit enim Deus assumere eam, quæ priùs fornicaria fuerat, non solùm ad usum, sed etiam ad matrimonium et in conjugem ; ut Hieronym. Theodor. et alii interpretantur, et Irenæus lib. 4, contra Hæreses, cap. 37, et August. 22, contrà Faust. cap. 80 et 85, et lib. contrà Secundinum Manich. cap. 21. Simili modo non *dispensavit* cum Hebræis quandò Ægyptiorum spolia illis concessit, sed vel tanquam Supremus Dominus donavit, vel saltem tanquam Supremus Judex reddidit eis mercedem laborum suorum ; ut dicitur Sapient. 10. Ità ergò in similibus omnibus intelligendum est ; neque potest aliter fieri, propter rationem adductam. Idemque applicari potest *ad præcepta affirmativa;* in quibus est res facilis, quia non obligant pro semper, sed stante opportunitate, quæ circa tale objectum inducat necessitatem. Potest autem Deus aut objectum mutare, cedendo Juri Suo vel hominum jura immutando, aut etiam necessitatem potest auferre, addendo novas circumstantias, quæ illam impediant : et nihilominùs Præceptum integrum manet, *ut ex se semper obliget pro debitâ opportunitate;* quod est signum, non fuisse factam dispensationem.

"Unde colligit D. Thomas in dictà solut. ad 3, hunc modum immutationis non solùm Deo, sed etiam homini, interdum esse possibilem. In negativis quidem præceptis, quando materia illorum cadit sub dominio humano, et per homines immutari potest, quomodo nos suprà explicuimus legem præscriptionis : in affirmativis autem, quando per homines possunt immutari circumstantiæ, quæ inducebant necessitatem operandi, *vel quandò possunt homines gravius præceptum imponere : ut si rex præcipiat filio non succurrere parenti extremè indigenti, ut subveniat reipublicæ periclitanti.* Deus autem ob Singularem Excellentiam potest, quandò

vult, uti absolutâ Potestate et Dominio.   Unde etiam intelligitur
ratio, ob quam non in omnibus Præceptis negativis potest talis
mutatio fieri per homines ex parte materiæ, in quibus potest fieri
à Deo : ut v. g. in præcepto non fornicandi : quia nimirùm non habet
homo illam potestatem in personam fœminæ, quam habet Deus, ut
possit alteri tradere in suam prout voluerit ; et ideò etiam potuerunt
leges humanæ per usucapionem mutare dominia rerum, non tamen
ita potuerunt mutare dominia uxorum.   Et ità, stante lege
humanâ, potest desinere esse furtum quod anteà fuisset ; non tamen
potest desinere esse adulterium, quod per se tale existit.

  " Præterea ex his obiter intelligitur, quotiescumque materia Præcepti talis fuerit, ut honestas vel turpitudo ejus non
pendeat ex Dominio Divino, tunc non solùm indispensabile esse
tale Præceptum, sed êtiam *ità immutabile, ut non possit ullâ rationè
licitum fieri id quod prohibet;* solùm enim *in negativis Præceptis hoc propriè invenitur.*   Hujusmodi est primum præceptum
Decalogi, quatenus negativum est, et prohibet habere vel colere
plures Deos : hoc enim nullo modo potest immutari ; quia est
contra rationem Ultimi Finis, et Excellentiam Dei, ac Unitatem
Ejus, quam Ipse mutare non potest.   Nec enim potest vel alium
Deum constituere, vel aliquid facere quod sit æquali honore
dignum ; mutatio ergò talis præcepti seu materiæ ejus, non cadit
sub Divinum Dominium. Idem est de Secundo Præcepto Decalogi :
tum quia involvit prohibitionem mendacii, quod nullâ ratione
honestari potest, si mendacium manet ; tum maximè, quia prohibet
facere Deum Auctorem mendacii, quod etiam includit irreveren-
tiam Dei, adeò repugnantem Divinæ Auctoritati, ut non possit in
hoc cedere Juri Suo (ut sic dicam).   Atque in hoc sensu verum
est quod intendebat Scotus, hæc aliis esse immutabiliora.

  " De tertio autem, cùm sit affirmativum, certum est posse
à Deo fieri, ut sæpe non obliget, quando aliàs secundum communem cursum rerum obligaret.   An verò possit homini licentiam dare, ut per totum vitæ tempus, et, quod difficilius est, per
totam æternitatem, nullum bonum motum circa Ipsum exerceat,
neque cultum aliquem proximum et directum exhibeat, non im-
meritò dubitavit Scot.   Nonnulli vero ex Thomistis censent hoc
non posse fieri, nec per propriam dispensationem, neque etiam
per mutationem materiæ. Si tamen consideremus absolutam ac
nudam potentiam, non apparet in hoc implicatio contradictionis :
quia inde non sequitur, non posse talem hominem bonos actus
morales circa objecta creata exercere ; quia eorum bonitas non
pendet ex prævio actu formali circa ultimum finem, et naturâ suâ
tendunt in Ipsum, et ita mediatè et remotè vel quasi materialiter,
possunt dici continere cultum Dei. At verò considerando Divinam Potentiam, ut conjunctam Infinitæ Sapientiæ et Bonitati
Dei, atque adeò loquendo moraliter (ut sic dicam), credibilius

est, non posse Deum in hoc cedere Juri Suo; quia esset veluti prodigalitas quædam irrationabilis : maximè respectu creaturæ rationabilis, et pro totâ æternitate. In aliis autem Præceptis non invenio hujusmodi immutabilitatem ex parte materiæ; solo excepto mendacio, ut jam dixi, in quo fortasse est specialis ratio, vel quia etiam respectu ipsius Dei malum est, vel quia de se non limitatur ad materiam creatam, nec pendet ex dominio Dei in illam vel in personam, sed in quâcumque materiâ et de quâcumque personâ dici potest; vel denique quia ejus deformitas non pendet ex alio dominio, vel Divino Jure, sed statim oritur ex dissonantiâ verborum ad mentem.

"Tandem ex dictis intelligitur, quo sensu dixerit Bernard. in lib. citato de præcept. et dispensat. ca. 5, ea, quæ pertinent ad Præcepta secundæ tabulæ, mutari posse auctoritate Dei præcipientis : loquitur enim non *de Præceptis ipsis formaliter sumptis*, ut sic dicam, sed *de actionibus circa quas illa·præcepta versantur.* De quibus ait, cùm per se nunquam liceant, auctoritate Dei præcipientis posse licere. Quod verum est in sensu explicato : illa tamen non est *dispensatio* in Præcepto secundæ tabulæ, sed est *mutatio materiæ* ejus; ut diximus. Tamen quia hæc mutatio, quandò fit ex peculiari Dominio et Potestate Dei, est (ut sic dicam) extra cursum naturæ et præter leges ordinariæ Providentiæ, ideò interdùm dispensatio appellatur; *non quidem propriè Præcepti Naturalis* (neque hoc dixit Bernard. si attentè legatur) sed *ordinarii cursûs et legis Providentiæ,* quæ à divinâ voluntate pendet : et in eodem sensu videtur loquutus Bonavent.; nàm sententiam Bernardi imitatur. Dices: 'ergò nulla 'erit tunc differentia inter Præcepta primæ et secundæ tabulæ, 'quam Bonavent. constituit, et favet Bernard. nam statim cap. 6, 'dicit, quædam ita esse immutabilia, ut nec à Deo Ipso mutari 'valeant.' Respondetur facilè ex dictis, in hoc esse differentiam, quòd Præcepta primæ tabulæ talia sunt, ut non solùm ipsa formaliter dispensari non possint, verùm etiam neque in actionibus quas prohibent possit talis mutatio fieri, ut liceant vel honestæ sint; ac subinde, ut neque etiam materialiter sumptæ honestari possint Auctoritate Dei præcipientis. Odium enim Dei nullo modo potest honestari, nec adoratio idoli, nec cultus alterius dei præter Deum Verum; quia ab his actionibus secundùm se sumptis inseparabilis est deformitas, si liberè fiant : quod non ita *semper* est in actionibus pertinentibus ad Præcepta secundæ tabulæ. Quod non universaliter, sed indefinitè, accipiendum est : aliqua enim Præcepta secundæ tabulæ, possunt esse immutabilia etiam hoc modo; ut apertè fatetur Bernard. dicto cap. 6, et in superioribus satìs explicatum est."—SUAREZ, *De Legibus,* lib. ii. cap. 15.

Viva takes the same view of the case with Suarez.

" Ex quibus deducitur, in quo sensu verum sit axioma illud theologorum, Deum scilicet dispensare non posse in Jure Naturæ; cùm tamen et Abrahæ dispensârit, ut vellet occidere filium innocentem ; et Israelitis, ut Ægyptios spoliarent ; et Oseæ, ut sumeret sibi uxorem fornicationum ; et Hebræis, ut plures uxores ducerent; necnon ut possent dare ex rationabili causâ libellum repudii, et vinculum matrimonii dissolvere. Etenim ex D. Th. 1, 2, quæst. 100, art. 8, in hisce actionibus non dispensavit Deus *sub iis circumstantiis, sub quibus sunt contra Jus Naturæ et ab intrinseco malæ;* non enim dispensavit in furto, ut fieret *invito Domino;* nec in homicidio, ut fieret *invito Domino vitæ,* qui est Deus; nec in fornicatione, ut fieret per accessum ad *non suam ;* sed dispensavit, *tollendo ab iis circumstantiam illam,* per quam essent intrinsecè et essentialiter malæ; et hoc pacto dispensavit etiam in polygamiâ et dissolubilitate matrimonii. Non potest tamen hoc pacto dispensare in iis, quæ sunt contra Jus Naturæ primo modo; puta in odio Dei, in mendacio, in mollitie, in peccato contra naturam, &c., quia hæc sunt intrinsecè mala, et essentialiter exigunt prohiberi simpliciter; eò quòd in *quâcumque circumstantiâ* sint contra Jus Naturæ, et illicita."—*De Matrimonio,* quæst. 3, art. 3, n. 6.—

And Billuart:—

" Potest tamen Lex Naturalis mutari impropriè, quatenùs ejus *materia* sic potest *mutari,* quòd desinat esse materia et objectum Legis : *v. g.* quamvis Lex dicat depositum esse reddendum, si tamen petatur in perniciem patriæ, redditio depositi desinit esse materia et objectum Legis ; quia Lex intelligitur de deposito reddendo circumspectè et prudenter.   Et de istâ mutatione legis impropriâ loquiter S. Th. dum hìc dicit Legem Naturalem, quantùm ad secunda Præcepta, posse mutari propter aliquas causas impedientes eorum observantiam.   Similiter, dum a. 4, præcedenti dicit Legem Naturalem, quantùm ad principia propria quæ sunt quasi conclusiones communium, non esse unam apud omnes secundùm rectitudinem,— S. Doctorem intelligere de mutatione Legis Naturalis *ex parte materiæ,* patet ex lectione utriusque articuli, et ab exemplo quod profert de lege depositi reddendi, quod, si repetatur irrationabiliter, desinit esse materia legis.

" Ad cujus et sequentium elucidationem observandum est, esse quasdam leges naturales, quæ exprimuntur terminis tam restrictis, ut à re per eos significata impossibile sit abesse turpitudinem vel honestatem ; ut ista : ' Non mentieris.'   Sunt autem aliæ, quæ terminis latioribus exprimuntur, ità ut, quamvis rem per eos significatam plerumque comitetur turpitudo vel honestas, potest tamen ab illâ abesse; ut in his : ' Depositum reddes,' ' Non occides.'   Ratio enim, seu Lex Naturalis, nihil aliud dictat, dictavit unquam, aut dictare potuit, quàm quòd 'depositum reddes' prudenter seu rationabiliter repetenti; et 'non occides' *privatâ auctoritate seu indebitè;* et id facile apprehendit quisquis prudens et intelligens: ex quo inferes, non in omnibus Præceptis Legis Naturæ posse fieri mutationem ex parte materiæ.

"Est itaque tantùm quæstio de mutatione Legis Naturalis per dispensationem; an scilicet aliqua potestas, humana vel saltem Divina, possit in eâ dispensare?

"Dispensatio, sicut dixi de mutatione, est duplex; propriè et impropriè dicta. Dispensatio propriè dicta, est relaxatio legis seu ejus obligationis, in aliquo particulari, facta ab habente potestatem, manente materiâ legis sic immutatâ, ut ejus obligatio remaneret si non accideret auctoritas dispensantis. Unde, quamvis dispensatio *supponat* aliquam legis interpretationem, ab eâ tamen differt, quòd ad *interpretationem* non requiratur auctoritas, sed sufficit prudentia et scientia.

"Dispensatio, impropriè dicta, est quando legislator vel alter sic *mutat materiam* legis, ut desinat comprehendi sub lege.

"Hinc dispensatio propria spectat *legislatorem* seu superiorem; dispensatio autem impropria spectat *dominum materiæ*, sive sit legislator et superior, sive non. Sic Deus, concedendo spolia Ægyptiorum Israelitis, egit ut Dominus, non ut Legislator. Sic privatus, qui remittit mihi debitum centum florenorum, agit ut *dominus* istius debiti, non ut superior. E contra, si Deus aut papa eximeret aliquem à lege jejunii vel sanctificationis Sabbati, ageret ut Superior et Legislator. Et indè sequitur aliud discrimen: quòd dispensatio propria directè *cadat supra legem;* impropria autem directè cadat *supra materiam* seu debitum: ita ut qui dispensatur propriè, *v.g.* in jejunio, non teneatur ampliùs lege jejunandi sicut tenentur alii: qui verò dispensatur impropriè, *v.g.* in redditione debiti quod remittitur, vel in ablatione alieni quod ipsi conceditur à domino, semper tenetur, sicut omnes alii, lege naturali non furandi, aut solvendi debita. Quòd si hic et nunc licitè aut alienum auferat, aut debitum non solvat, non est *quia eximitur ab istis legibus,* sed quia non remanet vel alienum, vel debitum, nec consequenter *legis materia.* Hæc, si bene perpendantur, tollunt æquivocationes, quibus multi decipiuntur in hâc materiâ.

"Circa propositam itaque quæstionem, Okam, Gerson, Petrus de Alliaco et pauci quidam antiqui opinati sunt, Deum posse absolutè dispensare in omnibus præceptis Legis Naturæ; imo totam illam legem abrogare; ita ut etiam odium Dei non esset peccatum. Sed hæc opinio meritò rejicitur ab aliis theologis et nunc inolevit.

"Scotistæ, cum suo duce, tenent Deum posse dispensare in Præceptis secundæ tabulæ tantùm; excepto Præcepto de mendacio.

"Communior aliorum theologorum sententia est, *neque Deum*

posse propriè dispensare in ullo Præcepto Legis Naturæ, sed tantùm
impropriè : cum quibus
   "*Dico,* Neque Deus ipse absolutè potest dispensare propriè in
Lege Naturali, benè tamen impropriè." (*De Legibus,* diss. 2. art. 4.)

Without further extending our quotations, the following passage from St. Bernard, to which Suarez
refers in his above-quoted chapter, deserves our careful
attention.   St. Bernard indeed appears to be one of
those, who hold that there can be dispensation, properly so called, in regard to some external precepts of
the Natural Law. Suarez, it is true, in the last number
of the above chapter, denies that this *is* his real
meaning; and at all events, if it be, so far of course
I am unable to follow the Saint's authority.   But
what appears particularly deserving of notice, is his
most clear and emphatic statement, as to the absolutely immutable character of *inward morality;* of that
type of virtue, which the Christian religion has publicly
exhibited to the world :

   " Necessarium . . . in tria hæc subdividatur, stabile, invio-
labile, incommutabile.   Et quidem *stabile* dixerim, quod ita est
necessarium, ut non cuilibet hominum illud mutare fas sit, nisi
solis dispensatoribus mysteriorum Dei, id est Præpositis : ut, verbi
gratiâ, regulæ Sanctorum Basilii, Augustini, Benedicti, necnon
et authentici Canones, et si quæ sunt alia ecclesiastica instituta
dignæ auctoritatis. . . . . . Necessarium deinde, quod *inviolabi e*
nominavi, illud intelligo, quod non ab homine traditum, sed di-
vinitùs promulgatum, nisi à Deo qui tradidit mutari omnino non
patitur : ut, exempli causâ, Non occides, Non mœchaberis, Non
furtum facies, et reliqua illius tabulæ legisscita ; quæ etsi nullam
prorsùs humanam dispensationem admittunt, nec cuiquam hominum ex his aliquid aliquo modo solvere aut licuit aut licebit,—
Dominus tamen horum quod voluit, quando voluit, solvit ; sive
cùm ab Hebræis Ægyptios spoliari, sive quando Prophetam cum
muliere fornicariâ misceri præcepit. Quorum utique alterum quid
nisi grave furti facinus, alterum quid nisi flagitii turpitudo repu-
taretur, si non excusasset utrumque factum Auctoritas Imperantis ?
Sanè ubi simile aliquid aliquando à sanctis hominibus fuisse legi-
tur usurpatum, Scripturâ non indicante quòd Deus ita præceperit,
— aut eos peccâsse fatendum est, sicut homines ; aut certè, sicut
prophetas, familiare Dei Consilium accepisse.   Unde et unum
exemplum pono quod occurrit de Samsone, qui seipsum unà cum
hostibus opprimens interfecit.   Quod utique factum si defenditur

non fuisse peccatum, privatum habuisse consilium indubitanter credendus est, etsi de Scripturâ hoc non habemus.

"Jam verò *necessarium incommutabile quid accipi velim?* Equidem nil congruentius, quàm quòd Divinâ ita constat et *æternâ ratione* firmatum, ut nullâ ex causâ possit, *vel ab ipso Deo, aliquatenùs immutari.* Sub hoc genere est omnis illa *sermonis Dominici in monte habiti spiritualis traditio; et quicquid de dilectione, humilitate, mansuetudine, cæterisque virtutibus, tam in Novo quam in Veteri Testamento spiritualiter observandum contraditur.* Hæc quippe talia sunt, quæ nec liceat nec expediat aliquando non haberi. Eò siquidem *immobiliter,* quo et *naturaliter* bona, *numquam nisi* innocenter, *numquam nisi* salubriter, aut imperantur aut observantur. *Omni tempore, omni personæ, mortem contempta, custodita salutem, operantur.* Primam ergò necessitatem sua cuique facit in promittendo voluntas, secundam præcipientis Auctoritas, tertiam *præcepti dignitas.*

"Differunt autem, ut jam dictum est, quibusdam à se invicem gradibus tres istæ necessitates, nec una omnes sequitur immutabilitatis firmitas. Nam ex primâ quidem quod efficitur, etsi non penitùs immutabile, tamen vix mutabile esse constat: dum solis illud liceat mutare prelatis; et hoc nonnisi fideli et providâ dispensatione. Quod verò fit ex sequenti, quæ et major ista, est *pene jam incommutabile;* soli quippe Deo esse mutabile superius demonstratum est. Porrò quòd de novissimâ fit, tamquam omnium maxima, omninò incommutabile est, utpote quod *ne Ipsi quidem Deo mutare liberum est.* Quod igitur nulli hominum fas est, nisi solis mutare prælatis, dici vix mutabile congruè potest; quod soli constat licere Deo, dicatur penè immutabile; quod *ne Ipsi quidem,* penitùs immutabile nominetur."—S. BERNARDI, *De Præcept. et Dispensati,* pp. 425, 426.

85. In the present Section we have spoken, almost exclusively, on that part of the ' Natural Rule,' which is precisely co-extensive with the Natural Law; that part, viz. which is concerned with the independent *sinfulness* of acts or their independent *obligation.* But we have used this phrase ' Natural Rule' in a wider sense (see n. 52, p. 117); we have used it to express, not merely the fact that such or such acts are independently *evil,* but that, among those which are *not* independently evil, *this* is independently better than *that,* or less good than *the other.* Our theory therefore will not be complete, unless we include in it this part also of the Natural Rule. The principles, however, which are here applic-

able, are most obvious and most simple.   How far, and
in what way, they may ever be reduced to *practice*, it
is not here our business to consider.

(1.) Suppose A and B are two acts, incompatible
with each other, between which I can now choose.
Neither of them is independently *evil ;* but subjectively
speaking (see n. 57, pp. 124, 5) A is independently
better than B.   Under all ordinary circumstances, I shall
act more virtuously, I shall more please my All-holy
Creator, by eliciting A than B.   But suppose God to
command B : then not only would A cease to be intrinsecally *better*, it would be *intrinsecally evil*, as being
incompatible with act B, which has become of *actual
obligation*.   This change of moral relation between these
two acts, comes of course from 'mutatio materiæ;' the
fact of God giving a Command, changes entirely the *circumstances* of that question which reason has to decide.

(2.) Suppose God, without giving a Command, inti-
mated to me His *Preference* 'hic et nunc' for act B : act
A would not in this case be an actual sin ; but act B
would be, to an indefinite extent, intrinsecally better.
The 'mutatio materiæ' would effect a total change of
relation, between the intrinsic character of these acts.

86. I have said that under such circumstances B is
intrinsecally better.   In like manner, if God commanded
me to retain the deposited jewel, or to keep the Jewish
Sabbath, obedience to such command would be of 'intrinsic' obligation.   This word 'intrinsic' may appear to
you superficially as somewhat perplexing, when so
used ; as tending to overthrow that very distinction
which it has been my purpose to advocate, between
the Natural and the Divine Positive Law.   It will
conduce then to clearness, if I explicitly answer any
such objection.

A Precept belongs to the Natural Law, when the
thing commanded is of *independent* obligation ; or (in
other words) of intrinsic obligation, *apart* from God's
Command : but the Precept belongs to the Positive Law,
when the thing's intrinsic obligation arises entirely *from*
God's Command.

In other words, the Precepts of the Natural Law do but add a fresh obligation, to one which exists apart from any such Precept; but the Precepts of the Divine Positive Law oblige to some act or acts, which, without those Precepts, would not be obligatory at all.

In other words again, God is necessitated by His Sanctity to impose those Precepts which belong to the Natural Law ; but those which belong to the Positive Law, flow wholly from His free choice.

I have reserved the phrase 'independent obligation,' to express exclusively an obligation which exists 'independently' of God's Will. But it is important (I think) from time to time to use the word 'intrinsic,' as applying to *either* case of obligation ; and this, for the purpose of keeping vividly in our minds the great truth, that God acts, as Moral Governor, in a way removed to the greatest possible extent from recklessness or caprice. He does not, and cannot consistently with His Sanctity, praise or censure, reward or punish, anything except what is *intrinsecally* good or evil respectively. His *gratuitous gifts* He, of course, imparts far more largely to this man than to that, on grounds often wholly irrespective of moral desert. But He cannot *praise or reward*, except that which is *intrinsecally good;* He cannot *blame or punish*, except that which is *intrinsecally evil.* Suppose *e. g.* He commands all men (as He does) to submit themselves to the Catholic Church. If I have no means of knowing that Command, it is inconsistent with the fundamental notion of Sanctity, that He should punish me for disobeying it. If I have the means of knowing and wilfully omit to use them, He punishes me for the 'intrinsic' sinfulness of such omission. If I know the Command and refuse to comply, He punishes me for the 'intrinsic' sinfulness of such disobedience.

And so, as to relative *degrees* of virtuousness; I cannot render my conduct *more acceptable to Him*, except by doing that which is *intrinsecally better.* A truth this, which is of course perfectly consistent with that other stated in the last number ; viz. that in various cases my *knowledge of His preference* renders an act *intrinsecally better*, which would otherwise be less good. This arises (as we have seen) simply from 'mutatio materiæ:' it arises from the fact, that such expression of His Preference changes the circumstances of the case; in other words, changes the matter, on which reason has to pronounce.

87. I will beg you now to study the Appendix to this Chapter; which, for mere reasons of physical convenience, is printed at the end of the book instead of here. You will find that the various propositions, discussed in the three last Sections, and also those contained in the Appendix to which I have referred, throw great additional light on the principles and arguments contained in Sections II. and III. I will beg you therefore, after having read the Appendix, once more to study those two Sections, from your new standing ground; for you will thus obtain a far more complete and systematic grasp of those truths, which it has been my object in this Chapter to set before you.

The importance of the truths in question is extremely great. The one main category, under which we regard men's acts in Theology, is as being right or wrong; more or less right; more or less wrong. Nor is it a small part of Theology, but more extensive than all the rest put together, which at every turn refers, both to human acts and to these their intrinsic qualities. Unless therefore you have most carefully studied the subject, you will fall for certain into one of the very worst intellectual habits, which can possibly come upon a philosophical or theological student; the habit of unconsciously using words, without precise corresponding ideas.

The principles which have here been established, will receive, as we proceed in our Theology, a constantly increasing development; and in this development we shall be very greatly assisted, by the Church's definitions, and by the labours of her greatest theologians. But I think (with the exception of one or two other truths which are to be comprised in our third

Chapter) all has here been stated, which is requisite as a *philosophical basis*, whereon that subsequent structure may be reared.

I will only remark in conclusion, that the matters handled in theological works under the head ' de principiis moralitatis,' are altogether different from those which we have been considering. This inconvenience however has not deterred me from using a title, which seemed more appropriate than any other I could think of, for expressing the contents of this Chapter.

CHAPTER II.

ON ETHICAL PSYCHOLOGY.

88. HITHERTO we have been regarding, under various aspects, those Precepts and Counsels, which God, as being All-holy, could not *but* propose to mankind. He is perfectly free, as we have so often remarked, not to create men; He is *not* free, having created them, to place before them Precepts or Counsels essentially different from these. We now turn our attention to His constitution of our own nature; we proceed to enquire, under what circumstances of advantage or disadvantage He has placed us men, by *giving* us that nature, towards the *fulfilment* of those Precepts and Counsels. The present Chapter then, however closely connected it may be in one sense with the former, yet belongs to a different part of Philosophy altogether. The former Chapter treated of necessary truth, this is to treat of contingent; the former was wholly metaphysical, this is to be wholly psychological. Let me explain my meaning in this statement, a little more at length.

Those truths, which were the object of our consideration in the previous Chapter, are truths of such a character, that it is intrinsecally impossible they should be other than they are: but those which are now to occupy us, are simply due to God's free appointment. There are various sciences, as you very well know, occupied with such truths; Astronomy, Chemistry, Botany, and the like. Just then as Botany contemplates the various properties which God has given to flowers, so Psychology contemplates the various properties which He has given to the human soul. In our former Chapter, we were not concerned at all with the phenomena of our soul, except so far as those phenomena enabled us to apprehend various truths *wholly external to the soul;* but here the phenomena of our soul are our direct object of enquiry. In every branch of human study, I need not say, our soul is the *contemplating subject;* but in Psychology, alone of all sciences whether necessary or contingent, it is also the *contemplated object.*

I make no profession however of carrying you through all Psychology. A very large proportion of mental phenomena, have no direct bearing on man's *moral* or *spiritual* action at all; and with these we do not here concern ourselves. What are the laws which regulate memory—or what is the true account of the sublime and beautiful—or what are the phenomena of the poetical temperament—these, and a thousand other psychological questions, may be of great moment to the philosopher as such; but they do not subserve the purposes of *Theology.* I call our present study then 'Ethical Psychology;' and include under it those facts of human nature, which are directly concerned with ethical truths. What means are given to each of us by nature, for knowing right and wrong?—what are the various impulses which lead in one direction and the other?—is it possible to do evil for the *sake* of evil, 'malè agere *propter* malitiam?'—are we so constituted that on the whole virtue and happiness coincide?—which is the stronger motive, and in what cases, desire of happiness or desire of virtue?—these, and many other enquiries of a similar kind, fall under our treatment. We may call it in one word the *map of our moral nature.* A historian, before he begins his narrative, prefixes an account of the country to which it refers. Here is a chain of mountains—there a rapidly-flowing river—here the soil has one important peculiarity, there another. And in like manner, before considering in order those various wonders of which man's moral nature is the theatre,—it is very con-

o

ducive to clearness, that we *first* investigate the conformation of *that nature itself*, as it came from its Creator's hands.

Such then is the character, such the limitation, of that portion of science which we here undertake. We must begin our treatment of it however, by stating various facts, which underlie the whole science of Psychology in its fullest extent.

SECTION I.

On the Three-fold Classification of Mental Phenomena.

89. I assume, from the ordinary philosophical books, a truth which is, I believe, pretty generally recognized. The soul is a perfectly simple substance. When this is said, it is very far from being meant (of course) that the soul is simple, as *God* is Simple. He is intrinsecally incapable of change; existing 'extra tempus;' "the Same yesterday, to-day, and for ever:" while the soul on the other hand, I need not say, is at every moment undergoing great changes or modifications. If I may use the expression then, I do not mean that the soul is 'extensively' simple, but that it is 'intensively' so; that it is incapable, from its nature, of any physical division. We may imagine a table or a chair, divided into its various constituent parts; we could *imagine* this, even though we were wholly unable to *effect* that division. But if we could see the soul, we should see that such division is wholly *un*imaginable, because there *are* no constituent parts into which it *could* be divided.*

90. It is also, I believe, universally recognized, that we have, and can have, no direct knowledge whatever of that substance which we call the soul. We know, and can know, no more of it, than those various successive modifications of which we are conscious. Here how-

---

* For a recital of authorities on this doctrine of the soul's simplicity, see Sir W. Hamilton's "Lectures on Metaphysics and Logic," vol. ii. pp. 5–9. Among theologians, he considers that St. Augustine, Scotus, and also the Nominalists held this view ; while St. Thomas and his followers denied it. I may add that Suarez considers it far the more probable opinion, that there is no real distinction, between the soul on the one hand and the intellect or will on the other ; and I think the later scholastics take the same opinion for granted. I imagine no one in the present day doubts it.

ever, lest this word 'conscious' be unduly contracted in its sense, I will anticipate one remark, which we shall have to make again and again hereafter.   Among the various mental phenomena whereof we are *conscious*, it is but a very small part on which we ordinarily *reflect*.   Hence it follows, that by carefully examining what passes in our mind, we are able to discover a very far greater number of phenomena than we had at all suspected.   My grounds for making this statement, will come before us as we proceed ; but I make it here, lest the word 'conscious' should be misunderstood, and limited to a sense far narrower than that which I intend.

91. Now these various mental phenomena or modi-fications of the soul, fall most obviously and irresistibly under three classes; intellectual acts, which I will call cognitions ; volitions ; emotions.   I say they fall into these three classes, obviously and irresistibly.   Any *emotion, e. g.* most strikingly resembles any *other* emo-tion, in the various laws to which it is subject; and no less strikingly *differs* in this respect from every *cognition or volition*.   Any *volition* again most strikingly resembles any *other* volition in the various laws to which it is subject; and no less strikingly *differs* in this respect from every *cognition and emotion*.   Cog-nitions are bound together precisely in the same way ; by mutual agreement with each other, and by distinction from all other phenomena.

It is of the very greatest importance, that this fundamental classification should be constantly kept before us in our psychological enquiries; and it will be a very great advantage therefore, if our very mode of speech constantly reminds us of its existence.   This service science has performed, by adopting the terms 'intellect,' 'will,' 'sensitive appetite.'   All volitions are spoken of, as proceeding from the will; all cognitions, as elicited by the intellect; all emotions, as experienced by the sensitive appetite.   We must not of course suppose for an instant, that there *is* any such thing as intellect, will, or sensitive appetite; that the soul, *e. g.* is compounded of those three elements, as a chair is compounded of legs, seat, and back.   They are but *abstractions*, used by science for the purpose of keeping constantly before our minds the great fact I have just explained — the threefold classification of mental phenomena.

92. Let us consider in order these various classes of phenomena. And first for emotions.

By emotions, as you well know, are signified all those modifications of the soul, wherein it experiences pleasure or pain of whatever character. All emotions therefore are either (1) pleasurable, or (2) painful, or (3) uniting both in various degrees. It is implied in our definition, that we include under the general term 'emotions,' what are commonly called 'bodily appetites.' And very conveniently; for it will be seen, as we proceed, that these are governed, in all essential respects, by the same laws which regulate *mental* emotions. It follows also, from what has been said, that all emotions are concerned necessarily with some *object;* the possession or thought of which causes pleasure or pain as the case may be. They move moreover *towards* such *pleasurable* object, or *from* such *painful* object, in this or that various manner. He who should enumerate every object, the possession or thought of which causes pleasure or pain; — and who should enumerate also our various feelings *in regard* to any such given object; — would tell us all that it is possible to know of the sensitive appetite.

93. I will use the word 'propension' to express our *susceptibility of pleasure or pain from the thought or possession of this or that object.* Thus my love of men's esteem, — or in other words my susceptibility of pleasure from a belief that men esteem me, — is a 'propension.' Again my love of food, — or in other words, my susceptibility of pleasure from the reception of food when I am hungry, — is a 'propension.' Once more; my hatred of bodily lesion, — in other words my susceptibility of pain from my flesh being in any way lacerated, — this is a 'propension.' And our various propensions are *gratified,* so far as we possess in some sense the various objects which give pleasure, or are free from those which give pain.

Now the very wording of the last paragraph, will

suggest a somewhat important classification of the propensions. Many of these, derive all the gratification of which they are capable, from the mere *belief* that their object exists. Take, as an instance of this, the propension which we call love of approbation. If I firmly *believe* that my fellow-creatures regard me with feelings of admiration, my propension enjoys its full satisfaction; the actual *fact* that they do so, literally adds *nothing* to that satisfaction. My enjoyment, I say, would be no whit the less, even though they held me in execration, so long as I confidently and undoubtingly *believe* the opposite. In like manner, the pleasure derived by a vindictive man from his enemy's misery, requires for its full existence nothing more than a confident *belief* that such misery exists: the *sight* of it only increases the pleasure, as making the *belief itself* more *vivid.* And there are very many other cases of a similar kind. But this is far from being true of all the propensions. I *believe, e. g.* that this is tender and nutritious food, having never tasted any better: but who will say that my appetite is as satisfactorily appeased by eating such food, as it would be if its quality were really what I think it? Still more, who will say that my appetite is satisfied, by a mere *belief* that the food *is before me?* Plainly a far closer contact with the object is here necessary, than is implied in the mere *belief* of its existence.

> Who can hold a fire in his hand,
> By *thinking* of the frosty Caucasus?
> Or cloy the hungry edge of appetite,
> By bare *imagination* of the feast?

This distinction is of sufficient importance, to require a distinct name for the two classes. Some of our propensions, we have seen, *possess* their object, by the mere fact of our *belief* that it exists; but others require a far closer contact. For want of a better name, let us call the latter 'physical propensions' and the former 'non-physical.'

St. Thomas, in one part of his " Summa," seems to imply, that the physical propensions are precisely identical with the bodily appetites; at least in that more extended sense of the word, which would include, *e. g.* love of music in that category.* I am not meaning to imply that there are *many* exceptions to this statement; but a very little thought will shew that there are *some*. Let us take what with some minds is among the strongest propensions they have,—love of adequate intellectual scope: to some minds, I say, the absence of such scope is among the keenest of miseries; the yoke of a false and narrow philosophy is a worse than Egyptian slavery. Now we may ask, are these men exempted from such suffering, simply by *believing* that their present philosophy is true and sufficient? Or rather is not the very opposite the fact? Never are they *so* miserable, as when (through misplaced reverence for authority) they undoubtingly *believe* in this false system; and their daring to doubt it is their first step, towards emancipation from this misery of intellectual bondage. Nothing then can be more certain, than that this propension is 'physical;' yet who can say that it is a *bodily appetite*, even in the most extended possible sense of that term?

Which of our propensions are physical, and which non-physical, is a question to be treated in a later Section, when we enter on a systematic consideration of our various propensions. This systematic consideration will lead, I think, to conclusions of much interest and importance; but before beginning it, it will be better to treat one or two preliminary subjects, which may be far more briefly despatched.

* 'Respondeo dicendum, quòd, sicut dictum est (a prec.) peccata recipiunt speciem ab objectis. Omne autem peccatum consistit in appetitu alicujus commutabilis boni, quod inordinatè appetitur ; et per consequens, in eo jam habito inordinatè aliquis delectatur. Ut autem ex superioribus patet (qu. 31, art. 3.) *duplex est delectatio. Una* quidem animalis, quæ consummatur in *sola apprehensione alicujus rei* ad votum habitæ ; et hæc etiam potest dici delectatio spiritualis : sicut cùm aliquis *delectatur in laude humanâ*, vel in aliquo hujusmodi. *Alia* vero delectatio est *corporalis*, sive naturalis, quæ *in ipso tactu corporali* perficitur ; quæ potest etiam dici delectatio carnalis.'—1, 2 qu. 72, art. 2. 0.

Section II.

On the Passions.

94. I observed just now, that he who should enunciate every object which causes pleasure or pain;—and should enumerate also our various feelings in *regard* to any such given object;—would tell us all that can be known of the sensitive appetite. Now to enumerate every object which causes pleasure or pain, is to enumerate our various 'propensions' (n. 93). To enumerate our various feelings *in regard* to any such given object, is to enumerate our various 'passions.' This latter is a far easier task than the former, and we at once proceed with it.

I say then, firstly, by way of definition, that whatever pleasurable or painful object be in question,—the passions are the various modes, in which my emotions *tend* to that *pleasure*, or *recede* from that *pain*. We must be on our guard here, against associations arising from the ordinary use of the term. In common parlance, the word 'passion' implies something violent and extreme: but in theological language the faintest emotion is a 'passion;' it is one or other passion, directed *to* one or other *pleasurable* object, or *from* one or other *painful* object.*

---

* The following passages from St. Thomas will, I think, sufficiently shew, that he intends to include, under the name of passion, *every kind* of emotion.

'Motus appetitûs sensitivi propriè *passio* nominatur ; sicut suprà dictum 'est.'—1, 2, quæst. 22, art. 3.

'Affectio autem *quæcumque*, ex apprehensione sensitivâ procedens, est 'motus appetitûs sensitivi.'—Quæst. 31, art. 1.

Again—'Stoici, sicut ponebant omnem passionem animæ esse malam, 'ita ponebant consequenter omnem passionem animæ diminuere actûs 'bonitatem : omne enim bonum, ex permixtione mali, vel totaliter tollitur, 'vel fit minùs bonum.

'Et hoc quidem verum est, si dicamus passiones animæ solum *inordi-*

95. The Aristotelic enumeration of the passions, which the scholastic theologians have followed, seems to me extremely good on the whole, though open to some criticism. I will first place it before you as it stands, and afterwards proceed to the requisite comments.

To fix our ideas by an instance. Let us suppose the particular propension before us to be love of approbation; or (in other words) let us suppose the pleasurable object, towards which the various passions are directed, to be the applause of our fellow-men. If I think of the fact that I am unpopular, I experience a painful emotion; 'how I long to be more admired:' this is 'Desiderium,' desire or longing. On the other hand, if I think of the fact that I am popular, I experience a *pleasurable* emotion; my spirits rise (as it were) and dance; I say to myself, 'How very delightful:' here is 'Delectatio.' I may think however of human applause, without particularly considering whether I do or do not possess it: and so I experience a much fainter emotion; 'what a pleasant thing to have:' this is 'Amor.' So here we have our three first passions; 'Amor,' 'Desiderium,' 'Delectatio.' Let us write them down, and place under them their three opposites. Thus

1. Amor.	2. Desiderium.	3. Delectatio.
4. Odium.	5. Fuga.	6. Tristitia.

These *latter* three passions are concerned with the corresponding *painful* object, unpopularity. If I think of unpopularity, without considering whether I am unpopular or not, I experience a faint emotion, 'Odium;' 'what a disagreeable thing!' If I reflect that there is great danger of my becoming unpopular, I experience the emotion 'Fuga;' 'oh that I might escape from that

' *natos modos* sensitivi appetitûs; prout sunt perturbationes seu ægritudines.
' Sed si passiones *simpliciter* nominemus *omnes* motus appetitûs sensitivi,
' sic ad perfectionem humani boni pertinet, quòd etiam ipsæ passiones sint
' moderatæ per rationem.'—*Ibid.* quæst. 24, art. 3, 0.

And he repeats the same statement almost verbatim quæst. 59, art. 5, 0.

Suarez again—' Omnis actus appetitûs sensitivi est et dicitur animæ
' passio.'

calamity.' If I reflect that I am already very unpopular,
' Tristitia' or ' Dolor :' grief at the depressing fact.

96. So far, I have no unfavourable comment whatever
to offer; nothing, I think, can be clearer or more satisfactory. I must add however one or two somewhat important facts; and firstly on the passion ' Delectatio.'

In the case of ' physical' propensions (see n. 93),
the passion ' Delectatio' may be experienced, without
our thinking in any way (explicitly or implicitly) of
its object. Thus (if it be not thought too trivial an
instance) there are many, to whom the process of
digestion is exhilarating; and who are consequently
(under ordinary circumstances) specially cheerful, immediately after dinner. This cheerfulness is none the
less experienced, though the mind is not thinking in
any way, either of the present digestion or the past
dinner. The keen and active thinker again, who has
found adequate intellectual scope, enjoys exquisite pleasure in consequence, even though he has never once
adverted to the fact.

From this it follows, that from these physical propensions, ' Delectatio' may be experienced in *three* different ways. If, *e.g.* I hear beautiful music, the sounds
give me great pleasure. If, in addition, I *advert to the
fact* ' what beautiful music I am hearing,' the *thought*
gives me further pleasure. Lastly, when it is all over,
I may *fancy* myself in imagination hearing the same
sweet sounds; and a real, though somewhat faint, ' Delectatio' then also ensues. Even in the case of non-
physical propensions, a twofold ' Delectatio' is possible.
Thus, though I know myself unpopular, I may indulge
in a *day-dream* of popularity; I may draw vivid pictures of the imaginary cheers which I receive; I may
sketch out in fancy addresses of admiration which are
to be voted me, and which are really to do some justice
at last to my admirable qualities. And so perhaps,
not unfrequently, a weak-minded man pursues this
very foolish course of thought, ' atque animum picturâ
pascit inani.' Or the native of a Southern clime again,
when unable to reach his enemy, may *imagine* him in

his power;—gloat over every detail of the *ideal* vengeance which he inflicts;—count the victim's supposed sufferings, and rejoice in his fancied groans.

These various distinctions of 'Delectatio' are sufficiently important, to deserve special names. First then, in *all* the propensions we may distinguish between 'Delectatio Apprehensiva' and 'Delectatio Imaginativa,' 'the delight of possession' and 'of imagination.' 'Delectatio Apprehensiva' will be the delight, which we experience, in *actually possessing* the object: in the case of non-physical propensions, it will be the delight which we experience in firmly *believing* that it exists; in the others, it will be the delight obtained by that far closer contact, which in their case is possible. 'Delectatio Imaginativa' will be the far fainter delight which we may derive, even when knowing the object to be absent, by *fancying* ourselves to possess it.

Then in the case of *physical* propensions, the 'Delectatio Apprehensiva' will be subdivided into 'Delectatio Physica,' the delight of *contact with the object;* and 'Delectatio Reflexiva,' the delight which ensues, from *adverting* to the circumstance that we are thus in contact. But there will be *no* such distinction as this latter, in the case of *non-physical* propensions.

There is another fact connected with this same passion, which a very little observation will suffice to establish. The pleasure caused, whether by the contact of a pleasurable object, or by the thought of its existence, often lasts for a *much longer period* than that during which such contact or thought *continues.* Let us take an instance already given of a physical propension; the delight of a keen intellect, which has found its adequate field of speculation. It is not merely that this pleasure is enjoyed, while the mind is *engaged* on that field; its possession diffuses enjoyment through the whole day. The pain which preceded was a *constant* pain, *affecting the whole current of life;* so also is the pleasure. The same truth equally holds in the case of non-physical propensions. The vain-glorious man, who has made a great hit in Parliament, or written a first-rate book, not merely enjoys the delight of praise while he is *thinking* of it; but has his whole life sweetened by it for some weeks to come.

The distinction, expressed in the respective words 'Apprehensiva' and 'Imaginativa,' is peculiar to the passion 'Delectatio;' but the other two remarks just made apply to *all* the passions. For (1) every passion, in the case of physical propensions, may be divided into 'physica' and 'reflexiva;' and (2) it is true of all the passions, that they often continue to possess us, long after the object which caused them has passed away. As an instance of the first remark, take a case of the passion 'Tristitia.' There is no more common remark, in reference to one who labours chronically under weak health, than this—how greatly his suffering is increased, if he indulges in the habit of *thinking* much on his own ailments; thus adding to 'Tristitia Physica' 'Tristitia Reflexiva.' The second remark may be illustrated by another passion. I may be wrought into a great access of rage, from the infliction of some stinging insult: this passion (as we shall soon see) is in fact 'Desiderium,' directed to the pleasurable object of *vindictive retribution*. Now it is evident, that this emotion of anger often continues, and unconsciously influences the whole current of my ideas, for a considerable period after all *thought* of vindictive retribution has ceased.

There is no need of pursuing the subject further, in its *general* shape; but there are particular reasons for saying a few words on the *particular* passion 'Desiderium,' and on its distinction (in the cases of physical propensions) into 'Desiderium Physicum' and 'Reflexivum.'

Thus take the phenomena of hunger. The bodily yearning for food may continue, and seriously affect the spirits, at times when we are not *thinking* of food at all. Here is 'Desiderium Physicum.' If, in addition, I turn my *thoughts* to my need of food, and begin *mentally longing* for the time when I shall get it, here is 'Desiderium Reflexivum;' a further suffering, and a very considerable one, in addition to the former.

To this statement perhaps exception may be taken; and it may be thought an improper expression, to say that I experience ' Desiderium' for a thing which has perhaps never entered my thoughts. This however is a purely verbal question ; on the *fact*, there is and can be no difference of opinion. I experience that uneasy sensation which we call hunger; a sensation which arises simply from the absence of food. Moreover the sensation is such, that simply in consequence of it, the sight or the thought of food leads me instinctively and at once to press towards the attainment of that object. I think that 'Desiderium Physicum cibi,' is not an unsuitable way of expressing this phenomenon; and therefore I use the expression. Those who differ from me, differ not on any question of *facts*, but on this mere question of verbal propriety.

Similiter et de motibus illis pudendis philosophandum est, qui sæpe in corpore insurgunt, dum intellectus ab omni turpi cogitatione penitùs liber est et immunis. Hi motus ad ' Desiderium' referri debent; ' Desiderium' autem ' Physicum' et non ' Reflexivum.'

And so in the other instance we have so often given : the longing for freedom from the bondage of a false philosophy. A sense of intellectual misery, and a yearning desire of escape, will often exist, when we are actually ignorant *what* is that evil which distresses us ; *what* is that relief which we seek.

Finally, it will be convenient if we here recapitulate, what are those cases in which an emotion may exist, *without any thought of its object.* We have found that these cases are of two kinds. First, in the case of physical propensions, when the passion has not been in any sense *caused* by a thought of the object; nay, when that thought perhaps has never existed. Secondly, in the case of *all* the propensions, when the passion has been caused indeed by a thought of the object, but continues long after such thought has ceased.

97. But there are five more passions in the Aristotelic catalogue; and to them I now proceed. The pleasurable object, says Aristotle, may perhaps not

only be simply a 'bonum delectabile,' but a 'bonum arduum;' an object which cannot be possessed without *danger* or *effort*. That we may derive our illustration from the same propension as before, let us take the case of military fame. Here there will be scope for further passions. Thus there may be 'Spes,' hope of obtaining this great prize ; and 'Audacia,' boldness in pursuing it : there may be also the contraries to these; 'Despera-tio,' despair of achieving so difficult an object, and 'Timor,' fear of the surrounding dangers. Thus :

| Spes. | Audacia. |
| Desperatio. | Timor. |

Further, he adds, there may be 'Ira;' rage against any one, who seeks to deprive me of this much-desired pos-session.

These last five passions are called 'irascible,' and so distinguished from the others which are called 'concu-piscible.' For what reason? Because men of sanguine and ardent, in other words of 'irascible,' temper, are quite specially disposed to 'Spes,' 'Audacia,' and 'Ira;' are disposed to them quite differently in degree from other men: whereas there is no such broad distinction among mankind, as to those who experience 'Amor,' 'Desiderium,' and the rest.

To complete the Aristotelic theory of passions, I should add one further statement. When I wish, in behalf of another, those very things which I wish in my own behalf;—dread for another those which I dread for myself;—delight in the possession by another of those very things which I delight myself in possessing;—I am said to experience for that other man the passion called 'Amor Amicitiæ,' or more generally 'Amor Benevolentiæ.' The passion which I called simply 'Amor' in n. 95, is called in full 'Amor Con-cupiscentiæ.' Opposed to 'Amor Amicitiæ' is 'Odium Inimicitiæ;' which I experience towards a person, for whom I desire those very things which I regard in my own case as evils. Opposite to 'Amor Concupiscentiæ' is 'Odium Abominationis:' such as a vain-glorious man feels for unpopularity ; or a musical man for harsh and discordant sounds.

98. All this latter part of Aristotle's theory is open (I think) to much criticism ; though the whole matter is of small moment. But first I will mention a little error, which is rather a blunder or hastiness of expression, than a philosophical mistake. He classes 'fear' and 'despair' among the 'irascible' passions : whereas of course they are of a precisely opposite character ; they are experienced *less*, in proportion as our temperament is *more* 'irascible.' But now for more important remarks.

(2.) It is surely an undeniable mistake, to speak of 'Hope' as peculiar to the pursuit of 'bonum arduum,' or as specially appertaining to men of 'irascible' temperament. Hope, in its various degrees, is common to every kind of 'bonum' and every kind of character. It may be said indeed with truth, that where the 'bonum' *is* 'arduum,' irascible men will be far more given to Hope than others : but there are numberless cases of 'bona non ardua' being very fervently hoped for, by very weak-spirited and ordinary men.*

(3.) Then the opposite to 'Hope' should rather (I think) be 'Fear' than 'Despair.' 'I hope for popularity :'

---

* Since writing the above, I have been interested in finding that Ripalda makes this same remark (de Virtutibus Theologicis, d. 21, sec. 4.) He is speaking indeed directly of 'Spes *voluntatis*,' but we shall see in the next Section, that whether the question be of Hope the *emotion*, or Hope the *volition*, the true answer, as to the arduousness of its object, must be precisely the same. Indeed Ripalda's arguments as often refer to the emotion as to the volition. I will extract a small portion of his remarks :—

"Ex quibus colligitur, Spem genericè sumptam *non* distingui à Desiderio *arduitate* objecti. Primò, quia non apparet in quo hæc arduitas objecti consistat. Secundò quia possumus *desiderare* bona ardua, quin ea *speremus;* quia ea non occurrunt [ut] futura : tunc autem datur Desiderium boni ardui, sine ullâ Spe et interdùm cum Desperatione. Tertiò quia sæpe *arduitate* objecti *crescit Desiderium et decrescit Spes :* conditio autem objectiva Spei, dividens ipsum à Desiderio, non potest *augere Desiderium et minuere Spem.*

"Hinc crediderim S. Thomam, vendicantem arduitatem ad Spem et ex ipsâ distinguentem à Desiderio, non agere de Spe *genericâ*, sed de Spe *pertinente ad partem irascibilem*, excitante bilim ad superandas difficultates objecti ardui. . . . . Unde spes non constituit in parte irascibili, quia ex conceptu *generico* Spes respicit *determinatè* bonum arduum, sed quia *capax est* ex tali conceptu bonum arduum expetere."—nn. 34, 35.

what corresponds to this on the opposite side? Surely this; 'I fear unpopularity.' And this statement is sanctioned by common usage; for Hope and Fear are always mentioned as opposed to each other.

(4.) If 'Audacia' is to be made parallel to the other passions, we must translate it 'Boldness in pursuit.' We have had 'Love' for such a 'bonum;' 'Longing' for it; 'Hope' of it: plainly then 'Audacia' will be 'Boldness in pursuit' of it.

(5.) My chief comments however must be made on 'Ira.' And here I will begin with a small criticism. It is not true (I think) that 'Ira,' in its prominent development, is peculiar to men of 'irascible' temperament. Anger exists quite as prominently and pervasively in the feeblest minds; though with them it takes a different shape, that of ill-humour, ill-temper, or peevishness. "That which in a more feeble temper," says Butler, "is peevishness, and languidly discharges itself on everything which comes in its way, this same principle, in a temper of greater force and stronger passions, becomes rage and fury. In one the humour discharges itself all at once; in the other it is continually discharging."

Next I make a remark, which goes more deeply in opposition to the Aristotelic enumeration of passions. It is obvious at once that 'Ira' does not appertain to the various 'bona,' or even the various 'bona ardua,' in the sense in which the other passions appertain to them. I experience 'Love' of military fame; 'Longing' for it; 'Hope' of it; 'Boldness in pursuit' of it; but not 'Anger' of it. Anger surely does not appertain to every 'bonum delectabile,' or even to every 'bonum arduum;' but only to one single 'bonum delectabile,' viz. 'vindictive retribution.' Anger then is no separate passion; but is one or other of the passions above named, exercised on that propension, which we may call for the present 'love of vindictive retribution.' The 'longing' for vindictive retribution; the 'hope' of it; 'boldness in pursuit' of it; finally, the 'delight' in it when attained;—all these represent the various phases of anger; they represent those phases, beginning with its commencement, and ending with its final result, where it vents itself in acts of vindictive infliction.

What was it then which led Aristotle to class it as a passion ? I imagine the following was his reason. Suppose I experience an emotion of 'Desiderium' for wealth, or power, or knowledge, — there is no very marked peculiarity, distinguishing the passion in *one* of these cases as compared with *any other*. Now on the contrary, no states of mind can be more signally distinct as phenomena, than 'Desiderium' of *wealth or power* on the one hand and 'Desiderium' of *vindictive retribution* (*i. e.* Anger) on the other hand. Hence probably it is, that Aristotle was induced to count the 'Desiderium' of vindictive retribution as a different passion from ordinary 'Desiderium.' But if this principle were to be acted on consistently — viz. of naming a distinct passion, wherever the emotion has a very distinct phenomenal character of its own, — the list of passions would be marvellously increased. Those emotions which we call *Envy*, and *Pride*, and *Vain-glory*, have quite as undeniably distinct characteristics of their own, as the emotion which we call Anger; and those emotions which relate to the Sixth Commandment, have still more peculiar characteristics. It is very far better then on every ground, that we keep once for all to the very plain and intelligible distinction, between passions and propensions.

(6.) And now we come to that part of Aristotle's theory, which represents 'Amor Amicitiæ' as a distinct passion. Plainly, like Anger, it is no passion, but a propension ; viz. my susceptibility of pleasure from my friend's interest being promoted. To this pleasurable object, or *from* the opposite *pain*, all the various passions may be directed; 'Longing' for the promotion of those interests; 'Hope' of their promotion; 'Boldness in pursuit' of their promotion ; and the rest.

(7.) Lastly, at a later period of this Chapter, I hope to shew that the passion 'Amor' is equally distinct from 'Amor Concupiscentiæ.'

99. Summing up the results of our criticism, we

P

may suggest the following re-arrangement of the ' passions.'   We will drop the distinction between irascible and concupiscible; which is indeed a very important distinction in regard to the temperament of different men, but cannot (I think) without inconvenience be introduced into the enumeration of the passions.   We retain ten passions, and may state them in the following order :—

1. *Positive.*   Amor,   Desiderium,   Spes,   Audacia,   Delectatio.
2. *Negative.*   Odium,   Fuga,   Timor,   Desperatio,   Tristitia.

On this arrangement, one only remark is necessary in conclusion.   'Desperatio' is opposed to 'Audacia,' in a way *differing* from that in which *the other* negative passions are opposed to their corresponding positives. 'Desperatio' and 'Audacia' are both exercised upon *the same* pleasurable object; whereas in the other cases the *positive* passion is directed *to* the *pleasurable* object, and the *negative* is directed *from* the corresponding *pain.*   Thus 'Desiderium' may be a longing for popularity; and if so, 'Fuga' will be a shrinking from the *opposite pain*, 'unpopularity.'   But if 'Audacia' be boldness in pursuit of that fame which is to be acquired by confronting danger, 'Desperatio' will be despair of any such fame.

Section III.

On the Relation between Will and Sensitive Appetite.

100. Whenever a passion exists, accompanied by a
thought of the pleasurable or painful object, then if no
special effort be put forth, a *corresponding act of the
will* is also elicited.   You will at once observe the
qualification, 'accompanied by a *thought* of the object.'
For *emotions*, as we have seen, frequently exist, without
our thinking in any way of the object which produces
them; * but no *act of the will* (as we shall see clearly
in due time) can ever be elicited without an accompanying thought.   And now to explain my general meaning,
in the statement which I just made.

I am by nature very susceptible of pleasure, from
being *generally liked ;* yet in fact I am but little known,
and not particularly attractive to those who do know
me.   Under these circumstances, the thought of popularity arises in my mind.   Forthwith the emotion of ' Desiderium ' is excited; that longing, yearning, emotion,
which we all so well know by experience.   I make no
effort whatever to interfere with the spontaneous course
of mental phenomena; but allow my mind to pursue its
natural course.   Under these circumstances, I shall
find on examination, that the *first* modification of the
soul, which we call the passion ' Desiderium,' has been
immediately succeeded by *another*.   This second modification is *an act of the will :* and it is truly analysed
in some such way as the following; ' I would go through
a good deal, in order to obtain popularity ;' or ' my will
cleaves to the absent pleasure of popularity, with a considerable degree of efficacity.'

* The two cases in which this may happen are enumerated at the close
of n. 96.

That this *is* in truth a second modification of the
soul, and quite distinct from the former,—would be
quite evident, were it only for the following reason.   I
have the power, as we shall soon see, to *separate* the
two *in fact;* by putting forth an effort, I can *prevent*
the act of will from following the emotion.   But
even if this were not the case, I have still the strongest
grounds possible for recognizing the two as distinct;
viz. a careful examination of my own consciousness.
In this branch of philosophy, it is simply unmeaning to
ask for any proof of a statement, except simply this:
all that a teacher can do, is to lead you (as best he
may) to fix your attention, each for himself, on those
particular facts of experience, of which he may wish to
obtain the recognition.   Now a very little of careful
self-inspection will sufficiently shew us, how totally
distinct are these two things; viz. (1) an emotion, and
(2) an act of the will.   'I am in high spirits' or 'in
grief;' 'I feel this pleasure' or 'that pain;' 'I am in
violent alarm at that danger' or 'I am yearning for that
enjoyment ;'—those various modifications of the soul,
which are *thus* truly analysed, are *emotions;* and appertain to the *sensitive appetite.*   On the other hand, ' I
am resolved on this,' 'I *choose* that,' 'I *intend* the
other with this or that degree of efficacity'—those
modifications of the soul, which are *thus* truly analysed,
appertain to the *will.*

It is important, in a degree which it is impossible to
exaggerate, that we should be most familiarly conversant with this distinction, between the will and
sensitive appetite.   We will therefore enlarge on this
part of our subject more than would otherwise be
necessary, simply for this purpose; viz. that we may
obtain of it the fullest and most familiar grasp.

101. Whenever an act of will follows any emotion
in the way which we have described, the will is said to
consent to that emotion; and the act or affection of the
will has commonly *the same name* with the passion
itself.   Thus the act of will already mentioned,—'I
cleave to the absent pleasure of popularity with such or

such a degree of efficacity'—this is called an act of 'Desiderium;' or more fully, of 'Desiderium voluntatis.'

I may here add, that an '*act* of the will,' and an '*affection* of the will,' are in Theology precisely equivalent. On the other hand, a '*disposition* of the will' is more commonly used, and by me will always be used, not to express a *present act*, but a *tendency or proclivity;* such as is generated by *habit*. Further, those acts or affections of the will, which correspond with the passions in the way we have described, may be called perhaps 'modal affections;' though I have not found them called by that, or indeed by any other, generic name.

102. Let us now go through some more of the passions, and see what the corresponding acts of the will will be. Thus the passion 'Spes' (let us suppose) is experienced in regard to the pleasure of popularity; I think of popularity as attainable, and a lively emotion of Hope ensues. Well—I put forth no special effort; and we ask what then will be the corresponding act of my *will?* The intellect, as we have seen, proposes the pleasure of popularity, as absent indeed, but practically attainable; the act of will then must be, 'I cleave to that pleasure, so proposed, with such a degree of efficacity.'

Next take 'Audacia.' I think of the fame which I may acquire by confronting danger; and my spirits rise high and swell for the encounter. Here is the passion 'Audacia.' What will be the corresponding act of *will* —the 'Audacia voluntatis?' The intellect proposes to me this pleasure of fame, as attainable by these arduous means; and my will cleaves to that 'bonum,' so proposed, with a degree of efficacity, sufficient (so long as it continues undiminished) to carry me through no small amount of trial and adventure.

Lastly, 'Delectatio.' I have at length gained that popularity which I so longed for; and my spirits dance, my heart beats with rapture, accordingly. Here is the passion 'Delectatio.' What will be the corresponding act of *will?* My intellect presents to me my popularity, as at length existing; and my will elicits an act, of which the true analysis is the following; 'I would endure many evils rather than lose this popularity at last acquired;' or 'I cleave to the thought of popularity, thus presented to me as existing, with such or such a degree of efficacity.' This affection of *the will* however is commonly called 'Gaudium' and *not* 'Delectatio.'

I might in like manner go through the other 'modal affections;' 'Odium voluntatis,' 'Fuga voluntatis,' 'Timor voluntatis,' 'Desperatio voluntatis,' 'Tristitia voluntatis,' and the rest. But after what has been said, you will find no possible difficulty in explaining their various significations.

In illustration of these remarks on the 'modal affections' of the will, three condemned propositions may be quoted : for these propositions contain mention of three modal affections ; viz. 'Tristitia,' 'Gaudium,' and 'Desiderium.'

Si cum debitâ moderatione facias, potes absque peccato mortali de vitâ alicujus *tristari*, et de illius morte naturali *gaudere ;* illam inefficaci affectu petere et *desiderare ;* non quidem ex displicentiâ personæ, sed ob aliquod temporale emolumentum.

Licitum est absoluto *desiderio* cupere mortem patris, non quidem ut malum patris, sed ut bonum cupientis ; quia nimirum ei obventura est pinguis hæreditas.

Licitum est filio *gaudere* de parricidio parentis, à se in ebrietate perpetrato, propter ingentes divitias inde ex hæreditate consecutas. (*Denz.*, prop. 13–15, p. 325.)

It is hardly necessary to say, that the 'gaudere,' *e. g.* in the first of these propositions, does not refer to the *passion* 'Delectatio,' but to that *affection of the will* which we call 'Gaudium.' There is a certain *act of will*, which the condemned writer declares is no mortal sin, and is condemned for so declaring. What is that act? It would be elicited thus : (1) my intellect would represent to me the death of such a person, as beneficial for the sake of some temporal gain; and (2) my will would simply and absolutely cleave to the object thus represented. My act might be truly analysed thus; 'I would choose, had I the power, that this man should have died, rather than that I should lose the temporal gain.' Any act, different from this, is not the 'gaudere' spoken of in the proposition. And a precisely similar analysis may be applied, to those *other* modal affections, 'Tristitia' and 'Desiderium,' which are spoken of in the three propositions.

Let us now take a few rather more complicated cases; where both propensions and passions are to be considered. Thus (1) what is meant by the will *consenting* to an emotion of *Envy?* or, in other words, what is 'Invidia voluntatis?' The *emotion* of Envy is the *passion* 'Desiderium,' directed towards some certain pleasurable object. What is precisely that object? Clearly, the bringing down A. B. somewhat more nearly to my own level. The *emotion* of Envy is a longing desire for the attainment of this pleasure. That act of the *will* then, which is rightly called 'Invidia voluntatis,' may be thus analysed ; 'I would gladly choose, if I could, that A. B. should be brought down more nearly to my own level.' Or again: 'My will cleaves with such a degree of efficacity to the pleasure, which my intellect represents to me as imaginable, of knowing that A. B. were brought down more nearly to my own level.'

What will be 'consent to the emotions of *ill-humour*,' or '*ill-humour of the will?*' We must here consider in the first place, what are precisely *emotions* of ill-humour; a question perhaps not quite so easy, as it appears on the surface. The phenomena of ill-humour, we may suppose, are such as the following. I rise up in a trying state of health, such as makes everything appear through an unpleasant medium; I feel in

fact restless and uncomfortable. Or again, little things go
provokingly wrong; I am just too late for the train, and
have to wait two hours for another, with nothing to do; or
the like. I receive the monstrous practical impression,*
that I am shamefully injured; and I consequently long
for retaliation. This state of mind leads me to feel, as
though every one I meet were a partaker in inflicting
this injury. The mere sight of a happy face is a sufficient excitement for wrath: 'How unfeeling towards
me! what a disregard to my feelings is displayed in
the fact, that this man should be happy, when I have
received such a trying annoyance!' In fact, I long to
relieve my uneasiness, by making every one I meet
uncomfortable so far as I dare. In one word then,
perhaps the emotions of ill-humour consist of the sour,
angry, desire which I experience (while the ill-humour
lasts) of inflicting small annoyance on every one I meet;
and again, of the pleasure which I feel in actually doing
so: all under the monstrous practical impression, that
they have in some way injured me. By *consent* to these
emotions, we express those acts of the will, which must
invariably be found in their company, unless I exert
myself to prevent such a result. It will consist therefore
of such acts as the following. 'I would annoy A. B.
in such a way if I could.' 'I choose to make C. D.
uncomfortable in such another way.' 'The thought of
the small disaster, which E. F. is now experiencing, is
a pleasurable thought; my will cleaves to the pleasure,
thus proposed, with such a degree of efficacity.' All
these acts being elicited, under the practical impression,
that A. B. and C. D. and E. F. are in a conspiracy to
treat me with neglect or contumely.

It is so very important rightly to grasp this distinction between emotions and volitions, that I will
give yet another instance for practice. Let us consider then, what is that act of the will, which we may
call a *murmuring against God's Providence.* And
here, as before, let us first consider the *emotion* itself.

* The precise nature of this difference, between a practical impression
and a speculative opinion, will be considered later; but the general meaning
of my statement is (I hope) sufficiently obvious.

No two emotions are more distinct from each other, than the two following. On the one hand, there is a loving and submissive desire that God may in some respects change the course of His Providence; save me from this or that temptation, from this or that calamity; or avert from His Church this or that impending evil. On the other hand, there is that emotion which we all know so well,—the repining and murmuring against God's appointments. From the first of these proceeds that loving spirit of prayer, which is always so welcome a sound to Almighty God, and which He often very signally rewards; but from the last (if unresisted) nothing issues, except sin of various kinds. I suppose that the acts of will corresponding to these two emotions,—and which will necessarily be elicited in their company unless we exert ourselves to prevent it,—may be thus respectively analysed. Act 1. ' I would choose ' this course of events rather than that, had I the power, ' *if God fully approved such a change.*' Act 2. 'Even ' though God continued to approve the present course ' of events, yet I would most certainly choose another, ' had I the power.' In the former act, the intellect proposes the object to the will, as *only desirable under the condition of God's Approval;* in the latter case such condition is wholly absent. It is the latter act, I need not say, and not the former, which is an act of discontent with God's Providence.

103. These will suffice as mere instances of the sympathy between will and sensitive appetite. But there is one particular case, which, on its own account, and not as a mere illustration, demands our direct and most careful attention.

The first remark which I wish here to make is the following. If my will cleaves to a pleasurable object as such, it is not for its *own* sake, but for the sake of the pleasure of possessing it, that we make it our choice. This is, in fact, a mere tautology; a simple truism. I choose then these pleasurable objects, for the sake of possessing them in their appropriate manner; in the case of non - physical propensions (see n. 93), for the sake of *believing* that they exist; in the case of physical propensions, for the sake of some closer contact. In the case then of non-physical propensions, that very statement, which we have just seen to be a mere truism, almost assumes the form of paradox; yet of course it is literally true. Why do I, who yield myself up to vain-glory, seek popularity? That I may have pleasure from it. How do I derive pleasure from it? by thinking that it exists, and dwelling on that thought. The very end then, which the vain-glorious man has in view when he seeks popularity, is not that he may *be* popular, but that he may *think* himself so. It is immensely *easier* to think himself popular if he *is* so, than if he is *not;* and for that reason alone he seeks popularity.

I now proceed to a further remark. We have already seen, that in the case of every propension, there are two different delights; Delight of possession, and Delight of imagination—'Delectatio apprehensiva' and ' Delectatio imaginativa.' (See n. 96.) Take first Delight of possession. The vindictive savage, who has his enemy under his power, orders the most exquisite torments to be inflicted; and gloats, though at a distance, over the thought, that this or that part of his command is being at this moment executed. Here we have delight of possession, exercised on that pleasurable object ' vindictive retribution.' The will, as we have seen, by not specially exerting itself on the occasion, elicits of course a corresponding act; called however, as I stated, an act not of ' Delectatio,' but of ' Gaudium.' ' I cleave, with such a degree of efficacity, to that pleasure which is derived from the thought, that my enemy at this moment is being tormented.' The more he thinks of this fact, that his enemy is being tormented,—the more keenly he derives from it that very pleasure, which was the end he aimed at in bringing that fact to pass.

But now, secondly, suppose I am such a savage, and that my enemy is dead or is otherwise out of my reach; still I may enjoy a subordinate and secondary pleasure. I may *fancy* him at my mercy; I may delight in the *visionary conception*, that I am inflicting the most exquisite torments; I paint to myself the expression of anguish, exhibited in his countenance; I *fancy* him appealing for mercy, and I fancy myself answering every such appeal by a fresh insult and a fresh wound. Now, suppose my soul puts forth no special effort—suppose, in other words, my will consents to this emotion—what would the act of will be called, which inevitably ensues? You see, my sensitive appetite here is not soliciting me at all to any *resolve;* it is not soliciting me, *e.g.* to meditate any *future plan of vengeance.* If *such* were the emotion, it would be ' Desiderium,' a *painful* passion; ' Oh, that I could punish my enemy !' Whereas *this* is ' Delectatio;' a *self-satisfied* passion ; a passion which desires nothing at all, unless it be its own continuance. The will's consent therefore will be simply an act of this kind; ' I choose the continuance ' of the thoughts which I am now eliciting, because of ' the pleasurable emotion which I thence derive:' or in other words, ' my will cleaves, with such a degree of ' efficacity, to the pleasure which I am now experi-' encing.' Yet this is not a case of ' *Gaudium ;*' for ' Gaudium ' is the will's consent to ' Delectatio *apprehensiva.*' ' Gaudium ' was analyzed in our very last paragraph, where we were supposing a *real* vengeance inflicted. What then is the theological phrase for the phenomenon we are *now* considering—the will's consent to ' Delectatio *imaginativa ?*' Where the act of consent (as in the supposed case) is *sinful*, it goes by the name ' Morose Delectation ;' *otherwise* it has *no* special name.

You may be surprised perhaps at the length to which I have gone, in this picture of the vindictive man. My reason is the extremely important part (alas!) held among sins, by this one of Morose Delectation, in matters of impurity. I could not go fully into particulars under that particular head; and yet I wished you clearly to understand the nature of the sin. In fact its consideration is an absolutely indis-

pensable part of the subject which we are treating;
viz. the relation which exists between will and sensitive appetite.

After all that has been said in this Section, you
will naturally ask; 'Supposing some emotion to be
' experienced which solicits to sin,—what is the most
' available way for us to *avert* the will's consent and
' *avoid* sin?' This question will very shortly come
before us, in detail and at length.

104. Before leaving however this earlier part of
our subject, one final remark should be made. We
have seen that whenever the pleasurable object is
thought of, and no special resistance is put forth, every
emotion of the sensitive appetite is invariably accompanied by a corresponding modal affection of the will.
But the converse by no means follows; and this is
carefully to be observed. Acts of the will are frequently
enough elicited, *without any corresponding emotions
at all.* Thus (to take a trivial instance), if I have
been accidentally rude to a man, I say very naturally
' I am extremely sorry for what I have done.' I don't
mean by this, that I experience the *passion* ' Tristitia;'
that I am at all out of spirits; that which I elicit, is
simply the ' Dolor voluntatis.' My intellect represents
to me the alternative of not having been guilty of this
rudeness, as a very desirable alternative; and my will
cleaves to the alternative, so represented, with this or
that degree of efficacity. In like manner (to go from
the least important to the most important instance) the
' Dolor,' required for Absolution, is not *depression of
spirits,* even the very slightest. My intellect represents the having offended God as a present evil; it
represents simultaneously the alternative of being free
from that present evil, as a very desirable alternative.
My will cleaves to that alternative, so represented,
with this or that degree of efficacity. All this you
will understand far more fully, when we come to that
extremely important subject, the relation between
intellect and will.

This statement then is undoubtedly true, and very

important; viz. that there are often acts of the will, without any corresponding emotions. Yet this very fact, undoubted as it is, is often most unduly pressed, and made the occasion of great self-deceit. Suppose I hear the lowest principles of life deliberately advocated; or I hear of acts wantonly done, most grossly injurious to the cause of God;—and suppose, in hearing such things, I experience no *emotion* at all of *holy resentment*. Well, it *may* be that I am none the less eliciting most efficacious *acts of the will*; that I am prepared at this moment to go through indefinite labour and exertion, if by such means I could avert those outrages against God's Majesty. I say, it *may* be so; but how *probable* is it that it *is* so? How should we judge of such probability, in any case where God is *not* thus directly concerned? If my mother for instance were grossly libelled, and I experienced no *emotion* whatever,— how far would you think it probable that my *will* is eliciting most efficacious acts of love towards her and zeal for her good fame? It is of course just as probable in one case as in the other.

I remember that I was once venturing to express an opinion, how odious and despicable is the character of those, who are content with avoiding Hell (as they hope) for themselves, and have no generous regard for God's interests, no zeal for promoting His general service. An objector replied; 'Oh, all that is a mere ' matter of sensitive emotion; men have no controul ' over that; it is most unjust to blame them for being ' without it.' The reply is obvious. Shew us men, of whom you will seriously state, that their *will* is most efficaciously directed to such ends;—that they are prepared to sacrifice this or that most important part of their worldly interest, in order that God may be the more honoured and served. Let *this* fact be admitted in regard to them, and the *further* fact, of their being destitute of *sensitive emotion* in the same direction, will but increase our admiration. Noble, heroic, souls, under the fearful chastisement of aridity! Surely the fact is, that in most cases, with these cold-hearted men, there seems but little sign of their *will* being in any degree more fervent than their *emotions*.

It is true no doubt, that some emotions are far more wayward and capricious than others in their visitation; and something will be said on this subject in our theological work. A man, *e. g.* may be interior, mortified and unworldly, who yet, from time to time, will think of his Saviour's sufferings with little or no sensible compassion. Yet if this were anything like a permanent *habit*, it would surely be a clamorous warning for him, to enter carefully into himself and see how things stand. It is very *possible*, that there is no fault of his in the matter; but the *presumption* would be all the other way. And this the rather, because (according to the common opinion) none but Saints are ordinarily visited with long-continued and enduring aridity. And the same principle holds, on the grief involved in repentance of our sins. If we find,—not sometimes and exceptionally, but always and habitually,—that the reflection on our past sins produces no *emotion* of grief,—it *may* be without fault of ours; and our 'Dolor voluntatis' *may* be very genuine: but we should carefully look into the question, and see if it really *be* so.

105. So much on the relation, between the passions and the modal affections of will. Now the questions of liberty and sinfulness cannot be considered in detail, till we come to our theological work; but it is very plain, and has been implied throughout, that *no* emotions can possibly be in themselves *sinful*, because they are not *in our own power*. On the other hand, those acts of will, which follow in the wake of such emotions, *are* very often sins; and in that case *the emotions themselves become temptations*. Yet there are *some* acts of the *will* which so far resemble *emotions;* viz. that they *cannot* be sinful, because the will has no power of withholding them. This shall be our next matter of consideration.

It is a remarkable fact in the constitution of our nature, that the action of our sensitive appetite greatly anticipates that of our will. My whole emotions are on fire, before my will has any real power of interfering in the matter ever so slightly. These *first* movements of the sensitive appetite last an extremely small portion of time; as we may say, for a single instant: and they are called ' *motus primò-primi.*' The scholastics are in the habit of saying, that in that single instant ' voluntas attrahitur quasi natura;' the will is drawn down by the sensitive appetite, like a piece of inanimate matter. Though you were the greatest of Saints, and though that emotion were the foulest of temptations, in that brief instant your will most unreservedly consents: most unreservedly, and yet *necessarily* (not freely) and so *without culpability.* Then follow a further number of instants, during which the emotions are called ' motus secundò-primi;' when the will has some *little* power to resist, but has no opportunity for collecting its *full* powers. In no case, as we shall afterwards see, can consent to the ' motus secundò-primi' exceed *venial* sin, however grave be the matter in which temptation takes place.

Bellarmine very ingeniously draws out this whole doctrine, from St. James, c. i. v. 14, 15. " Every one " is tempted," says the Apostle, " being drawn away " and enticed by his Concupiscence :" here, says Bellarmine, is consent to ' motus primò-primi.' " But Concupiscence conceives and brings forth sin :" here is consent to the ' motus secundò-primi,' which is *venial* sin. " And sin when consummated brings forth death :" here the Apostle represents that consent as become complete and consummated ; as become perfectly deliberate ; and so as bringing forth death, or becoming *mortal.**

---

* Accedat his testimonium S. Jacobi Apostoli, qui in 1 cap. v. 14, 15. suæ epistolæ, distinguit tentationem à peccato, et peccatum à crimine : ' Unusquisque,' inquit, ' tentatur à Concupiscentiâ suâ abstractus et illectus. ' Concupiscentia verò, cùm conceperit, parit peccatum ; peccatum verò cùm ' consummatum fuerit, generat mortem.' Ubi S. Jacobus non distinguit motus concupiscentiæ in involuntarium et voluntarium ; nec dicit, omnem motum voluntarium esse peccatum mortale, omnem involuntarium esse

106. It will be very useful to use a phrase, when speaking of intellect and will, parallel to that which we have just been considering; and to speak of ' *actus* primò-primi' and ' secundò-primi.' By ' actus primò - primi' then, we will designate those acts, which come as it were upon the intellect or will (as a heathen would say) by mere *chance;* those which the faculty elicits, before the will has the slightest power of interfering. By ' actus secundò - primi' we will designate those acts which the faculty elicits, before the will has opportunity of putting forth its *full* power.

107. Having now then mentioned those cases, where the will has either no power whatever, or very insufficient power, of resisting the sensitive appetite,— let us finally consider by what means the will can resist, when it *has* arrived at the period of mature deliberation. This question is far most commonly met with in a somewhat narrower form; viz. what power has the will of resisting *temptation?* And as this is not only the more common form but immeasurably the more important, I will treat the question at length, under that particular point of view. We shall be afterwards able, with great ease, so to state the principles we shall have evolved, that they shall be applicable to the whole general question above stated.

Aristotle has stated an extremely important psychological fact, when he says that the will governs other parts of us ' despotically ;' but that it governs the

veniale, ut Philippus Melancthon voluisset ; sed distinguit *tres* motus Concupiscentiæ. Unum involuntarium, quo quis ad peccatum incitatur, sine ullo suo consensu ; cùm ait : 'Unusquisque tentatur à concupiscentià suà ' abstractus et illectus.' Et hunc motum non dicit Apostolus esse peccatum, sed *causam* peccati ; si nimirùm accedat consensus. Alterum motum vult esse imperfectè voluntarium, cum addit, ' Concupiscentia verò, cùm ' conceperit, parit peccatum.' Esse autem hunc motum imperfectè voluntarium, et proinde peccatum, sed veniale, patet, quia nominatur peccatum, et tamen distinguitur à peccato consummato et mortem generante. Ex quo intelligimus, hunc secundum motum non esse peccatum consummatum ; nec generare mortem ; ac per hoc non esse peccatum mortale. Tertium denique adjungit perfectè voluntarium : et hunc motum esse peccatum mortale declarat Apostolus, dicens, ' Peccatum verò, cùm consummatum fuerit, generat mortem.'—BELLARMINE, *De Amiss. Grat.* lib. i. cap. 9. n. 12.

sensitive appetite ' politically.' Let us draw out the meaning of this statement.

First then, in regard to every other part of our soul and body, the will governs, either despotically or not at all. If I say ' hand, move up;' ' finger, move down ;' ' foot, walk ;' the result straightway ensues. If I say, ' intellect, turn yourself from thinking on ma-' thematical subjects, to dwelling on this parliamentary ' speech ;'—so long as I continue the command, the desired act also continues. On the other hand, if I say, ' body, become thin ;' or ' hair, grow more quickly ;' or ' stomach, digest more agreeably ;' no result ensues of any kind. Or if, without having studied mathe-matics, I say, ' intellect, contemplate the properties of ' conic sections ;'—again no result ensues. In all these cases, you see, the will either commands despotically, or commands not at all.

What is the difference between despotical and poli-tical government ? Without attempting complete pre-cision, it may be said perhaps that the distinction turns, rather on the character and circumstances of the people, than on the form of government. If the people are barbarians, trained to be mere passive tools in their go-vernors' hand, the government is despotic ; otherwise it is political. The difference which we mean to express is of the following kind. If a despot once obtains a clear view, that such a measure is important for the well-being of his country,—nothing remains, but to enact that measure and execute it. How different with a ' political' sovereign ! He sees clearly that a measure is very good and important ; but it will shock public opinion. ' I must exercise management here,' he says ; ' I must conceal my ultimate projects ; I must veil what ' I do under an acceptable appearance ; nay, I must ' cease from attempting what is best, that I may secure ' what is practicable.' Or to go in my illustrations, from one extreme of human life to another, look at the angler who has hooked a large fish. His power over it is ' political' and not despotic. If he tries by main force to land him, the line will break and the fish escape altogether.   Yet he has a very real power over the fish, if he will only understand that it is 'political.'   He draws the fish quietly backward and forward, till its strength is exhausted ; if it struggles a good deal for deliverance, he allows it a little free play for a few moments, and then begins again.   At length his efforts are crowned with success, and the fish is safely deposited in his basket.

Now this is a model for the fit way of dealing with our sensitive appetite, when we wish to controul it. I am frantic with an emotion of rage, at some stinging insult which I have received.   By help of prayer indeed and God's answering grace, I keep my *will* most firmly fixed in the right direction ; but can I compel my inflamed passions to be suddenly cool ? can I say, ' violent emotions, cease and leave me to repose ?'   I might as profitably address my command to the swelling and raging ocean.   Am I powerless then in quelling the storm ?   Very far indeed from it ; I may govern it to a very great extent, if I will only be content to do so ' politically.'   For instance, I fix my thoughts in a careful and sustained way on the fact, how immeasurably fouler and baser are those outrages which God has received at my hand, than are any which I have been called on to endure.   Or I think of the very many extenuating circumstances attending the injury I have received.   Or I think how far more deserving of pity than of anger, is the poor man who has inflicted on me this blow.   And so, in the very process of such thoughts, a gradual change takes place in my emotions ; my sensitive appetite comes into harmony with my will ; and God remains master of the whole field.

This being understood, I proceed to answer the question before us.   In every case, as we have seen, the will *consents* to the emotion, if it elicit *one particular act :* strictly speaking therefore, it *resists*, if *instead* of that one act it elicits any other act whatever. Thus it often happens, as St. Augustine says, that ' vitia vitiis vincuntur ;' a temptation to *sloth, e. g.* is overcome on the motive of *avarice*. Yet in the ordinary theological sense we are not said to *resist* temptation, unless we elicit some *virtuous*, or at least *indifferent* act, in place of that *sinful* act to which the temptation solicits.

What kind of act we may in each particular case most profitably choose, is a matter of spiritual prudence ; and to decide it is an important portion of the ascetical art. But more commonly, I suppose, it is better to fix our own mind on thoughts of the most opposite character. So, if we are suffering under strong emotions of ill-humour (see n. 102), a very good way of resistance will be, to work particularly at doing good turns to the various persons on whom our ill-humour seeks to vent itself; or if we have no opportunity for that, *wishing* them definite blessings. Under an emotion of envy, it may be well to pray earnestly that this or that definite good may befall the object of our envy ; and to do what may lie in our power, towards promoting that good. Under the temptation of vain-glory, it will always be useful to ponder carefully and in fullest detail, on various circumstances in my past life, under which I have cut a most contemptible figure ; nay sometimes perhaps to pray for still further humiliations. If the emotion be of pride, let me dwell on some fact of my life so humiliating, that I should be crushed at the very thought of the world knowing it ; in order that I may sufficiently taste my own contemptibleness. Yet, though this is perhaps the more common rule, there may be occasions often enough, when we shall act more prudently in turning our thoughts to matters altogether heterogeneous ; to mathematical studies, or to a game at cricket.

But this truth also must be carefully observed. We may be really and truly refusing our *consent* to the emotion, while we are taking no steps whatever towards *diminishing* or *subduing* it. This is evident on the surface, from what has been said. So long as my will refuses to elicit that act to which the temptation

solicits it, so long I am *resisting* the temptation.   Here
then again is a question of spiritual prudence.   Generally, no doubt, it is better to adopt measures of one
kind or another, towards *removing* the dangerous emotion altogether; yet, sometimes we shall do more
wisely, in despising it (as it were) and leaving it to
itself.   So long as the emotion be not accompanied
with the *thought* of an evil object, no effort at all will
be necessary (as we have seen)* to prevent the will's
consent: but even when the thought *is* present, much
less exertion is required for merely *averting that consent*, than would be requisite if we attempted the
further task of *subduing the emotion*.   And this very
question is often asked and thus answered in books of
Moral Theology.   Thus, St. Alphonsus (de peccatis in
genere, c. i. n. 6,) enquires, ' An peccet graviter qui
' *negativè se habet*, et positivè non resistit motui
' appetitûs sensitivi circa objectum sub mortali pro-
' hibitum.'   He takes for granted, either that there is
no *thought* of this mortally sinful object, and so (for
the moment) no temptation; or else, that at all events
the will is firm in refusing to elicit that act, to which
it is solicited.   And, supposing this, he asks, whether
a man is *further* bound to aim at subduing the emotion
itself.

One thing however is evident, and has a very important bearing on the question immediately before us.
So long as the emotion remains unsubdued, there is a
constant and most imminent *danger*, of an evil *thought*
entering the mind, and of the active temptation thus
recurring.   Suppose, *e.g.* the emotion be one of fiery
rage, occasioned by some galling insult.   There is
most imminent danger, lest ' actus primò-primi ' of the
intellect make continual incursions, representing how
pleasurable it would be to punish our foe.   If, indeed, we are faithful to grace, these thoughts, constantly recurring, are constantly put away; but then,
perhaps, *as* constantly they return again.   Under
a very violent emotion, there may be an almost un-

* (n. 100.)

broken series of intellectual 'actus primò-primi:' like
those curves of which we read in mathematics, abound-
ing in what are called conjugate points ; in other
words, made up to a great extent (as one may say) of
a number of points, which are infinite in number, and
yet *no two of them exactly in contact with each other.*
Nay, there may be an *absolutely* unbroken continuation
of foul images; specially where diabolical agency is at
work.   The will, at every instant, is occupied in rejecting the intellectual ' actus-primò - primus ' of the
former instant, while suffering in this very new instant
from a fresh intellectual incursion.   Such miserable
facts as these, often make it difficult for a holy man to
know, whether he *is* firmly resisting temptation; and
such facts accordingly have from time to time caused
most bitter anguish to the highest Saints.   ' Viri timo-
rati' are tempted to regard the very continuance of this
intellectual picture, as a proof that they have in some
degree consented; whereas the fact has very probably
been, that they have been simply acquiring great treasures of merit.

On the *particular* case then of resisting *temptation*,
the sum of our remarks will appear to be this :—

(1) In the great majority of cases, it will be very
desirable to aim, by such ingenious devices as have
been illustrated at length, to subdue the emotion.
(2) The temptation, however, may be faithfully resisted, without *any attempt to subdue the emotion;* if we
take pains to elicit some good or indifferent act at each
instant, in place of that evil act to which we are solicited.   (3) However highly inflamed be the emotion,—
so long as there is no *thought* of the evil object, there
is no *present* temptation; though we are in most imminent and momentary *danger* of temptation arising.

And on the *more general* question, of the will's
power to withstand the sensitive appetite, two propositions will state all that is important.

(1.) At every moment the will possesses the physical power, of resisting those solicitations which arise
from the sensitive appetite; or in other words, of

putting forth some different act, from that to which those solicitations invite him. The will possesses this power, through its despotic government of the intellect; by means of turning the thoughts, with an effort, into this or that totally distinct direction. How far this power is always a *moral* (as well as physical) power—as, for instance, where the emotion is a strong temptation and there is no recourse to prayer—this is quite a separate consideration, and belongs to a much later portion of our work. We have not yet treated on the difference between moral and physical power; and (though we had done so) the question just stated does not appertain to the relation between will and sensitive appetite, but turns rather on the intrinsic strength or weakness of the will itself. There is no question of more vital importance; but it does not find its fit place here.

(2.) To resist the solicitations of the sensitive appetite is one thing; to aim at *subduing those emotions themselves*, is quite a different and a further thing.

Section IV.

On Certain other Phenomena of the Will.

108. Here we close this series of enquiries, concerning the relation which exists between will and sensitive appetite. There are other enquiries, which are even much more important, concerning the will's relation to the *intellect*. But these are so indissolubly mixed up with the great doctrine of Liberty,—and this again with the most controverted portions of the 'Grace' treatise,—that we must defer their methodical investigation till we enter on Theology. Several truths, indeed, which are then to be fully and methodically considered, will by necessity be partially implied and taken for granted in the earlier part of the course; as, in fact, they have been already. But the full statement and development of those truths must come later.

There are certain propositions however, in regard to the will, over and above those treated in the last Section, which even at this early stage require to be stated with some degree of definitiveness and clearness. To do this will be our purpose in this present Section.

The 'modal affections' of the will, 'Amor,' 'Desiderium,' and the rest, are comparatively seldom spoken about, I think, eo nomine in Theology; except when the relation between will and sensitive appetite is being considered. Different phrases are commonly used, whether to express the same or other phenomena; such phrases I mean, as 'Intentio finis,' 'Fruitio finis,' 'Electio mediorum.'

109. By 'Intentio finis' is signified something more than '*Amor* finis;' it is more nearly analogous perhaps to the modal affection 'Spes.' The intellect proposes the end, not merely as desirable, but as in some degree

' hìc et nunc' attainable. To the pursuit of this end, the will cleaves with greater or less efficacity ; in other words, I resolve at once to aim in some way or other at some attainment of the desirable end. Then comes ' Electio mediorum;' out of the various means conducive to that end, I choose this or that according to my innate freedom. Lastly, so far as I succeed, comes the ' Fruitio finis.' This, precisely and in every respect, corresponds to the modal affection ' Gaudium.' My intellect represents the pleasurable end, as in greater or less degree attained; and my will cleaves to that end, so represented, with greater or less efficacity. In other words, I elicit an act of which this is the true analysis; ' I would go through this or that amount of ' exertion, rather than lose this pleasure which I have ' thus attained.'

The whole of this statement, which we find in the books, must be understood in a sense, not inconsistent with the following undoubted fact. It happens again and again, that it is the suggestion of *media*, which changes the ' *Amor* finis' into an ' *Intentio* finis;' that the thought of the means comes in fact *first*, and the intention of the end is *later*. For instance, I am a very vain-glorious man : so often therefore as I think of popularity, I elicit a very energetic act of the will, under the head 'Amor finis.' A particular *means* of acquiring fresh popularity offers itself; the going up to town, to speak at a public meeting in favour of some popular question. Immediately I elicit an ' intentio finis;' a resolve to increase my popularity in the way suggested : and I adopt the requisite *means* accordingly.

110. In order to attain my end, a *connected chain* of means is often necessary. I live four miles from a railway-station, and that station is eighty miles from London. I walk to the railway, that I may be carried to London. Here then (1) I walk to the railway, in order that I may obtain the convenience of the train. (2) I desire the convenience of the train, that I may more comfortably go to London. (3) I desire to go to London, in order that I may attend a meeting which

will be held there.   (4) I desire to attend that meeting, in order that I may be the more popular.   (5) I desire to be more popular, in order that I may *think* myself so.   (6) I desire to think myself so, because of the great pleasure which that thought gives me.

In this connected chain of ends, the last named is that which we call the '*absolute*' end; viz., 'that I may enjoy the pleasure of thinking myself more popular.'   The other ends are '*relative*' or '*intermediate*.' Instead of 'absolute end,' the phrase 'ultimate end' is more commonly adopted; but there is such very great variety of usage, as to the sense of this phrase 'ultimus finis,' that I must prefer 'absolute end.'   I propose therefore universally to adopt that phrase.

On ' Fruitio finis' and ' Electio mediorum,' nothing more need be said; but ' Intentio finis' must be considered under some further aspects.

111. If I am really doing or resolving on A *for the sake of* end B, I am at this moment *desiring and intending* end B.   This is so very obvious, that no explanation or argument can make it more so.   If I am not at this moment desiring B *at all*, how *can* I be resolving on A for its *sake?*   I may be desiring A; but my reason for doing so at this moment will be something *else*, and not my desire of B, if I am *not* desiring B at this moment at all.*

It is most important however to observe, that I may be most really *desiring* B, and yet not *consciously thinking* of B.   The full consideration of this most important fact, belongs of course to the general question of the relation between intellect and will; yet even at this early stage, some general notion of what is meant seems indispensable.   Take then the following hints, from the illustration already given, where I am walking to the next town to catch the train.   Suppose a friend

* " Impossibile est aliquid actu appeti prout *utile est*, et non ex voluntate aliquâ *quæ actu maneat* circa finem, saltem confusè apprehensum. Quòd si nec maneat voluntas finis confusè apprehensi, jam medium non *poterit* appeti prout utile [sc. *ut* medium], sed quatenùs honestum aut jucundum seu delectabile *secundùm se* [sc. ut *finis*]."—VASQUEZ, in 1m 2æ, d. 4, c. 2.

is with me, in whose conversation I am very greatly interested. I will suppose that there are a great number of different turns in the road, which I am quite as often *in the habit* of taking, as that *particular* route which leads to the town. My friend and myself pursue our walk, quite engrossed in the interesting matters which we are discussing ; and we are quite surprised to find how quickly the time has passed, and that here we are at the station. Now it is plain (completely as we seem to have been engrossed by our conversation, little as we have *explicitly* been thinking about town or railway,) that the intention of going to the town *has really and actively influenced us throughout.* How otherwise can you possibly account for the fact, that we have steadily pursued *that one road*, neglecting the innumerable turns which I have supposed to exist? Will you say that the *habit* of going to the town is enough to account for it? Not at all; for I have supposed that there is none of the turns, which I have not equally been in the *habit* of taking. There must have been an intention, *really inflowing* into my acts ; really, practically, energetically, influencing me;—and yet such, that I have not been *reflecting or thinking of it* at all.

This unconscious intention may be very *definite ;* or it may be *vague* to almost any imaginable extent. In the above case evidently it is most definite. So definitely are my intentions fixed on that particular town, that in every single instance,—without so much hesitation as would reinstate a conscious reflection on what I am doing,—I choose, as a matter of course, the one road thither leading, in preference to any other alternative. But why do I wish to catch the railway and go to town? It may well be that *this* consideration is not at all definitely before my mind. It may well be, that I am not definitely aiming at all at the pleasure of popularity to be gained at the public meeting. It may well be, that I have no more definite *thought* of my motive for going to London, than that it is for the sake of some end or other, *vaguely remembered*, as having been thought by me pleasurable when I formed the intention. But if this be so, then it is not strictly true to say that I am at this moment desiring to go to town for the sake of acquiring popularity. The act, whereby, during my walk to the town, I desire to reach the train, will be truly analyzed thus ; 'I 'desire to catch the train, for the sake of some end, of 'which I merely remember that I thought it pleasurable 'when last I distinctly thought of it at all.'

It will be in accordance with theological usage, if we call the intention 'implicit' while it remains (without our thinking of it) in a *definite* shape; and 'virtual' when it is only the *vague memory of it* which continues. Meanwhile we may keep the term 'unconscious' intention for the present, as a *common* term ; as including *both* 'implicit' *and* 'virtual.'

The statements of theologians on this subject will be more suitably introduced, when we treat the subject itself at length ; *i. e.* when we treat definitively the relation between intellect and will. On the other hand, the *facts*, here stated, have their appropriate evidence of course in our own consciousness.

112. We have hitherto spoken, as though I aimed but at *one absolute end* in the same instant. But this is *most rarely* the case; and in general a *considerable number* of absolute ends are *simultaneously* inflowing into the Will. If I go to town, it will probably not be *merely* for the sake of attending that meeting: there will be some interesting matters to talk over with my lawyer; and some old friend to see, from whom I have long been separated. Even when these are *most* vaguely represented, my will will be aiming, not at 'one end' but at *various* ends ; of which I remember that I *thought* them pleasurable, when I last distinctly thought of them at all.

The common theological usage is to consider only *one* absolute end as appertaining to *one* 'actus humanus.' Hence in those very numerous cases where more than one absolute end is influencing my will, as many different *acts* are considered to be simultaneously proceed-

ing, as there are different absolute ends. Suppose, *e. g.*
that I help a poor man, through a mixed motive of
virtuousness and vain-glory : it will be considered that
two acts of mine are simultaneously proceeding ; one
virtuous, the other vicious under the head of vain-glory.

113. You will at first be more than a little surprised, at the notion that intellectual acts, so important
and so influential, can proceed in the mind with so little
reflection.   This fact indeed is one of the most important in all Psychology ; and when we treat on the
relations of intellect and will, it must receive our most
careful attention.

This will be a convenient place for stating more
distinctly, that the phrase ' Intentio finis ' is used quite
as properly, in regard to a ' relative or intermediate' end,
as in regard to an ' absolute' end.   Thus in the instance
of walking with a friend to catch the railway, the end
was merely ' relative or intermediate;' yet we have said
that the ' implicit intention ' of that end influenced me
throughout the walk.

114. We have considered hitherto *two* kinds of intention, directed towards an end; ' explicit' and ' unconscious.'   There is a third kind very frequently met
with in Theology ; viz. ' habitual.'   The habitual intention of an end which has once been proposed, is
considered to continue so long, as it is not explicitly or
implicitly *revoked*.   Thus suppose a priest forms the
intention to-day, of offering all his masses for the next
month for some definite object.   He thinks no more
about it; the intention in no sense inflows further into
his acts, neither explicitly nor unconsciously; but still
his ' habitual intention ' is not on that account considered to cease.   But suppose, at the end of a week,
totally forgetful of his former intention, he makes
the intention of offering all his masses of the next
week for a purpose altogether different.   This is an
implicit *revocation* of his former intention ; because,
though he has lost all memory of that intention, the
latter intention is directly inconsistent with the former.
The former intention then is said to be implicitly re-

voked; the habitual intention is said no longer to remain. The former intention may also of course be *explicitly* revoked; but this is too plain to need illustration.

Now this theological use of the word 'habitual,' is very different from that which ordinarily obtains. In ordinary parlance, the phrase 'habitual intention' would be considered as implying a *far* closer connection with *present action* than it does in Theology. For instance, I should naturally say 'I have an *habitual intention* of avoiding mortal sin;' but this would mean a great deal more than, 'I once intended it, and have not since intended the contrary.' It would mean nothing less than this; 'so soon as I am for a moment tempted to 'mortal sin, that intention of avoiding it, which *was* 'latent, becomes apparent; that which *was* dormant is 'roused into action.' Or consider, if it be not too light an example, the kind of intention which I have to wind up my watch at night. I should naturally call it an 'habitual intention;' yet plainly it is much more, than that merely I *once* intended to do so, and have never *revoked* that intention. As soon as the ordinary time for the process arrives, by a sort of habit or instinct, the *actual* intention is awakened, and the act succeeds as a matter of course. Or take the kind of intention which is engendered by any virtuous habit; the habit of temperance, for instance. Suppose that by long self-discipline I have become temperate in a high degree. Well, I am not eliciting acts of temperance all day long; yet all day long I *do* possess a certain quality of soul, in virtue of which, so soon as the *opportunity* of temperance arises,—so soon as I sit down to table, —various temperate intentions actually influence and direct my will.

I think it is of great importance for various theological purposes, that this particular kind of intention should be carefully recognized; and in order that it may be so recognized, it will be far better to give it a separate name. Let us call it therefore a 'prevalent' intention. I am said accordingly to have a 'prevalent' intention of doing this or that, when I have no intention indeed of the kind (explicitly or unconsciously) *at this mo-*

ment influencing my will; but when my soul is *in fact so constituted,* (whether by nature or habit,) that on the suitable occasion such an intention *would* quite certainly and spontaneously arise. A 'prevalent intention' then is, in fact, *one particular species* of 'habitual' intention; but a species possessing many important properties of its own. A 'prevalent intention' implies that some certain quality exists at this moment in the will; but a 'merely habitual' intention by no means implies this.

We had better (to prevent confusion of ideas), sum up here, and place in one view the various subdivisions of 'intention' which have been suggested. There is at first starting a three-fold division; viz. into 'explicit,' 'unconscious,' and 'habitual' intention. Then 'unconscious' is further subdivided into 'implicit' and 'virtual;' while 'habitual' is also subdivided into '*merely* habitual' and 'prevalent.' Lastly, going back to the original threefold division, 'real' includes *both* 'explicit' and 'unconscious,' as *distinct* from 'habitual.'

115. I must not close for the present this matter of intention, without begging you again carefully to distinguish 'Intentio' from 'Amor' or 'Desiderium.' 'Intentio' always implies (as we have already observed) that we propose to *aim* at the end. Whenever our will cleaves to the end as desirable, without any purpose or notion of ourselves *aiming* at it, our act is either one of 'Amor' or 'Desiderium.' Look, for instance, at the two first, out of those three condemned propositions already quoted in n. 102:—

Si cum debitâ moderatione facias, potes, absque peccato mortali, de vitâ alicujus tristari, et de illius morte naturali gaudere, illam *inefficaci affectu* petere et *desiderare,* non quidem ex displicentiâ personæ, sed ob aliquod temporale emolumentum.

Licitum est absoluto *desiderio cupere* mortem patris, non quidem ut malum patris, sed ut bonum cupientis ; quia nimirùm ei obventura est pinguis hæreditas.—DENZ. prop. 13, 14, p. 325.

In the second of these occurs the phrase, 'absoluto

desiderio cupere mortem patris.'   The question is not at all, in regard to the least thought of *murdering* his father; but simply of his will cleaving to his father's *death*, as to a desirable object.   And, in the first propo- sition, the words '*inefficaci* affectu petere et *desiderare*' do not refer at all to what is called '*Intentio* inefficax,' but simply to 'Desiderium;' as the very words shew. The same remark applies to the '*absoluto desiderio* cupere' of the second proposition.   On the other hand, the distinction between '*Intentio* efficax' and 'ineffi- cax' cannot possibly be, that in the latter case we do not *aim* at the end; that 'Intentio inefficax' does not ordinarily result in action; for if it did not, it would not *be* 'Intentio' at all.   No: the distinction between '*In- tentio* efficax' and '*inefficax*' turns on *the greater or less degree of firmness or tenacity* with which the will resolves on aiming at the end.   As this distinction is one of no slight importance, I hope carefully to consider it in our work 'de actibus humanis.'

116.   This will be a convenient place, for stating an- other very important proposition in regard to the will. This proposition is so obvious, when stated, that you will wonder at me for taking the trouble to enunciate such a truism; and yet I hardly know one doctrine so frequently neglected.   It is this:— *Good and bad acts of the will are what they are, and not what we reflect on them as being.*   Notwithstanding the obvious un- deniableness of this proposition, I will add a few words to explain its meaning.

In order that any act of the will may take place, a certain object must be represented by the intellect, as possessing this or that combination of qualities; as in- vested with these or those accompanying circumstances. To the object, thus presented, the will freely tends in a certain intrinsic mode; and thus the act is complete. Many such acts take place, without the intellect re- flecting on them in the slightest degree.   But it often happens that the case is otherwise; that the intellect *does* reflect on the act itself, and analyzes it truly or falsely as the case may be.   My thesis is this: that the

act is what it is; and that, supposing the intellect were
to analyze it ever so mistakenly, such an intellectual
error could in no possible way affect the real character
of the act itself.

Now the neglect of this very plain truth, often leads
us to think our acts better, and often worse, than they
really are.   For instance, we desire to make acts of
faith, hope, and charity; and many men unaffectedly
think, that if we have recited (with seriousness and
attention) the words put down for us in our prayer-
book, we have accomplished our end.   I will give you
at once a 'reductio ad absurdum' of this most wild
misconception.   It is theologically certain (as we shall
see in due time) that every sinner, even the foulest,
who elicits a real theological act of 'Amor super omnia,'
is at once justified 'extra sacramentum.'   Now from the
notion which I am attacking, this strange result would
follow; that the foulest sinner, who should with seriousness and attention recite the words put down in the
prayer-book for a theological act of love, would be
ipso facto justified without a moment's delay;   an
adopted son of God; an heir of Heaven.   A short and
easy road indeed to that happy abode ! *

You will ask at once, what conditions are necessary,

---

* So the most lenient Francolinus—'Peccatoribus, ut *facile* est ore
pronunciare formulam contritionis, ita perdifficile est *verè et ex corde* talem
actum facere.'   *De Dolore requisito*, l. 1, c. 1, n. 38.   He draws attention
to the same distinction, in regard to attrition also, between reciting the due
formula and eliciting the due act.   *De Pæn. Disc.*, l. 3, c. 3, sub finem.
Lugo, '*Quis* certò scit *veram fuisse* contritionem quam habuit ?'   *De
Pænitentiâ*, d. 7, n. 266.   Turlot, 'Nolim putes contritionis actum consistere
aut perfici *verbis quibusdam studiosè conceptis ;* v. g. *dicendo*, 'Domine Deus
doleo,' &c. . . . . . sed in *cordiali affectu* sub ejusmodi verbis supposito.'
Catech., pars 4, c. 5, lec. 2.   F. Vaubert, S. J., 'La première chose dont il
faut se garder, c'est de s'imaginer avoir fait un acte de foi ou d'espérance
ou de quelqu'autre vertu que ce soit, lorsqu'on en a *prononcé du bout des
lèvres* quelque formule, ou qu'on l' a seulement repassée dans sa mémoire.
. . . . . Il y a autant de différence entre un acte de vertu, et ces formules
qu'on sait par cœur ou qu'on lit dans les livres, qu'il y en a *entre le roi et
son portrait*.'   *Traité de la Communion,* par. 4, n. 2.   Ripalda, '*Ægrè
potest* homo *discretionem* facere *rationum* formalium *quæ ipsum movent* ad
suos actus.   Ego experimento cerno id haud facile fieri.'   *De Ente Super.*
d. 45, n. 13.   Ripalda quotes Suarez to the same effect : 'Nunquam
homo scit evidenter, an ex purâ supernaturali ratione moveatur et opere-
tur ?'   *De Gratiâ*, l. 2, c. 11, n. 35.

that our acts may *really* be acts of faith, hope, and love.* It is impossible of course to exaggerate the importance of this question; both that you may yourselves elicit such acts, and that you may hereafter teach your people how to do so. We shall consider it therefore in its due place, with a care and completeness, not disproportioned (I hope) to its most vital practical moment.

So much on the case, where we think our acts better than they really are. But we often think them worse. A good man, again and again, elicits real acts of faith, hope, and love, from the very depths of his believing, hoping, and loving heart, without reflection of any kind. And here non-theological men are continually apt to fancy, that these are not *true* acts of faith, hope, and love at all. Having in the former case said of an act, that it *is* what it is *not;*—here they begin to say, that it is *not* what it *is:* just as if a lion were not a lion, nor a tiger a tiger, unless ticketed and labelled as they might be in a menagerie! Among all the various acts of love, which our Blessed Lady was eliciting without intermission in viâ, I should like to know how many she *reflected upon* or analyzed. Of course, her thoughts were so absorbed in God, that she had neither leisure nor inclination to turn, from the thought of Him, to the thought of herself and her own acts.

Our proposition, however, must be carefully guarded against misconception. Any act of will depends of course essentially, for its character, on that intellectual act which *preceded* it; I am only saying, that it does *not* depend for its character in the slightest degree on any intellectual act which *follows* it. It depends, for its character, essentially on the mode in which its object was intellectually represented; I am but saying that it does *not* depend at *all*, for its character, on any *other* intellectual act, *except* this. Take two instances in illus-

---

* Acts of faith, being intellectual, might appear as not strictly in point: but the ' pia affectio voluntatis' *is* of course an act of will ; and the act of faith follows from that ' pia affectio ' as a matter of course.

R

tration. Suppose acts A and B are precisely similar, in
regard to the thing externally done; for instance, eating meat on a Friday : but that they differ totally in
the preceding intellectual representation.   In performing act A, I remembered the Church's prohibition; but
in performing act B I totally forgot it.   Or more generally, in one case the thing done was intellectually proposed as sinful; in the other case not.   It is plain that
these two acts are as different from each other in character, as any one act can well be from any other.

But now suppose (and it is the case contemplated
by the proposition we are considering) that you and I
both commit an act, which we perfectly knew at the
time we did it to be mortally sinful ; which, in both
cases, the intellect represented as such *at the time of its
commission*. You and I, however, are most different in
character and habits.   You are a *novice* in sin; and for
that very reason, the remembrance of what you have
done haunts you through the day.   But for myself, I
am from long habit callous and obdurate; I am constantly *in the habit* of doing things which I know to be
mortally sinful; and the result is, since this particular
act had nothing specially to distinguish it from a hundred others done in the day, that I have never *reflected
on it for a moment*, either as being sinful or otherwise.
It is obvious on the very surface, that this distinction
between you and me, a distinction wholly *external* to
the act, cannot by possibility be a ground for any distinction, between the respective character of *these two
acts themselves.**

117. We are now in a position to draw out the
various kinds of ' bonum.'   To enter on the full mean-

---

* I am not here meaning to imply an opinion, that for mortal sin
it is always necessary, that the object *should* be explicitly proposed
by the intellect as sinful.   This is a question much controverted in
the schools ; and my own opinion on it is, that in the case of obdurate
sinners such explicit proposition is *not* requisite for mortal sin.   This
opinion I shall defend to the best of my power, in its proper theological
place, by such arguments as appear to me cogent.   Still it must always
remain true, that an act, in which the object was *not* proposed by the intellect as sinful, possesses a very important intrinsic difference from one in
which it *was*.

ing of the word 'bonum,' would lead us to philosophical enquiries, which are important indeed, but
somewhat complicated.   This is in no sense requisite,
for the sake of that part of Theology, to which our
present work is an introduction.   We may answer
all our necessary purposes here, by defining 'bonum'
simply as 'that at which the human will can aim.'
Of how many kinds then are 'bona?'

118. First, as we have already seen in many instances, the human will can aim at *pleasure;* or in
other words, one class of 'bonum' will be 'bonum
delectabile.'   We may aim either at 'positive' or at
'negative' pleasure; by 'negative pleasure,' meaning
'relief from pain.'   Moreover we can pursue pleasure,
whether positive *or* negative, in two different stages;
we may pursue *present* or *future* pleasure.   And now
to give examples of these different phenomena.

If I eat of some attractive dish, which I know will
make me ill next day, I am pursuing 'present positive'
pleasure.   If, when next day comes, I refuse to take
the medicine, which has been rendered necessary by
that indulgence, I again pursue *present* pleasure; but
here it is *negative.*   If I rise early, and go to bed late,
and deny myself sufficient food and recreation,—all for
the purpose of amassing vast wealth, in order that I
may derive therefrom every kind of comfort and indulgence—I am pursuing 'future positive' pleasure.
You will say perhaps, that the *prospect* of that *future*
pleasure is itself *present* pleasure.   During great part
of my labour it is so; but even then, a very little consideration will shew that this accounts only for *part* of
my will's energy (see n. 112).   One absolute end may
be the *present pleasure* of looking forward to future
wealth; but another absolute end, quite as influential
or probably much more so, is the *future* pleasure,
which I consider as promoted by this present toil.
Indeed there are commonly periods, not inconsiderable
in duration, when the *present* pleasure quite ceases;
periods which correspond, in the Devil's service, to
times of aridity in the service of God: during *these*

periods we are working *exclusively* for future positive
pleasure.   Lastly, perhaps I work hard day and night,
to get up my defence in some trial, which threatens my
fortune or my life : in such case I am working for
future negative pleasure.   So far indeed as I labour
for the purpose of appeasing my *present* emotion of
fear, so far no doubt I am pursuing a *present* negative
pleasure; but when this emotion of fear is for the
moment away, I am still able to work very energetically and consistently ; and I am thus pursuing 'future
negative' pleasure.

So we see that the human will can pursue bona
delectabilia in four different shapes : (1) present positive pleasure ; (2) present negative pleasure ; (3)
future positive pleasure ; (4) future negative pleasure.

Again, we may further subdivide 'bonum delectabile,' according to the particular nature of that propension, to which any such 'bonum' respectively appertains.   Some propensions, as we have seen, are
satisfied by our merely *thinking* that their object
exists ; others require a far closer contact (see n. 93).
Those 'bona delectabilia' which belong to the latter
class, we may call 'bona physicè delectabilia;' the rest
'mentaliter delectabilia.'

118. Secondly, we are able (in some degree at least)
to pursue virtuousness for its own sake; or in other
words, a second kind of 'bonum' will be 'bonum honestum.'   This will be most evident by giving a few
instances.

Take that case of the deposit, which we had so
constantly before us in the last Chapter.   Plainly I
have the full power of giving back my friend his jewel,
for no reason in the world, except simply because I am
under the obligation of doing so.   Or if I have contracted a small debt, the payment of which is in no way
inconvenient, I am fully able to make such payment
on demand, for no reason in the world except because
it would be *dishonest* to refuse.

Now take a further instance.   Suppose I am assailed by a violent temptation against the Sixth Com-

mandment; suppose all my emotions, the whole of my sensitive nature, enlisted for the moment on the side of sin. I kneel before a crucifix; and while praying earnestly to my Saviour for help, I ponder at the same time with so much earnestness on the baseness of repaying His bounteous love with ingratitude, that I am sustained for a while against temptation simply by this prayer and this thought. Presently perhaps, in order to strengthen my resolution, I call before my mind such *further* thoughts, as the fearfulness of Hell suffering, and the various appalling torments which would there await me; and when I *have* done this, my *emotions* no doubt are in some degree helping me on the side of virtue. But let us confine our attention to the earlier part of this resistance; to the part which elapsed, *before* this appeal to sensitive fear. During that earlier part, I was performing an admirable act, under the head of purity: and for what end? Simply the virtuousness of shewing gratitude for my Redeemer's love. What other end can be named? It was in no degree for the sake of any devotional sweetness; for my whole sensitive appetite was at the time playing the Devil's game, and acting directly against the cause of virtue. I repeat, the end was, and could be, no other, than the virtuousness of shewing gratitude for my Redeemer's love.

Here you may make the objection, that this act of virtue was (1) supernatural and (2) rendered possible only by prayer. As to its being supernatural, this plainly does not affect the question. Reason shews us that the act above described is good; and experience shews us that it may exist. These two truths are in no way interfered with by a third truth; viz. that this act is not *good* only, but *supernatural* also. Indeed it may be well here to state briefly a fact, on which, under the head of Grace, we shall have to enlarge. God takes care always to adjust His grace to the fixed and recognized laws of our nature; according to that well-known maxim of the schools, 'Gratia se accommodat Naturæ.' Why does He so act? Because the whole

Christian religion is based on *faith;* and if we could *experience* the Supernatural, there would be no *room* for faith.

Now for the second supposed objection: viz. that the act was only rendered possible by prayer; that by prayer only was I able thus manfully to acquit myself in the conflict; that, had prayer (at least implicit prayer) ceased, my will would soon have surrendered to my bitter enemy. This fact undoubtedly *is* an observed fact of human nature, and not known merely by Revelation; viz. that when I make use of prayer, I am able to do ten thousand good acts, which without prayer I could *not* do. No more important fact than this can be named in all Psychology; and it is one, on which we shall lay the very greatest stress in all our work. Still this fact in no way interferes with our conclusion. It was a fact undoubtedly, that I was praying; but it was no less a fact, that I was eliciting a most energetic act of purity, from the pure end of gratitude to my Saviour.

You will ask, as I can aim simply at a *future* 'bonum delectabile,' can I also aim simply at a *future* 'bonum honestum?' The question is of some nicety, and shall be treated under 'de actibus humanis.' But it is of no practical importance; for no act can be *virtuous*, unless it be done for the sake of *present* 'bonum honestum;' for the sake of that virtuousness which is inherent in the act itself. (See n. 56, p. 123.)

In the catalogue then of 'bona,' we are fully warranted in adding 'honestum' to 'delectabile.'

120. Before going further, it may be asked, can there be an *unconscious* intention of 'bonum honestum,' as we have seen there so often is of 'bonum delectabile?' A very little observation of what passes in our mind, will shew that this *is* a *most common* phenomenon. Perhaps the following illustration will help us in making the necessary introspection.

Some fifty years ago, men of the world were in the habit of using most foul and obscene language, in conversation with each other; yet they always thought it most ungentlemanly to use such expressions in the presence of ladies. I will suppose two gentlemen of the period to be most busy in conversation with each other, while ladies are present. They are wholly engrossed, so far as they are themselves conscious, with the subjects which they are upon ; politics, or the stock-exchange, or sporting. They are not explicitly *thinking* of the ladies at all; and yet, if they are really gentlemen, the presence of the ladies exercises upon them a most real and practical influence. It is not that they find themselves to *fall* into bad language, and then apologize. No ; they are, during the whole time, so restrained by the presence of the ladies, that they *don't dream of such expressions.* Yet on the other hand, no one will say, that the freedom of their thought and conversation is perceptibly influenced at all.

If it be so common a thing to preserve an unconscious remembrance of our *fellow-men's* presence, how abundantly practicable must it be, to preserve a remembrance, precisely similar in kind, *of our Creator !* And interior men, by reflecting on their daily life, will find that this is altogether so with them; that they preserve a practical impression of God's presence, which really inflows into their thoughts and powerfully influences them. They know at the same time that this is no matter of *conscious reflection ;* nor does it in any perceptible degree affect their power, of applying freely and without encumbrance to their various duties as they successively arise.

It will be further asked, is there, in the case of ' honestum,' the same distinction between 'implicit' and ' virtual,' which we have recognized in the case of ' delectabile ?' The question is of no great practical moment, but I think that there *is* this distinction. By one illustration, I shall be able both to explain my statement, and sufficiently to evince its truth.

Suppose I set myself carefully to elicit that important act, which is called one of ' Amor super omnia,' or ' sovereign Love.' What the necessary requisites are for such an act, is a question of extreme moment, to be considered in our theological course; but we will suppose that they have been attained.   While my mind remains in this posture, or (in other words) while this act proceeds, I apply myself to the performance of various incumbent duties.   For some little time, in all probability, the act remains unchanged; the various duties are performed on the highest of all possible motives.   By degrees however, my remembrance of God becomes more vague, though still most real; this *special* act of sovereign *Love* is changed into a combination of *other* acts, of which God is more or less directly the Object; such as those which we shall consider in Theology, under the name 'acts of obedience,' 'religion,' and the like.   So soon as this is the case, there ceases to be an intention of that *peculiar* end which is appropriate to sovereign *Love;* for that special end (by hypothesis) no longer inflows into the will. And yet that very end *virtually* remains; for the ends, which now actuate my will, are but the present *effect and echo* of that *former* end.

121. Returning now to our catalogue of 'bona'— are there any other absolute ends at which the human will can aim, besides those two which we have considered, viz. virtue and pleasure ?   For instance — can we ever act 'propter *malitiam*,' for the mere *wickedness* of an act ?   It is agreed by all Catholic theologians and philosophers, that we can*not;* according to the phrase so constantly quoted by St. Thomas, 'nemo intendens ad malum operatur.'   And this statement is undeniable. Take the very wickedest man in the whole world, and get him to fix his thoughts carefully on such topics as these : 'what foul ingratitude to neglect my Redeemer;'—'how exquisitely base and mean to ruin the friend that trusts me.'   Will it be found that such considerations *spur him on* to evil action? that his spirits *rise* with the contemplation ? that he enters with increased vigour and refreshment, into further acts of sin ?   On the contrary, he knows most thoroughly, to the very depth of his heart, that the *reverse* will take place; and for that very reason, *we can't get him to dwell on such thoughts at all.*

We all of us know,—he knows and we know,—that if we can only get him duly to *ponder* on such thoughts, our success in reclaiming him will be secure.

Man then is physically unable to act wrongly '*propter* malitiam;' quite as unable as he is to cross a bridge of paper or fly up into the moon.

It may be said perhaps, 'Surely there are cases of ' very abandoned sinners, where *the mere fact of dis-* '*obeying God* is found to imbue sinful pleasure with ' quite a *peculiar zest.*' No doubt this is true; and there is something indeed of the same kind, even in men who are very far from abandoned sinners. But these cases present no kind of difficulty in the way of my statement. In such cases, let us grant, men act simply for the pleasure of defying God. Still it *is* a pleasure. Put the case that there were *no* pleasure in disobeying God—could a person *then* act for the mere motive of disobedience; '*propter* malitiam?' Clearly not. But you see, on the other hand, men *do*, again and again, act against the *whole current* of present pleasure, 'propter *honestatem;*' for the sake of the virtuousness of so acting.

No one then can act simply for the sake of *wicked-ness*: nor is there any need to occupy any time in shewing, that *neither* can any one act for the sake of *pain*, simply as such, and as an absolute end. We conclude therefore, that 'bonum' is rightly and exhaustively divided, as it always is in Theology, into three kinds; 'honestum,' 'delectabile,' 'utile.' * Whenever we act for any end at all, we act either 'propter bonum *honestum,*' for the sake of *virtue;* or else 'propter bonum *delectabile,*' for the sake of *pleasure;* or else 'propter bonum *utile,*' for the sake of some object which is useful as a *means*, towards one or other *absolute* 'bonum.' Our absolute end will invariably be either 'honestum' or 'delectabile;' our relative or intermediate end will be 'bonum utile.'

* See, *e. g.* St. Thomas' Summa, 1, q. 5, a. 6.

Section V.

*On the Adaptation of our Nature to Virtue.** *

123. You may regard this, if you please, as the cul-
minating truth of this Chapter; as the truth, to which
every earlier remark is prefatory and subservient. In the
first Chapter we established, that by intrinsic necessity
such and such acts are virtuous, such and such vicious.
It will be very suitable then, if we establish in the second,
that God by His free Will has so created us, that our
nature is adapted to the *practice* of what is intrinsecally
virtuous and the *avoidance* of what is intrinsecally
vicious. At the same time, in point of fact many of the
phenomena, which we shall adduce in behalf of this proposition, are far more important in *other* respects, than
in their bearing on our conclusion. Still, by adducing
them in this shape, we shall have (as it were) a thread to
string them together; and we shall be able to remember
them much more distinctly, than might be otherwise possible. Here then is our thesis, to be argued in the present
Section. It is plain that the eye was formed for the
purpose of seeing, and the ear for the purpose of hearing;
yet it may often happen, that the very organ, given for
the purpose of seeing or hearing, not only fails in effecting
that purpose, but is the occasion of severe and terrible
suffering. In like manner, we maintain that our nature
was formed for the practice of virtue; and yet to maintain this, is quite consistent with the admission, that multitudes have *perverted* their nature to the practice of *vice*.

124. The first argument for our thesis, shall be a

* Those who are acquainted with the 'Sermons' of Butler, the great
Anglican philosopher, will observe how many thoughts in this Section
are taken from them. I have annexed a few quotations from him; but
these will give no adequate idea of the amount of matter due wholly to
that great work.

very remarkable fact which we have already established (see n. 121). We can, and frequently do, pursue virtue, because it *is* virtue; but the wickedest man alive has not so much as the physical power, of pursuing vice because it *is* vice. Here is a most striking superiority allotted, in our moral nature, to virtue over vice.

125. Secondly. The only absolute ends, which the will *can* pursue, are 'bonum honestum' and 'delectabile:' now observe the circumstance that these are also the only two *legitimate* ends of action. That 'honestum' is a legitimate end of action, is self-evident; that 'delectabile' is so, will be made clear (I hope) in ' de actibus humanis;' meanwhile, to a Christian at least, the principle is conclusively established, so soon as he remembers how very virtuous are such motives as these, — hope of Heaven and fear of Hell. It is a metaphysical truth then, that these two ends 'honestum' and ' delectabile' are the two legitimate ends of action. And we have the psychological fact, *corresponding* to that metaphysical truth, that they are the only two ends, which have the physical power of influencing our will.

126. Another psychological fact, most strongly to our present purpose, has been mentioned in the First Chapter. (See n. 51, p. 116.) God has so constituted our nature, and so arranged the circumstances in which we have been placed,— that there is no one class of thoughts, brought more constantly before the minds of all, even the most hardened sinners, than those of *moral obligation* and *moral preferableness*. But these thoughts, from their very nature, *claim* to be the *ruling* thoughts of our whole life. (See n. 66, p. 133, 4.) With such clamorous urgency does God, in the constitution of our nature, summon us to virtue.

127. Already then I have put before you three arguments for our thesis: our fourth shall be the following. The pleasures of *reflection* are all on the side of virtue. To explain.

The good man derives great enjoyment, from pursuing a virtuous course; as we shall see fully established in the remaining part of this Section. On the other

hand, the vicious man carries on his evil course, simply
for the sake of that pleasure, which is thence to be
derived.   So far then, let it be conceded for argument's
sake,   both   are   equal   in   point   of   enjoyment;   the
virtuous   man   deriving   pleasure   from   the   thought   of
virtuous objects, and the vicious man of vicious.   But
how as to the pleasures of *reflection?*   The thought of
vicious *objects* is pleasurable to the bad man; but is
the thought *of his love for them* pleasurable?   Is it a
happy thought, *e. g.* to the voluptuary, that he is the
mere slave of sensual enjoyment?   So very far otherwise,—the exact opposite holds so very universally,—
that spiritual writers use the phrase, 'to enter into one's
self,' as simply expressing the idea 'to lead a virtuous
life.'   'Peccator odit animam suam;' the sinner is unable
to bear the thought of his own interior, and shrinks
from the very idea of steadily contemplating its state.
On the other hand, so far as the good man has reason
to believe that he is really advancing in the interior
life, really growing in the love of God,—the thought of
this fact is among the sweetest pleasures which nature
affords.

In one word.   The good man loves good objects,
and the bad man bad objects; but the good man loves
his own *love* of good objects, whereas the evil man *hates*
his own love of things which are evil.

128.   Our fifth argument may be introduced as
follows.

Every separate 'bonum delectabile' corresponds of
course to a separate propension.   The propension '*Love*
of Knowledge' turns on that 'bonum delectabile,' the
pleasure of knowledge; the propension '*Love* of Praise,'
on the *pleasure* derived from praise.   Now (1) if we
never aimed at 'bonum delectabile,' we should always
aim at 'bonum honestum;' we should lead lives of (languid perhaps but of) faultless virtue.   And (2) were it
not for our propensions, we *could* never aim at 'bonum
delectabile.'   The logical conclusion is, that the *propensions* are the *one disturbing force in our nature;* that
were it not for them, a deflection from virtue would be

physically impossible. It becomes then a matter of great interest, to examine carefully the nature of these propensions.

(1.) First we have to make on them one most obvious remark. No reason can be given, except God's free appointment, why we have these propensions rather than those. We derive pleasure *in fact* from acquiring knowledge ; but God might (had He so pleased) have made that process simply painful : and so with the rest.

(2.) Further, happiness of course is only obtainable, through gratification of the propensions; it is simply unmeaning to make any contradictory statement. Suppose then God had so acted, that the circumstances, under which He has placed us, should afford no object, capable of gratifying those propensions which He has given us. It is plain that, on such a supposition, all happiness, even the very slightest, would be impossible. Nay,—if our propensions had been such as to *make themselves felt* and *clamour* for gratification,—then, in the supposed case, misery, awful and unmitigated, must have been our unavoidable doom. Now various arguments, as you well know, have been drawn with great force from the visible world, as proving an Intelligent and Benevolent Creator through the plain marks of benevolent design. Here is another most important addition to such arguments ; viz. the fact that every propension, which makes itself felt, has in fact *an object suited to its gratification*, in those circumstances under which God has placed us. The proof of this statement will be found, in what is immediately to follow.

But (3) much more than this may be said. *Every propension, of whose existence we are aware, has a real and legitimate place in helping us forward to virtue.* Christian mortification consists on the whole,—not in thwarting, in checking, in endeavouring to *root out*, our various propensions,—but rather the very contrary. Mortification, I say, on the whole, with exceptions presently to be mentioned in detail, consists not in *stinting* our various propensions, but in giving them *fuller and wider scope;* in directing them to those Objects, which yield them a far higher and deeper satisfaction, than any other objects can give. And our propensions, when they *are* thus directed, become (as I said) an invaluable help to us, in our attempts to practise virtue.

This then is my fifth argument for the thesis of our present Section. To sustain and illustrate it, will occupy a very much longer space, than will the united treatment of all our other arguments. But it will (in my humble opinion) amply repay such lengthened consideration, by the extreme importance of those results to which it will lead. My first business will be, to *establish* the above statement; viz. that every propension, of whose existence we are aware, has a real and legitimate place in helping us forward to virtue. When the truth of this statement is made clear and undeniable, it will be a very simple and easy matter to shew its *cogency,* as an argument for our immediate thesis.

129. Now here, that I may the better explain my meaning, let us suppose an objection. ' How can the ' path of virtue be rendered easier,' asks the objector, ' by becoming more *pleasurable?* A good act must be di- ' rected to the *virtuousness* of its end; (see n. 56, p. 123), ' whereas a propension *can* only draw us towards the ' *pleasure* of that end. A propension, then, may help ' us indeed in the performance of that *external act,* ' which is virtuous; but not in its *virtuous* perform- ' ance. Take, for instance, that propension already ' mentioned, our love of knowledge. We are *virtuous* ' in studying, only so far as we study *for the sake of* ' that virtue; whereas the propension, love of know- ' ledge, inclines us to study on quite a different motive, ' viz., the act's *pleasurableness.'*

Certainly it cannot be denied, that when an emotion of pleasure is excited by the thought of study, and I put forth no special resistance,— my *will* also tends to such pleasurableness as an immediate end. But does it at all follow, that my will's *whole* energy tends towards this end? There is one act undoubtedly, directed to ' bonum delectabile;' but does it follow, does it tend ever so remotely to follow, that there is not another act (and possibly one far more energetic and efficacious) directed to ' bonum honestum ?'   In the case before us, I am plainly not studying *merely* for pleasure; for I see from my window that a game of cricket is proceeding, which would give me much greater enjoyment.   I refrain from that pleasure, because I believe study to be that employment, in which God at this moment prefers that I should engage.   The objection, then, does not tend ever so remotely to overthrow that statement, against which it is directed.   We admit most fully, that an act *is* elicited at this moment, wherein my will tends towards ' bonum delectabile ;'   we only maintain in addition, that the existence of this pleasure gives my will the power, of eliciting *simultaneously* a far more energetic act than would otherwise be possible, *in the direction of ' bonum honestum.'*

Before proceeding to defend this allegation, one word may be useful, (in order to avoid misconception,) on the *concomitant* act directed to ' bonum delectabile.' It by no means follows, nor is it by any means probable, that this act is sinful; though it is impossible fully to explain our meaning on this head, till we come to the theological treatment of ' actus humani.' Firstly, the ' bonum delectabile ' need not be its *absolute* end ; the pleasure itself may be directed, unconsciously indeed yet most really, to some further 'bonum honestum.'   The act may be of *this,* or some cognate, kind; ' I choose the pleasure of study, as a means of ' serving God more cheerfully and more effectually.' Whenever I am deeply impressed with the thought of God, whenever the implicit remembrance of His presence is acting powerfully on my will, it is probable that most acts of mine, which are directed *immediately* to pleasure, are directed *absolutely* to some such virtuous end; a truth, which I hope to defend and illustrate at sufficient length, in our theological course. But secondly, even though pleasure *were* the act's absolute end, the act need not be *sinful;* it might be simply *indifferent.*   Nay lastly, and to take the most extreme

case, though my act *were* directed to pleasure with that
degree of inordination which constitutes venial sin,——
(you must allow me to use these expressions, though
you cannot yet understand their meaning;) — still this
evil might be most abundantly counterbalanced, by the
simultaneous good which I obtain the power of effecting.   To the consideration of this good then, let us next
proceed.

The immense advantage, gained for the practice
of virtue through the *pleasure* which accompanies it,
consists ordinarily in two principal particulars.   First,
the lessening of temptation.   Under the head of Concupiscence, we shall treat in detail the effect produced by *temptation* on the will : but it may here
be assumed, as sufficiently obvious on the surface, that
temptation acts upon the will like a heavy weight,
drawing it in the wrong direction ; thwarting and im-
peding it, to an indefinite extent, in its struggles towards good.   *Everything which lessens temptation,
strengthens pro tanto the will's actual power to good
at the moment.*   Now taking the particular instance we
have chosen, and which is indeed a sample of numberless others, see how vastly temptation is diminished, by
the *pleasure* which accompanies the virtuous act.   It
is God's Preference, that at this moment I shall sit
down and study; but how urgent and violent would
be my temptation to engage rather in the game of
cricket, if the study were *simply* a dry, dreary, and
disgusting occupation.   And this temptation would
increase in strength every instant ; until at length
(and indeed before very long) it would reach that degree, which an ordinary man's will has not the moral
power of resisting.   The pleasurableness, which accompanies virtuous practice, is often in fact a most important part of that grace given us by God, (part of what
is called 'exterior grace,') enabling us to fight manfully
against temptation, in His service and for His sake.

The second benefit, which we derive from the accompanying pleasure, is connected with an important
phenomenon of the human will.   Except in the case of

men who are practised and disciplined in austere virtue, the *will has not the moral power of tending for any length of time to 'bonum honestum,' while the sensitive appetite remains without gratification.* In a state of long-continued and simple ' tristitia,' its powers to good are withered and paralyzed. It is not at all too much to say, that if other phenomena of our nature remained as they are now, the consistent practice of virtue would be simply and absolutely impossible,—morally impossible in the strictest and completest sense of that word,— were it not for the various, and frequently keen pleasures, which our Holy and Merciful Creator has strewed in our path.

Here we are able to see the force of a phrase, frequently used by St. Thomas and the Thomists ; ' delectationes propter operationes, non contrà.' These pleasures, so mercifully imparted by God, should be used for the purpose intended by Him ; for the purpose of more strenuously and virtuously performing those acts to which they are annexed. On the other hand, if we engaged in these operations *for the sake* of the pleasures, we should *invert* the order of nature. Suppose I sit down to study in a quasi-*gluttonous* way ; simply seeking the pleasure of that intellectual treat which it affords, without considering at all whether God at this moment prefers it ;—here is the quasi-sensuality of a highly intellectual man.

130. But there is another case of virtue being assisted by concomitant pleasure, which has so very special and distinct an importance of its own, as to require separate treatment. I refer to the case of what is commonly called *sensible devotion; i.e.* when the accompanying pleasure arises *directly* from a contemplation of those Objects, which should be the polestars of our Christian course. This pleasure, I need hardly say, reaches very different degrees in different men ; or in the same men at different times. It ranges from that cheering consolation which is so often felt by an ordinary Christian, up to those high degrees of rapture and delight, which are the frequent heritage

s

of Saints; such as made St. Francis Xavier exclaim,
'It is too much, O God, it is too much!'

A false mystic, of whom you may have heard,
named Molinos, has been condemned for the following
proposition :—

Qui desiderat et amplectitur devotionem sen-
sibilem, non desiderat nec quærit Deum, sed
seipsum.—DENZ. p. 337, prop. 27.

And this condemnation surely gives no slight
sanction, on the Church's part, to the great importance
of sensible devotion in the interior life. We are not
of course denying, that there may be *abuse* of this ;
spiritual writers are loud in saying that there *may* be,
and that there often *is*. But it is an extremely trite
remark, that a thing's *abuse* is no argument against
its *use;* and our own present argument leads us rather
to consider its inestimable service in the promotion of
true piety.

Observe then that sensible pleasure, *i. e.* emotion of
an intense kind, unless we strenuously resist its tendency, penetrates the intellect with a most vivid apprehension of its object. Now the objects which produce
sensible devotion are such, that in proportion as the
intellect contemplates them more keenly, the will
elicits higher and nobler acts of virtue. What are the
kind of thoughts which constitute the very life of
sensible devotion ? I suppose such as these : the
wonderful and unwearied love of God, as contrasted
with man's ingratitude and insensibility ;—the treasures of tenderness stored up in the Sacred Heart ;—
the rapturous joys reserved for us in Heaven ;—and so
with many others. As our emotions rise more highly
from such thoughts as these, the thoughts themselves
take a far deeper and more powerful hold of the intellect, and thus lead to the highest and choicest acts
of the will. In other words, the sensitive appetite acts
on the will, in the way of rendering its acts far more
efficacious, through the intermediate agency of the

intellect.   This will be made still clearer, when we consider the relation between intellect and will; meanwhile I would earnestly recommend you to study Father Faber's chapter on the subject, which makes part of his ' Growth in Holiness.'*

131. We have now gone through our preliminary enquiry ; we have sufficiently seen how perfectly *conceivable* it is, that the propensions may be of invaluable service to the cause of virtue.   We now come to our direct and immediate statement, that they *are* so; insomuch that, of those various propensions which are the *sole occasion of sin*, there is *not one* which may not in its way *importantly promote the glory of God*.   It will of course be impossible for us to enumerate *all* the propensions ; but I am confident we shall be able to establish so large an induction, that no doubt will remain in your minds on the truth of what we affirm. Indeed if not sufficiently satisfied, you have but to task your ingenuity,— to think of any propension which I shall not have named,—and call on me to prove my point in regard to that propension.   But first, of course, you must hear patiently to an end my own enumeration.

I will begin with the propension of *Duty*.   It is a plain fact in human nature, that we derive pleasure from the mere consciousness of doing what is

* P. 422–451.   The following passage particularly deserves attention. " [During periods of sensible devotion], all trains of thought which concern heavenly things display a copiousness and exuberance which they never had before.   Meditations are fluent and abundant.   The virtues no longer bring forth their actions in pain and travail, but with facility and abundance, and their offspring are rich, beautiful, and heroic.   There are provinces of temptations always in discontented and smouldering rebellion.   But [now] we have a power over them, which is new, and which is growing.   We have such a facility in difficulties as almost to change the character of the spiritual life ; and a union of body and spirit, which is as great a revolution as agreement and peace in a divided household.   All these blessings are the mutations of the Right Hand of the Most High.   Even to beginners, God often vouchsafes to give them, not merely as sugar-plums to children, as some writers have strangely said, but to do a real work in their souls, and enable them to hold their way through the supernatural difficulties proper to their state.   But proficients should ardently desire them, for they fatten prayer ; and the perfect can never do without them, as they can never cease augmenting their virtues and rendering the exercise of them pleasant."— Pp. 428, 429.

right. This is so undoubted, that many Protestants, who fully hold the intuitiveness of moral truth, have introduced great error into their speculations, by confusing these two totally distinct facts : (1) our *intuition* of what is right; and (2) our *pleasure* in practising it. Now it is remarkable that their opponents, those who deny altogether our intuition of moral truth, yet never deny the other fact; viz. the *pleasurableness* of moral practice. They never deny, I mean, that we *do* derive a real gratification, from the simple belief that we are doing our duty.

The strength however of this propension, appears to be very far greater on the negative than on the positive side. The *misery* of doing what we know to be *evil,* is far keener and more poignant, than the *pleasure* of doing what we know to be *good.* It has sometimes happened, that even the most wicked men, having committed some extraordinary crime, have felt a remorse so bitter that life has been intolerable. In the case of all newly plunged in sin, the pain of remorse accompanies and sullies all those enjoyments which their sin may purchase. But much more, as men grow in goodness, does this propension increase in strength. To a Saint, the deliberate commission of one venial sin is anguish almost unsupportable.

It needs no argument to shew how extremely important is this propension in the cause of virtue.

132. The next propension I will name, shall be that of ' Self-charity;' the propension whereby we feel pleasure at the thought that our happiness is being promoted, and pain at the thought that it is being lessened. How far this is a strong and unintermitting propension, we shall consider in the next chapter; but so *far* as it exists, its effect on all Theists must be simply and greatly good. Nay take even the exceptional instance of those who believe in *no* punishment after death — even on *them* this propension has one beneficial effect; it will often cause vicious pleasure to be accompanied with a pang, which arises from the remembrance, that their permanent happiness even on this earth suffers

from their wicked courses. But in all who believe a future state of retribution, it is plain that this propension works constantly and uniformly on the side of man's highest good.

133. I must now call your attention to an extremely strong propension, or rather union of propensions; the treatment of which will occupy some little time: we may call it the propension of 'Personal Love.' Following St. Thomas's language, we may subdivide this into three propensions;—'Amor Concupiscentiæ,' 'Amor Amicitiæ,' and 'Amor Benevolentiæ:' though St. Thomas is speaking of them as *virtues*, and not as propensions. We shall find indeed, as we advance, that *two* of these three are more properly counted as *the same ;* but we will begin by explaining the three, as St. Thomas understands them. First then for 'Amor Benevolentiæ.'

It frequently happens, that I may hear anecdotes of some living man, or read his life, or in some other way come to a knowledge of his character;— and I may feel my affections drawn to the subject of these anecdotes, in a way quite unlike that, in which they are drawn to any one else. I may most fully recognise that others are as good men, or better; but there is some quality in *this* man's goodness, which specially finds an echo in my own breast ; some inexplicable sympathy on my part towards him, which it is quite hopeless to analyse. He for his part (we will suppose) knows nothing of me whatever ; nor has he so much as heard of my existence. Still what singular pleasure I receive, in contemplating the success he meets with in his various undertakings ! How overjoyed I am to know of his well-doing ! What delight should I experience, in going through indefinite effort and privation, for the sake of promoting his interests ! Or again, suppose that (without knowing me personally) he expressed some *wish or preference*, as to the conduct to be pursued by his friends and well-wishers,—how keen would be my pleasure in *conforming* my conduct to the wishes so expressed! The propension, which makes me susceptible of these various pleasures, and of their opposite pains, may be called 'Amor Benevolentiæ.'

But now put a further case. Let us suppose, that the object of my affections becomes acquainted with me. Let us suppose, that just as *his* peculiarities of character have attracted my affections towards him with such singular warmth,—so he should become acquainted with corresponding peculiarities of *mine*, which draw him with equal tenderness towards myself. What then ensues? My feeling of Amor Benevolentiæ to him becomes at once indefinitely stronger; or in other words, the pleasure which I feel, in promoting his interests or conforming to his wishes, becomes indefinitely greater. Here is 'Amor *Amicitiæ ;*' ' amatio et *redamatio* :'—that disinterested love for another, which is accompanied and intensified by the consciousness that I am loved in return. We can hardly find a more suitable instance of this feeling, than the relations between a widowed mother and me her only child. Our characters were in no small degree similar; and her education of me has rendered that similitude closer and more exquisite. Consider, on the one hand, the keen appreciation with which I dwell on those many loveable points of her character, which speak so peculiarly to my feelings. Consider, on the other hand, my deep abiding consciousness, how tenderly she loves me; how open to her is my whole character; how fully she understands its various peculiarities. Is it not plain that all this will produce in me the liveliest and deepest emotions of disinterested attachment? With actual delight and joy would I go through a world of labour, if I could save that dear heart one single pang.

At the same time, and as the necessary companion of this propension, I have another quite different in kind, 'Amor Concupiscentiæ.' I delight in my knowledge of her love; her praise is among my sweetest rewards ; that we shall exchange unrestrained confidences and grow in knowledge of each other, is among my happiest active employments; to gaze on her sweet smile and loving countenance, is like entering into a tranquil and secure harbour from the storms of life.

You will at once see, from what has been said, that 'Amor Amicitiæ' is but one species of 'Amor Benevolentiæ;' whereas 'Amor Concupiscentiæ' is wholly different in character. 'Amor Benevolentiæ' and 'Amicitiæ' derive their respective gratifications from *precisely the same* objects; viz. the well-being and well-doing of the beloved person: whereas 'Amor Concupiscentiæ' is satisfied by objects totally different from the former. Without as yet accurately defining our terms, we may say that 'Amor Benevolentiæ' is a 'disinterested' propension; 'Amor Concupiscentiæ' an 'interested' one. What is meant by this? The pleasures, which I derive in virtue of my propension 'Amor Benevolentiæ' or 'Amicitiæ,' result from the *well-being* of its object *in himself;* but those which I derive from 'Amor Concupiscentiæ,' result from his *demeanour* towards *me.* The knowledge that my friend is happy, or that his interests are being promoted, suffices in itself to cause all those delights which result from the *former* propension; whereas the *latter* propension derives its satisfaction from a knowledge of *my own* position in that friend's favour and affection. Indeed the 'Amor Concupiscentiæ' often clashes more than a little with the 'Amor Benevolentiæ:' I am far from feeling that pleasure which I otherwise should, in my friend's well-being or the promotion of his highest interests, because I long for more of his society or warmer manifestations of his regard.

The following quotation from Billuart, St. Thomas's most approved commentator in his own school, may suffice to shew, that I have accurately stated the Angelic Doctor's use of these expressions; with only the qualification already mentioned, that he speaks of them as virtues, not as propensions.

" Observandum 1°. cum eruditissimo magistro nostro P. Henneguier, in suo opusculo De Absolutione Sacramentali, du-

plicem attendi posse in nobis erga Deum amorem: scilicet amorem
concupiscentiæ, quo *volumus Deum nobis bonum Ejusque beatitudinem nobis appetimus;* et amorem amicitiæ, quo *Deo bonum
Ejusque beatitudinem et perfectionem volumus.* Hic iterum est
duplex: unus secundum quid et inchoatus, alter simplex et abso-
lutus.   Primus dicitur benevolentiæ simplicis, alter benevolentiæ
amicabilis.   Neque enim idem sunt, ut plerique existimant, benevolentia, et amicitia seu charitas: benevolentia est alterius principium seu effectus; nam ex eo quod alicui volumus bonum,
disponimur ut ipsum amemus et ad ipsum amicitiam habeamus;
inde etiam quòd aliquem amemus et ad ipsum amicitiam habeamus, fit ut ipsi bonum velimus: unde S. Th. 2, 2, q. 27, art.
2, ad. 1, dicit quòd cùm philosophus definit amare, quod est
velle alicui bonum, ‘definiat amorem, non ponens totam rationem
‘ ipsius, sed aliquid ad ejus rationem pertinens, in quo maximè
‘ manifestatur dilectionis affectus.’
     “ Est igitur hoc discrimen, secundùm D. Th., inter bene-
volentiam et amorem amicitiæ, quòd benevolentia sit simplex
actus voluntatis, quo volumus alicui bonum *sine redamatione ex
parte ejus;* ut dum videmus duos pugiles in certamine aliunde
nobis ignotos, quorum unum vellemus vincere; est exemplum
S. Thomæ loco citato: amor autem seu amicitia addit benevolentiæ redamationem, seu *unionem affectuum* ad invicem; *amicus
enim est amico amicus,* ut fert commune adagium.   Placet verba
S. Doctoris referre loco citato in corpore articuli; ubi inquirens
utrùm amare, prout est actus charitatis, (quam paulò ante de-
finierat esse amicitiam, ut dicam modò), sit idem quod benevolentia, sic respondet: ‘ Dicendum quòd benevolentia propriè
‘ dicitur actus voluntatis, quo alteri bonum volumus.   Hic autem
‘ voluntatis actus differt ab actuali amore, tam secundùm quod
‘ est in appetitu sensitivo, quàm etiam secundùm quod est in
‘ appetitu intellectivo, quod est voluntas.’   Tum paucis inter-
jectus prosequitur: ‘ Amor (seu amicitia) importat quamdam
‘ *unionem secundum affectum* amantis ad amatum, in quantum
‘ scilicet amans æstimat amatum quodam modo, ut *unum sibi
‘ vel ad se pertinens,* et sic movetur in ipsum; sed benevolentia
‘ est simplex actus voluntatis, quo volumus alicui bonum, etiam
‘ non præsuppositâ prædictâ unione affectûs ad ipsum.   Sic ergò
‘ in dilectione secundùm quod est actus charitatis (hoc est ami-
‘ citiæ, ut mox dicam), includitur aliqua benevolentia; sed dilectio,
‘ sive amor, *addit unionem affectûs;* et propter hoc philosophus
‘ dicit ibidem, quòd benevolentia sit principium amicitiæ.’
     “ Unde vulgò à theologis assignantur tres conditiones requi-
sitæ ad amicitiam: prima, quòd sit amor benevolentiæ, non concupiscentiæ; secunda, quod sit mutuus; tertia, quòd fundetur in
aliquâ communicatione, sive bonorum, sive secretorum, &c. inter

amicos : sicque benevolentia et amicitia conveniunt in primâ conditione, differunt in secundâ et tertiâ."—BILLUART, *De Pœn.* diss.
4. art. 7. par. 1.

I may also add however the following references :
2, 2, q. 23, a. 1, 0 ; q. 27, a. 2, 0, ad finem.

Some few Catholic writers, Bossuet being one, maintain that, according to St. Thomas, even in 'Amor Amicitiæ' we are aiming at our own advantage : but the
more suitable place for refuting this strange opinion,
will be found under the head of the theological virtues
in the subsequent part of our course.

134. This will be the proper opportunity for shewing (see n. 98.) how totally distinct is the *passion*
'Amor,' whether from 'Amor Benevolentiæ' or ' Amor
Concupiscentiæ;' though I admit that St. Thomas seems
in some sense to identify it with the latter.

The passion 'Amor' is that emotion which I experience, whenever the thought enters my mind of *any
object which is to me at this moment a 'bonum delectabile.'* On the other hand it is simply in virtue of my
propensions, that *this* object rather than *that,* is to me
a 'bonum delectabile.' To say that the propension
'Amor Benevolentiæ' has been called out in me towards
A. B. is simply to say in other words, that the *well-
being and well-doing of A. B.* is to me ordinarily a
' bonum mentaliter delectabile.' To say that the propension 'Amor Concupiscentiæ' has been called out in
me towards him, is to say that the *possession of his
favour and love* is to me ordinarily a ' bonum mentaliter
delectabile.' When I think indeed on either of these
objects, I ordinarily experience the *passion* 'Amor;' but
I experience it in no other sense, and in no other degree,
than when I think of *any other* 'bonum delectabile' in
the whole world. There is, I say, literally no more connection between the passion 'Amor' and the propension
'Amor Concupiscentiæ,' than between the said passion
and the propension, 'Love of Praise,' ' Love of Acquisition,' or any other which can possibly be named.

And the same remark may be made, mutatis mu-
tandis, on the *modal affection* ' Amor.' This is simply

that *act of Will* which, unless I make special resistance, *infallibly accompanies* the passion 'Amor,' when I think of any 'bonum delectabile.' (See n. 100.)

135. Returning to the two propensions before us, we may call their *union* by the name 'Personal Love;' and it is plain at once, how great an assistance they give in many respects to the cause of virtue, even if lavished on human objects. They raise the heart above low and grovelling desires; they open to the mind ideas of far higher and more exalted pleasures, than would otherwise be dreamt of; they tend to form the character in habits of generosity and disinterestedness.

But are our fellow-men, specially our fellow-men in this visible world, objects at all adequate to this propension, as God has implanted it in our hearts? Surely, though we had no more than unaided *reason* to guide us, we never could think so. The following most beautiful passage may serve here to express my meaning.

" The thought of God, and nothing short of it, is the happiness of man; for though there is much besides to serve as subject of knowledge, or motive for action, or instrument of excitement, yet the *affections* require a something more vast and more enduring than any thing created. What is novel and sudden, excites, but does not influence; what is pleasurable or useful, raises no awe; self moves no reverence; and mere knowledge kindles no love. He alone is sufficient for the heart who made it. I do not say, of course, that nothing short of the Almighty Creator can awaken and answer to our love, reverence, and trust. Man can do this for man; man doubtless is an object to rouse his brother's love, and repays it in his measure. Nay, it is a great duty, one of the two chief duties of religion, thus to be minded towards our neighbour. But I am not speaking here of what we *can* do, or *ought* to do, but what it is our *happiness* to do; and surely it may be said, that though the love of the brethren, the love of all men, be one-half of our obedience, yet this love exercised by itself, were that possible, (which it is not) were no part of our reward. And for this reason, if for no other, that our hearts require something more permanent and uniform than man can be. We gain much for a time from fellowship with each other. It is a relief to us, as fresh air to the fainting, or meat and drink to the hungry, or a flood of tears to the heavy in mind. It is a soothing comfort to have those whom we may make our confidants; a comfort to have those to whom we may confess our faults; a comfort to have those to whom we may look for sympathy. Love of home and family in these and other ways is sufficient to make this life tolerable to the multitude of men, which otherwise it would not be; but still, after all, our affections exceed such exercise of them, and demand what is more stable. Do not all men die? are they not taken from us? are they not as uncertain as the grass of the field? We do not give our hearts to things inanimate, because these have no permanence in them. We do not place our affections in sun, moon, and stars, or this rich and fair earth, because all things material come to nought, and vanish like day and night. Man, too, though he has an intelligence within him, yet in his best estate is altogether vanity. If our happiness consists in our affections being employed and recompensed, ' man that is born of a woman' cannot be our happiness; for how can he stay another, who ' continueth not in one stay' himself?

" But there is another reason why God alone is the happiness of our souls, to which I wish rather to direct attention. The contemplation of Him, and nothing but it, is able fully to open and relieve the mind, to *unlock, occupy, and fix our affections*. We may indeed love things created with great intenseness; but such affection, when disjoined from the love of the Creator, is like a stream running in a narrow channel, impetuous, vehement, turbid. The heart runs out, as it were, only at one door; it is not an expanding of the whole man. Created natures cannot open to us, or elicit, the ten thousand mental senses which belong to us, and through which we really live. *None but the presence of Our Maker can enter us; for to none besides can the whole heart in all its thoughts and feelings be unlocked and subjected.* ' Behold,' he says, ' I stand at the door and knock ; if any man hear my voice and open the door, I will come unto him, and will sup with him, and he with me.' ' My Father will love him, and We will come unto him, and make our abode with him.' ' God hath sent forth the Spirit of His Son into your hearts.' ' God is greater than our heart, and knoweth all things.' It is this feeling of simple and absolute confidence and communion, which soothes and satisfies those to whom it is vouchsafed. We know that even our nearest friends enter into us but partially, and hold intercourse with us only at times; whereas the *consciousness of a perfect and enduring presence, and it alone, keeps the heart open.* Withdraw the object on which it rests, and it will relapse again into its state of confinement and constraint; and in proportion as it is limited, either to certain seasons or to certain affections, the heart is straitened and distressed. If it be not over-bold to say it, He who is Infinite can alone be its measure; He alone can answer to the mysterious assemblage of feelings and thoughts which it has within it.   'There is no creature that is not manifest in His sight, but all things are naked and opened unto the eyes of Him with whom we have to do.'"—*Newman's Parochial Sermons,* vol. v. pp. 357–361.

The fact which we are considering, is one of such extreme importance in a great number of ways, that I must ask your indulgence for what might seem an impertinence.   It might seem, I say, an impertinence, if I ventured to add anything of my own, when your memories are filled with that beautiful passage which I have just quoted; and yet it will serve (I hope) to give us a still firmer and deeper possession of the truth before us, if we consider in some detail those various particulars, which Father Newman has united in his most attractive picture.   Let us consider then the warmest mutual affection, that can exist towards a visible human friend.   And in order to fix our ideas by one instance, let us compare that affection, with the friendship which may be sustained, between the Sacred Humanity of Our Lord Jesus Christ, and a soul which gives itself generously to God.

First consider *devotion to the cause of that friend.* Who could dare make it the chief wish of his life, to promote the cause or desires of any earthly friend? Who might even surrender himself for one moment *without restraint* to such a purpose?   You see then that our devotion to any earthly friend (1) must be *occasional,* and not pervasive of our whole life; while (2) it must be measured and not unreserved.

Next, consider the *foundation* of the friendship, according to that theory on Personal Love which we have drawn out; in other words, those particular qualities of heart and character, which specially attract our love.   In studying the mysteries of our Saviour's life on earth, or the various aspects under which His different offices towards us are represented by the Church,—one man is drawn specially to one class of such exhibitions, another to another.   One man is singularly affected by His Infancy; another by His

Passion; a third by the Sacred Heart; a fourth by the Precious Blood.   One Christian dwells with tenderest devotion on His acts, another on His words; one is more affected by His compassionate love towards the worst sinners, another by His most tender familiarity with the beloved Apostle.   And so we might indefinitely proceed.   But we may safely assert that there is no one human being, among all the inexhaustible varieties of character, but will find more than one feature specially to win and attract him.   It matters not to our argument *what* that special feature may be: for in all there is the same Divine Saviour; in all there is a certain quality, unparalleled and unapproachable; in all (I need not say, for to doubt it were blasphemy; in all) there is that, to which no development of our earthly friend's character can bear the most distant comparison.

Thirdly, consider that important ingredient in friendship, mutual confidence and appreciation.   With earthly friends I can exchange but half confidences; to the most sympathetic and congenial friend I can open but a small part of myself, and should only be misunderstood if I attempted more.*   But the Soul of Christ views my whole character in all its lights and shades;

* "And even with our fellowmen—are they adequate objects for our thoughts and affections?   Practically, it is a plain matter of fact, that they are not.   How are our affections and sympathies broken up and given away in fragments!   We do not trust our whole heart to our nearest friend. We give part of our confidence to one man, part to another; we cannot give more, and should be stared at if we tried.   When we wish really to sympathise with another's deep feelings, or to explain our own, how hopelessly do we fall short; and by what a chance does it seem to be that we succeed at all!   Those burnings of the heart which we occasionally experience, on having sure signs that others do thoroughly feel what we do, or when a great system opens upon us, or when one whom we love performs a noble action, or when one whom we revere shews us unexpected affection, at once shew us the emptiness of our ordinary sympathies, and are earnests of something greater.   Such passing emotions betray to us capacities for a state of habitual feeling, in which must be the highest happiness, and which we are as yet as unable and unworthy to feel as our friends are to excite. Is it conceivable that this union of high capability with actual unworthiness should be meant merely to point us forward to a future life?   Surely, rather it sanctions *those present desires* which it causes; that blind craving after the supernatural, that worshipping of the unknown God, of which the highest and the lowest minds give common witness."—*British Critic*, 1838, p. 217.

sees in every particular my difficulties, my sorrows, my temptations; understands the cause of this peculiarity, which repels my dearest earthly friend; does justice to my conduct under that emergency, when my nearest intimates felt themselves bound to condemn me. You will object at once, that my faults also and imperfections are exposed with fearful openness to His piercing gaze. Ah! we do little justice to His loving tenderness, if we regard this as an objection. If there be but the real *wish* of doing right, if there be but a true *desire* of dealing generously with Him, it may be said in a most true sense that our miserable short-comings and infirmities are even incentives to his love. In our theological course this most touching truth will be handled at length.

Fourthly, friendship with our Lord is a friendship, which, if I am but faithful to myself and to His grace, is sure, steadfast, and eternal. If my dearest friends in many things misunderstand me now, what constant danger there is lest, under some future contingency, they may far more grievously misunderstand me! If St. Paul and St. Barnabas, among the most holy of God's servants, and endeared to each other by common labour in their Redeemer's service — if these holy Apostles could cool and separate, what earthly friendship can be accounted secure? Here then is one mode in which earthly friendships may be dissolved; and another is the very condition of this life. My tastes may change, nay they are ever changing; my friend's tastes change; circumstances remove us from all active communication with each other; till we meet again after a long interval, and find that our mutual sympathy is gone. But look at the opposite picture. Jesus Christ is 'the same yesterday, to-day, and for ever;' and for myself, as I advance in piety, I do but increase in sympathy with Him. Nay, as Father Newman most justly remarks, His very greatness keeps me back from that rude familiarity, which sometimes brings earthly friendships to a speedy end.*

* " Fear is allayed by the love of Him, and our love sobered by our fear

Fifthly, in earthly friendships, as we have already remarked, the ' Amor Concupiscentiæ' is ever clashing with the ' Amor Benevolentiæ:' in heavenly friendships alone are they fully harmonious and complementary of each other.   In proportion as I enjoy with greater zest that *one* pleasure, of working for my dearest Lord and consulting His Preference in all things,—in that very proportion do I the more enjoy that *other* pleasure, of basking in the sunshine of His presence, and rejoicing in the thought of His approbation and love.

Then lastly, friendship presses towards *union* with the beloved object; almost, as it were, towards corporal union; as the very marks of friendship which we spontaneously exhibit, embracing and the like, sufficiently testify.   But what other union of friendship can bear a moment's comparison, to that miraculous union which we enjoy with the Sacred Humanity, in the Sacrament of our Saviour's love, the pledge of His undying tenderness?

So here are six points of contrast.   First, the love to our Saviour is more pervasive and ungrudging; secondly, those qualities which are its foundation are more attractive; thirdly, the mutual confidence is greater; fourthly, the friendship is more permanent and stable; fifthly, in this friendship alone the ' Amor Benevolentiæ' and ' Concupiscentiæ' are brought into harmony; sixthly, the union is closer.   In every one of these particulars the superiority of Divine friendship is vast and incalculable.

It may unthinkingly be urged, in objection to all

of Him.   Thus He draws us on with encouraging voice amid the terrors of His threatenings.   As in the young ruler's case, He loves us, yet speaks harshly to us, that we may learn to cherish mixed feelings towards Him. He hides himself from us, and yet calls us on, that we may hear His voice as Samuel did, and believing, approach Him with trembling.   This may seem strange to those who do not study the Scriptures, and to those who do not know what it is earnestly to seek after God.   But in proportion as the state of mind is strange, so is there in it, therefore, untold and surpassing pleasure to those who partake it.   The bitter and the sweet, strangely tempered, thus leave upon the mind the lasting taste of Divine truth, and satisfy it; not so harsh as to be loathed; nor of that insipid sweetness which attends enthusiastic feelings, and is wearisome when it becomes familiar."—*Par. Serm.* vol. i. p. 350.

this, that friendship requires for its perfection a certain *exclusiveness;* and that He who loves all mankind with such exuberant tenderness, can be no sufficient object for this propension.   A moment's thought gives the reply.   In human friendship exclusiveness is necessary, simply because the will, the intellect, the affections of men are in themselves so limited and confined: we have not *enough* of our friend's thoughts, if his friendship be shared with multitudes.   In Divine friendship this holds not in the slightest degree.   So the Protestant poet answers this very objection:—

> "Thou art as much His care, as though beside
>   Nor man nor angel lived in heaven or earth ;
> Thus sunbeams shed alike their glorious tide,
>   To light up worlds or wake an insect's mirth :
> They shine and shine in unexhausted store ;
> Thou art thy Saviour's darling, ask no more."

The sun, Mr. Keble implies, puts forth its *whole* influence towards enlivening a poor worm, just as though there were no gorgeous palaces, or majestic scenes of natural beauty, to receive its gladdening light. And so the Sun of Justice sheds His *whole* rays on me, a miserable worm of the earth, as fully, as absolutely, as though there were no mortified priests or holy ascetics, who look to His light as their very life.   That human soul of His, as we shall see when we study the Incarnation treatise, is occupied, at every instant, as simply, as intently, in reading my heart and considering my thoughts, as though there were no other object to engage it.   The objection then is not merely answered; it is actually retorted.   One chief prerogative of Divine Love as compared with human, is the constant *thought* and *consideration* which we receive from the Beloved Object.

Another objection may be ingeniously raised, against part at least of the above argument.   Who would venture, I asked, to throw himself unreservedly and pervasively into any human friendship?   'Certainly,' replies the objector, 'no *good* man could do so; but ' might not a bad man ?   And why may not he so far

' obtain the very same pleasure, which the *pious* man
' gains by his friendship with our Lord?' Now there
have been from time to time various men, with hearts
far removed from God, who *have* more or less attempted thus to make idols of their fellow-men : and
what has been the result ? The very attempt shews
weakness of character, as all would admit; that love,
which *can* be a *strong-minded* man's *one* object, *must*
be a divine and not a human love. But look at this
weak-minded idolator of a fellow-man, and see what is
the course of his history. He is in constant alterna-
tions, flux and reflux, of rapture and despondency.
To-day he has found the very idol, for which he has
so long been seeking in vain; he is in transports of
delight. Next week he finds that his idol is but an
ordinary man, and he falls into an agony of disappoint-
ment. These men, in fact, more signally than any
others, illustrate the truth which I am putting before
you ; they display every imaginable symptom, of lavish-
ing a strong propension on objects utterly and con-
temptibly unable to afford it gratification.

We now proceed to further illustrations of our
principle. My love for my Redeemer viewed in His
human nature, leads me (in proportion to its growth)
to a constantly increasing love for the Triune God ;
for God contemplated in His own Original and Infinite
Nature.* Here is indeed an adequate object for my
keen affections.

Again, the love of Mary is an ever fresh and inexhaustible well of joy and delight. Love to her indeed, such as we find it in the greatest Saints, is that
very reality, of which the highest (perhaps) and purest
among human affections,—a child's love to his mother
—is but the faint and inadequate type.

Then again, from among the Saints I choose this
or that one in particular; not from believing him to be
the holiest in that blessed assemblage, but because his
is that particular exhibition of sanctity, to which (from

* " Ut dum visibiliter Deum cognoscimus per hunc *in invisibilium
amorem rapiamur.*"

T

some occult sympathy) I am instinctively drawn. It is not merely one indeed, but a certain small number, towards whom for this reason I cherish a special and tender devotion.

Lastly, love for my Guardian Angel has something in it which reminds me of human friendship; for this loved being stands to *me* in a relation which he holds to no other creature, and loves me therefore with a certain *exclusiveness* of affection.

And thus we see, in strong corroboration of our general thesis, a very important fact, as to those who are called by the Holy Spirit to the noble vocation, of steadily and systematically renouncing all particular attachments on earth. These men, we see, are in no sense called upon to *subdue* this propension of Personal love, but the very contrary. Their love is directed with all the more intensity and delight to its *legitimate* Objects; who belong indeed to the Invisible World, but whom the eye of faith so keenly and lovingly discerns.

136. The next propension which deserves our notice, is *General* Love of our fellow-men, as *distinct* from *Personal:* and this again exists under the same two divisions, ' Benevolentiæ,' and ' Concupiscentiæ.' I say we have a certain love to our fellow-men *as such:* this propension may be thwarted by various causes ; such as a sense of injury received, or some special antipathy; but where such disturbing influences are absent, the propension shews itself unmistakeably. Man, as is so constantly remarked, is a social animal. We seek the society of our fellow-men *as such*, by a tendency quite distinct from that, which leads us to seek the society of our *personal friends.* And when we are in this general society, we feel a certain genial cordiality as our normal attitude of mind. In other words (1) we experience a certain feeling of general goodwill to our companions;—' Amor Benevolentiæ:' and (2) we take for granted, and have pleasure in the thought, that they *respond* to that feeling;—' Amor Concupiscentiæ.' * That ' Amor Concupiscentiæ ' indeed towards

* " Mankind are by nature so closely united, there is such a correspond-

our fellow-men is *negatively* a most strong propension, is manifest from this. I suppose no man could live (unless supported by most singular supplies of grace) under the impression that all his fellow-men regarded him as a monster of depravity. And this misery would evidently be totally distinct from any fear for his personal safety; it would arise simply from believing himself an object of universal detestation.

This propension, even in its rudimental state, is of manifest advantage to the cause of virtue; in that it directs our thoughts, from purely selfish ends, to the promotion of the common good. In holy men it assumes far greater prominence; and develops into that intense feeling of brotherly love, so characteristic of the saintly character. The holy missionary or parish priest is no doubt *chiefly* animated by personal love for his Creator and Saviour; yet no slight support is afforded him in his holy enterprises, by this burning love of the brethren. A remark has often been made, sometimes indeed by the enemies of Christianity as a reproach to it, but it seems certainly just: it is this. The tendency on the whole of growth in sanctity is, that our personal love

ence between the inward sensations of one man and those of another, that disgrace is as much avoided as bodily pain, and to be the object of esteem and love is as much desired as any external goods: and in many particular cases, persons are carried on to do good to others, as the end their affection tends to and rests in; and manifest that they find real satisfaction and enjoyment in this course of behaviour. There is such a natural principle of attraction in man towards man, that having trod the same tract of land, having breathed in the same climate, barely having been born in the same artificial district or division, becomes the occasion of contracting acquaintances and familiarities many years after: for anything may serve the purpose. Thus relations merely nominal are sought and invented, not by governors, but by the lowest of the people; which are found sufficient to hold mankind together in little fraternities and copartnerships: weak ties indeed, and that may afford fund enough for ridicule, if they are absurdly considered as the *real principles* of that union: but they are in truth merely the *occasions*, as anything may be of anything, upon which our nature carries us on *according to its own previous bent and bias;* which occasions therefore would be nothing at all, were there not this prior disposition and bias of nature. Men are so much one body, that in a peculiar manner they feel for each other, shame, sudden danger, resentment, honour, prosperity, distress; one or another, or all of these; from the social nature in general, from benevolence, upon the occasion of natural relation, acquaintance, protection, dependence; each of these being distinct cements of society."— *Butler's Sermons.*

shall more and more be *taken from* our visible companions here below, and fixed on the Invisible World. I am far from meaning by this, that all men, or more than a comparatively small portion, are called by God to a state in which particular earthly friendships are to cease. But I do think it true, that, as we advance towards perfection, such friendships become less absorbing and less engrossing; we grow more and more towards regarding our friend, as in some way a special representative to us of our brethren in general.

137. The next propension to be noticed is 'Misericordia'—Compassion. In addition to this General Love of our fellow-men which we have just considered—a propension which, in its rudimental state, and on its positive side, must be regarded as somewhat faint—in addition to this General Love (I say) we have a propension, far keener, far more irrepressible, far more powerfully influential, which draws us to the relief of *misery as such*. We meet a fellow-man whom we never before saw; and experience (it may be) some calm emotion of general benevolence. Let him unfold a tale of bitter distress, and give us ample means for knowing its truth, far different is our emotion. The most hard-hearted men can only save themselves from this pain, by resolutely shutting their ears to the melancholy story; it is not in human nature, that we shall *know* our brother's griefs, and not grieve ourselves.*

* " Of these two, delight in the prosperity of others, and compassion for their distresses, the last is felt much more generally than the former. Though men do not universally rejoice with all whom they see rejoice, yet, accidental obstacles removed, they naturally compassionate all, in some degree, whom they see in distress ; so far as they have any real perception or sense of that distress : insomuch that words expressing this latter, pity, compassion, frequently occur ; whereas we have scarce any single one, by which the former is distinctly expressed. Congratulation, indeed, answers condolence : but both these words are intended to signify certain forms of civility, rather than any inward sensation or feeling. This difference or inequality is so remarkable, that we plainly consider compassion as itself an original distinct particular affection in human nature ; whereas to rejoice in the good of others, is only a consequence of the general affection of love and goodwill to them. The reason and account of which matter is this : when a man has obtained any particular advantage or felicity, his end is gained ; and he does not in that particular want the assistance of another : there was therefore no need of a distinct affection towards that felicity of another already obtained ; neither would such affection directly carry him

Now it is quite unnecessary to remark in detail, on the powerful assistance given by this propension to the cause of virtue, and its powerful tendency against selfishness and indolent sensuality. It is more pertinent, to point out the singular *suitableness* of this propension in a world like ours. In a world where sorrow is so general, what plain mark of benevolent design is seen in the fact, that God has given us a propension which tends so powerfully to alleviate sorrow !

One of you has here interposed a very ingenious objection; let me state and answer it. ' God created us ' in a perfectly happy state; excluding all possibility ' (except through sin) of pain or grief. Hence,' argues the objector, ' a Catholic philosopher is *precluded* from ' such a line of argument as the above; he is precluded ' from supposing, that God created our nature with ' express reference to the circumstance of our being ' encompassed with grief.' I reply as follows. Catholic doctrine teaches, as you will see in due time, that Adam was preserved in his state of happiness, not by any peculiarity of his nature, but by a series of constant and watchful operations exercised by God *upon* that nature. Two alternatives were put before him ; and for that very reason, his *nature* was so created as to suit *either* alternative, and inclusively therefore the less happy one. Since, *on* that alternative, misery was to abound,— it was suitable that our nature should include this special propension of Mercy or Compassion. More will be said in this very Section, on the relation between Adam's original state and our fallen condition.

It is a fact by no means to be forgotten, and which no one to be sure could antecedently have imagined, that under the Gospel *God Himself* becomes an Object

on to do good to that person : *whereas men in distress want assistance ; and compassion leads us directly to assist them.* The object of the former is the present felicity of another ; the object of the latter is the present misery of another. It is easy to see that the latter wants a particular affection for its relief, and that the former does not want one, because it does not want assistance. And upon supposition of a distinct affection in both cases, the one must rest in the exercise of itself, having nothing further to gain ; the other does not rest in itself, but carries us on to assist the distressed."— *Butler's " Sermon on Compassion."*

to this propension. In contemplating our Blessed Lord's sufferings, and particularly the various stages of His Passion, the feeling of *Compassion* occupies a very prominent place.

138. The last propension of this class which I shall mention, is 'Gratitude;' the peculiar pleasure we derive, from requiting in kind any favours we have received. A mere allusion will suffice, on so plain a matter, (1) to the great assistance derived from this propension to various acts of social virtue; and (2) to the great degree in which it cheers and consoles all work done for *His* sake, 'Who, being rich, *for our sake* became poor.'

139. We have now recited six propensions; (1) Duty; (2) Self-charity; (3) Personal Love; (4) General Love; (5) Compassion; (6) Gratitude: and we have seen the immense assistance which they give us in living for Almighty God. Our general thesis, you remember, is this; that all our propensions without exception are calculated, each in its own way, to give us help and support in that holy enterprise. As yet certainly we have done very little to demonstrate that thesis. 'No one ever doubted,' an objector may reply, 'that ' *many* of our propensions lead towards *good;* the only ' question worth considering is, whether there are not ' *others* which with *equal* force lead towards *evil.* On ' this, the only important question, nothing has yet been ' said.' I reply, by fully admitting the force of the objection. My object hitherto has chiefly been, to put before you a map (as it were) of these essentially beneficial propensions, and of the place which they occupy in the interior life; thus shewing the careful provision made by our Creator, for giving us rest and joy in His service. My object, I say, as yet has been *this* rather than any very strong controversial argument in behalf of our thesis. Our next step however will advance us considerably in the way of proof. For I proceed to ask, *what* are those propensions, which on the whole are most widely and deeply influential—have put forth the most permanent and sustained power—in leading men away from God. I will shew you that *those*

very propensions are capable of rendering *most important assistance* towards His love and service.

You will at first perhaps answer, that the propension of the flesh (as I may call it),—the propension which tempts us to violate the Sixth Commandment,—is the most pervasive and powerful enemy to virtue.   I do not think that would be a true answer ; for fearful as have been the effects produced by that propension, it cannot from its very nature have that *constant, unrelenting, pervasive power*, which is exercised by certain other propensions.   We will not of course leave it unnoticed ; but, on the contrary, we will consider it in its due place, with a care proportioned to its importance. But first we will direct our attention to those propensions, which often become the main-spring of a man's *whole conduct of life ;* which often colour the *whole tissue of his existence.*   Of this kind, spiritual writers prominently mention three : (1) Love of Honour or Fame ; (2) Love of Power ; (3) Love of Wealth.   I commence then with the Love of Honour.

140. This propension certainly acts, with a constancy and intensity which perfectly amazes one, in leading men to direct their conduct towards an end quite distinct from their Creator's service.   It is often remarked, how miserably *impurity* clouds the intellect ; but *this* propension clouds it immeasurably more.   Men will tell you, as of quite an honourable fact, that they look on infamy as the greatest of evils, and that the approbation of their fellow-creatures is their one paramount end of action.   Well do I remember a veteran Protestant politician, writing a letter to the newspapers, which professed quite a tone of conscious and indignant virtue.   It ran in substance thus : ' True, I am an ' old man ; I must soon leave this visible scene ; but ' *for that very reason*, it is a more sacred duty that I ' leave my *reputation* intact.'   He was a man who firmly believed in the doctrine of a future state ; and he was (I take for granted) fully confident, of being pretty sure after death to be admitted into Heaven and the company of Saints and Angels.   And yet, for *that very reason*

forsooth, it was the *more* his sacred duty, to leave his
reputation intact on this sinful and miserable earth.   It
is just as though a crawling worm were on the point of
being raised by God to the dignity and privilege of a
rational creature; and were to say, '*for that very reason*
it is *the more* a sacred duty, to preserve my reputation
among my fellow crawlers unsullied and intact.'   But
the same motive animates all classes and all professions.
So a soldier will go through deeds of fabulous daring,
and (which is more strange) will undergo sufferings of
most fearful severity,—sustained throughout by one
sweet hope, that of his fellow-countrymen's applause. Or,
(going to an extremely opposite instance) a philosopher
will give his whole energy to the working out of
some grand intellectual system, in the hope of one
principal reward—posthumous fame.   It is related, I
believe, of that profound thinker Kant, that he was
quite thrown off his balance with anxiety and distress,
when some danger appeared, lest he should lose with
posterity his fair claim to originality of discovery.

A more monstrous, more frantic, antagonism to God,
than this idolatry of human honour, cannot well be
imagined.   He placed us men on earth, that we might
make His Will and Preference the ruling principle of
our lives.   We, the creatures of His hand, give hardly
so much as a passing thought through the day to that
Will and Preference.   So far as we are slaves to this propension, our main motive of action is avowedly, professedly, the approbation of our fellow-worms, our fellow-
sinners.   The whole world is seated in wickedness; and
yet we do not blush to make the applause of that world
the incentive to our whole conduct.   The *extensiveness*
of this idolatry, is as amazing as its *intensity*.   It extends from such cases as the great soldier or illustrious
philosopher, through all intermediate ranks, down to
the very school-boy; who is ashamed to express his
own sense of what is due to God,—not from fear of being
molested by his fellow-boys, for the same thing takes place
where there is no *danger* of molestation;—no; but from
simple alarm at the thought of their *sneers*, their *deri-*

sion. And long after we have ceased to be school-boys, how often have we felt (some of course more, others less,) that before the sneer and derision of our fellow-men, we become almost ashamed of our strongest principles, almost distrustful of our highest aspirations. Even men aiming at perfection, during the lower stages of their growth at least, are infested by this deadly foe; which forces itself as it were into companionship with their best ends, and sullies with its foul presence many of their highest actions.*

* On some of the more ordinary and petty manifestations of this vice, how accurate is Surin's description; and how amusing if it were not so sad! "Le second effet de la vanité est l'amour et le désir des louanges. Quand un homme est occupé de lui-même, et que ses propres perfections sont l'entrétien ordinaire de son esprit, il désire que ses perfections soient connues et louées. La complaisance qu'il a en lui-même ne manque point de produire ce désir; et quand on le loue, *il se repaît de cette fumée.* L'approbation du monde, l'applaudissement, les louanges, sont pour lui un breuvage délicieux, qui l'énivre de l'amour de lui-même. Il est toujours auprès à écumer les jugemens qu'on fait de lui, et quand il a fait quelque action publique, quand il a composé quelque pièce, il est toujours *en ardeur de savoir ce qu'on en dit.* Si l'on n'en parle pas avantageusement, il en sent une vive douleur, qui vient de sa vanité. Si l'on en juge favorablement, *il se fera dire et redire sans cesse ce qui flatte, pour se repaître de ce vent.* Il se *blame, pour s'attirer de louanges, afin qu'en le contredisant, on lui verse plus abondamment de cette liqueur qu'il boit avec tant de plaisir* dans la coupe de la vanité.

"Mais quand deux esprits vains *se rencontrent ensemble, et se mettent à se louer à l'envi,* c'est alors que vous voyez la vanité dans son triomphe. Ecoutez deux poëtes qui se louent : ils se placent l'un auprès de l'autre dans le temple de mémoire ; ils se donnent de l'encens à pleines mains, et se traitent comme des dieux. S'ils louent leurs héros, ils en font des divinités.

"C'est la coutume de flatter ainsi les grands par des louanges excessives pour leur complaire ; car rien ne touche plus les esprits foibles des gens du monde que les louanges. Les femmes sont ravies d'être louées de beauté ; les courtesans de politesse, et de galanterie ; les guerriers, de bravoure ; les ministres d'état, de grand génie. *On leur représente la postérité occupée à les admirer.* Tous ces vains discours vont à leur persuader, que ce souvenir avantageux qu'on aura d'eux, est la *plus douce chose qu'il y ait au monde.* Et cela, n'est-ce pas une vanité deplorable? Pendant que les hommes les loueront sur la terre, *ils seront peut-être dans les flammes éternelles.* 'Laudantur ubi non sunt, torquentur ubi sunt.' (S. August.) L'amour propre les enchante tellement, qu'encore qu'ils soient malheureux en eux-mêmes, ils se font un plaisir imaginaire des louanges qu'on leur promet après leur mort.

"Quels efforts ne fait-on pas pour avoir place dans l'histoire? On sent une agréable satisfaction de voir son nom dans une Gazette. C'est un plaisir bien mince qui tournera peut-être à votre confusion : mais enfin cela contente ; et en même temps qu'il contente, il fait d'étranges ravages dans l'âme : *il éloigne de la vérité ; il bannit l'humilité chrétienne.* Aussi ceux qui marchent dans la lumière de la vraie sagesse, fuient cela *comme le poison qui fait mourir toutes le virtus.*"—*Dialogues Spirituels,* vol. 2, pp. 3–5.

Yet consider well this very remarkable fact. We have seen that this propension, as usually directed, more than almost any other is God's deadly foe. We may now add, that in that very degree it is among the most unmistakable illustrations of our general principle. We are maintaining, that all our propensions have an important place in the cause of virtue : and that, in regard to most of them, our work here below is, not to aim at *lessening* their force in the very slightest degree; but singly and exclusively to aim at *fixing* them on their proper *objects*. In the present case, is there not an Object ready at hand, which is as manifestly, as undeniably, *adequate* to the intense strength of this propension, as its ordinary objects are grotesquely *inadequate*? Our Creator is more closely present to us, than we are to each other; the Soul of our most loving Saviour penetrates every hidden corner of our hearts; Mary sees in God all that most closely concerns us; Our Guardian Angel, the Blessed Saints, all know in various degrees what we do, and what we think. How *can* we, who have the approbation of the whole Court of Heaven as a prize to contend for, so *demean* ourselves, as to open our hearts mainly to the vain, transitory, delusive, praise of our fellow-men?

Here we see an ascetical truth of some little importance. If I am at this moment fluttering with vain glory; my emotions highly enflamed; my very body throbbing, as it were, under the magnetic influence of human applause; I am not called to aim at *lessening* that emotion. No : let me contemplate, with the eye of faith, my Creator, my Redeemer, my Heavenly Mother, the whole blessed Company of Angels and Saints, looking down on me, and prepared to approve or censure me as my conduct may deserve. In that vision of faith I am wrapped securely. That very propension, which was the devil's chief engine of attack, becomes the Holy Ghost's most powerful weapon in putting Him to flight.

This contrast is from time to time expressed in the New Testament. Thus John, c. xii. v. 43. " Dilexerunt " enim *gloriam hominum* magis quàm *gloriam Dei ;*"

and Romans, c. ii. v. 29, " Sed qui in abscondito, " Judæus est: circumcisio cordis in spiritu, non litterâ ; "*cujus laus non ex hominibus, sed ex Deo est.*"

You will not of course suppose me to deny for a moment, that the approbation of *good men* in all ordinary cases is to be greatly prized; and specially in this point of view, as the pledge and representative to us of *God's* approbation. In this, as on so many other matters, it will appertain to our later course to complete what our earlier begins. When we come to consider the morality of human acts, we shall be led to some definite and important results, on the principles of judgment here to be adopted; on the principles whereby we may distinguish, that idolatry of human applause which is so dangerous and detestable, from that love of *good men's* approbation, which is in itself perfectly legitimate, and in its results inestimably valuable.

141. The next propension to be treated is Love of Power. This does not seem comparable to the former, either in intensity or pervasiveness; indeed it is but a comparatively small portion of mankind, who are in a position to gratify it at all in the more ordinary sense. It is quite plain however, that every man who is in a position to gratify it by influencing others to his own private ends, may equally gratify it by influencing them towards *public ends* and towards *their Creator's service.* The propension before us is gratified, in proportion as we know that we are able to move at will a large number of our fellow-men : it is plain then that the gratification is precisely the same, whether that power be exerted in this or in that direction. He who fulfils his duty, by using the full influence of his station or circumstances to the promotion of God's Glory, is in no slight degree assisted and cheered in that holy work, by the propension which we are considering. Certainly there is great need of watchfulness, lest this gratification be tainted with pride ; still in itself it is undeniably legitimate.

But a further remark is still more in point. The Gospel assures us, of what reason alone would render

very probable, the great efficacy of *intercessory prayer.*
And it is most important that we should perform this
duty, not in a dry perfunctory way, but with a keen
and lively interest. Now such keen and lively interest
must necessarily arise, in proportion as we have a
practical and living persuasion, that our prayer will
as really and truly promote God's Glory, tend to the
salvation of souls, affect the course of events, redress
ecclesiastical evils, move the whole fortunes of the
Church, as the most lively and energetic work can
possibly do. It is plain then how very desirable it is,
that we cherish in ourselves this practical and living
persuasion; and it is no less plain, that we are indefinitely
assisted in doing so, by the keen pleasure which the
propension before us experiences from that persuasion.
This I take to be the primary and truly legitimate
scope of this propension;—the stimulating us to intercessory prayer.

142. There remained *Love of Money.* This however
must be decomposed into two separate elements.
Money is chiefly sought as a mere ' bonum utile ;' as
serviceable towards further ends. There is an indefinitely large number of pleasurable or serviceable
things, of which I have learnt by experience that they
are purchaseable by money. The desire of all these
things inflows virtually (see n. 111) into those various
acts of mine, whereby I desire money ; and (to come
more immediately to our present subject) the thought
of money is made pleasurable, by the combined and
confused thought of these various pleasures. This it
is no doubt, which chiefly causes the intensity and
universality of money-hunting : it is a sort of *com-
pound* propension, uniting the force and strength of so
many simple ones.

This is the sense in which love of riches is de-
nounced by our Lord in terms of such astounding
severity. It is most important, that we should preserve
a clear and constant memory of these denunciations;
and I will therefore say some little to remind you of
them. At the same time you must understand, that I

have neither leisure nor (indeed) ability to do them anything like justice.

Three different Evangelists have recorded our Lord's saying, that it is easier for a camel to go through a needle's eye than for a rich man to enter the kingdom of Heaven (Matt. c. xix. v. 24.   Mark, c. x. v. 25. Luke, c. xviii. v. 25); and all three record that He proceeded to declare, 'with man it is impossible, but with God all things are possible.'   A rich man's salvation *tests* (if we so express ourselves) the Omnipotence of God.   Again (Luke, c. vi. v. 24, 25), ' Verumtamen ' væ vobis divitibus, quia habetis consolationem vestram. ' Væ vobis qui saturati estis, quia esurietis.   Væ vobis ' qui ridetis nunc, quia lugebitis et flebitis.'

Observe also, as has been frequently remarked, in the parable of Dives and Lazarus, how closely connected with eternal perdition is the mere possession of wealth.   Nothing more is said of Dives, than that he was clothed in purple and fine linen, and feasted splendidly every day (Luke, xvi. v. 19).   Then as the natural result of this we are told (v. 22) that after his death he was buried in Hell.

In all such passages, our Blessed Saviour is speaking (no doubt) of riches in *their natural tendency*.   He who is abundantly supplied with all the necessaries and many superfluities of life;—who seems to be so circumstanced, that the slightest wish or whim can be readily gratified;—what is the state of mind into which such a man will naturally fall?   He will become, unless he makes very special resistance, proud, self-satisfied, luxurious ; above all, and characteristically, he will look on this world as his home.   There can hardly be a character more deeply hateful in the eyes of God.   Consider in this connection, Apoc. c. iii. v. 17, 18, ' Quia dicis : Quòd dives sum, et locu- ' pletatus, et nullius egeo ; et nescis quia tu es miser, et ' miserabilis, et pauper, et cæcus, et nudus ; Suadeo ' tibi emere à me aurum ignitum probatum, ut locuples ' fias, et vestimentis albis induaris, et non appareat

' confusio nuditatis tuæ; et collyrio inunge oculos tuos,
' ut videas.'

On the other hand, a poor man feels at every step
his utter and abject dependence; and having little
solace in this world, he is the rather disposed to seek
such solace in the things of God. Of course the rich
man may contend against his special temptations, and
the poor man may throw away his special advantages;
but the *tendency* of the two conditions respectively
is as above stated.

Elsewhere indeed our Lord explains His words.
He explains them, as applying not so much to the
wealthy or poor *person*, as to what may be called the
wealthy or poor *spirit.* Thus in St. Mark, immediately
before his statement on the camel's eye, he explains
what he means by the rich man; viz. one who *trusts*
in riches (c. x. v. 24): ' Discipuli autem obstupes-
' cebant in verbis ejus. At Jesus rursus respondens
' ait illis; Filioli, quàm difficile est, *confidentes in*
' *pecuniis* in regnum Dei introire.' Again, whereas
in Luke, c. vi. v. 20, He says, ' Blessed are ye poor;'
in Matt. c. v. ver. 3, it is, ' Blessed are the poor *in
spirit.*' And whereas in Luke, c. vi. v. 21, He says,
' Blessed are ye who now hunger,' in Matt. c. v.
v. 6, it is ' Blessed are they who hunger and thirst
after justice:' those, *e. g.* who, from the very fact of
being without comfort and rest *here*, are led to *seek*
them in the *service of God.*

On the whole however, we cannot surely, in any
fairness, draw from these awful statements a milder
conclusion than the following. If there be any rich
man, who is not sensitively alive to the special temptations of his state;—who does not carefully examine how
far he is exposed to them;—who does not (if he *be* so
exposed) carry out carefully some special discipline in
regard to those temptations;—such a man has reason
to be in most serious alarm, as to his attaining final
perseverance. Even though he be in Habitual Grace
now, he has reason for the most anxious doubts, whether

this will continue to the last. To this subject we shall have more than once to recur.

There is another form taken by this compound propension, love of money : it not only leads those who have money in abundance, to be proud and worldly; it leads those who have it *not*, to seek it in a restless, feverish, absorbing, spirit. Against this also Our Blessed Lord directs his strongest warnings. Thus Matt. c. v. ver. 25, 26. ' Ideò dico vobis, ne solliciti ' sitis animæ vestræ quid manducetis, nec corpori vestro ' quid induamini. Nonne anima plus est quàm esca? ' et corpus plus quàm vestimentum? Respicite vo- ' latilia cœli, &c.' And the same thought is pursued for several further verses to the end of the chapter. Again, Matt. c. xiii. v. 22 : ' Qui autem seminatus est ' in spinis, hic est, qui verbum audit, et sollicitudo ' sæculi istius, et *fallacia divitiarum*, suffocat verbum, ' et sine fructu efficitur.'

This exercise of the propension before us,—the laborious and unrestrained *working* for wealth,—produces in the spiritual life effects, not less disastrous perhaps than the former, but plainly of quite a different kind. The restless occupation, the breathless anxiety, the feverish excitement, all these present as broad a contrast as can well be imagined, to that tranquil, recollected, interior, spirit, which is the atmosphere wherein alone prayer and meditation can breathe. The great majority of mankind undoubtedly are, from circumstances, obliged to labour in weariness and uncertainty for their daily bread. What is that kind of spiritual discipline, whereby they may best be preserved from these terrible spiritual dangers—this is one of the most important, and perhaps one of the most difficult, questions, on which Ascetic Theology has to treat.

As one of my chief objects in this Section, is to give the best map I can of our various propensions, it was of course out of the question that I should omit one, so vitally important in its bearing on spirituality as this compound propension. It is equally plain however, that it cannot come within the scope of our immediate argument; not being an *original* propension at all. So far as we have yet treated it, it is not a propension which God has implanted in our nature, but one which we form for ourselves, by our mode of *exercising* those which He *has* implanted. Our thesis only calls on us to prove, that all those which He *has* implanted are capable of most virtuous use ; and as this is not one of their number, it is not included in the statement. In proportion as we shall have exercised our *original* pro-pensions according to God's wish and desire, this com-pound and derived propension will not have been called into existence.

It is commonly held however by psychologians, and I think with truth, that the desire of money is not *wholly* analyzed, by ascribing it to the desire of those various gratifications which money can purchase. It is held that there is a propension, implanted by God in our nature, which we may call ' love of acquisition;' that we are susceptible of a special pleasure, from hoarding and accumulating what we can call *our own;* from guarding and adding to a store of *property.* In-deed this seems clear in the extreme case of a miser; since he loses his relish for those enjoyments which money can procure, in his idolatry of money itself. What then is the legitimate use of this propension ?

Our Saviour Himself seems to tell us (Matthew, c. vi. v. 19), 'Nolite thesaurizare vobis thesauros in ' terrâ, ubi ærugo, et tinea demolitur, et ubi fures ' effodiunt et furantur; thesaurizate autem vobis the- ' sauros in *cælo;* ubi neque ærugo neque tinea de- ' molitur,' &c. Even apart from Revelation, Reason would shew that there are many things which are more specially *ours* than *money* can ever be; which may more truly be called *property;* which will more ade-quately satisfy our love of accumulation : virtuous habits, a contented disposition, a disengaged heart— these are treasures indeed. First, they are intrinsic to ourselves, and cannot by physical possibility be snatched from our grasp; and secondly, when once gained, they are not diminished but increased, in proportion as we draw upon our store. There is a pleasure, which is undoubtedly attainable, by hoarding and accumulating;— here a little and there a little;—so much to-day and so much more to-morrow;—by watching for every opportunity, and taking sedulous advantage of it, which may be made the means of further accumulation. But I maintain that this pleasure can be far more satisfactorily enjoyed, in the gradual acquirement and increase of *virtuous habits*, than of *perishable gold*. And now let us consider, in addition to this, what the Gospel discloses, as to these spiritual and heavenly treasures. Let us ponder on that great Gift of Habitual Grace, which is increased by every supernatural act we do. Let us carry on our thoughts to those future treasures in Heaven, spoken of by Our Blessed Saviour; those treasures, whereof Habitual Grace is the seed and the measure. Such thoughts will soon make clear to us, what is the full and adequate object of the propension before us.

143. I said that the chief obstacles to piety enumerated by ascetical writers are, (1) Love of Honour or Fame; (2) Love of Power; (3) Love of Wealth; and these three propensions we have now considered. Perhaps indeed there is a fourth, which both is, and is commonly admitted to be, an equally (or a more) powerful antagonist: I mean Pride. What is that propension whereof *pride* is the *perversion*, and what is its legitimate scope, I will consider somewhat later in the present Section. That which I will *next* treat, shall be Love of Knowledge; or (as it may perhaps be more suitably called) Love of Intellectual Exertion: a propension, which exercises its full power indeed over extremely few; but almost makes up, by its violence and intensity, for the narrowness of its operations. Nothing, *e. g.* is more commonly remarked, than the very close and (as it were) natural connexion, between great mathematical power and extreme infidelity. How is such a fact to be explained? There are few questions in Ethical

u

Psychology more important than this; and I incline to think the true explanation is as follows.

There is a certain small number of men, endued with singularly high intellectual gifts, on whom various choice intellectual processes confer a degree of pleasure, resembling that which ordinary men derive from sensual indulgences. I mean such processes as these; viewing a large field of truth in its mutual relations; pressing judgments to their various consequences; analyzing the more recondite phenomena of the mind, &c. &c. These indulgences however differ from sensual, in this most important particular; viz. that they are capable of very protracted and sustained continuance. The sensualist obtains but transient and fitful excitements; and in the interval feels languor, perhaps remorse. But these intellectualists may give themselves up for an indefinite period to their darling pursuit. If then they choose to do this in a reckless inordinate way, simply for the sake of the pleasure thence to be derived, and with no reference to moral duty or the will of God, what is the result? They become more thoroughly obdurate—more thoroughly insensible to higher and more spiritual motives—than perhaps any class of men which can be named. The principle, on which this result takes place, will be considered in our work ' De Actibus Humanis.'

Next ensues a further result — diabolical pride. The intellect is an instrument of tremendous power. ' Instrument' is exactly the proper word to express my meaning: the intellect is an *instrument*, just as any mechanical power is one. It is as simply absurd, to make the quality of a man's intellect in itself the matter either of praise or blame, as to praise or blame a steam-engine: the *true* matter for praise and blame, is the *use* which he makes of this powerful instrument; whether in God's service or the Devil's. But I say, the *power* of this instrument is enormous; immensely greater than unintellectual men can even imagine. Consider then, how great must be the intoxication of wielding a power of this kind, in the case of such men as I suppose; in the case of men, who do not so much as *attempt* any practices of religion,— meditation, or examen of conscience, or the like,— and who are free from severe bodily sickness or other temporal trouble. They know by experience the wonderful influence of intellectual power; and they look up to themselves intensely for possessing it. Here again is another distinction, which separates these men for the worse from the class of sensualists. No sensualist can *respect* himself,— *look* up to himself,— on the ground of his bestial excesses; whereas pride is the ordinary, nay the necessary accompaniment of great intellectual power, whenever the humbling exercises of piety are neglected.

Here then are two qualities which naturally ensue: (1) insensibility to all spiritual motives; and (2) pride. How easily do these two united lead to unbelief. The pride of these men would .be most painfully wounded, by the manifest *contradiction* involved, in believing one thing, when they practise another; while of course their indisposition to *practise* religion is the greatest imaginable. This being so, how obvious that they should have recourse to a most easy and simple alternative! They ponder on the various objections (in themselves surely most plausible) which may be brought, not so much against Christianity in particular, as against Theism in general. At the same time, they give no careful thought at all to those replies which have been made by Christian writers; contenting themselves with the conclusion, that the whole thing is buried in hopeless uncertainty.

Here is one obvious cause of their unbelief; another will be found in the following consideration. The mysteries of the Gospel, nay the doctrines of Natural Religion, appear, to their blind, carnal, grovelling, and proud intellect, quite low and contemptible; such as it is impossible to believe, without doing violence to their whole nature. ' A fit story,' they think, ' for the ' cradle and the nursery; for the earliest years of each

' individual, or the earliest years of the human race:
' man has *outgrown* these puerilities.'

Indeed all, who are conscious of great intellectual
power, and who have any kind of interest in their own
perfection,—must be most painfully aware by experience, how troublesome and anxious an element is
such intellectual power in their mental composition.
It may be made no doubt an invaluable *servant :* but
it is ever trying to rise into the position of *master;* and
on no account must this be permitted.

If then this propension be not comparable, as to the
extensiveness of its evil effects, with those which we
considered immediately before—with Love of Honour,
of Power, of Money —almost in the same proportion it
exceeds these propensions in the *intensity* of its mischief; in the utter ruinousness of those effects which
it produces, on men who unreservedly surrender themselves to its influence. It makes a perfect wreck of
their spiritual character : it degrades them to the very
lowest moral level possible on earth; to that state of
mind, known in Theology as 'obduratio' and 'excæcatio.'
If then it can be shewn, that even *this* propension is
capable of important service to morality,—certainly no
inconsiderable addition will have been made to the
progress of our argument.

Now those frightful results of this propension which
we have been considering, are seen only in those, who
give themselves up to it almost *exclusively.* They are
commonly but little gifted with the propension either of
Personal or of General Love; and they allow this Love
of Intellectual Exertion to override despotically all the
rest. There may be an exception to this statement, (not
however affecting our argument,) so far as it is true,
that various persons of great intellectual power have
from time to time yielded themselves slaves to a low
sensuality. But at all events, in the hardened men we
are considering, all the *higher* propensions except the
one before us are dormant; and the Love of Intellectual
Exertion reigns paramount and supreme. It is obvious
then to enquire, what are the effects of this propension, on

those who gratify it,—not in this reckless, inordinate, overbearing way,— but with due moderation, and merely as *one part* of their moral nature.

In regard to those who must support themselves by the labour of their hands, hardly any answer can be given to this enquiry; the main current of their life is such, as to disable them altogether from gratifying this propension, except in the most partial and occasional manner.   The main case to be considered then, is that of the *leisured classes;* and I do not think it too much to say, that if this propension were away, and no other change wrought in human nature, the immense majority of these classes would find the consistent practice of virtue morally impossible.   In behalf of this conclusion I argue thus.

How many men are there, so created by God, that they can keep up through the day a constant course of Divine contemplation?   Just so many, as have a vocation to the purely contemplative life; *i. e.* an extremely small minority.

Now let us turn our thoughts again to the labouring classes; and I will use this word in its *widest* sense, so as to include *all* whose day is spent, either in *manual* labour, or in *other* active and practical work of a busy and external kind.   How are these men able to serve God,—through the day, through the month, through the year,—consistently and perseveringly?   For our answer let me refer to n. 129 (p. 257).   They may aim at referring their various acts virtually and most really to God; and the quiet tranquil gratification, which their Creator has ordinarily attached to the orderly performance of their regular duties, will cheer and sustain them in their course. If this gratification were away, there would be ordinarily (I suppose) no sufficient moral power, of referring the course of their lives really to God.

I ask then, what *substitute* for this gratification is available to the *leisured classes?*   Take away this one propension which we are considering, I believe that no other can be named.   The propension of Personal Love, as directed to one or more of our fellow-creatures, is

certainly very far from being one which can be called
into active exertion through the day; the very attempt
to do so, does but land us in deep misery, unreality,
and false sentimentality. Will you propose æsthetic
employments — music, drawing, and the like? I believe
the number is but small in the leisured classes, who
could derive enjoyment from making such occupations as these the business of their lives; most charm-
ing and refreshing though they be as *recreations*, and
as affording a grateful vicissitude to severer studies.
According to God's merciful design however, the whole
field of science and literature is open to these classes;
each one may cultivate that, which best suits his taste,
his circumstances, his powers, or the degree of his
intellectual acquirements; and most beneficial is the
result. That very peculiarity of the propension, which
constitutes (as we have seen) its chief evil, — I mean
its singular power of receiving *long-continued and
protracted gratification* — this very peculiarity confers a
most important service in the way we have described.*

* Father Newman had the same truth in view, I suppose, when he
wrote the following most powerfully expressed passage. He has not, indeed,
made it sufficiently clear, whether he is speaking of *mankind in general*
or exclusively of the *leisured classes*. If the former, I venture to think its
wording is open to great exception; for it would (on that interpretation)
seem to state, that few Christians of uncultivated intellect *have the moral
power of avoiding mortal sin:* though of course he could not possibly have
meant this. If we take it as applying to the leisured classes alone, it
conveys, I think, an important truth.

"Now on opening the subject, we see at once a momentous benefit
which the philosopher is likely to confer on the pastors of the Church. It
is obvious that the first step which they have to effect in the conversion of
man and the renovation of his nature, is its rescue from that fearful subjection to sense which is its ordinary state. To be able to break through the
meshes of that thraldom, and to disentangle and to disengage its ten
thousand holds upon the heart, is to bring it, I might almost say, half-way
to Heaven. Here, even divine grace, to speak of things according to their
appearances, is ordinarily baffled, and retires, without expedient or resource,
before this giant fascination. Religion seems too high and unearthly to be
able to exert a continued influence upon us: its effort to rouse the soul, and
the soul's effort to co-operate, are too violent to last. It is like holding out
the arm at full length, or supporting some great weight, which we manage
to do for a time, but soon are exhausted and succumb. Nothing can act
beyond its own nature; when then we are called to what is supernatural,
though those extraordinary aids from heaven are given us, with which
obedience becomes possible, yet even with them it is of transcendant difficulty. We are drawn down to earth every moment with the ease and
certainty of a natural gravitation, and it is only by sudden impulses and

Here is the first benefit, and surely an inappreciable one, conferred by the propension before us: it gives (as it were) forcible plunges that we attempt to mount upwards. Religion indeed enlightens, terrifies, subdues; it gives faith, it inflicts remorse, it inspires resolutions, it draws tears, it inflames devotion, but only for the occasion. The sinful spirit repents, and protests it will never sin again, and for a while is protected by disgust and abhorrence from the malice of its foe. But that foe knows too well, that such seasons of repentance are wont to have their end: he patiently waits, till nature faints with the effort of resistance, and lies passive and hopeless under the next access of temptation. What we need then is some expedient or instrument, which at least will obstruct and stave off the approach of our spiritual enemy, and which is sufficiently congenial and level with our nature to maintain as firm a hold upon us as the inducements of sensual gratification. It will be our wisdom to employ nature against itself. Thus sorrow, sickness, and care are providential antagonists to our inward disorders; they come upon us as years pass on, and generally produce their effects on us, in proportion as we are subjected to their influence. These, however, are God's instruments, not ours; we need a similar remedy, which we can make our own, the object of some legitimate faculty, or the aim of some natural affection, which is capable of resting on the mind, and taking up its familiar lodging with it, and engrossing it, and which thus becomes a *match for the besetting power of sensuality*, and a sort of homœopathic medicine for the disease. Here then I think is the important aid which intellectual cultivation furnishes to us in rescuing the victims of passion and self-will. It does not supply religious motives; it is not the cause or proper antecedent of anything supernatural; it is not meritorious of heavenly aid or reward; but it does a work, at least *materially* good (as theologians speak), whatever be its real and formal character. It expels the excitements of sense by the introduction of those of the intellect.

" This then is the *prima facie* advantage of the pursuit of knowledge; it is the drawing the mind off from things which will harm it to subjects which are worthy a rational being; and, though it does not raise it above nature, nor has any tendency to make us pleasing to our Maker, yet is it nothing to substitute what is in itself harmless for what is, to say the least, inexpressibly dangerous? is it a little thing to exchange a circle of ideas which are certainly sinful, for others which are certainly not so? You will say, perhaps, in the words of the Apostle, 'Knowledge puffeth up:' and doubtless this mental cultivation, even when it is successful for the purpose for which I am applying it, may be from the first nothing more than the substitution of pride for sensuality. I grant it. I think I shall have something to say on this point presently; but this is not a necessary result, it is but an incidental evil, a danger which may be realised, or may be averted, whereas we may in most cases predicate guilt, and guilt of a heinous kind, where the mind is suffered to run wild and indulge its thoughts without training or law of any kind; and surely to turn away a soul from mortal sin, is a good and a gain so far, whatever comes of it. And, therefore, if a friend in need is twice a friend, I conceive that intellectual employments, though they do no more than occupy the mind with objects naturally noble or innocent, have a special claim upon our consideration and gratitude."— *Newman on University Education*, pp. 295 to 298.

It may be objected perhaps that, in certain states of society, the leisured classes may not have the means of intellectual cultivation. Such cases however, if they exist, are in the highest degree exceptional; and God no doubt gives exceptional grace to meet them.

the leisured classes the moral power of consistently obeying God. But the great majority, alas ! whether of the leisured or any other class, do not choose to aim at consistent obedience. Let us consider then, secondly, the benefit conferred by this propension, even on this indevout majority. As things are now, the leisured class are the greatest benefactors of mankind ; they apply their energies, in fifty different ways, to the investigation of principles and truths, from which spring the greatest advantages to society. But let the propension before us cease, what would this class become? they would sink into the selfish and sensual recipients of bodily enjoyment. Now plainly this latter state, as compared with the former, is a most formidable barrier to the efficacious entrance of Divine Grace. The former state is not a state of *piety,* or a state which leads to *salvation ;* — very far from it : but it surely opposes indefinitely less *obstacles* than the latter, to the Holy Ghost's pressing solicitations.

A third benefit of this propension, and not yielding in importance to any, is the assistance which it has given in forming the Church's Theology ; — Dogmatical, Moral, Ascetical, and the rest. I must reserve, to its proper place in the second Book, the task of putting before you the great importance of Theology ; an importance, which it is difficult indeed to exaggerate, and of which every additional opportunity for experience and reflection will but increase your sense. But consider the great labour and self-denial through which this work has been accomplished ; consider the great pain often involved, in those processes of abstraction, generalization, observation, comparison, which are the necessary conditions of success ; consider the many hours of painful perplexity and anxious hesitation ; consider the pressure of bad health, and sacrifice of more easily obtained enjoyments. What could possibly have supported a body of thinkers through this exhausting labour, except the gratification afforded by the propension before us? This or that man, saintly in attainment, may have been able so to labour, for the pure love of God and performance of duty; but what *large succession* of men could have been found so to act?

144. In closing our consideration of this propension, we close that of our whole second class; for we have treated those which (with one exception*) have of all the greatest strength in drawing the soul from God. Our thesis will next be corroborated, and even more strongly, by moving onward to a further class; to those propensions, which at first sight seem of all the most inevitably and exclusively *evil* in their result. Of these we may specially single out three; Anger, Envy, Pride: the two first would seem to have no scope, except injury to our fellow-creatures; nor the third, except rebellion against our Creator. If these three propensions have legitimate gratifications, *à fortiori* (it may be inferred) must all others have such.

The instance of Anger is so important, that we must treat it at some little length; the other two will be far more briefly dispatched.†

That Anger is not necessarily evil, is plain enough from Scripture. Thus St. Paul (Eph. iv. 26) quoting from the Psalms, says, 'Irascimini, et nolite peccare;' while nevertheless in verse 31 he adds, 'Omnis ... ira ... 'tollatur a vobis:' implying evidently that there is a lawful and an unlawful anger. And our blessed Lord Himself is represented as vouchsafing to experience the emotion of anger (Mark, iii. 5): 'circumspiciens eos 'cum irâ, contristatus super cæcitate cordis eorum:' He experienced the emotion of *holy resentment*, at their base hypocrisy, their deep, malicious, blind, bigotry. So again (John, ii. 14–17) He drove the money-changers and others from the Temple; shewing such marks of visible resentment, that the Apostles remembered that Scripture, 'Zelus domûs tuæ comedit me:'

---

* I mean that of Pride; which we are very soon to consider.

† The whole treatment of ' Anger,' which follows in the text, is taken from Butler's ' sermon on Resentment;' which I am often inclined to think both the most original and the most valuable of all his writings. It should be read in connection with his ' sermon on Forgiveness of Injuries.'

as if they paraphrased it ; 'zeal for the honour of Thy
' House, and consequent resentment at its contumelious
' treatment, have devoured me.' *

We shall see indeed, as we proceed, that this propension is simply identical with 'Love of Justice.' It
is simply identical, I say, with a desire, that *goodness
as such may be rewarded*, and that *wickedness as
such may be punished ;* and with a resulting pleasure
when that consummation takes place. What I have
to say upon it will therefore be divided into two parts.
First, I will explain to the best of my power the extremely important purposes, which this propension,
' Love of Justice,' subserves ; and secondly, I will shew
you that it is the very same propension, which, in its
irregular manifestations, has wrought such extensive
misery, under the shape of Anger or Malevolence.
First then for the former of these two subjects.

The Love of Justice is so intimately associated with
our whole life, that it requires the greatest effort of
abstraction, to imagine how strange would be the scene
presented here below without it. Consider the great
majority of mankind. These men follow simply the
impulse of their various propensions, as they are successively awakened ; like a ship, left, without rudder,
to the movement of each successive gale. They are
simply passive in the matter ; they take no consistent
pains whatever, to follow that one definite course which
Reason prescribes. These men however, as things are,
are led by this propension to *sympathize with virtue as
such, and abhor vice.* Their idea, indeed, of what *constitutes* moral virtue, is vague and indefinite enough ; so
deplorably low is the cultivation of their Moral Faculty:

---

* " Surely, unless we had this account given us by an inspired writer,
we should not have believed it ! Influenced by notions of our own
devising, we should have said, this zealous action of our Lord was quite
inconsistent with His merciful, meek, and (what may be called) His
majestic and serene temper of mind. To put aside form, to dispense with
the ministry of His attendant angels, to act before He had spoken His
displeasure, to use His own hand, to hurry to and fro, to be a servant in
the work of purification, surely this must have arisen from a fire of indignation at witnessing His Father's House insulted, which we sinners cannot
understand."— *Newman's Parochial Sermons,* vol. iii. p. 198.

still it is something.   They admire, even though they do not practise, generosity, self-devotion, probity, and the like ; they will do something to reward such qualities ; they will do a great deal to punish their opposites.

What would be the world's aspect, if this propension were suddenly removed ?   The most active imagination cannot follow this supposition into all its various consequences ; I will take only one instance.   We have seen how completely the great mass of men are ruled by the Love of Honour.   Now suppose Love of Justice were absent, society would dispense its favour and approbation, without any reference to *virtue* at all.   Popular applause would be bestowed on men, without any reference at all to their merit ; simply in proportion to the degree in which (by whatever low arts and devices) they should be able to curry favour (as we say) with their fellows.   No degree of heroic devotion to their country's cause, or self-denying generosity and benevolence, would have even a *tendency* to obtain for men the admiration of mankind.   And consequently, that enormous mass of men, who are powerfully swayed by this desire of being greatly admired, would simply pursue such low arts and devices as are alone available for their purpose.   You see at once—faintly indeed as compared with the truth, yet very clearly,—the total *wreck* which must ensue.   This propension then is one of the very links which hold society together ; take it away, society collapses.

In the case of *good* men, nothing like this could of course ensue ; because they proceed on *principle and reason*, not by mere inclination.   Yet in their case too, the evil inflicted by loss of this propension would be very considerable.   As an introductory sample of what I mean, conceive a meditation on the Passion, in which Our Blessed Lord's *Innocence* should have no effect of its own in intensifying our emotions !   As things are, we dwell on His spotless Purity ; and our *indignation* is excited against those cruel and pitiless men, who could see it unmoved, and continue their unrelenting afflictions.   But suppose the propension before us were eradicated, then we simply *love* these most wicked men as *God's creatures* and as *Christ's redeemed:* this is *the whole account* of our feeling in regard to them. You see, it is as though our moral nature were lopped of an integral part; as though it went on three legs instead of four. Or take another instance. Consider the immense advantage to our spiritual growth, which arises from viewing our sins, one after another, with loathing and bitter indignation, as outrages against our Holy Creator. Such emotions of indignation could not exist, if this propension were withdrawn from our nature.

Then I ask further—what is it which is the animating principle of holy men, missionaries, parish-priests, nay laymen, in their zealous and sustained endeavours for the perfection of themselves and others? Will you say *Love?* I reply—Love, in proportion to its higher excellence, is a plant of far slower growth: in the earlier stages of our course, it is rather this *pious zeal* which is our help and encouragement. What image does S. Ignatius put before us, when he would start us on our course with energy and ardour? The feeling of *military ardour:* he puts before us 'the two Standards;' and calls on us to fight bravely, under Jesus as our Captain, against the embodied hosts of His enemies. Now what is the motive of military ardour? Partly no doubt, it is the desire of honour and fame; and so far it does not fall under our present consideration. But in no less a degree military ardour is made up of *this* propension, Love of Justice: each man identifies his own course with that of right, and this inspiring thought gives animation to every blow. So in the case before us. What are the feelings called up in our mind, by that glorious meditation on the Standards? Partly no doubt, that we are fighting under the very eyes of the Heavenly Host, and are receiving our due meed of praise: but fully as much also, that *other* feeling, that we are engaged on the side of Eternal Truth; and that every blow we give tells against the forces of evil. Whether we are assailing evil within or without,— fighting against a corrupt self or a corrupt world,—in either case *this* it is which gives spirit to our exertions, that it *is* evil against which we are privileged to fight. We see then how vastly our practical work is aided by this propension.

But if we would really understand the place occupied by it in our moral nature, let us ask, what would be the feeling of *Christian Charity*, if Love of Justice were away? in other words, what effect would be produced on our character by that *other* propension of General Benevolence, Christianly directed, if *Love of Justice* were not also present to qualify and direct it? Our feeling would be simply that of *love to sinners*, without any *zeal* at all *against sin;* without any emotion of hatred against their principles. Our pleasure would be fully as great, in rescuing the greatest criminal from the justly deserved punishment of his offences, as in defending the most saintly Christian from the unjust oppression of an unfeeling persecutor. Now it is plain, without adding another word, that to act *in accordance* with such a feeling as this, would simply be to turn the whole moral world upside-down. He who should aim, in his social dealings, *simply* at increasing the pleasure and lessening the pain of his fellow-men ;—he who should do this, I say, without any reference whatever to their comparative *deserts*, without any sustained attempt at promoting virtue and discountenancing vice ; — this man would act simply as God's open enemy.

It is no exaggeration then at all, but the simple truth, to say that that very propension, General Love, which might seem of all the most undeniably and inevitably beneficial in its character, would be simply and grievously *injurious* to the cause of virtue, unless this other propension, Love of Justice, were found in its company. Take either of these most powerful propensions *separately*, they lead us to *evil*. If Love of Justice had full sway in our social dealings, isolated from the General Love for mankind, — it would lead us to every species of harshness, violence, inconsiderateness, uncharitableness, pride ; it would lead us to feel, as though we were to be the pitiless judges of our fellow-men.   On the other hand, if Love for mankind carried us away, without our being acted on equally by Love of Justice,— our social career would be that of traitors to Our Creator and recreants to His cause. Either one then, taken by itself, would be simply evil in its effects, and lead us from virtue: but taken in harmony, just as God has implanted them, they lead us precisely in the true direction; they give precisely that one legitimate and desirable impulse, or rather series of impulses, to our whole dealings with mankind, which God desires at our hands.

Such was the picture exhibited, as those tell us who have studied Church History, by the great ancient champions of the faith, S. Athanasius, or S. Leo, or S. Augustine. These great Saints, we are told, combined qualities which might appear on the surface irreconcileable: they experienced most keenly the emotion of *holy resentment*, in regard to heretics considered as God's enemies; while they felt the most lively *tenderness* for them one by one, as the creatures of God and the redeemed of Christ.*

Enough then has been said (though very much more might be added) to vindicate the first of those two propositions with which we started; viz. that this propension, Love of Justice, is of inappreciable importance as part of our moral nature. The other proposition was, that it is this very propension, and no other, which, in its perverted state, becomes personal malice —public faction—in fact enmity and hatred, whether

---

* " O that there was in us this high temper of mingled austerity and love! Barely do we conceive of severity by itself, and of kindness by itself; but who unites them? We think we cannot be kind, without ceasing to be severe. Who is it that walks through the world, wounding according to the rule of zeal, and scattering balm freely in the fulness of love; smiting as a duty, and healing as a privilege; loving most when he seems sternest, and embracing those most tenderly whom in semblance he treats roughly? What a state we are in, when any one who speaks the plain threats of our Lord and His Apostles against sinners, or ventures to defend the anathemas of His Church, is thought unfeeling rather than merciful; when they who separate from the irreligious world are blamed as fanciful and extravagant; and those who confess the truth, as it is in Jesus, are said to be bitter, hot of head, and intemperate!"—*Newman's Sermons*, vol. iii. pp. 204, 205.

on a large or a small scale.   By far the greater part of all the misery which man 'aggressively' inflicts on his fellow-men, is due to nothing else than the perversion and degeneracy of this one propension.   I say the misery which he 'aggressively' inflicts; and I beg your particular attention to the sense of this word 'aggressive.'   When I speak then of the misery which man 'aggressively' inflicts, I mean the misery which he inflicts as *being* misery; *for the sake of* inflicting it; for the *pleasure* which is thence produced.   There is a fearful mass of evil, *non*-aggressively inflicted by man on man; inflicted, that is, whether consciously or unconsciously, in pursuit of some end altogether different. Thus parents, who give themselves to brutal intemperance, inflict on their children indefinite evil ; bad example, neglect of their education, and many others : indeed *almost all* wickedness causes a vast amount of social mischief.   But I am speaking here, of that misery which is inflicted on others, as *being* misery ; *for the sake of* that wretched gratification, which results from the infliction of evil as such.   Part even of this no doubt may be put down to the account of *Envy*, which is next to be considered; but I maintain that far the *greater* part arises from the propension before us.   In other words, the gratification which men derive from the sufferings of their fellow-men, simply as such, is far most commonly a gratification (of course a most detestable and perverted gratification) of this propension, Love of Justice.

That we may see this more clearly, let us begin by imagining a particular case.   You will grant of course, that, almost universally, those men who are not really pious and interior, think far more highly of their own claims than truth will warrant.   The same principle further applies to their children, their friends, their country ; for all these objects they entertain a far higher value than simple reason can justify.   Suppose now I receive some severity of treatment, which is in accordance with *the strictest justice*.   It is far most probable that I shall regard it as *grossly injurious*.   Here then the propension before us is at once called into play. Suppose I am one of those, who on the whole act simply *according* to their propensions, and not on principle; I proceed immediately, in accordance with this particular propension, to *retaliate* on the aggressor for his supposed injury. Now if when we receive *just* treatment we consider ourselves aggrieved, what will be our thoughts on receiving *unjust* treatment? The attacked party then, being *unjustly* assailed by me, thinks *more seriously* of the injury he has now received, then *I did* of my *original* ground of complaint. And so here you see at once a very remarkable scene opening before us; blow and counter-blow, action and reaction, increasing without limit in the way of violence and intensity. But this is only a small part of the case. *My* relations and friends see the whole thing on my side; *his* on his side. And similarly, on a greater scale, when countries contend; England, *e. g.* and France. Englishmen look on it almost as a matter of plain undeniable common sense, that England is in the right; and can't in any way be got to imagine that the case even admits of another interpretation. Frenchmen are equally obstinate and equally one-sided. However extensive then is the class of phenomena to which we are referring—the phenomena of mutual hatred and aggressive injury,—here is plainly a broad principle, which will account for the whole.

And a proof that this is a *true* account,—that Anger (as distinct from Envy) always implies a notion of *injustice* done,—may be derived from this fact. Shew me that the injury which I received was not in any way intentional;—*e.g.* that the other party was *intending* to do something totally *different*, and by accident hurt me; or that he was out of his right mind at the time; or the like:—what ensues? I may be unwilling to *believe* that it was unintentional; this is very common:—but let me once *believe* it to be so, and yet retain my *resentment*, I should be looked on by all mankind as simply beside myself. It is true indeed, that I may greatly resent what is caused by mere *carelessness;* but this (as Butler well observes) is because I consider *observance* as my *due,* and regard carelessness towards me as *in itself* faulty and injurious. It is true again, that I may be angry with those who are not free agents; as children or brutes: but this (as any angry man may observe by looking back on his past consciousness) is because, in the blindness of my rage, I was under the practical *impression* that the object of my wrath was free and responsible.   If I can only be brought carefully to *consider* and *ponder* on the fact that he is *ir*responsible, my anger begins to subside as a matter of course.

Look then over the whole expanse (and it is a very wide one) of human hatred and malice;—put aside those comparatively few cases, which are explained by Envy;—and what do we find?   There is not one single instance, in which hatred and malice are not connected with a feeling of *moral disapprobation:* we regard those whom we hate, as in this or that respect *faulty,* and *therefore* we hate them.   We consider them as faulty, for having injured us; or for having injured those whom we love; or for sympathizing with those who have so acted; or we regard them as in some other respect wilful offenders.   Man is not capable of any feeling towards his fellow-man, simply *as such,* except that of Benevolence.   Hatred, I say, cannot be felt against our fellow-men simply *as such;* but either as objects of *Envy* (which is another matter) or else as in this or that way *blameworthy.*   Take even the extreme case of the misanthrope, and what is its true analysis?   He regards all mankind as conspiring and banded together for his injury, and *therefore* he hates them.

One of you has objected, that men are sometimes driven into shocking cruelties, from the motive of *fear;* as in the case of certain slave-owners.   But this objection proceeds on a misconception of my whole statement.   An injury, inflicted from the motive of fear, is not an '*aggressive*' injury; it is not done for the

x

pleasure of inflicting evil, but for the negative pleasure of myself *escaping* such infliction. It is true indeed, that in such a state of things real hatred and malice often arise; but it will be found that this very fact confirms our theory. In order to justify to myself those cruelties which I inflict,—in order to persuade myself that they are due to some higher motive than mere pusillanimity and terror,—I resolve with blind obstinacy to believe, that those objects of my dread are possessed with monstrous and enormous faults. Then, by dwelling on these imaginary faults, I rise into a sentiment of indignation against the offenders, and thus perpetrate my cruelties under the agreeable delusion that I am but occupied in inflicting a just retribution.

It may perhaps be objected, that malice and hatred often exist as cool settled dispositions of the will; quite apart from this *feeling* of anger. This however is only one particular case of a general phenomenon; of a phenomenon, which *must* be explained to you at one time or another; and which may as well therefore be explained now. The propensions may be said to reside primarily in the sensitive appetite, and secondarily in the will. Primarily in the sensitive appetite, because our susceptibility of pleasure appertains exclusively to the sensitive appetite. Secondarily however in the will, for the following reason. Suppose, *e. g.* I have worked for some time at money-getting, under the influence of a strong and lively *emotion* tending in that direction. These various emotions, as we saw in the third Section, have all been accompanied by corresponding acts of the will. These various acts of the will have generated a *habit;* and the *habit* of aiming at pleasure will enable the will to act, not languidly but with great steadiness and efficacity, in the same direction, even when the sensitive excitement is away. And the same truth holds of this propension also. Every *feeling* of resentment which I have not resisted, is accompanied by an act of the will; these various acts generate a *habit* of hatred or malice; and this *habit* may enable the will to act with the most determined and implacable malignity, even apart from any paroxysms of sensitive excitement.

On the whole then, there can be no doubt, that that very propension, which would appear on the surface as tending far more than any other to the disruption and overthrow of society,—the feeling of mutual animosity and hatred,—is really on the contrary, if but rightly directed, one of those necessary links which hold society together. *

By means of this propension, we can explain a phenomenon which we have already admitted to exist (see n. 121, p. 249); viz. that extreme reprobates feel a certain pleasure in the mere fact of disobeying God.   Let us put the case this way.   Suppose I were to hear of some distinct universe, under the controul of a being who should be perfectly good, so far as my own inadequate ideas of goodness extend.   There can be no doubt that, in virtue of this propension, I should sympathize with his government, rejoice in his success, grieve over his failure.   But now let me become a *member* of that universe, and a different kind of feeling ensues.   This being's goodness brings him into collision with myself; he forbids me what I wish, and restrains my liberty. My pride is at once wounded; a practical sense of injustice takes possession of me; and I feel pleasure in a certain kind of retribution.   I disobey his commands, as it were to *spite* him.   This is St. Thomas's account, and I think a true one, of the cause which produces 'odium Dei;' though here, as in other cases, he is considering habits of the will, where I am speaking of emotions. †

* " The indignation raised by cruelty and injustice, and the desire of having it punished, which persons unconcerned would feel, is by no means malice.   No, it is resentment against vice and wickedness: it is one of the common bonds by which society is held together: a fellow-feeling, which each individual has in behalf of the whole species, as well as of himself. And it does not appear that this, generally speaking, is at all too high amongst mankind.'—BUTLER *On Resentment.*

† Respondeo dicendum, quòd, sicut ex supra dictis patet (1. 2. quæst. 29, art. 1) odium est quidam motus appetitivæ potentiæ, quæ non movetur nisi ab aliquo apprehenso.   Deus autem dupliciter ab homine apprehendi potest: uno modo secundum Seipsum, puta cùm per Essentiam videtur; alio modo per effectus suos, cum scilicet " invisibilia Dei per ea quæ facta sunt, intel-

This propension, as has been so often said, finds its legitimate gratification in justice being done ; in goodness being rewarded, and wickedness punished. It would appear then, that one-half of its legitimate gratification is found in the misery of our fellow-creatures ; or rather indeed much more than one-half, since wickedness greatly preponderates over goodness. Here then arises a most difficult question ;—in what cases may the ' vindictive ' emotions of this propension be legitimately indulged ? To give this question a fullness of treatment, commensurate with its difficulty and importance, would carry us quite too far : moreover it is an ethical, not a psychological question, and therefore does not in strictness belong to this Chapter. Still some brief remarks may be desirable.

First, the most legitimate of all gratifications to the vindictive emotions of this propension, is the punishing our own sins. Those who undergo severe austerities, e. g., may make unlimited use of it in animating their zeal, to inflict still greater punishment on their wicked

lecta conspiciuntur."   Deus autem per Essentiam Suam est Ipsa Bonitas, Quam nullus habere odio potest, quia de ratione boni est ut ametur : et ideò impossibile est quòd aliquis videns Deum per Essentiam, Eum odio habeat. Sed effectus Ejus aliqui sunt qui nullo modo possunt esse contrarii voluntati humanæ ; quia esse, vivere, et intelligere est appetibile, et amabile omnibus ; quæ sunt quidam effectus Dei.   Unde etiam secundum quod Deus apprehenditur ut auctor *horum* effectuum, non potest odio haberi.   Sunt autem *quidam effectus Dei qui repugnant inordinatæ voluntati;* sicut inflictio pœnæ, et etiam cohibitio peccatorum per Legem Divinam ; quæ repugnant voluntati depravatæ per peccatum : et quantùm ad considerationem talium effectuum, ab aliquibus Deus odio haberi potest, inquantùm scilicet apprehenditur *peccatorum prohibitor et pœnarum inflictor.*—2. 2. quæst. 34, art. 1.

It is not merely *by accident,* that in so many cases our own enumeration of the propensions coincides with St. Thomas's of the virtues. The two ideas in themselves indeed are totally distinct, as is most manifest.   By propension (as we have so often observed) we mean simply man's susceptibility of pleasure or pain from any particular class of objects.   On the other hand, a *virtue* is that *habit* of the *will* which disposes it to pursue its various objects in due measure and degree: as we shall see in our theological course. Still St. Thomas expressly tells us, that for every separate propension he counts a separate virtue ; and this fact readily accounts for the coincidence above mentioned.

These are St. Thomas's words :   ' Virtutes perficiunt nos ad prosequendum debito modo inclinationes naturales quæ pertinent ad jus naturale. Et ideò *ad quamlibet inclinationem naturalem determinatam, ordinatur aliqua virtus specialis.*'—2, 2 quæst. 108. art. 1, in corp.

and offending selves. All indeed who are at all zealous for their perfection, adopt some self-chastisement or other; whatever it may be, the vindictive emotions of this propension will assist them greatly in its sustained use.

Another very legitimate exercise of vindictiveness, is against evil, whether in the abstract, or as personally realized in the evil spirits, or again as embodied in material objects. Holy men may well thus stimulate themselves against the Devil and his hosts, while actively and earnestly engaged in converting heretics or reclaiming sinners; in hewing down idols; destroying criminal pictures; or the like.

Now to take an extremely opposite case. We know that those in mortal sin are fully deserving of eternal torment; yet what more intolerable course could there be, than the yielding consent to an emotion,* which finds pleasure in the prospect, that this or that wicked man will probably be damned? We need not determine what may be the case on the Day of General Judgment;— how far those who are to be saved may *then* laudably exercise this propension, in sympathizing with God's judgments. This is a separate question altogether: but it is plain that here 'in viâ' to rejoice ('gaudere,' see n. 103, p. 218) in my neighbour's probable damnation, will be the surest means possible of securing my own.

It may be asked then, is there no legitimate scope for this propension, in contemplating an open and unblushing sinner? There is more than one such scope: there are many inflictions, which on the one hand are chastisements for sin, and yet on the other hand are most salutary for moral improvement. These we may most legitimately wish for sinners. Suppose a wicked worldling has used the power given him by high station, as a means for oppressing and demoralizing the poor;— it is most lawful to admit a vindictive pleasure, when we hear that he has been hurled down *from* that high

* What is precisely the yielding consent to an emotion has been explained in n. 100 and 101, pp. 211, 212.

station by the course of events.   And so where we have
to govern others,—as parents or schoolmasters *e. g.*
govern children,—we may most suitably make use of
this feeling, to help us in our bounden duty of inflicting such punishments, as we judge really conducive to
the moral improvement of those committed to our
charge.   To go *beyond this* towards *others*, would
plainly be to adopt towards them a most different
measure, from that which we apply to ourselves.   In
our own case, we may take a vindictive pleasure in
looking *e. g.* on the discipline, as a well-deserved infliction on our sins ; but we can never say, ' Oh, that Hell
had been my lot, as I richly deserved ! '   We wish to
ourselves those inflictions *only*, which are *corrective* as
well as punitive ; to others also we should wish the
same.

Here then we also see, how great a degree of resentment may innocently be allowed, in the case of an injury
inflicted on ourselves.   An injury done to ourselves, is
as truly deserving of punishment as one done to others.
We cannot then be said to exceed, so far as we allow
ourselves in no more than that *degree* of resentment,
which we should experience, if another, wholly uncon-
nected with us, were the party injured.   Nay we may go
perhaps a little further ; for where we are ourselves the
sufferers, we are the more able to *understand*, intellectually to *appreciate*, the extent of the injury, and so the
wrongfulness of the act.   Yet on the other hand, in
proportion as we move towards perfection, we shall
feel much *less* keenly an injury done to ourselves ; because our practical impression will the more be, that
we *deserve* nothing better.   However, as a help towards
aiming at perfection, it will be well to discipline ourselves from the first in the habit, of never consenting
to an emotion of resentment, for any injury which we
may ourselves suffer.   It is by such means, that we
shall the more quickly grow to the desired degree of
self-hatred and self-contempt.

Finally, as we become holier and better, we shall
more and more cease to dwell on injuries, as being

inflicted against our *fellow-creatures*, any more than as against ourselves. We shall be more and more absorbed in the thought of God; and feel in regard to *all* evil-doing, as towards an injury done to God.

It will be interesting, in illustration of all that has been said, if you are disposed to read St. Thomas's treatment of the virtue ' vindicatio' 2, 2, q. 108 : though it would carry us much too far, to examine precisely how his statements stand in regard to ours.

145. A very ingenious objection has been made by one of you, against the whole theory which I have drawn out on the origin of malice and cruelty. In order the more fully to meet that objection, I will here consider *another* propension, of a totally different character from Love of Justice, and which otherwise would have been treated in a later part of the Section. The propension to which I allude, may be called, for want of a better name, ' Love of the Marvellous;' for I speak of that delight which is experienced, from coming in contact with something, which is most broadly and strikingly contrasted with our every-day experience.

As an instance of what I mean, consider the rapturous enjoyment of a child, when he first sees a play or some other gorgeous and magnificent spectacle : for weeks afterwards he can think of nothing else. It is this propension, which leads feebler minds to that constant longing for novelty and change, which is so very common ; and deeper minds are influenced by it, to foreign travel and the search after rare and unusual objects.

It is equally plain, that there is nothing in this visible scene which can afford such a propension any stable or sufficient gratification. Its full and legitimate Objects, can be nothing less than those great and awful Truths, which concern God and the Invisible World. Apart from Revelation, the contemplation of what Reason has to tell concerning our Infinite Creator, will afford it a far more adequate enjoyment than can any earthly scene ; but the marvels revealed by *the Gospel* are such, as to give it the keenest and most exquisite delight. He who lives by faith, is able to feed his soul on the most transporting mysteries, even while going faithfully and punctually through the most ordinary business of every-day life. A God Incarnate! A God dying to redeem us! A God dwelling within the Holy Tabernacle, and patiently awaiting our prayers! What amount of meditation can ever exhaust such marvels? Nay, and this heavenly-minded Christian looks forward also from time to time, with beating heart and throbbing expectation, to that future period, when he shall awake as it were from the darkness and slumbers of earth, to full light and wakefulness; to the actual vision of those wonders, which "eye hath not seen, nor ear heard, nor has it entered into the heart of man to conceive."

146. I now approach the objection to which I just now referred. Hatred and Malice, I had said, are but perversions of that vitally important propension, the Love of Justice. Whenever we inflict suffering on our fellow-men, for the sake of that pleasure which we derive from such suffering,—there is always (putting aside the case of Envy) a practical impression (however monstrous) of injury received and retaliation justly inflicted. There is no such thing as hatred of our fellow-men *as such.* 'You forget,' replies the objector, 'a whole class of facts. Take such a series of ' atrocious cruelties, as those perpetrated, *e.g.* by the ' worst Roman Emperors, or by the miscreants of the ' first French Revolution. How could Robespierre ' imagine that he had received *injury* at the hand of ' those helpless multitudes, whom he ruthlessly slaugh- ' tered?' Let us take then Robespierre and his associates as our instance; for whatever may be said in their case, is most easily applicable to any other of similar appearance.

Now (1) such a man as Robespierre undoubtedly would consider his opponents to be in some sense morally culpable; for in his fanatical blindness he regarded the enemies of republicanism as the enemies of the human race. Add to this, that a wicked man (as already explained) receives the monstrous practical impression, that those who oppose *himself* deserve whatever vengeance he can inflict. I doubt not therefore, that his cruelties did in some degree proceed from this propension, Love of Justice, in that frightfully perverted state to which his wickedness had reduced it.

But (2) his *fear* was added, as an extremely strong motive : to a great extent his cruelty proceeded, *not* from any pleasure he received in the suffering of his *victims*, but from his anxiety to protect *himself*. To pause in his frenzied course for one day is, as he fancies, to give his prostrate enemies time to recover themselves, and to conspire against him. He feels how justly he has deserved their hatred ; and is ever dreading its explosion. This is one of the curses attendant on social guilt, that in some sense past evil deeds necessitate future. What does Macbeth feel after Duncan's murder ?

> ' I am in blood
> Stepped in so far, that, should I wade no more,
> Returning were as tedious as go o'er.'

And so a craven and panic fear possesses him, of the terrible retribution which he must expect, the moment he intermits, even for the shortest period, his bloody career.

Still I think we shall by no means do justice to the phenomena of the case, unless we introduce into our analysis the propension treated in the previous number; the delight which accrues, from that which is broadly and strikingly contrasted with our every-day experience. In virtue of this propension, the constant practice of cruelty generates a kind of nervous excitement, which more and more possesses the whole mind. Just as they say that a tiger, having once tasted blood, cannot again forbear;—so to these men, after this career of wild excitement, ordinary existence appears vapid, insipid, commonplace, to an intolerable degree.

Take these three facts : (1) these men's fanatical idea that they are inflicting on their opponents a just retribution ; (2) the panic fear caused by their most critical position; and (3) the strange attractiveness of

that nervous excitement which is kept up by the pro-
longation of these shocking cruelties;—all will admit,
I think, that such cases as those before us are fully
accounted for, without at all supposing any hatred of
mankind *as such.*

147. Next to consider *Envy:* and I begin with these
preliminary remarks. What is more wholesome, more
admirable, more bracing to the spiritual strength, than
such an exercise as this ;—to ponder on the lives of holy
men, and strive to lessen the distance between them
and us, by advancing in all virtues and by imitating
their holy example ? God has given us a special pleasure, in the performance of this holy exercise ; or in
other words has implanted in us the propension *Emulation.*

But we may seek to gratify this propension,—in
other words we may strive or desire to lessen the distance between others and ourselves,—by trying or
desiring, *not* to raise *ourselves,* but to *depress them.*
Emulation then and Envy are in fact the very same
propension : rightly gratified, it is Emulation ; wrongly
gratified, Envy. Nothing can be clearer or more
simple. *

---

* 'Respondeo dicendum, quòd, sicut dictum est (art. præc.) invidia est
tristitia quædam de alienis bonis. Sed hæc tristitia potest cotingere quatuor
modis.

'Uno quidem modo, cùm aliquis dolet de bono alicujus, inquantùm ex
eo timetur nocumentum, vel sibi ipsi, vel etiam aliis bonis ; et talis tristitia
non est invidia, ut dictum est (art. præc.), et potest esse sine peccato. Unde
Gregorius 22. Moral. (cap. 6. ante med.) ait : "evenire plerumque solet ut non
amissâ caritate, et inimici nos ruina lætificet, et rursùm ejus gloria sine in-
vidiæ culpâ contristet ; cùm et ruente eo quosdam bene erigi credimus, et
proficiente illo plerosque injustè opprimi formidamus."

'Alio modo potest aliquis tristari de bono alterius, *non ex eo quod ipse
habet bonum,* sed ex eo quod *nobis deest bonum illud quod ipse habet ;* et
hoc propriè est *zelus,* ut Philosophus dicit in 11. Rhetor. (cap. 11. circ.
princ.) ; et *si iste zelus sit circa bona honesta, laudabilis est,* secundùm illud
1 Corinth. 14. 1, "Æmulamini spiritualia." Si autem sit de bonis tempo-
ralibus, potest esse cum peccato, et sine peccato.

'Tertio modo aliquis tristatur de bono alterius, inquantùm ille cui accidit
bonum, est eo indignus : quæ quidem tristitia non potest oriri ex bonis ho-
nestis, ex quibus aliquis justus efficitur, sed sicut Philosophus dicit in
11, Rhet. (cap 14.), est de divitiis, et de talibus quæ possunt provenire
dignis et indignis : et hæc tristitia secundùm ipsum vocatur *nemesis,* et
pertinet ad bonos mores. Sed hoc ideò dicit, quia considerabat ipsa dona
temporalia secundùm se, prout possunt magna videri non respicientibus ad

There are various corruptions of this propension. (1) Where the sphere of action (if I may so express myself) is changed. This takes place, when we emulate others in *worldly*, not in *spiritual* advantages ; when we try to outstrip others in the race of ambition ; or vie with those richer than ourselves, as to ostentation, command of equipages, and the like ; or indulge in any other kind of worldly emulation. (2) Not only the sphere of action may be changed, but the propension itself perverted into envy. Needy men may rejoice, in the calamities of those who were richer than themselves ; or a politician, in the total downfall of one who was his opponent.

It may seem at first strange, but it is most undoubtedly true, that very far the *worst* perversion of this propension, occurs where the sphere of action is *not* changed. Envy of our neighbour's *spiritual excellence;* the desire that it might be less, because it overshadows and shames our own;—where can there be a more odious feeling than this ? *

The will's deliberate consent to such an emotion, is numbered by Catholic writers as among the most heinous of sins.

148. We have now therefore seen, that those propensions which are far the most powerful of all (with one exception) in drawing souls from God — Love of Approbation, of Power, of Knowledge, of Acquisition — may do most important work in directing them towards His service. We have seen further, that those very

æterna. Sed secundùm doctrinam fidei, temporalia bona quæ indignis proveniunt, ex justâ Dei ordinatione disponuntur, vel ad eorum correctionem, vel ad eorum damnationem ; et hujusmodi bona quasi nihil sunt in comparatione ad bona futura, quæ servantur bonis. Et ideò hujusmodi tristitia prohibetur in Scripturâ Sacrâ, secundùm illud Psal. 36. 1, " Noli æmulari in malignantibus, neque zelaveris facientes iniquitatem :" et alibi Psal. 72. 3, "Pænè effusi sunt gressus mei, quia zelavi super iniquos, pacem peccatorum videns."

'Quarto modo aliquis tristatur de bonis alicujus, in quantum alter excedit ipsum in bonis ; et *hoc proprie est invidia ;* et istud semper est pravum, ut etiam Philosophus dicit in 11. Rhetor. (cap. 10), quia *dolet de eo de quo est gaudendum, scilicet de bono proximi.*'—St. Thomas, 2. 2, quæst. 36, art. 2.

* I mean of course odious in its results, when the will consents to it. No emotion in itself can strictly be called odious, because it is not in our own choice whether we experience it or not.

propensions, Anger and Envy, which might seem most undeniably and exclusively *evil* in their tendencies, may be put to most excellent account. Nay the former of them, as we have seen, is so vitally important to our moral nature, that if it did not exist, the very propension of General Benevolence would be mischievous in its effects on our conduct. All this reasoning gives the greatest antecedent probability, to the thesis we are maintaining; insomuch that even if we were not able as yet to see its full truth in the case of any *particular* propension, there would be the greatest probability that more careful observation would place *this* propension on the same footing with so many others.

I prefix these remarks to my treatment of *Pride*, which is the next case to be considered. I am not doing this indeed, because there is any difficulty at all in ascertaining, *what* is that propension, and what its legitimate application, of which Pride is the perversion; for the case is otherwise. Still it must be admitted, I think, that the *evil* effects of this propension when *perverted*, exceed and overweigh its *good* effects when *rightly directed*, very far more than in the case of any other propension. And though I think I shall be able to give a perfectly satisfactory reason for this fact, still it seemed better to preface my treatment of this most important propension with the above remark. I should add indeed, that there is another propension, of which some may think that the evil effects of its perversion exceed the good effects of its legitimate application in even a greater degree; I mean the propension which tempts us against the Sixth Commandment. But so far as this statement is true, it stands upon totally different grounds; as will be explained in its due place.

That propension, of which Pride is the perversion, is the ' Love of Self-assertion ;' the propension which finds its gratification, in contemplating our own personal importance, and acting with a view to its vindication and promotion. In order to explain the place of this propension in our moral constitution, I proceed as follows :—

(1.) The personal importance of us men is incalculably great. If we consider only what unaided reason can tell us, we have grounds for this statement.   Each one of us possesses true liberty ; in other words, each one possesses what might have seemed the inalienable prerogative of God, (and which on this very ground is denied to man by many sectaries,) in being (as it is expressed) a self-originating principle of causation.   This statement will be explained and illustrated, in our theological work on Liberty; but its general meaning is (I trust) sufficiently clear to you. Each one of us then is entrusted with the charge of that most precious deposit,—his own moral character, his own permanent and eternal interest. It rests simply with *himself*, whether he shall grow towards the Holiness of God, or in the precisely opposite direction ; it rests precisely with *himself*, whether he shall be for ever happy or for ever miserable.

But let us introduce into our picture the truths of Revelation, and this statement becomes far more emphatically true.   For each one of us God died; it rests then with each one to determine, whether in his regard that death shall have been efficacious, or shall have been frustrated of its desired results.   To each one, supernatural grace is imparted, abundantly sufficient for raising him to the Facial Vision of God; he has the unspeakable privilege therefore, the awful responsibility, of either co-operating with God or directly resisting Him. Those in a justified state moreover possess, seated in their soul, certain inward permanent gifts, the very thought of which is most elevating and transporting.

(2.) It is of extreme importance that we *dwell upon*, that we *realize*, this our great personal importance. You remember, when we were speaking of vain-glory, the weak-minded youth at school ; of whom we said, that he shrinks from giving expression or effect to his most certain religious convictions, from fear of his companions' sneers.   What was immediately wanting to him? precisely this ;—*a realization of his own personal importance*.   In every instance where men are drawn from their true End, whether by vain-glory or by any

other earthly shadow, a true sense of their own personal importance would infallibly save them.   And so
the great writers of the Church have ever felt.   S. Leo
for instance, as quoted in the Breviary, ' agnosce Chris-
tiane *dignitatem* tuam;' ' ponder on the great dignity to
which you have been called, and refuse for very shame
so to act as to degrade it.'   One instance however, from
a contemporary writer, will be more to our immediate
purpose, than the multiplication of such quotations as
this; and I will give therefore a most interesting quotation from Father Newman.

Every Christian student of Aristotle is struck with
his description of μεγαλοψυχια: that very quality, which
he paints as the highest and noblest of virtues, appears
to ordinary readers most closely allied to that most
detestable sin of Pride, which flows from this very propension we are considering.   Various critics, defending
Aristotle, deny indeed this statement; and with the
philosophical or personal controversy thence ensuing
we have no kind of concern.   Father Newman however,
in one of his later Protestant sermons, has based on
this Aristotelic description, a complete sketch of the
Christian character.   From this sketch two inferences
at once follow; and they are the very two propositions
which I am occupied in maintaining.   First it follows,
that this habit of self-assertion *is* most important to the
Christian life; and secondly it follows, that this is the
very principle, of *which Pride is the perversion.*   I will
quote in the note one long passage from this most
striking composition, and shall be very glad if I thereby
induce you to study the whole.*

---

* "He then, who believes that, in St. Paul's words, he is 'joined to the Lord'
as 'one spirit,' must necessarily prize his own blessed condition, and *look
down upon all things,* even the greatest things here below,   ' Ye are of God,
little children,' says   the beloved disciple, ' and have overcome them;
because greater is He that is in you than he that is in the world.   They are
of the world ; . . . . we are of God. He that knoweth God, heareth us ; he
that is not of God, heareth not us.'—1 John, iv. 6.   Here is the language of
saints ; and hence it is that St. Paul, as feeling *the majesty of that new
nature which is imparted to us,* addresses himself in a form of indignation
to those who forget it.   ' What !' he says, ' what ! know ye not that your
body is a temple of the Holy Ghost ?'   As if he said, ' Can you be so mean-
spirited and base-minded, as to *dishonour yourselves* in the devil's service !

(3.) Seeing then that this habit of Self-assertion is thus vitally important, our ultimate conclusion at once results. That there *is* a certain, not inconsiderable, pleasure, derivable from dwelling on our personal importance, the phenomena of pride themselves most amply prove. Such pleasure therefore is capable, in proportion to its intensity, of giving us valuable assistance in our Christian course.

You will ask perhaps, is this a *different* pleasure from that which appertains to the propension of *Self-charity?* A little consideration will shew that it is

Should we not pity the man of birth, or station, or character, who degraded himself in the eyes of the world, who forfeited his honour, broke his word, or played the coward ? And shall not we, from mere sense of propriety, be *ashamed to defile* our spiritual purity, the *royal blood of the second Adam*, with deeds of darkness ? Let us leave it to the hosts of evil spirits, to the haters of Christ, to eat the dust of the earth all the days of their life. Cursed are they above all cattle, and above every beast of the field ; grovelling shall they go, till they come to their end and perish. But for Christians, it is theirs to walk in the light, as children of the light, and lift up their hearts, as looking out for Him who went away, that He might return.'

"For the same reason, Christians are called upon *to think little of the ordinary objects which men pursue*, wealth, luxury, distinction, popularity, and power. It was this negligence about the world, which brought upon them in primitive times the reproach of being indolent. Their heathen enemies spoke truly ; indolent and indifferent they were about temporal matters. If the goods of this world came in their way, they were not bound to decline them ; nor would they forbid others in the religious use of them ; but they thought them vanities, the toys of children, which serious men let drop. Nay, St. Paul betrays the same feeling as regards our temporal callings and states generally. After discoursing about them, suddenly he breaks off as if impatient of the multitude of words ; ' But this I say, brethren,' he exclaims, ' the time is short.'

"Hence, too, the troubles of life gradually affect the Christian less and less, as *his view of his own real blessedness*, under the Dispensation of the Spirit, grows upon him ; and even though persecuted, to take an extreme case, he knows well that, through God's inward presence, *he is greater than those who for the time have power over him*, as Martyrs and Confessors have often shewn.

"And in like manner, he will be calm and collected under all circumstances ; he will make light of injuries, and forget them *from mere contempt of them*. He will be undaunted, as fearing God more than man ; he will be firm in faith and consistent, as 'seeing Him that is invisible ;' not impatient, who has no self-will ; not soon disappointed, who has no hopes ; not anxious, who has no fears ; nor dazzled, who has no ambition ; nor bribed, who has no desires.

"And now, further, let it be observed on the other hand, that all this greatness of mind which I have been describing, *which in other religious systems degenerates into pride*, is in the Gospel compatible, nay rather intimately connected, with the deepest humility."—*Sermons on Subjects of the Day*, pp. 163-166.

altogether different. Suppose I believed myself destitute of all freedom; of all real power either to promote or obstruct my own well-being; well — the propension Self-charity would, by such a supposition, lose *no part of its adequate object*. It would still be a matter of joy to me, if I believed happiness is in store for me on the whole; and of grief, if I believed that misery would preponderate in my lot. On such a supposition I say, the propension of *Self-charity* would lose *no part at all* of its adequate object; whereas the *propension before us* would in that case *have no legitimate object whatever left*. This fact alone, shews how absolutely and entirely distinct is the legitimate object of one of these propensions from that of the other. But again, that *personal responsibility*, which is my only true personal importance, and consequently the only legitimate foundation for this propension's gratification — this responsibility (I say) reaches (as we have seen) not only to the promotion of my own *permanent happiness*, but still more prominently and importantly of my own *moral perfection*. But as to this latter, it is evident on the surface how utterly it is beyond the scope of Self-charity.

Thus far, on the legitimate application of this propension. But we now come to a matter far more important, and deserving far more careful consideration; I mean the process of its perversion. The *legitimate object* then of this propension, is our *personal importance*, in the sense of our *vast personal responsibility;* of our great spiritual gifts and endowments. Everything which Reason or Revelation tells us, as to the preciousness of that deposit committed to our charge,—our own sanctity, our own eternal destiny, — every such intelligence gives a fuller scope for such legitimate application. The propension is *perverted*, in proportion as it seeks some gratification *different* from this. So far therefore as I dwell with complacency on my (real or supposed) *moral excellence*, I am making a perverted use of this propension. And very far more, so far as I dwell with complacency on things which make no pretension to be morally excellent ;— my intellectual powers, or my ancient lineage, or my acquired wealth.   *Moral* pride (see n. 68, p. 140) is very bad ; but pride which is *not* 'moral' (as I hope to shew in our theological work) is far more detestable.

Now so long and so far as my will is abjectly submissive to the will of God, in that proportion pride is impossible.   It will be a very interesting task hereafter, to prove this statement ;— to shew clearly the power possessed by moral virtue, of necessarily expelling pride : here let us take for granted, what you are all of course quite willing to admit.   On the other hand, so far as at any moment the energy of our will towards good abates, an entrance is opened to pride.   This being assumed, I here further maintain, that so soon as an *opening* is made for pride, pride will infallibly *make use* of that opening, and obtain entrance ; and I beg your most particular attention to the reason which I give for this statement.

The Propension, which we are now considering, differs from every other most signally, in this one particular ; the *extraordinary ease with which it obtains gratification.*   Let us contrast it in this respect, for instance, with another, which in many respects resembles it, Love of Approbation.   It is a very difficult thing to obtain the approbation of *others;* but it is the easiest thing in the whole world to obtain *our own:* to dwell in thought on this or that (real or imaginary) excellence.   Now the mass of men, so far as they do not aim at 'bonum honestum,' are perfect slaves to present and immediate 'bonum delectabile ;' they clutch, unreflectingly and instinctively, at every gratification which comes within their reach.   But *here* is a gratification, which is within their reach at every moment of their existence ; how certainly therefore it ensues, that they will eagerly seize it!   And thus it comes to pass, that this one pleasure mixes itself unconsciously with the whole current of their daily life, and works at every instant more deeply into their soul.   All these innumerable emotions of pride are accompanied as a matter of course

Y

(n. 100, p. 211) with innumerable acts of will, precisely parallel; and these acts of will, from their very number, constitute in such men a habit, more intense and more deeply rooted, than any other evil habit which can be named.

Even a pious and interior man, who sincerely aims at perfection, at every step of his upward progress is startled and horrified, at the great abysses of pride which he discovers in his own heart. All those acts of will, which have generated this habit, have passed from his remembrance, or more probably were never distinct objects of reflection; they have been elicited, spontaneously and as a matter of course, at those moments, when the will was either altogether idle, or at all events less energetic, in a virtuous direction.

We are now able to explain the remarkable fact above stated, that the *good* effects of this Propension when *rightly* directed, bear so comparatively small a proportion, to its *evil* effects when *perverted*. In order to understand the reason of this, observe first, that all which has been said on the extreme ease of gratifying this propension, applies to it only in its perverted exercise. This is quite manifest: the thought of our personal importance, in the sense of our great *personal responsibility*, is *not* a pleasing but a *most painful* thought, except to those who are really labouring for their own sanctification. That thought, which is at once so gratifying and so easily elicited, is the thought of some (real or supposed) *excellence ;* and to take pleasure in this thought, with full consent of the will, is that very perversion which we call pride.

In order the better to fix our ideas, let us choose some other Propension, with which to contrast this in the particular above stated. No more suitable one can be chosen for this purpose, than that which we have already contrasted with it in another aspect; Love of Approbation.

I say then firstly, that the Love of Approbation is an incomparable keener and more powerful propension, than the Love of Self-assertion. This is plain, whether we compare the two in their legitimate or their perverted exercise.   How immeasurably more lively and transporting is the delight which we receive, from believing that our dearest Redeemer approves our conduct, than that which ensues from our conviction that we are really promoting our own true importance!   On the other hand, consider the incredibly and almost fabulously inspiring effect, produced *e.g.* on soldiers, who possess the full spirit of their profession, by the prospect of receiving praise and gratitude from their countrymen at home.   Such is vain-glory; and if we view *pride* in comparison with it, how languid and (as it were) *sullen* a pleasure it is which the latter confers.

Why then is it that pride is ordinarily so far more powerful and deeply rooted a habit?   Evidently, because the Propension far more than makes up, by the *frequency* of its gratifications, for their comparatively small *intensity*.   Those acts, which engender the habit of pride, are in the mass of men almost or altogether *unceasing;* * those which make up the habit of vainglory, are comparatively rare and intermittent.   Acts of virtuous Self-assertion are *by no means more frequent*, than acts wherein we aim at, or rejoice in, God's approbation; and the latter Propension, being immensely the stronger, gives far greater help to virtue than the former.   But acts of *pride* are *immeasurably* more frequent than acts of *vain-glory;* so much so, as to do much more than compensate, for the immensely less *pleasure* which appertains to the former propension.

One final remark may be interesting, before we quit this Propension.   It has been assumed, in our treatment of it, that so long as the will is kept in due subordination to God, the entrance for any long time of that emotion which we call pride is impossible.   Now further I ask, what did we find, in treating of Resentment, to be the one principal source, from whence proceed hatred, malice and all 'aggressive' injury to our fellow-men?   A small amount, it appeared, was due to

---

* That is, of course, during their *waking* hours.

the action of envy ; but far the greater part, to perverted Love of Justice.   Lastly I ask, how does this love
of Justice *become* perverted ? how is it transformed
into personal anger and unholy resentment ?   Simply
through pride ; through our monstrous practical exaggeration of our own just claims to respect and deference.
So long then, it appears, as the will is duly subordinate
to God, pride even as an emotion can for no long time
remain ; and so far as pride is absent, personal anger,
and hatred, and malice, will be non-existent.   In other
words, it is only in proportion as they fail in *due reverence to their Creator*, that creatures ever experience
any continued emotions of mutual hatred and vindictive
malice *against each other.*

149.   The Propensions, which we have hitherto considered, all agree with each other in this respect ; viz.
that every growth in virtue does but give increased
scope for their gratification.   It is requisite indeed, that
we take great pains in fixing them carefully on their
legitimate objects.   It is requisite also, that a certain
definite *proportion* should be preserved, between various
Propensions of the number, as to the degree in which
we respectively cherish and foster them.   To labour at
these two tasks indeed, is the principal and most important office of *mortification;* as we shall see in our theological course.   But so only that they are fixed on
their legitimate objects, and fixed in the right relative
proportion, it is absolutely impossible that we can
exceed in our *degree* of calling them into exercise.
These, and whatever others there may be which agree
with them in this particular, I call by the name of the
higher Propensions.   Let us recapitulate those which
we have mentioned, in that order in which they occurred.

  I. Love of Duty.
 II. Self-charity.
III. Personal Love, (1) Amor Benevolentiæ and (2)
        Concupiscentiæ.
IV. General Love, (1) Amor Benevolentiæ and (2)
        Concupiscentiæ.

    V. Compassion.
   VI. Gratitude.
  VII. Love of Approbation.
 VIII. Love of Power.
   IX. Love of Acquisition.
    X. Love of Knowledge.
   XI. Love of Justice.
  XII. Love of the Marvellous.
 XIII. Emulation.
 XIV. Love of Self-assertion.

150. Let us still linger on these Propensions, before passing on to the rest; not for the sake of any additional argument for our thesis which we may thence derive, but rather for the sake of imprinting them more deeply on our memory, and becoming more conversant with their character.

And first let us enquire, are there any of these Propensions, which receive gratification from *every* virtuous act which we perform? Evidently the first does so: it is not (as we have stated in treating of it) a powerful propension on its positive side; still a *certain* pleasure is derived, from the consciousness of acting rightly, on every occasion when we know ourselves so to act.

Is there any other Propension, which is of necessity thus universally gratified by virtuous conduct? You will say perhaps that Self-charity is so, not to mention others; because every good act really tends to our own happiness. True; but we are not, in every good act, *thinking* of our own happiness: as we shall see in the next chapter. The first Propension then is the only one, to which we can assign this universality of gratification in the practice of virtue.

Next, that we may see more clearly what benefits are derived from these Propensions in our Christian course, let us take the ordinary division of duties. Let us divide our duties then, into those which are (1) towards God; (2) towards ourselves; and (3) towards our brethren. And among our various Propensions, let us consider *which* are those calculated to give us special help, in fulfilling the first, the second, the third, of these three classes.

First, duties towards God. It is a very trite remark, that *all* our duties may in a very true sense be called duties to God. Those which are called *in particular* by that name, are on the whole reducible to this;—the fixing our thoughts at due times, and commonly with particular effort and abstraction, on the thought of God, in all His various aspects. And this is important for two reasons. First, that we may preserve through the day our implicit memory of His presence; or in other words, that our various successive acts may be really, even if unconsciously, directed to His love and service (see n. 120, p. 247). Secondly, that by such habits of familiar conversation with our Creator, we may be the more certainly and effectually transformed into His likeness. The same duty is also incumbent on us, in regard to other Objects of the invisible world;—the Sacred Humanity, our heavenly Mother, Saints, and Angels. It will perhaps then be more conducive to completeness, if we call these duties, duties towards God *and* the Invisible World.

The chief Propension which will give us energy for this task, and joy in fulfilling it, is (I need not say) 'Personal Love,' in its two great branches; but hardly less important service will also be rendered by ' Love of Approbation.' ' Love of the Marvellous' also enjoys signal delight in these high contemplations. 'Gratitude' and 'Compassion' give (as we have seen) subordinate assistance; and it is perhaps not an undue refinement to say, that even such theological considerations, as are in place during direct prayer and meditation, give a real gratification (with educated Christians) to their ' *Love of Knowledge.*' 'Emulation' also stirs us up towards following those high examples, whom we study at such periods.

The second class of duties—those towards ourselves—are no whit less indispensable than the former. Under this head are included such exercises, as periodical examen of conscience;—the labouring to discover remedies, for those hitherto hidden sins which we may have discovered;—the practice of penance and satisfaction, by way of self-revenge;—the watching over ourselves through the day, that we practise faithfully, in all these respects, what we may have resolved wisely.   These exercises, I say, are no less important, than those of the former class ; or rather are absolutely indispensable, in order that the others may be really performed at all.   Unless there be this constant interior watchfulness and discipline, our contemplation of Heavenly Objects will be *delusive;* will not truly correspond to the great Realities.   It is for this very reason, that so many misbelievers have fallen into such terrible abysses of evil, under pretext and imagination of heavenly contemplation.   It is for this reason, that so many have mistaken the dictates of pride and bitterness, for true zeal in God's behalf; and the untempered heats of fanaticism, for the fervours of genuine devotion.

What then are those Propensions which will specially cheer us, in the fulfilment of these laborious and otherwise wearisome obligations ?   So far of course as the motive for their performance has reference to God, those Propensions last recited have their place also here. But we are rather inquiring, what Propensions will be *specially* called into play, by that *special* part of God's service, which consists of these interior duties.   We may answer as follows.

(1.) 'Self-charity' will be of most powerful assistance in the cause : the very fact that we are thinking of our own interior, will remind us how essentially we are promoting our own happiness by so acting.   (2.) 'Love of Self-assertion' in like manner will be gratified, in proportion as we faithfully acquit ourselves of that responsibility which rests upon us ; and still more, 'Love of Acquisition,' when we find our evil habits sensibly diminish, while our various virtues are healthily advancing towards maturity.   In regard to *one* side of these duties—the discovery of hidden sins, and self-chastisement in vindictive requital,—we have seen how very powerfully the ' Love of Justice' will both stimulate us to the task, and sustain us in its performance.

There remains the third class of duties, those towards our brethren. These indeed are not so absolutely essential to the very *idea* of true religion, as are the two former; yet in those circumstances wherein God has placed us, it will ever remain true, that ' he who loves God will love his brother also.' What are those Propensions which will give us special help in *this* branch of obligation? On these duties indeed, as in regard to the former, it is to be noted, that so far as the motive for their performance has reference to *God*, the Propensions bearing on the *first* class have their place here also. But the meaning of our question is, what Propensions will *specially* be called into play, as often as our working for God takes the special shape, of aiming at the conscientious discharge of our social duties.

The first place will be held, in partnership, by those two most important Propensions,—' General Love' (in its two branches) and ' Love of Justice.' So far as either of these unduly preponderates over the other, social *mischief* tends to ensue: it is the *resultant* of their united action, which will speed us forward in the due direction. In proportion as we possess these two Propensions, (1) in the right mutual proportion, and (2) in strength and intensity, in that proportion we shall be well equipped by nature for our social duties. Both ' Compassion' and ' Gratitude' are also of great assistance to these duties; but far more the former than the latter. ' Love of Approbation' also should be enlisted in the same cause: for though, when directed to our fellowmen, there is need of great watchfulness, lest it exceed and become inordinate;—yet (as we before observed) it may have a perfectly legitimate gratification, in the applause we receive from good and pious Christians. Finally it may be remembered, that in one very important part of our social duties,—intercessory prayer,—the ' Love of Power' is an invaluable stimulus to its due performance.

151. Another course of remarks on these Propensions will be desirable, in consequence of a deep and vital difference which exists on this head, between Catholics and Protestants. In speaking of Protestants, I refer to those who may be called '*formal* Protestants.' There are certain Protestants, be they more or fewer in number, whose interior life is such, that were the Catholic Church to be truly exhibited before their eyes, in her doctrines, her precepts, her rule of life, they would speedily recognize her Divine authority: their Protestantism is due to their ignorance of Catholicism in its real nature. But there are other Protestants, of whom a most different account must be given; and whom a clearer apprehension of Catholic doctrine and practice, would but drive into a more determined and uncompromising opposition.* And it is such Protestants as these, of whom I intend speaking. They would regard this whole treatment of our Propensions as simply illusory, and even fanatical. And as you will probably come often enough into contact with such opponents, it is better you should at once understand their view of the case.

I cannot better explain their general meaning, than by a single very characteristic illustration : their opinion on monasteries and convents. You will constantly hear them urge, that convents are such *dreary* places; and that the unhappy victims, there immured, must pine away in desolation and misery. You will reply of course, that a convent would indeed be a dreary place for one who had no vocation; or, in other words, who was so constituted (by nature or habit) as to have no sufficient power of realizing the invisible. But as to one who *has* such a vocation, you will add, no place can be so happy as a convent ; for God, and the other objects of the Invisible World, are a far more adequate rest whereon the affections may repose, than any beings

---

* It may be asked, whether this distinction be equivalent to that between 'vincible' and 'invincible' ignorance ; but no intelligible answer could be given in a few words. 'De Ignorantiâ' will be one important part of our theological work.

of this earth can possibly be.   Now the reception,
which such a reply will meet from Protestants, is deeply
instructive.   It is not merely that they will not admit
its force: they will be angry with you, for having the
' effrontery ' to urge it; they will look on it as a mere
juggle of words; they will regard it as a mere superficial plausibility, invented for the purpose of controversy, the truth of which you yourself no more believe
at the bottom of your heart than they do.

Now how can we account for this their strange demeanour?   They cannot possibly mean, *e.g.* that our
Propensions are incapable of being gratified by invisible
objects.   Take, for instance, a fact to which we have
often adverted; the incredible delight which a soldier
receives, from the praise of his countrymen.   Does this
delight spring only from the praise of those, among his
countrymen, whom he has *seen and known?*   The supposition is simply ridiculous.   He is in the Crimea, and
they at home; those with whom he is personally acquainted are but an infinitesimal part of the whole; yet
the praise of that unknown mass is the sweetest music
in his ears.   How can it then be called unmeaning or
paradoxical to maintain, that he whose thought dwells,
not on his unseen *countrymen* but his unseen *Creator,*—
that such a man will derive a similar gratification from
that Creator's praise and approbation ? or rather indeed
a much greater gratification; by how much the Creator
has him with immeasurably greater constancy in His
thoughts,* and knows with immeasurably greater in-
timacy his whole course of life.   This is however but
one Propension out of many : consider others also;
consider, *e.g.* Compassion.   If I hear a most touching
tale of woe, who will say that I have no pleasure in
relieving it, because I never *saw* the sufferer ?   Or,
taking Gratitude as an instance, that I have no pleasure
in requiting a service, unless I personally *know* my
benefactor ?   Or consider General Love.   Is not the
hatred of my fellow-men one of the keenest sufferings
imaginable ?   And who will say that it is lessened,

---

* I express myself, of course, ' more humano.'

because the great majority of those men are external to my acquaintance?

Our opponents then cannot possibly mean, that man's Propensions are incapable of being gratified by invisible objects: we must seek some deeper ground of difference, between them and ourselves. Nor is it very difficult to discover this ground. I was once arguing this very point of doctrine, with a very candid and intelligent Protestant; and the answer which I received shed quite a flood of light on the real matter at issue. ' Seclusion from the world,' said my antagonist, ' must ' by absolute necessity be a wretched and dreary con- ' dition, whatever you say about such persons realizing ' the Presence of God. How is it possible to find con- ' tent and comfort, in the thought of an *abstraction?*' This, I am persuaded, leads us to the real truth; they do not *practically* believe in a *Personal* God at all.

Now on *this* supposition, nothing can be more intelligible than the above statement. A heathen philosopher calls on his hearers to live justly, temperately, beneficently,—not for the sake of human applause, but for the pure love of virtue. ' Virtue,' he adds, ' is its ' own reward, and will support us in the absence of all ' human consolations.' This is very specious and plausible, so long as his disciples are content with admiring and *listening* to his fine sentiments; but let them once try and *put them into practice*, the fallacy of his reasoning will force itself on their notice. ' What ' is meant at last by virtue? simply a certain state of ' my own mind: how can a *state of my own mind* be ' any gratification, to those most powerful Propensions, ' which rest on *external objects* for their satisfaction? ' How can my Love of Approbation, or my desire for ' another's affection, be satisfied by a mere *abstraction?* ' Such talk is mere insult or mockery.' These will be the very natural and just comments of a heathen auditor; and in proportion as any men (whatever they are called) *agree* with heathens, in (practically at least) ignoring the very notion of a Living and Personal Creator,—in that proportion the very same reclamation will be natural and (in one sense) reasonable in *their* mouths also. To speak of God as a really satisfying Object to the heart, is to give *them* a stone when they ask for bread; it is to call on them to rest their affections on a mere abstraction. This then I believe to be the real ground of difference, between Catholics and these Protestants; this it is, which perplexes both the Catholic and the Protestant controversialist. Each arguer is amazed and bewildered, when he finds his opponent doubting or denying, what to him appear the most obvious and elementary of truths. And each is tempted consequently, to charge the other with conscious and flagrant disingenuousness; whereas the real truth simply is, that they mutually differ as to principles, far more fundamental and pervasive, than any which have been directly subjects of disputation.

Protestants, I say, in proportion as they are 'formally' such, do not *practically* realize the existence of a Living and Personal Creator, wholly distinct from, and external to, ourselves; of a Being, who has Acts, Thoughts, Affections, of His own; of a Being, who may be just as truly and legitimately the Object of our various propensions, as any other external being can be; of a Being, 'Who, though the highest, yet in the 'work of creation, conservation, government, retribu- 'tion, makes himself, as it were, the minister and ser- 'vant of all; Who, though inhabiting eternity, allows 'Himself to take an interest, and to feel a sympathy, 'in the matters of space and time.' * They consider themselves of course,—sincerely consider themselves,— to believe most firmly in His existence; but all their views and opinions on religious matters imply, by necessary inference, the *contradiction* of that belief. To suppose that the real difference between Catholic and Protestant, lies in opposite intellectual convictions on the existence of Purgatory, or on the cultus of Our Blessed Lady, or on the efficacy of sacraments, seems to me a most inadequate view indeed of the real gulf between them and us. We start from, and throughout

* Newman's Discourses on University Education, p. 93.

proceed upon, an essentially different view from them, on the very foundation of all religion;—on the nature, the character, the claims, of our Almighty Creator.   On this the very foundation of all religion, the doctrine of God,—the Protestant's practical belief is one thing, the Catholic's another and most opposite.   ' No one,' says Father Newman, ' can really set himself to master ' and to teach the doctrine of an Intelligent Creator in ' its fulness, without going on a great deal farther than ' he at present dreams.' *   ' Let him really and truly, ' not in words only, or by inherited profession, or in ' the conclusions of reason, but by direct apprehension, ' be a Monotheist, and he is already *three-fourths of the* ' *way towards Catholicism.*' †   I am not speaking of

---

* Newman's Discourses on University Education, p. 100.

† I am not saying that this will tend to remove those various obstacles, which prevent his regarding the *historical arguments* in favour of Catholic Doctrine as satisfactory ; that is another matter.   But I say, it will tend most powerfully to remove the innumerable objections to Catholic Doctrine *in itself*, which are felt by the mass of Protestants.

On the general statement in the text, as to Theism being the main point at issue between Catholics and Protestants, I may say that I had come to the clear conviction of its truth, before I was aware how far any other Catholics were in agreement.   The following quotation therefore expresses a judgment, of which my own was altogether independent.   ' This is the doctrine which belief in a God implies : if it means anything, it means all this, and cannot keep from meaning all this, and a great deal more ; and, though there were nothing in Protestantism, as such, to disparage dogmatic truth (and I have shewn there is a great deal), still, even then, I should have difficulty in believing that a doctrine so mysterious, so peremptory, approved itself as a matter of course to educated men of this day, who gave their minds attentively to consider it.   Rather, in a state of society such as ours, in which authority, prescription, tradition, habit, moral instinct, and the influences of grace go for nothing ; in which patience of thought, and depth and consistency of view, are scorned as subtle and scholastic ; in which free discussion and fallible judgment are prized as the birthright of each individual ; I must be excused, if I exercise towards this age, as regards its belief in this doctrine, some portion of that scepticism, which it exercises itself towards every received but unscrutinized assertion whatever.   I cannot take it for granted, I must have it brought home to me by tangible evidence, that the spirit of the age means by the Supreme Being what Catholics mean.   Nay, it would be a relief to my mind to gain some ground of assurance, that the parties influenced by that spirit had, I will not say, a true apprehension of God, but even *so much as the idea of what a true apprehension is.*

' Nothing is easier than to use the word and mean nothing by it.   The heathens used to say, " God wills," when they meant " Fate ; " " God provides," when they meant " Chance ; " " God acts," when they meant " Instinct " or " Sense " ; and " God is everywhere," when they meant " the Soul of Nature."   The Almighty is something infinitely different from a principle, or a centre of action, or a quality, or a generalization of pheno-

course, as though a sharp and definite line could be drawn,—between those who are 'formally' Protestants and those who are but accidentally so,—on this spirit (as it may be called) of practical atheism. Here, as in all other cases of the same kind, one doctrine melts into the other through numberless intermediate gradations. There is the class of Protestants (be they many or few) who are not 'formally' Protestants at all; who realize God's Personal Existence, as firmly as ordinary Catholics realize it; and who are truly on their way to Catholicism, if it were but adequately exhibited before their sight. There is on the other hand that numerous body of extreme Protestants, whose practical doctrine has been described above. Lastly, there is a large number of intermediate persons, who are in a greater or a less degree of agreement with the former or with the latter.

This also must be observed. I am not here engaged in vindicating the deep harmony which exists, between the most undoubted facts of our nature on the one hand, and the monastic institute on the other hand; though I hope indeed, that the proposition which we are here defending, will be found a most important *premiss* for that *further* conclusion. To vindicate that harmony, is to shew that certain souls possess such keen power of apprehending the Invisible, that God and other heavenly Objects suffice *of themselves* to satisfy their highest Propensions. This is not our *present* thesis. In the earlier part of our remarks on the Propensions, we maintained, that to all those who choose to feed their thoughts on the great Truths of Faith, the constitution of their nature gives two singular advantages. First, God is an Object which is suited to

mens. If, then, by the Word you do but mean a being who has contrived the world and keeps it in order; who acts in it, but only in the way of general Providence; who acts towards us, but only through what are called laws of Nature; who is more certain not to act at all, than to act independently of those laws; who is known and approached indeed, but only through the medium of those laws; such a God it is not difficult for any one to conceive, not difficult for any one to endure.'—*Newman's Discourses on University Education*, p. 594.

Father Faber, in various parts of his work on 'The Creator and the Creature,' most powerfully enforces the same great truth.

the satisfaction of their highest Propensions, in precisely the same sense in which any earthly object can furnish such satisfaction; and secondly, the thought of Him gives a far deeper, more solid, more permanent gratification to these Propensions, than any earthly object has to offer.   To this whole course of reasoning various Protestants reply, that the very allegation of God being a real *rest* to the affections is simply sophistical ; is founded on a mere equivocation.   Our digression then has been occupied, in dealing with that Protestant reply.

Let us now then consider, what are those various arguments, which may be adduced in this controversy. How far indeed arguments are likely in ordinary cases *to be of avail,*—against a principle, so widely and deeply pervading the Protestant mind, so unsuspiciously imbibed and taken for granted as self-evident,—this we are not here to consider : it would require a separate treatise of itself.   But such arguments as the following, are in themselves surely very cogent and irrefragable; however little our opponents may choose to give them a candid and dispassionate consideration.

(1.) One answer to our opponents is contained in all the preceding discussion.   Their whole statement implies the denial of a Personal God : once admit a Personal Creator, external to ourselves, it is simply ludicrous, to assume as *self-evident,* that the thought of Him may not be found a most real and keen gratification to our highest propensions.   Strange however as it must appear, they do assume this position as self-evident ; and thus imply a denial of God's Personal Existence.   Yet so far are they from *professing* any such denial, they are most indignant at being even suspected of it.   Since therefore their reasoning undoubtedly implies a certain proposition ;—and since they indignantly deny that they *hold* any such proposition ;—their whole intellectual position is simply self-contradictory.

(2.) A second answer to them may be given, even more direct and fundamental than the former.   They say, that the thought of God *cannot* thus satisfy the human affections; we Catholics know, as a matter of certain fact, that in numberless cases it has and does so satisfy them. There is no fact on earth more certain, than that great numbers of monks and nuns have, in every age, been able, with joy and delight, to renounce all human and earthly attachments altogether, and satisfy every longing of their souls by communion with the Invisible World.

" What are the humble monk, and the holy nun, and other regulars, as they are called," asks Father Newman, " but Christians after the very patterns given us in Scripture? What have they done but this,—continue in the world the Christianity of the Bible? Did our Saviour come on earth suddenly, as He will one day visit, in whom would He see the features of the Christians He and His Apostles left behind them, but in them? Who but these give up home and friends, wealth and ease, good name and liberty of will, for the kingdom of heaven? Where shall we find the image of St. Paul, or St. Peter, or St. John, or of Mary the mother of Mark, or of Philip's daughters, but in those who, whether they remain in seclusion, or are sent over the earth, have calm faces, and sweet plaintive voices, and spare frames, and gentle manners, and hearts weaned from the world, and wills subdued; and for their meekness meet with insult, and for their purity with slander, and for their gravity with suspicion, and for their courage with cruelty; yet *meet with Christ everywhere,—*Christ *their all-sufficient, everlasting portion,* to make up to them, both here and hereafter, all they suffer, all they dare, for His Name's sake?" *

And as so many monks and nuns have ever found God ' their all-sufficient portion,' so many ordinary Catholics also have ever felt towards Him a real personal affection. In the following passage, Father Newman expresses, what had been to me a most striking fact of observation, from the time when I became acquainted with Catholic books of devotion; and of course therefore, long before I read the passage in question. He expresses this fact, I need hardly add, with incomparably greater clearness and force than I could hope to reach; and his words therefore will be far more suitable than any of my own.

* Sermons on Subjects of the Day, p. 328.

" And what the Church urges on us down to this day, Saints and holy men, down to this day, have exemplified. Is it necessary to refer to the lives of the Holy Virgins, who were and are His very spouses, wedded to Him by a mystical marriage, and in many instances visited here by the earnests of that ineffable celestial benediction, which is in heaven their everlasting portion? The martyrs, the confessors of the Church, bishops, evangelists, doctors, preachers, monks, hermits, ascetical teachers,—have they not, one and all, as their histories shew, *lived on the very name of Jesus*, as food, as medicine, as fragrance, as light, as life from the dead?—as one of them says, ' in aure dulce canticum ; in ore mel mirificum ; in corde nectar cœlicum.'

" Nor is it necessary to be a Saint thus to feel : this intimate, immediate dependence on Emmanuel, God with us, has been in all ages the characteristic, almost the definition, of a Christian. It is the ordinary feeling of Catholic populations : it is the elementary feeling of every one who has but a common hope of heaven. I recollect, years ago, hearing an acquaintance, not a Catholic, speak of a work of devotion, written as Catholics usually write, with wonder and perplexity ; because (he said) the author wrote *as if he had ' a sort of personal attachment to our Lord; it was as if he had seen Him, known Him, lived with Him*, instead of merely professing and believing the great doctrine of the Atonement.' It is this same phenomenon, which strikes those who are not Catholics, when they enter our Churches. They themselves are accustomed to do religious acts simply as a duty; they are serious at prayer-time, and behave with decency, because it is a duty. But you know, my brethren, mere duty, a sense of propriety and good behaviour, these are not the ruling principles present in the minds of our worshippers. Wherefore, on the contrary, those spontaneous postures of devotion? why those unstudied gestures? why those abstracted countenances? why that heedlessness of the presence of others? why that absence of the shamefacedness which is so sovereign among professors of other creeds? The spectator sees the effect; he cannot understand the cause of it. *Why* is this simple earnestness of worship? *we* have no difficulty in answering. It is because the Incarnate Saviour is present in the tabernacle ; and then, when suddenly the hitherto silent church is, as it were, illuminated with the full piercing burst of voices from the whole congregation, it is because He now has gone up upon His throne over the altar, there to be adored. It is the visible sign of the Son of Man which thrills through the congregation, and makes them overflow with jubilation." *

Here again, I am not considering how we can best

* Occasional Sermons, pp. 47–49.

z

convince Protestants of this fact, which is so familiarly known to us Catholics ; that is another matter : I am but saying, that this fact is in itself a most absolute answer to their argument. When we speak of personal affection for God,—personal in the very same sense in which our affection for each other is personal,—they reply, not that such affection is *undesirable*, but that it is *impossible.* If you allege that a thing is impossible, in no other way can you be so irrefragably answered, as by my shewing you that it *exists.*

(3.) The next argument may be drawn, from the New Testament Scriptures ; which Protestants ordinarily hold to be inspired by God.* How very much, on the surface at least, these inspired writings appear to favour our side of the question, is plain from the comments made on them by infidel writers. It has been urged again and again by the opponents of Christianity, that the New Testament overlooks such virtues as friendship and patriotism, in its earnest inculcation (1) of personal love for God and (2) of general love for all mankind. This has been urged, I say, again and again : many Protestant controversialists have considered the objection; but I never heard of one who attempted to deny, that at least *far greater stress* is laid in the New Testament on love for God, than on any love for our earthly friends.

In attempting any citation of individual passages, the real difficulty is, lest, in contemplating individual passages, we omit to consider the general spirit. No one, I am quite certain, can read the New Testament with any approach to fairness, and fail to see, how simply it takes for granted throughout the very proposition for which we are contending; the proposition, that God is a real Object for our affections, in the very same sense in which we are objects of each other's affections. The following passages then must be taken merely as samples of an indefinite number.

Thus, that God's love to us is no mere figurative

---

* In this and various other parts of the present book, for convenience' sake, the limits of strict philosophy have been exceeded.

expression, but is entirely analogous to an earthly father's love of his children, is stated expressly in Luke, xi. 11–13. ' If our earthly father,' argues our Blessed Saviour, ' will give to his children good gifts and not bad, *how much more* will our Heavenly Father so act !' The argument, from our earthly father's love to God's Love, implies of necessity what I just stated; otherwise it is simply unmeaning. So, in the Parable of the Prodigal Son, God is represented under the figure of an earthly father, who, on his son's return, is moved with compassion, and falls on his neck, and kisses him. (Luke, xv. 20.) In another place, His joy over the return of a repentant sinner is imaged by the shepherd's delight in recovering his lost sheep.* Then consider John, xvi. 26, 27, ' Non dico vobis quia Ego rogabo Patrem de vobis : Ipse enim Pater amat vos, quia vos Me amâstis.' Here we see first, that God loves them, *in that very sense in which they love our Blessed Saviour.* But no one ever doubted (as I shall presently urge at greater length) that those disciples, who actually lived with our Lord in the flesh, loved Him *in the same sense in which they loved each other.* It is in *this* sense therefore that God loves *them.* And we see, secondly, in this passage, that our Blessed Lord takes for granted, that the same results follow from God's Love, which would follow from that of an earthly friend ; and that He will therefore readily hear their prayers. The love of God for man therefore, if the New Testament can be trusted, is altogether analogous to the love of an earthly father for his children.

Next, that our Blessed Saviour, in His human nature, loves His disciples with a human affection (though this, at all events, no one can have ever doubted), is plainly stated in innumerable instances; of which the few following may be taken as samples.

---

* Matt. xviii. 12–14. "Quid vobis videtur ? si fuerint alicui centum oves, et erraverit una ex eis, nonne relinquit nonaginta novem in montibus, et vadit quærere eam quæ erravit ? Et si contigerit ut inveniat eam, amen dico vobis, quia gaudet super eam magis quam super nonaginta novem quæ non erraverunt. *Sic non est voluntas ante Patrem vestrum Qui in cœlis est,* ut percat unus de pusillis istis."

" Et extendens manum in discipulos suos, dixit: *Ecce mater Mea et fratres Mei.* Quicumque enim fecerit voluntatem Patris Mei Qui in cœlis est, ipse Meus *frater, et soror, et mater est.*" (Matt. xii. 49, 50.) " Quam cùm vidisset Dominus, *misericordiá motus super eam*, dixit illi: Noli flere." (Luke, vii. 13.) " Majorem hâc dilectionem *nemo habet,* ut animam suam ponat quis pro amicis suis." (John, xv. 13.) " Ante diem festum paschæ, sciens Jesus quia venit hora ejus ut transeat ex hoc mundo ad Patrem, cùm dilexisset Suos qui erant in mundo, in finem dilexit eos." (John, xiii. 1.)

And now for the chief point of all; viz. that Christians are to love their God and their Saviour, in the very sense in which they love each other; in the same sense, but of course in a higher degree, and with more unreserved adherence of affection.

Thus, " Qui amat patrem aut matrem plusquam Me, non est Me dignus; et qui amat filium aut filiam super Me, non est Me dignus." (Matt. x. 37.) Here is the very comparison, between love of Christ on the one hand, and love of father, mother, son, daughter, on the other hand. Unless the word 'love' is used in *the same sense* as applied to the contrasted objects, our Lord's sacred words become a simple absurdity; parallel to that which is involved in the question, ' which of the two is longer, an hour or a mile?' You cannot *compare* the length of an hour with that of a mile, because the word 'length' is used in two totally different senses; and no less utterly absurd would it be to compare love of Christ with love of father and mother, if the word 'love' were used in two different senses.

Again, consider the well-known summary of the Law. " Ait illi Jesus: Diliges Dominum Deum tuum ex toto corde tuo, et in totâ animâ tuâ, et in totâ mente tuâ. Hoc est maximum et primum mandatum. Secundum autem simile est huic: Diliges proximum tuum, sicut teipsum. In his duobus mandatis universa Lex pendet et prophetæ." (Matt. xxii. 37–40.)

Here the same word is used for love of God and love of our neighbour.

Still more to our general purpose is the following. "Et cœpit ei Petrus dicere : Ecce nos dimisimus omnia, et secuti sumus Te. Respondens Jesus, ait : Amen dico vobis : Nemo est, qui reliquerit domum, aut fratres, aut sorores, aut patrem, aut matrem, aut filios, aut agros, propter Me et propter Evangelium — qui non accipiat centies tantùm, nunc in tempore hoc, *domos, et fratres, et sorores, et matres, et filios, et agros*, cum persecutionibus, et in sæculo futuro vitam æternam." (Mark, x. 28–30.) No one maintains, that all who give up earthly goods and relations for God's sake, *literally* receive them back again; that he, for instance, who, for God's sake, leaves father and mother, obtains literally two new human objects for his filial affections. What then *can* be meant, except that very proposition for which we have been arguing? viz. that those very affections, which we tear, for God's sake, from their immediate earthly gratifications, receive satisfaction ' a hundred times' greater, in *those higher Objects* which our faith will bring within our reach.

Then what can St. Paul mean in such passages as the following, except that his love for Christ was similar to our love for a human object? similar, though of course immeasurably higher and more pervasive. " Mihi *vivere Christus est*, et mori lucrum." (Philip. i. 21.) " *Desiderium habens* dissolvi et *esse cum Christo*." (Ibid. i. 23.) " *Quis ergo nos separabit à charitate Christi?* tribulatio? an angustia? an fames? an nuditas? an periculum? an persecutio? an gladius?.... Sed in his omnibus superamus propter Eum *Qui dilexit nos*. Certus sum enim, quia neque mors, neque vita, neque angeli, neque principatus, neque virtutes, neque instantia, neque futura, neque fortitudo, neque altitudo, neque profundum, neque creatura alia, poterit nos separare à charitate Dei, quæ est in Christo Jesu Domino nostro." (Rom. viii. 35, 37–39.) And St. Peter, "Si tamen *gustâstis quoniam dulcis est Dominus*." (1 Pet. ii. 3.)

St. Peter's own Supremacy indeed had been based on his exceeding the other Apostles in love of Jesus. "Cùm ergo prandissent, dicit Simoni Petro Jesus: Simon Joannis, *diligis Me plùs his?* Dicit ei: Etiam, Domine, Tu scis quia amo Te. Dicit ei: Pasce agnos Meos. Dicit ei iterùm: Simon Joannis, *diligis me?* Ait illi: Etiam, Domine, tu scis quia amo Te. Dicit ei: Pasce agnos meos. Dicit ei tertiò: Simon Joannis, *amas me?* Contristatus est Petrus, quia dixit ei tertiò, Amas me? et dixit ei: Domine, Tu omnia nôsti: Tu scis quia amo Te. Dixit ei: Pasce oves meas." (John, xxi. 15–17.) And St. Paul dwells on that very connection between love of Christ and love of each other, on which his Master laid such repeated stress. "Et ambulate *in dilectione*, sicut et *Christus dilexit nos*, et tradidit semetipsum pro nobis oblationem et hostiam Deo in odorem suavitatis." (Eph. v. 2.)

Again, earthly love, in proportion as it is more deeply rooted in the whole feelings and affections, does not content itself with emotion, but issues in a careful compliance with every *wish* of the beloved person. In this respect also love of God and of Christ is to resemble it; for it is to shew itself in punctual performance of the Divine Commandments. "Qui habet mandata Mea, et servat ea, *ille est qui diligit Me.* Qui autem diligit Me, diligetur à Patre Meo: et Ego diligam eum, et manifestabo ei Meipsum. . . . . Respondit Jesus et dixit ei: Si quis diligit Me, *sermonem Meum servabit*, et Pater meus diliget eum, et ad eum veniemus, et mansionem apud eum faciemus. Qui non diligit Me, sermones Meos non servat. Et sermonem quem audistis, non est Meus: sed Ejus qui misit Me, Patris." (John, xiv. 21, 23, 24.) "Sicut dilexit Me Pater, et ego dilexi vos. *Manete in dilectione Meâ. Si præcepta mea servaveritis, manebitis in dilectione Meâ*, sicut et ego Patris mei præcepta servavi, et maneo in Ejus dilectione." (John, xv. 9, 10.)

(4.) So much on the inferences deducible, from the plain statements of Scripture. We may derive a further argument from the fact itself of the Incarnation ; an argument which will be cogent, not indeed against all our opponents, but at least against those Protestants, who consider themselves to believe that great and most august Mystery.

No one, I suppose, who believes in any sense the New Testament facts, ever doubted that St. John, *e. g.* "who lay on Jesus's breast" had a real personal love for Him ; or St. Peter, who wept bitterly when He turned to look on him ; or St. Mary Magdalen, when she was unable to apprehend any other thought, except the one pervasive and absorbing impression, "They have taken away my Lord, and I know not where they have laid Him." Now no one will dream of maintaining, that Personal Love, once formed, is lost, merely because its object departs from this visible scene; and it follows therefore, that all those pious men, who mixed familiarly with our Lord during His earthly ministry, retained for Him a life-long Personal Love. But those who believe the Incarnation, hold necessarily that Personal Love for Jesus, is Personal Love for the Incarnate God ; in their judgment therefore, all these favoured disciples had a life-long Personal Love for the Incarnate God.

Now I ask, can there be an hypothesis more absolutely incredible, than that this was purely an *exceptional* case ? that those indeed who lived with our Lord *in the flesh* retained for Him a Personal Love, but that no other Christians could ever have the power of sharing their blessedness ? that the humblest of the seventy could enjoy this high privilege, but that St. Paul had not even the physical possibility of arriving at it ? yet this *must* be maintained by those who say, that a real Personal Love for Him is now impossible.

Further, there is a fact, perhaps the most remarkable fact in all the world, which throws a flood of light on this whole matter. There are preserved to us *authentic records* of our Blessed Saviour's life. We are able, by a truly amazing disposition of God's Providence, to study one by one the very acts and words of Almighty God ; to trace Him through each various event of His earthly ministry ; and to share, with those

who were actually present, its salutary effect.   Surely
it is most incredible that so marvellous a Providence
shall have been put forth, except for some most important end.   We know of course that the end, for
which God the Son became Incarnate and died, was
the salvation of us men.; but I am now inquiring into
the end of this *further* fact, that His words and deeds
in the flesh have been so extensively recorded, and are
authenticated by inspiration itself.   And I say that this
fact is eminently suited for the vitally important purpose,
of engendering in us that personal knowledge of our
dearest Lord, on which personal affection can be reared.

See then whither we are led.   It is most incredible
that Personal Love for our Lord should be the peculiar
privilege of one solitary Christian generation ; and
this inspired record of His life is eminently *suited* to
give *every successive generation* of believers the fullest
means of attaining that Love.   On the other hand, it is
most incredible that this inspired record can have been
put forth, *except* for some most important purpose ;
and yet no *other* purpose can be even suggested, except
the very one which we are considering.   Here then is
a two-fold ground for our conclusion, that it is our
great duty and blessedness so to meditate on His life
and actions, as to rise into His love.

And now we are able to answer an objection, which
Protestants might have made with some superficial
plausibility, to our original reasoning.   ' True,' they
might have said, ' many of our Propensions may be
' abundantly satisfied by invisible objects : our Love of
' Approbation may be so satisfied; or our Compassion;
' or our General Love of mankind.   But *Personal Love* is
' essentially different ; Personal Love requires personal
' knowledge.'

To this our reply is now obvious.   First indeed I will
observe, that this reasoning only professes to meet *one*
out of the *four* arguments adduced for our proposition.
But secondly, even in regard to that one, the reply is
inefficacious.   No doubt, in human friendships, personal
knowledge supplies the firmest and surest basis for

tenderness of personal affection : yet even in them it is far from indispensable. That I may take instances which Protestants will admit, consider such a personal knowledge as we obtain e. g. of Johnson from Boswell's life, or of Dr. Arnold from Mr. Stanley's. What student is there of these biographies, who is not conscious of personal regard, and that indeed in no inconsiderable degree, towards the remarkable men there commemorated ? But supposing we had reason to know that Johnson and Arnold appreciate us as we appreciate them ; — that they know our various thoughts, and sympathize in our various troubles ; — what then would be wanting to a very complete personal friendship ? The application is apparent. And I may refer in this connection to the comparison drawn out at length in n. 135, (p. 268–271) between Personal Love to our blessed Saviour and Personal Love to any human object whatever.

You will object, that at least, in order to cultivate such Personal Love, we must give great and constant effort to the task of realizing the invisible world. ' Since we cannot actually see, and hold palpable con-' verse with, our Blessed Lord, it will be the more ' requisite to supply the deficiency, by specially fixing ' our thoughts on His various works and actions ; the ' study of which brings home to our feelings and ' imagination His personal character.' The whole practice of the Catholic Church is in full accordance with this statement. Meditation is recognized, as a most important integral part of the Christian life ; and the great majority of meditation-books occupy far the greater part of the year, in a study of the various Mysteries relating to our Lord. The truth alleged is indeed most undoubted. Let any one consider the terrible hold which the world has on our affections, (1) from the very fact that it *is* so importunately visible, and (2) from the tendency of our corrupt nature towards all those things which are antagonistic to God,— and what will be his certain inference ? this, that unless we direct special and sustained efforts to this very purpose,—the purpose of realizing the invisible, of making ourselves practically and influentially conversant with the things of faith,—the things of sight, this dazzling and delusive world, will infallibly draw us into its vortex.

Of all our higher Propensions, this of Personal Love is the only one, in regard to which any objection, ever so superficially plausible, could be alleged against our statement, that they may find their highest and most adequate gratification in the great Objects of faith. Any such objection has now (I trust) been entirely overthrown; but what is most remarkable is, that it is precisely this very Propension of Personal Love, in regard to which Scripture speaks with such singular frequency and emphasis.

It may be said, that there is one class of Protestants at least, to whom we cannot with any truth ascribe such opinions as those which we have been combating; the 'Evangelicals.' 'These religionists,' it will be urged, 'preach, as their very characteristic doctrine, the abso-'lute necessity of personal trust in our Saviour.'

Now I will most willingly make the same distinction in their case, as in that of other Protestants : among them, perhaps even more than among others, there are various men, who are not 'formally' Protestants; whose interior life is such, that if Catholicism were really and purely presented to their notice, they would be at once efficaciously moved by grace to embrace it. I am most eager to think, that among those who have in various times professed 'Evangelical' opinions, there are very many, who have had a most real love for their Redeemer. But speaking of 'Evangelicals' as *a class*, it is most remarkable, notwithstanding all their professions, how little they display of Personal Love for our Lord. Their favourite scriptural study, *e. g.* is not the Gospel narrative, which speaks throughout simply of *our Lord;* but rather the Epistles, which speak of *faith and love* towards Him, far more prominently than of Himself. And so, generally, it is not when *our Lord* is mentioned, but when *faith* is mentioned, that your true 'Evangelical' feels his interest awakened, his affections inflamed, his attention keen and eager. If I am a Catholic, my love for my Saviour leads me to follow Him *e. g.* step by step, through all the various stages of His bitter Passion ; and accompany each step by its appropriate affections.   Catholic books of devotion on this plan are simply innumerable ; what single one is there of the kind, which has issued from the ‘Evangelical’ quarter ?   Protestants of a ‘high   church’   complexion   have   occasionally   thus written ;   witness   *e. g.*   Jeremy   Taylor :   but   what ‘Evangelical’ has so done ?

149. The same doctrine which we have been treating in the last two numbers, may be put forth in a slightly different shape as follows.

All spiritual writers are of course unanimous in telling us, that our one way to perfection is the mortifying our evil and corrupt affections.   In proportion as we do so, they tell us, heavenly and spiritual affections grow up within us ; we become changed beings ; our joys and sorrows, our hopes and fears, all are essentially different from what they were ; we live in a new world ; no phrase in fact can so well express the change wrought within us, as St. Paul’s significant and emphatic statement, that we become ‘a new creation.’   No doctrine of course can be more true, or more fundamental, than this.   And yet not unfrequently it is understood, in a sense totally *different* from that which these writers ever imagined, and directly at variance with the most certain psychological facts.   Such language is not unfrequently understood, as though there were certain evil passions in our nature, which it is our simple business to extirpate ; and as though, in proportion as we do so, certain totally different affections, hitherto dormant, were sure to start into existence, and become the animating principle of our lives.

There cannot, I say, be a more extravagant supposition than this ; nor indeed could any one entertain it, who in any sufficient way mastered the meaning of his words.   Our natural constitution is simply good ; it contains no one evil passion.   There can be un-

doubtedly no more essential discipline, than that of mortification ; but the work of mortification is wholly misunderstood, wherever such a theory is held as that just
stated.   Our lower propensions no doubt,—those which
we are *presently* to consider,—are to be more and more
stinted of gratification.   But the *main* office of mortification, is not to *stint* or *check* the exercise of our Propensions, but the very contrary ; it is to tear them
away from objects utterly unworthy of them, that they
may be the more undividedly fixed on Those, which
alone can give them any deep or permanent satisfaction.
I am not professing to prove this statement ; for I consider that the whole of the present section has been one
continued proof of it.   I am but shewing you, under a
different point of view, what that conclusion is, at which
we have been aiming throughout.

An objection however may be started against this
whole doctrine, which at first blush has a somewhat
plausible appearance.   ' Is it not the commonest remark
' in the world,' you may ask, 'that to the Saint everything
' which is most painful to the natural man,—the world's
' hatred and the world's reproach, contempt and bodily
' pain,—are not tolerable merely but delightful ?   And
' does not this clearly shew, that there *is* that very
' change of Propensions, which you deny ?   that the old
' assemblage has been extirpated from his nature, and is
' succeeded by others of a directly opposite character ?'

I reply, first by asking,—is it indeed true that the
old Propensions have been extirpated from his nature ?
Take Love of Approbation, *e. g.* is it indeed true, that the
thought of God's disapproval gives the Saint no pain ?
or less pain than it gives ordinary men ?   or rather does it
not give him immeasurably more ?   Take again Personal
Love—has the Saint *less* of this feeling towards God
and Christ, than ordinary men for each other?   A
moment's consideration suffices to shew, that such a
statement as the above is so preposterous, so contradictory to the most obvious facts, that nothing can possibly
be more so.   If then *e. g.* the Saint has become indifferent to *men's* approbation — nay if he even delights

in their reproach,— it is for some reason most widely different from the supposition, that the Love of Approbation has been eradicated from his nature.

We will continue to take Love of Approbation as our sample Propension ; and whatever is said of this, may be most easily applied to the other Propensions also. And it is obvious to remark, that the account to be given of the Saint's *indifference* to human applause is most simple. His mind is pervaded with the thought of God, not of man ; and it is divine, not human, approbation therefore, which he earnestly covets.

But we have further to explain why it is, that he is not merely *indifferent* to human applause, but that he rather *rejoices in its opposite.* This will lead us back to a psychological remark, already made in a different connection. In treating on Love of *Money*, I explained that when a single object is serviceable for a vast assemblage of further ends, those various ends so completely colour our thought of the bonum utile, that it seems as though *a new Propension arose, directed to that bonum utile itself* (see n. 142, p. 284 and 288.) This is not of course really the case ; it is the various *ends*, which really and virtually influence us, *through* the intermediate object. Only, since the object is one and the ends are very many ; —since the object is constantly and explicitly before our mind in our attempts at gaining it, and the ends not so ; —they are merely presented to our mind in a vague and confused mass.

Now, on the side of good, the same phenomenon is seen. Human contempt, *e. g.* is felt by holy men as so intensely conducive to ends which they have inexpressibly at heart, that a new Propension seems to spring up within them; they derive the keenest pleasure from that object, which they have so long coloured with the combined attractiveness of those various ends.

The following indeed is but a most brief and imperfect portion, in that great catalogue of ends. (1.) Human contempt saves the good Christian from all those temptations to vain-glory, which are otherwise so trying, and which require such constant watchfulness. (2.) By freeing him from such an impediment, it enables him to gaze more directly and with more unclouded vision on Heavenly Truth. (3.) It consequently enables him to grow far more quickly in love of God and in every virtue. (4.) Such growth is not only an object of love to him for its own sake, but also as increasing his heavenly reward ; as intensifying the degree, in which he will see and love God for all eternity. (5.) This same growth gives his intercessory prayer greater weight with God, and (6) enables him to satisfy more efficaciously for his own sins and those of others. Then (7) human contempt is a fresh mark of resemblance to his crucified Lord, who is the deepest Object of his affections ; and (8) it is welcomed by him also as the suitable lot for such a sinner as he feels himself to be. And the list, as I have said, might be quite indefinitely prolonged.

It is not therefore that a new Propension springs up within him, *Love of being disapproved :* — what can be more absurd ? It is not this, but a most different fact. His love of approbation is most abundantly satisfied, by the thought of God and of other Heavenly Objects ; and contented with this, he seeks no such comparatively worthless food, as his fellow-creatures' praise on earth. And at the same time, to be despised by his fellow-creatures, is recognized by him as eminently serviceable towards various ends, to which his other propensions are powerfully attracted. Just so in regard to every parallel case.

150. I have spoken thus at length on the higher Propensions, because they are far more important to my subject than the rest. Yet the others also must not go without some degree of attention ; for the thesis, which I profess to prove, is that *all* our propensions are most usefully available in the cause of virtue. I will proceed then to the extremely opposite class, the Bodily Propensions.

The chief Bodily Propensions will be Love of Eating ; of Drinking ; and that which tempts against the Sixth Commandment, which we may call the Propension of the

Flesh.   To these may be added such others, as the Love of Warmth when we are cold, and of Coldness when we are warm ; the Love of Bodily Rest when we have worked too much, and Love of Activity when we have rested too much.   In the same class also, should be placed the pain caused by bodily lesion, to which we have already referred (see n. 93, p. 197).   In the same class also, that most delightful feeling, which we call a sense of good health; which is experienced, when our various bodily organs are in that state, which most fits them for active and serviceable work.   That each one of these Propensions has some important office, in soliciting us to the performance of this or that duty, — this is so obvious on the surface, that it would be impertinent to shew it in detail.   Yet something more should be said about these Bodily Propensions ; and I will take, as their sample and representative, the pleasure which we derive from eating and drinking.   On the other hand, the Propension of the Flesh is in many respects of most exceptional character ; and so far from being available as a sample of others, requires quite a separate treatment of its own.   I will speak of it here, as soon as I have said what seems desirable of the others ; but there will be a further treatment also, appertaining to the next Section.

We have more than once referred, to those pleasures and refreshments, which, by God's merciful appointment, accompany all our innocent worldly engagements.   Every process of manual work or industry, — every intellectual process, — every occupation in short, — has ordinarily and normally its concomitant enjoyment.*   This appointment of God is in deepest harmony with the facts of our nature.   In proportion indeed as men advance towards the heights of perfection, (1), their higher Propensions receive ordinarily, a far keener and far more constant enjoyment from the Invisible World;

* " Dieu, par une sage disposition de Sa Providence, a mis de la facilité et du plaisir en tout ce qui est nécessaire à l'entrétien de la vie ; et il n'est point de la douceur de Sa Conduite, qu'une chose, de laquelle on ne se peut passer, devienne laborieuse et pénible."—SURIN, *Lettres Spirituelles*, vol. i. p. 233, 234.

and (2) even were it otherwise, their moral power is far greater, of pursuing God's work under aridity. But ordinary persons are most differently circumstanced. I am not denying (God forbid!) that the merest beginner in spirituality is really cheered and supported,—and that to a very appreciable extent,—by the rest of his propensions in God ; yet (putting aside cases rare and utterly exceptional) his joy in God is neither at all continuous, nor at all sufficient by itself to carry him forward. This being so, the conclusion is manifest. His good habits are so fresh, and his evil tendencies so strong, that it is morally impossible for him to continue perseveringly to resist temptation, unless various refreshments and recreations be furnished as he proceeds. Were it not then for this merciful dispensation to which I have just referred, he would be morally unable to resist successfully those various temptations which cross his path.

And here, be it observed by the way, is one of the greatest injuries which those inflict on their own happiness, who give themselves up unreservedly to the pursuit of keen and violent pleasures of a sensual character. Such pleasures, by the constitution of our nature, can be but sparingly obtained ; while on the other hand indulgence in them indefinitely impairs our relish for those tranquil, yet most really enlivening, enjoyments, of which we have been speaking. And this is one of the reasons, why it is so terrible a calamity to have once begun such a course ; why the temptation to *repeat* the indulgence is so woefully greater, than was that which induced us first to pursue it.

Returning then to the matter before us, I proceed thus. As the various other innocent occupations of life, are invested by our merciful Creator, each with its own appropriate gratification ;—so particularly this is the case, with the necessary duty of supporting bodily life. Not merely is the gratification of hunger in itself a matter of enjoyment, but there are various pleasures of palate also, which necessarily accompany it. I am far of course from denying, that there is here much

danger of sin, and that temperance is a great duty ;
indeed in our theological work, we shall have to consider precisely, *what* is that mode of surrendering ourselves to any gratification, which *renders* the act sinful.
But I maintain most confidently, and shall in that part
of our work give reasons for the statement, that it is a
most serious mistake to suppose, that the deliberately
accepting such gratification is in itself at all sinful ; or
even that to persons of ordinary spiritual attainments,
the abstaining from it is subjectively preferable (see
n. 57, p. 124). Again, I admit freely, or rather urge
most earnestly, that in proportion as we advance towards
perfection, it becomes more and more our duty to
resist and repress the lower propensions. But I utterly
and absolutely deny, that it is either obligatory or
preferable, to *begin* by the attempt at refusing them
all satisfaction ; and in denying this, I am confident
that I am speaking in harmony with the Church's
spirit. It is certain, that as on the one hand she has
ever most loudly maintained the heroic excellence of
austerity, so on the other hand she has been no less
watchful against any intrusion of rigorism and harshness. Consider this one fact alone ; the habit, prevalent throughout the Church, of celebrating the
greater festivals by greater delicacies than are enjoyed
on ordinary days. Why, on the view which I am
opposing, such a procedure would change the most
holy periods of the year into the mere occasions of sin
and imperfection. And the Church has in every age
been censured accordingly. Just as one class of men
have regarded her as possessed with an unnatural love
of human suffering, so another class has ever de-
nounced her as lax and compromising : so that, from
the very first, she has been permitted to inherit her
Lord's reproach ; " Behold a man that is a glutton and
a drinker of wine, the friend of publicans and sinners.
And [yet] wisdom is justified by all her children." *
The notion, which I am opposing, is pregnant with immeasurably greater and more fearful evil, than we

* Luke, vii. 34, 5.

A A

should at first suppose. Consider what has been already said, that those who are novices in piety (1) certainly do not obtain keen and constant enjoyment from the thought of God; while (2) they have not the moral power of persevering for a long period in His service without sensible solace. Suppose then a certain small number of such men were really persuaded, to aim at renouncing all these innocent pleasures ; what must ensue ? They would be actually driven to seek their solace, in the sinful pleasures of pride and vainglory; and in the more subtle forms of worldliness.

And observe how fact corresponds with this theory. In every age of the Church, characters of the following kind present themselves to our notice. We find men who, at first sight, challenge our reverence, as glorious models of superhuman austerity. Their doctrines are condemned by the Church, or in some other way they are strictly sifted ; and then what do we behold? They display themselves in their true colours, as monsters of diabolical pride.

What has now been said, will suffice to explain the view which appears to me true, of all our various bodily Propensions. It remains to say a few words on that exceptional one, which I have called the Propension of the Flesh. The direct purpose, for which this has been implanted by God, is of course plain enough : the propagation of mankind ; the continued existence of men, who are Christ's redeemed and capable of sanctification. Undoubtedly it is appalling, and again it is heart-breaking, to consider the terrible amount of sin to which this Propension has led. Yet other circumstances being as they are, some Propension of the kind was requisite, in order that mankind should continue to exist in undiminished numbers. It is true (no doubt) that the Propension of Personal Love, — taken in connection with the mental peculiarities of the two sexes, so supplementary of each other, — would in very many cases lead to such exclusiveness of affection, between one man and one woman, as exists under the holy sacrament of Matrimony.

Perhaps the cases are far more than is sometimes supposed, when this Propension of Personal Love has been the main impulsive cause of marriage. But consider the great burden which children are, to the great majority of men ; consider the great anxiety, and great pecuniary pressure, which they cause. Consider this, and you will see very plainly, that unless some most powerful instinct had been implanted which tends to the generation of children, there would have been no security at all, with the mass of men, that marriage would have attained its very principal end.

There seems however the strongest reason for thinking, that this Propension does not now exist in us according to its natural state, but rather under a most miserable and morbid exaggeration. A more detailed consideration therefore of its phenomena, must be reserved for the next Section, which is to treat expressly on the degradation of our nature. Yet one concluding remark on it will here be in place.

There are several, who are called by God to the admirable height, of refusing all gratification to this Propension : even to them—which might seem strange —it performs most important services. There can be no doubt, that through the arduousness of that conflict which they have to sustain, habits of humility and watchfulness are engendered, in a far greater degree than would otherwise be the case. Then secondly, a great additional motive is supplied them for the practice of perfection; viz. the fear, lest God should otherwise refuse them that grace, whereby they shall in fact triumph over the assaults of this Propension. And lastly, by the triumph itself, (in those who are victorious) an invaluable element, both of heroism and of tenderness, accrues to the character.

151. The last class of Propensions to which I shall refer, may be called by one compendious name the ‘Love of Beauty.’ I include under this head, love of beautiful scenes, of architecture, of music, and the like. We may conveniently also include, love of those enjoyments, which are derivable from the sense of smell.

There is a very great diversity, as to the degree in which this or that person is susceptible of these various pleasures ; but the vast majority of mankind are in greater or less degree under their influence. The benefit afforded by these propensions to the increase of virtue is so obvious, that the only difficulty is, to marshal in due order the various thoughts which throng the mind.

(1.) By increasing the amount of innocent recreation, they very considerably lessen the temptations to sin, and increase the facility of practising virtue. This advantage is far greater, than might at first blush appear ; as will be most evident, if we consider what I have recently urged, on the great difficulty experienced by ordinary men, when they try to persevere in God's service under circumstances of dullness and aridity.

(2.) They are of great service in lessening the undue domination of the bodily Propensions. No one will doubt, that we are far less unfavourably circumstanced in regard to piety, that we present a far less powerful barrier to the Holy Spirit's operations,—in proportion as we pursue the enjoyment of beautiful scenery or music, rather than the lower pleasures of sense.

(3.) These Propensions are capable of being enlisted much more directly, and with much greater efficacity, in the service of our Lord : and the Church has very largely availed herself of them for this purpose. Who can exaggerate the beneficial effects of music, towards producing sensible devotion in the more ordinary class of Christians ? What exercises are more animating and inspiriting, than congregational hymnody ? What external appliance can be named, which is so serviceable in drawing the mass of men from worldly thoughts, and for the time bringing them (as it were) close on the gate of Heaven, as some touching strain on the organ, or some sweet and soft harmony of voices ? Again, consider the use ever made by the Church of painting ; not only indeed for the purpose of stimulating sensible devotion, but also of bringing the Mysteries of Faith more definitely and more interestingly before the mind.

Nay the very sense of smell has its place in the beautiful whole ; as in the use of incense at Mass and Benediction.

(4.) What has been hitherto said, applies to the great mass of men. But there are certain souls, gifted with a far keener and more sensitive organization, in whom this perception of beauty seems quite different *in kind* from that experienced by their fellow-men ; and in *them* a still further religious effect is to be observed. Such remarks as the following, have more than once been made in various shapes, by such gifted men.

'Suppose I am engaged in gazing on some en- ' chanting scene of loveliness. First, my emotions are ' absolutely undescribable ; so thrilling are they, so ' subduing, so overwhelming. If you have yourself had ' no experience of such emotions, in vain should I ' attempt to describe them ; any more than I could ' explain the nature of light to one born blind : simply ' I have a sense, which you have not. This is my first ' remark : and my second is, how this beauty with holy ' violence draws me to God ; how peremptorily it refuses ' to be rested in as an end. I feel a pensive, melancholy, ' yearning, for something still absent. I wish, as it were, ' to embrace this beauteous scene before me ; but it ' eludes my grasp : if I try to draw nearer, it vanishes ; ' it is dissolved into rocks, trees, and water, which are ' its component parts indeed, but which in themselves ' have no such beauty. Thus it bears witness against ' itself, that it is a shadow and not a reality.'

The conclusion, drawn from these considerations, is one surely, which recommends itself to the judgment of the philosopher, no less than to the feelings of those who are thus sensitively organized. 'Surely,' it is argued, ' these exhibitions of natural beauty point to ' something altogether beyond and above themselves ; ' they are but adumbrations, adapted to our present ' perceptive powers, of the Eternal and Supreme ' Beauty ; of that Beauty, which is so transcendant and ' so ravishing, that its contemplation will be our all- ' sufficient Beatitude throughout endless ages.'

There is a striking passage in the "British Critic" of 1838, which briefly expresses this view of the case.

"All [*i. e.* the whole constitution of the physical world] is magnificent promise, unsubstantial and encouraging. Is there not something very strange and pregnant in the mere fact, that an assemblage of lifeless, senseless, atoms, should be enabled to excite in moral beings those apprehensions of beauty and sublimity, with which the physical world doubtless does overpower us? Can these apprehensions be more, or can they be less, than indications of great spiritual truths; a temporary and arbitrary system, for training our minds to receive notions which are as yet beyond us? They surely are too baseless to be more; too noble to be less. . . . . . All nature seems to invite our affections but to reject them, and to testify of a" Greater Who is behind.*—Jan. 1838, p. 216, 7.

And the same general doctrine, thus expressed in regard to the beauty of natural scenery, has been put forth by Father Newman in the case of music.

"To many men, the very names which the science employs are utterly incomprehensible. To speak of an idea or a subject seems to be fanciful or trifling, and of the views which it opens upon us to be childish extravagance; yet is it possible, that that inexhaustible evolution and disposition of notes, so rich yet so simple, so intricate yet so regulated, so various yet so majestic, *should be a mere sound, which is gone and perishes?* Can it be, that those mysterious stirrings of heart, and keen emotions, and strange yearnings after we know not what, and awful impressions from we know not whence, should be wrought in us by what is unsubstantial, and comes and goes, and begins and ends in itself? It is not so; it cannot be. No; they have escaped from some higher sphere; *they are the outpourings of eternal harmony in the medium of created sound;* they are echoes from our Home; they are the voice of Angels, or the Magnificat of Saints, or the living laws of Divine Governance, or the Divine Attributes; something are they besides themselves, which we cannot compass, which we cannot utter,—though mortal man, and he perhaps not otherwise distinguished above his fellows, has the gift of eliciting them."—*Sermons before Oxford University,* p. 349.

We have now gone through so large a list of our various Propensions, that no doubt (I think) can

* In the original—" of a greater *system* which is behind."

remain in your mind, on the truth of our general proposition.   And thus we complete the fifth argument adducible for our thesis.   We have seen, that our Propensions alone are the cause of our not leading lives of simply spotless virtue; and we have also seen, that there is not *one* of these Propensions which has not important service to perform, in the interests of virtue. Can there be a stronger proof, that virtue is the end for which our nature has been constituted ?

152. I prepare the way for our sixth argument, by a general remark, which follows at once from the map of our Propensions that has been just drawn out.   Each Propension of course aims immediately at its *object;* Hunger aims at food ; Anger at vindictive retribution; Love of Popularity at popularity.   But in *some* cases that object is in itself and primarily beneficial to *ourselves,* in *other* cases it is in itself and primarily beneficial to *others.*   As an instance of the first class, take Self-charity, or again Love of Knowledge.   These Propensions lead me to promote respectively *my own* happiness, and *my own* possession of knowledge ; in other words, they lead me to pursue objects, which are mainly and directly beneficial to *myself.*   As a very strong instance of the second class, take Compassion : this *can* only be gratified at all, by benefiting a *fellow-creature.* The same may be said on the Propension of Gratitude. Or again consider the Love of *Communicating* knowledge ; the great pleasure which many men derive, from imparting to others their intellectual acquisitions : *this* pleasure cannot by possibility be enjoyed, without exerting ourselves for the advantage of others.   In the case of Personal and of General Love, we have already drawn this very distinction : we have divided them into ' Amor Benevolentiæ,' which leads us directly to the benefit or service of *another;* and ' Amor Concupiscentiæ,' which leads directly to *our own.*

There are several cases no doubt, in which it is difficult to decide, whether a Propension belongs to the former or the latter class ; whether its object primarily tends to others' benefit, or to our own.   And in all cases, there is a very important reciprocity of benefit : those objects which primarily benefit myself, ultimately benefit others also ; those which primarily benefit others, ultimately benefit myself. Thus (confining our attention to merely earthly results) if I gratify my Love of Knowledge, I primarily benefit myself; but unless I am unusually reserved, I ultimately benefit others also. On the other hand, if I gratify Compassion, I primarily benefit another : yet in so doing I obtain myself a two-fold advantage ; viz. (1) the elevation of my own character, and (2) the raising up friends for myself against any future time of trouble or distress. Still on the whole, the two-fold division of Propensions, in accordance with this principle, is undoubtedly a just division.

Let us call the former of these classes ' self-regarding :' the latter then would be suitably expressed by the term ' extra-regarding ;' but as this is rather cumbrous, let us drop a syllable and call them ' ex-regarding.' So ' Amor Benevolentiæ' is ex-regarding Love ; ' Amor Concupiscentiæ,' self-regarding.

On counting over these Propensions respectively, we shall find that, according to the *average* condition of human nature, the ex-regarding are fully as strong, fully as importunate, as the others. Still many persons are of course in a class, either below or above this average condition. So you have *selfish* men in great numbers ; that is men, with whom the self-regarding more or less preponderate in strength over the others. A selfish man by *temperament,* is one in whom *by nature* this is the case ; a selfish man by *habit,* is one who has *cultivated* the former and *neglected* the latter. And here we are led to one obvious conclusion : viz. that selfishness ' does not *pay;*' that it defeats its own end. Happiness *can* only be proportionate, to the degree in which our various Propensions are gratified. But the selfish man, so far as he is such, refuses all gratification to one-half of his propensions, and those perhaps naturally the strongest. What kind of happiness can be his, who hardly ever enjoys the pleasure, and never in a great degree, of gratifying Friendship, Compassion, Gratitude?

And so your selfish men, with long-headed maxims of shrewdness ever in their mouths,—' I will never neglect my own interest; no such fool as that:' and the like;—are (to say the least) far from being that class of men, who really attain the greatest degree of earthly happiness.

Here then we may draw out our sixth argument. It is a metaphysical truth, that (circumstanced as we are) we act most sinfully in living only for ourselves: the great majority are called on to live also for their fellow-men,* and all to live chiefly for God. Now parallel with this metaphysical truth, is a psychological fact; viz. that *unless* we live in great degree for our fellow-men and for God;—*unless* we keep Him and them habitually in our thoughts;—we cannot lead thoroughly happy lives: for one half at least of our natural cravings will be violently thwarted and repressed. Here surely is a reason of great strength, for holding that our nature has been formed for virtue.

153. The seventh is a still more cogent argument. Trace the progress of a holy man towards perfection,—what are those Propensions which he will more and more gratify? what are those which he will more and more repress? Of course I am not for a moment forgetting, the indefinite difference which exists between this and that man's vocation ; how immeasurably greater in that amount of worldly gratification which A. is called to resign, than that whose abandonment falls within B.'s vocation. Still on the whole, in proportion as we advance towards perfection, in that degree our life tends in a greater proportion to consist of these two things : 1st, contemplating God and Heavenly Objects ; and 2ndly, working for them. In other words, in proportion as we advance more towards perfection, we more and more gratify those Propensions (1) which are satisfied by the direct contemplation of God and Heavenly Objects; and (2) those, the satisfaction of which is absolutely inseparable from the very fact of

---

* I speak of *external* life : of course even *solitaries* are called on to *love* their fellow-men, and pray for them.

working for God.   These two classes, I say, we shall more and more gratify; the others we shall more and more repress.   Now let it be most carefully observed, that those which we shall more and more *repress*, are precisely those which even worldly men can gratify but *occasionally and at intervals ;* whereas those which we shall more and more *gratify*, are those which may pervade our whole life.   This will at once be evident, on turning to the respective catalogues.   It is Love of Honour, *e.g.* or Power, or Money, which colours *the whole* of a godless man's Life ; not Love of Sensual Pleasures nor even of Æsthetical Enjoyments.   But it is precisely Love of Honour, of Power, of Acquisition, which any one may and does gratify more and more deeply, more and more without stint or measure, in proportion as he gives himself up more entirely to God.

Now who can be so wild as to maintain, that this most remarkable fact is due wholly to *chance?*   Yet if it be *not* due to chance, what can it manifest, except a most remarkable and distinct provision, on our Creator's part, tending to the result, that the path of virtue and of happiness shall be made identical?

This deep and tranquil rest of our most powerful and pervasive propensions, in God and God's service, would seem to be that most precious gift, so often commemorated in Scripture under the name of ' Peace.' To this again refers St. Augustin's often-quoted address to God : ' Thou hast made us for Thyself : and our heart is restless and unquiet, till we find our repose in Thee !'   It has always drawn me specially to Lombez's great spiritual treatise, that he makes this great and paramount blessing the central figure (as it were) in his picture ; the point from which all his ascetical principles radiate, and to which they converge.   Hear again St. Alphonsus, quoting in his own favour another great Saint also.

" S. Franciscus Salesius, ut Deo alliceret peccatores, potissimùm curabat, ut ipsi cognoscerent *pacem quâ fruuntur illi qui Deo adhærent,* et vitam infelicem quam ducit qui à Deo alienus est . . . . . Curetur ut pœnitens cognoscat *pacem interiorem,* quâ donantur, *qui Dei amicitiâ fruuntur;* et infernum quem ante tempus experiuntur, qui alieni sunt à Deo: additâ pernicie temporali, quam secum trahit peccatum.'—*Praxis Confessarii,* nn. 5 and 15.

The same general truth is contained in the various statements, made by theologians, on that 'beatitudo imperfecta' which is attainable here in viâ. Thus Bellarmine declares it as a thing quite evident (cùm *satis constet*) 'beatitudinem in hâc vitâ in *virtute perfectâ* sitam esse:'* and declares that, even on this ground alone, 'ratio postulat, ut magno studio in hanc rem (virtutem) incumbamus.' Other theologians do not speak quite so clearly and distinctly as this; nor do they attach to the subject an importance approaching that, which (in my humble judgment) it really deserves: still the general drift of their statements is in the same direction.

154. This whole consideration leads at once to an enquiry, very closely related to it. How far has God (1) so constituted our nature, and (2) so providentially arranged external circumstances, that virtue and earthly happiness are coincident? For a satisfactory discussion of this matter, I consider that we have not sufficient data; at all events I do not feel myself competent to attempt it. Yet something may be said perhaps, both true and important; though it will fall far short of a complete and thorough investigation.

And first I will say, that there is hardly any subject, on which it is of more extreme importance to avoid anything like exaggeration; while there are few, on which moralists have greater tendency (most unintentionally) to exaggerate. They are most keenly conscious, how great is the peace implanted in them by a Christian life;—how absolutely satisfactory to their highest affections are those Objects, to which they have given their hearts;—how low and contemptible are those idols, on which worldly men squander their affections; and all this leads them, most unaffectedly and sincerely, to regard such men as plunged in deepest misery. Yet if the fact really be not so, or at least not universally so, then (as I just now observed) there is more than one

* De Amissâ Gratiâ, l. 6. c. 10, n. 6.

reason, why it is of very great importance not to make any allegation on the subject, which facts will fail to sustain.

(1.) One reason why this is so important, is the great danger of the ‘ incredulus odi.’ Worldly men are certainly not naturally disposed to regard their condition as so lamentable; if therefore the picture be too highly coloured, there is great danger that they will not even look at it; if facts are stated which their own experience falsifies, they will not give due attention to *other* facts, which their own experience (if they would but consult it) would most completely confirm.

Then (2) there is real danger, if we press too far the necessary coexistence of piety and earthly happiness, lest we transgress an important point of doctrine. There is no more fundamental tenet of Christianity than this; that by *way of the Cross* we advance to our Crown, and that suffering is the chief instrument for strengthening and perfecting our virtue.

And now for such remarks on the general subject, as may seem warrantable and safe. It would appear certainly at first sight probable, from the facts brought together in the preceding numbers, not merely that the pious man must immeasurably exceed others in earthly happiness, but that those others must be utterly miserable. Yet candour obliges us to admit, that many worldly men do on the whole lead lives of great enjoyment : particularly if they be gifted with good health and pecuniary competence ; and if they are exempt from the more violent and passionate emotions. It is true indeed that this happiness is most precarious and insecure. For first, even so far as this world is concerned, it is at the mercy of a thousand accidents, which may occur at any moment, and the like of which do constantly occur. And secondly, their prospects as to the next life are such, as must absolutely appal them, if they would but steadily contemplate the facts of the case. But it is truly wonderful how great a power such persons possess, of *refusing* to contemplate the facts of the case ; of giving themselves up to this or that worldly enjoyment; and, in the pursuit or possession of such enjoyment, of forgetting altogether both God and themselves.   This power is simply owing, as I believe, to the corruption of our nature, on which in the next Section I hope to speak ; but whatever its cause, its existence is undeniable.

Now in comparing the happiness of good and bad men, we must put out of account those, who are called by God to the highest paths of Sanctity, and who are faithful to that vocation.   Of such men, both the griefs on the one hand, and the consolations on the other, are in a most special sense the immediate work of God's hands, for the direct purpose of their sanctification. These griefs and consolations, I say, do not come from the action of *circumstances* on the constitution of their *nature*, but by God's direct and immediate agency ; their frequency and their degree does not depend on any action of general laws, but on the special circumstances of that individual soul.   This then is *one* reason, why there would be no meaning in any attempted comparison between their earthly happiness and that of worldly men : and *another* reason is, because their sorrows and their joys are so utterly heterogeneous from those of worldly men, that no kind of comparison is even possible.

It must not of course be supposed, that God exercises a less *watchful and minute* Providence over ordinary Christians than over Saints.   Yet in the former case that Providence is carried on, in a very far greater degree, by and through *general laws ;* and it is therefore quite intelligible to inquire whether, *according to* these laws, virtue is or is not ordinarily more conducive to happiness, than is the opposite course of conduct.   It is true again, in ordinary Christians as in Saints, that their joys and sorrows are on the whole different in kind from those which befall worldly men. Still this holds in a far less degree in ordinary Christians than in Saints; and in the former case it by no means holds to so great an extent, as that every kind of comparison is rendered impossible.

There are various considerations then which, in my

humble judgment, will lead us most gravely to doubt, whether real advancement in virtue can ever be opposed to increase in earthly happiness.

Thus (1) according to the very trite remark, worldly men are most happy at those times when we see them; interior men at those times when we do *not* see them. It is impossible therefore to draw any trustworthy inference, on the happiness really appertaining to a worldly man, by merely observing him in the general intercourse of society.

(2.) There are the strongest grounds for believing, that worldly men carry about with them the constant sense, how utterly hollow and unsatisfactory are their real state and prospects. We have already (see n. 127, p. 252) drawn attention to the fact, that such men ever avoid the contemplation of their own interior, as carefully as that of the most disgusting object in nature. But it is very observable, by how *constant and spontaneous an instinct* they do this. It is not, that from time to time they turn their thoughts within, and then recoil from the spectacle which they behold : they never for a moment do so. How is this to be explained, except by the hypothesis above stated? viz. that they bear about with them a constant, unceasing, inextinguishable sense, of their own miserable plight? More will be said on this most remarkable phenomenon, in our theological course; here we advert to the fact, for the sake of its obvious bearing on our present argument. Surely this sense of inward unsatisfactoriness and of most serious peril, must be a most serious drawback from their *enjoyment*.

Then consider (3) how little they value those very things, to the acquisition of which their whole life has been devoted; whether their object has been wealth, or power, or whatever else. To fix our ideas, let us take the instance of an ambitious politician. Though he be at the highest point of preferment;—though he have squandered his best years in working actively for its attainment;—when once gained, it crumbles within his grasp: its *pursuit* was intoxicating, but its *possession* is disappointing. Where shall we find such a politician, who will contemplate the high position he has attained, and then say to himself with perfect sincerity,—' this is indeed a sufficient reward for all the pains devoted to its pursuit?'

The only case which, even on the surface, can seem an exception to this general remark, is the case of sensual men. Yet is there any one of *them*, who, on looking back at the end of life on his past enjoyments, will say that they were really purchased at no extravagant price, by such sacrifice of labour, of wealth, of reputation, as has been involved in his career?

Contrast with this the interior man. Suppose him to recognise unmistakeably, that—comparing his state with that of a year or two back—he sees, far more clearly and constantly, the depth of his own sinfulness; that by help of prayer and grace he is able to triumph far more constantly over this or that temptation; that he realizes the invisible world far more keenly and pervasively. Well : he rejoices in this increase of piety, as in a most precious possession. He regards it indeed (1) as intrinsecally excellent, and (2) as greatly conducive to His eternal interests; and so far, the fact does not bear on our argument: but he rejoices in it also, and cherishes it most joyfully, as contributing most importantly to his present happiness.

(4.) Our fourth consideration shall be based on what has been said in this Section, as regards the completeness with which all our Propensions can be gratified in the service of God. In the case of worldly men, *this* propension ever conflicts with *that*. What worldly career is possible, in which *all* these various propensions, above recited, can receive their due food and nourishment? or even in which any approach is made to such a result? If a man surrenders himself to one tyrant Propension—if, *e. g.* for the sake of ambition, he sacrifices Duty, Personal Love, Popularity, and the rest,—these various unsatisfied Propensions must inflict on him more or less of serious suffering. If on the other hand he aims at giving to *all* a *little*

gratification, they clamour painfully for more.   Let it
be said again.   Those *earthly* objects, which correspond
to these various Propensions, are mutually *antagonistic:*
if therefore we thus indulge those propensions a little,
they clamour for more; if we indulge them much, they
clash with each other.   In either case, they produce
jar and conflict in our mind ; and afford the most
striking contrast to that union and harmony, wherewith these very Propensions enjoy their appropriate
objects in a good man's life.

(5.) Then consider, lastly, the great peace and
serenity of mind, which the good man's resignation to
God's Will must ever tend to engender.   He firmly
believes, (remember) and realizes the truth, that everything which happens to him, great and small, is specially
appointed by a God, Who tenderly loves him and most
earnestly desires his eternal happiness.   Surely then,
under even the very heaviest trials, he has a ground
for the deepest peace and tranquillity; and a ground,
to which the worldly man, even in the lightest mischances of every-day life, is a total stranger.   Such
light mischances (as daily experience shews us) inflict
on the latter class of men immeasurably greater pain,
than we should at all have expected from their trivial
character.   It is astonishing, how mere a trifle will
destroy the happiness of a vain-glorious, or again of an
ambitious, man, for a day or for a week.

Hitherto we have spoken of those worldly men,
who are able to secure considerable enjoyment; those
worldly men (in other words) who are well circumstanced in regard to health and money, and who are
troubled with no deep and violent emotions.   But
these at last are a comparatively small number.   Piety
imparts its best consolations to the sick and the poor;
what comfort do *these* men receive from the world?
Or take again the worldly man, who loses that very
object to which he has devoted his life : a soldier, who
lies under the unanswerable imputation of cowardice;
a money-getting man, who has lost his whole substance, and has no means of replacing it; an intel-

lectual man, whose eye-sight fails him or whose faculties decay. What is the predicament of such as *these*, if they have not learnt to seek their happiness in God? Or lastly, consider men who have been endued by God with keen and deep sensibilities: what are they without piety? Father Newman here brings out what I would say, with insurpassable force and accuracy of expression. He is speaking of St. Augustine's conversion, and these are his remarks.

" Men of ordinary minds are not so circumstanced as to feel the misery of irreligion. That misery consists in the *perverted and discordant action of the various functions and faculties of the soul*, which have lost their legitimate governing power, and are unable to regain it except at the hands of their Maker. Now the run of irreligious men do not suffer in any great degree from this disorder, and are not miserable; they have neither great talents, nor strong passions; *they have not within them the materials of rebellion*, in such measure as to threaten their peace. They follow their own wishes; they yield to the bent of the moment; they act on inclination, not on principle; but their motive powers are neither strong nor various enough to be troublesome. Their minds are in no sense under rule: but *anarchy is not in their state a case of confusion, but of deadness ;* like what is said to be the internal condition of Eastern cities and provinces at present, in which, though the government is weak or null, the body politic goes on without any great embarrassment or collision of its members one with another, by the force of inveterate habit. It is very different, when the moral and intellectual principles are vigorous, active, and developed. Then, if the governing power be feeble, all the subordinates are in the position of rebels in arms; and what the state of a mind is under such circumstances, the analogy of a civil community will suggest to us. Then we have before us the melancholy spectacle, of *high aspirations without an aim ; a hunger of the soul unsatisfied; and a never-ending restlessness and inward warfare of its various faculties.* Gifted minds, if not submitted to the rightful authority of religion, become the most unhappy and the most mischievous. They need at once an object to feed upon, and the power of self-mastery; and *the love of their Maker, and nothing but it, supplies both the one and the other.* We have seen in our own day, in the case of a popular poet, an impressive instance of a great genius, throwing off the fear of God, seeking for happiness in the creature, roaming unsatisfied from one object to another, breaking his mind upon itself, and bitterly confessing and im-

B B

parting his wretchedness to all around.   I have no wish at all to compare him to St. Augustine; indeed, if we may say it without presumption, the very different termination of their trial seems to indicate some great difference in their respective modes of encountering it.   The one dies of premature decay, to all appearance a hardened infidel; and if he is still to have a name, will live in the mouths of men by writings at once blasphemous and immoral: the other is a Saint and Doctor of the Church.   Each makes confessions; the one to the Saints, the other to the powers of evil.   And does not the difference of the two discover itself in some measure even to our own eyes, in the very history of their wanderings and pinings?   At least, there is no appearance in St. Augustine's case of that dreadful haughtiness, sullenness, love of singularity, vanity, irritability, and misanthropy, which were too certainly the characteristics of our own countryman. Augustine was, as his early history shews, a man of affectionate and tender feelings, and open and amiable temper; and, above all, he sought for some excellence external to his own mind, instead of concentrating all his contemplations on himself.

     " But let us consider what his misery was : — it was that of a mind imprisoned, solitary, and wild with spiritual thirst; and forced to betake itself to the strongest excitements, by way of relieving itself of the rush and violence of feelings, of which the knowledge of the Divine Perfections was the true and sole sustenance.   He ran into excess, not from love of it, but from this fierce fever of mind.   ' I sought what I might love,' he says in his Confessions, ' in love with loving, and safety I hated, and a way without snares.   For within me was a famine of that inward food, Thyself, my God; yet through that famine I was not hungered, but was without all longing for incorruptible sustenance; not because filled therewith, but the more empty, the more I loathed it.' "—*Church of the Fathers*, pp. 226, 7, 8.

     We shall better see the force of these various considerations, if we state precisely the question before us. For the question is not precisely, whether good men are on an average happier than worldly men; but whether this individual man, with the *same* temperament, in the *same* state of health, under the *same* external circumstances, will or will not be happier, if he has consistently sought his rest in God, than if be has sought it in the world.   I have said ' under the same external circumstances;' though of course the argument fairly requires me to add,—except so far as those circumstances would be changed by the mere fact of living interiorly.

Now in considering such a question as this, great regard must be had to the peculiarity of different individuals. There is no psychological fact in the whole range of them more remarkable, than the wonderful difference of men from each other, as to their natural susceptibility of happiness. No doubt, bodily health has a great deal to do with this; and past circumstances also may greatly affect our present capabilities of enjoyment. Yet on the whole I strongly incline to think, that its chief cause is far deeper than either of these explanations would suggest. God has made one man joyous, and another melancholy, by natural temperament; and as God has made him, so he will remain.

Yet even here something may be said on a good man's happiness. Observation will certainly shew, that in many good men there is a certain most strange and impressive union often found, of this natural melancholy with inward peace ; the deep happiness, engendered by a good life, becomes more remarkable, from the superficial sadness below which it is to be found.

And as this is true in regard to natural temperament, so is it also in regard to external circumstances. It is very remarkable, how great a degree of external agitation and excitement, is compatible with real and true enjoyment of that great gift of peace. There is plainly no inconsistency at all in the supposition, that while two or three Propensions are causing grief or excitement, the great body of Propensions may at the same moment be enjoying a deep and tranquil gratification. And this will be made still more intelligible, by considering an important psychological fact; a fact which we shall have to treat carefully, in the very important discussion hereafter to be attempted, on the relations between Intellect and Will. I allude to the great number of *implicit* acts ever proceeding in the mind : acts, which bear most importantly on the agent's happiness and character, and of which nevertheless he is wholly unaware. It will be remarked also, that the enjoyment which results from the thought of this or that happy object, continues long after the thought itself has come to an end. See n. 96, p. 203.

I have already said that the question before us comes in fact to this:—Will *the same individual man* ordinarily gain or lose as to earthly happiness, in proportion as he pursues the interior life? But we may in fairness add even a second qualification. Let us suppose, that a man has for years been plunged in worldliness, or even in great and gross sin. The grace of God efficaciously touches his soul, and he turns from his evil ways. Supposing it were true that, during the earlier period at least of his new course, there were a real diminution of enjoyment;—this fact in all fairness should be put down, not to his present piety, but to his past recklessness and irreligion.

On the whole then it may well be doubted, whether in any one case it can truly be said that earthly happiness is diminished by the practice of virtue. That in the immense majority of instances at least, great *increase* of such happiness is so obtained, cannot admit of fair doubt.

I may add however in conclusion, that this whole question is not a very practical one. The essential happiness, to which a good Christian looks, belongs to Heaven and not to Earth; nor would it in any way take him by surprise, if it were necessary to make some sacrifice of temporal happiness, in order to his attaining eternal. There are two collateral matters indeed which *are* of *great* moment ; but on these, after all which has been said, there can be no possible doubt. They are the two following:

(1.) We have been occupied, during this Section, in drawing out arguments for the proposition, that our nature has been formed for virtue. One of these arguments is, that God has so specially, and in such various ways, provided for the happiness, even for the earthly happiness, of those who give themselves to Him. This proposition at all events will (I think) be denied by none, who have considered what we have urged in its behalf.

(2.) We have often adverted to the fact, that ordinary Christians have in so small a degree the moral power, of persevering in their interior course, without the help of pleasurable emotion. This being so, it is a fact of very great importance to the spiritual life, that such men can always obtain quite enough of rest and solace in the service of God, to give them the fullest moral power of persevering in their high enterprise. And this has been (I hope) most abundantly shewn in the present Section. It is quite manifest, from what has been said, that every one has full moral power (if he pleases) to make God's service his one central and pervasive object: the object, which influences all his deeper emotions; which gives zest and animation to the main current of his life.

155. Some Catholic philosophers, in considering the imperfect beatitude attainable on earth, seem to consider it as consisting, very far more in the prospect of future felicity, than in the enjoyment of present peace : nay they speak of it, as though they placed it *almost exclusively* in the former.* A few words should be said on this statement, were it only in deference to the authority of those Catholics who have maintained it. Now this proposition, that our present happiness *mainly* consists in our hope of future Bliss, may be understood in three different senses. Let us consider them in order.

First it may be understood (so to speak) in a negative sense. The statement intended may be this ; that the happiness of a good man would be utterly destroyed, if he had not solid and substantial grounds for expecting its continuance ; nay, and that it would be most terribly diminished, unless he had grounds for

---

* So Solimani : " Vitæ hujus felicitas sita *potissimè* est in *præmii* post obitum obtinendi *spe* minimè fallaci, quæ morum integritate nitatur." Vol. ii. p. 232. On the other hand, Dmowski speaks of " imperfecta beatitudinis species, quæ *in vitá ex virtute* et rationis præscripto peractá, *cum* spe futuræ et perfectæ felicitatis assequendæ, consistit." Vol. iii. p. 29.

expecting after life that completeness and intensity of Bliss, to which we look forward under the Gospel. In this sense, no thoughtful Christian can doubt the proposition. It is true that a *worldly* man is able to possess great enjoyment, though he have means of knowing that nothing can be more gloomy than his prospects after death. But this is because of the phenomenon to which we have so often referred ; viz. that worldly men have a wonderful power of *totally forgetting* themselves and their own interior, while they throw themselves eagerly, for gratification, on the various objects of sense or of worldly pleasure. It is the characteristic of a *good* man, that he *does* look within ; that he *does* contemplate his own state and prospects. If then that state and those prospects are of so miserably gloomy a character as above supposed, his wretchedness must be intolerable.

A second sense, in which the above proposition may be understood, is the following. ' Of all those ' various spiritual enjoyments, which render Christ's ' yoke easy and His burden light, the one main and ' principal enjoyment, is the looking forward to our ' future Reward.' In this sense the proposition appears to me very doubtful. It is quite certain of course, that the prospect of Beatitude is a most important *constituent* in the good man's present happiness ; but is it the *chief*, the *almost sole*, constituent ? This is the precise question which we are here asking.

That the prospect of heavenly Bliss is a most important constituent in the just man's happiness, is (I say) quite certain. The Propension of *Self-charity* is gratified almost exclusively by this thought. Self-assertion also receives much gratification from looking to the future. Personal Love again receives pleasure, from the thought of that time, when the mutual love of God and man will be so far more perfect. Love of the Marvellous looks with keenest delight to the thought of those wonders that are to be revealed. All our Propensions, so far as they agree in seeking pleasure and recoiling from pain, are drawn most powerfully to the thought of that happy Life, where all suffering shall be absent and all joy abound.

All this is undoubtedly true: yet still I cannot but think it doubtful, whether this thought be the *chief* part of a good man's earthly happiness.   I cannot but think that an interior man would speak somewhat as follows.   ' Truly it is a happy thing, the looking for-
' ward to future Bliss; and yet the chief part of my
' present happiness arises less from this than from
' other things.   It arises rather from the close bond
' of love, which now unites me to my dearest Saviour;
' from my consciousness of His tender affection, and
' my power of in some degree returning that affection.
' It arises from my basking in the sunshine (as it
' were) of my Creator's approval.   It arises from that
' communion with God in prayer, which I so constantly
' enjoy ; and from that far closer communion with Him,
' which is imparted in the Holy Eucharist.   It arises
' from my consciousness of a will, at peace with itself,
' and submitting with absolute resignation to the Pro-
' vidence of God ; a will, not torn asunder by conflict-
' ing emotions, but fixed undividedly on my True End.'
I am inclined to think this would be the true account of the case ; though I am far from speaking with any confidence, and the matter at last is of small moment.   An argument for my opinion may be grounded on this fact.   Suppose a good man is oppressed by some most severe trial ; bodily torment, or mental anguish.   What is that thought, to which he has instinctive recourse for alleviation ? does he turn his thoughts to the Bliss which is in store for him here-after,—the wonders of the Beatific Vision,—the absence of all pain, which is to be his endless privilege ?   Surely he rather turns to the contemplation of Christ Crucified; of his Saviour dying, and dying for his love.   What is the special charm of that thought ?   Doubtless, that it enables him to value that Saviour's *present* love, and to elicit happy acts of open-hearted confidence and colloquy.

(3.) We have now considered two different senses, in which the proposition before us may be intended. In the first sense, it is most undeniably true; in the second, I am inclined (though with diffidence) to dissent from it. But there is a third sense also imaginable, of the following kind. It may have been intended then to say, that at last the possession of *present* enjoyment is no matter of great moment; that all men have full moral power (by means of grace) to work steadily for God, with a future reward in prospect, even though there were little or no *immediate* happiness to cheer them in their course. From this view I most strongly and confidently dissent; and I am quite certain that a very little examination of phenomena will suffice to disprove it. But on this head I need not here enlarge; as everything which has been said, or will be said, on the moral inability of ordinary Christians to carry on an interior life through long-continued gloom and depression, is really said in opposition to any such view.

156. You will remember a criticism which we made early in the Chapter, (see n. 93, p. 198) on a psychological proposition implied by St. Thomas. It is this: that all those pleasures, which are not obtained by bodily contact, are enjoyed by means of no closer possession, than our mere *belief* in the existence of their object. Thus the pleasures of vain-glory are fully enjoyed, through my *confident belief* that others admire and value me: nor is it possible to obtain a closer contact with the pleasurable object, than this mere *intellectual conviction* of its existence. On this we remarked, that St. Thomas certainly makes too broad and general a statement: for instance Love of Knowledge is not really and solidly gratified, by our mere *belief* that we possess a true and deep philosophy; the philosophy must *be* true and deep, or else the Propension (in the case at least of all higher intellects) is the cause of suffering instead of gratification.

We are now enabled to add one or two further instances of the same truth. Thus, consider that peace, which pious men enjoy, from the harmonious rest of their Propensions in God.   This great blessing is not really enjoyed, by our merely *believing* in its existence. A self-deceiving fanatic, *e. g.*, may be very *confident* that he possesses this heavenly gift, when he is really a prey to the tormenting emotions of pride, envy, and a hundred others.   In order to enjoy this deep repose, our propensions must *be* resting harmoniously in the invisible world; and it will by no means suffice, that we *believe* the case to be so.   Or take again that happy temperament which many men possess, and to which I have alluded in n. 154 (p. 371).   We do not enjoy the pleasures thence accruing, by merely *believing* that ours is such a temperament; unless it really *be* so, those pleasures escape our grasp.

It is not clear however that in either of these cases we have added to the number of those Propensions (see n. 93, (p. 198), which are physical without being corporeal; of those Propensions, in other words, which require for their gratification some far closer contact with their object than mere *belief* in its existence, while yet that contact is not of a corporeal kind.   It is not clear, I say, in regard to either of the two instances just given as exceptions to St. Thomas' statement, that they enable us to enlarge our list of those Propensions, which are thus ' physical ' without being ' corporeal.'

The first instance most certainly does *not* enable us to do so : for this blessing of inward peace (as we have abundantly seen) is not obtained by the gratification of any one special Propension, but by the harmonious agency of all those which are more powerful and pervasive.

In regard to the second instance, there may be greater doubt.   It may be said, and perhaps with truth, that persons, possessing this happy temperament, do really receive enjoyment from a separate Propension.   We may assign, perhaps, a Propension, distinct from any other, which we may call ' Love of Existence;' and which expresses the susceptibility of pleasure which such men possess, from the mere fact of *living*, so long as there is no special bodily or mental anguish to destroy that pleasure. This Propension, if it be justly assigned, is undoubtedly 'physical;' and yet probably not 'corporeal.' It is probably not 'corporeal;' for these men's happy temperament seems attributable to some far deeper reason than mere bodily health. Yet, on the other hand, it is undoubtedly a 'physical' Propension; for it derives its pleasure, not from the fact that such men *believe* themselves to be living, but from the fact that they *are* living. One thing however should be added. Even if this theory of a special Propension be true, still the principal superiority, in point of earthly happiness, which these men possess over others, does *not* consist in their possessing this special Propension ; but far more, in the singular degree of enjoyment which *each one* of their Propensions receives, from possessing its appropriate object.

At last then, the exceptions to St. Thomas' statement would appear to be but few ; and the cases are still fewer, of a physical Propension which is not corporeal. All the Propensions indeed, which we have called *bodily*, are undoubtedly 'physical;' and so are all those which we have called by the general name ' Love of Beauty.' But all these are ' corporeal ' also; they are gratified by the *bodily* contact of their objects, and can be *fully* gratified in no other way. The sound of the music must reach our bodily ears ;— the sight of the beautiful scenery must reach our bodily eyes ;—or our enjoyment is incomplete. On the other hand, those which we have called the 'higher Propensions,' are certainly not 'corporeal;' but then neither (with one exception) are they 'physical.' If we look through the catalogue given in n. 145, we shall find that Propension so often cited by us, the 'Love of Knowledge,' to be the only one, which is not most adequately and amply gratified, by *belief* in its object's existence. I gratify Love of Approbation, by firmly *believing* that I am approved by God or men ; nor can I derive from that Propension any fuller gratification. I gratify Personal ' Amor Concupiscentiæ,' by firmly *believing* that my Divine Friend, or my human, returns my affection ; nor

is closer contact possible, between that Propension and
its object.   It will be desirable, that you should yourselves take the trouble of going through the whole list,
and satisfying yourselves that I have spoken truly in
what I have now asserted.

This fact is sufficiently remarkable, to serve as the
basis of a further argument (and it will be the 8th) for
our general proposition; viz., that human nature was constituted for the practice of virtue.   It might have been
thought beforehand, that earthly objects, from being so
much nearer at hand, would be able to come into far
closer *contact* (if I may so express myself) with our
various Propensions; and that our happiness would
therefore be far greater, from fixing them on visible,
than on invisible, objects.   We have found, however, in
regard to all those Propensions which are really of great
importance to happiness, — in regard to all those Propensions which unite power with pervasiveness, — that
(with one single exception) the case is totally otherwise.
The ambitious, the vain-glorious, nay, even the covetous
man, cannot by possibility come into closer contact with
the object of his desire, than is obtained by *belief* in its
existence.   But this is the precise nature of that contact with *Heavenly* Objects, which every believer has
within his power.   To believe firmly, to realize keenly,
the truths of religion; — this befalls every individual, in
proportion as he advances in virtue.   In proportion
therefore as we do so advance, all our higher Propensions receive in a greater degree that very gratification,
which is literally the only kind of gratification permitted
them by their very constitution.

There is one exception, as we have seen; viz., Love
of Knowledge.   If it were really true then, that the doctrines of Christian Philosophy and Theology are less in
agreement with those necessary truths, which reason
declares, — or with those deep facts of human nature
which experience testifies, — or that they are less concor-
dant and mutually harmonious, — than the doctrines of
some unchristian philosophy, then undoubtedly the mere
fact of our *believing* the case to be otherwise would not

avail us.   But I may here assume, that the fact is widely otherwise ; and since it *is* widely otherwise, this Propension also, Love of Knowledge, affords far deeper gratification to the genuine student of Christian Theology, than to the student of any human philosophy which has ever been devised.

The general fact which we have been treating, — I mean the dependence of our higher Propensions, for their gratification, merely on our *belief* in their objects' existence, — is closely connected (as we shall see in our theological course) with that great doctrine, Justification by Faith; a doctrine, on which St. Paul lays such prominent and such singular stress.

Eight arguments then have been adduced for our proposition, that human nature is formed for virtue. In the course of evolving those arguments, various psychological facts have been stated and dwelt upon, which you will find, I think, of extreme value, in our subsequent theological enquiries.

Section VI.

On the Marks of Moral Degradation in our Nature as it now exists.

157. The considerations of the last Section lead to an obvious difficulty. If our nature is so unmistakeably, indeed so eminently, formed for virtue and perfection, how is it, that imperfection and forgetfulness of God are so widely, so awfully, prevalent throughout the world? Here indeed we are brought face to face with that master difficulty,—so saddening to the heart, and so perplexing to the intellect,—the existence of evil. In every part (I might almost say in every corner) of Theology, this difficulty meets us in one or other development; and, even in its least formidable shape, is utterly insoluble. Let us take a review then of this difficulty, as it here encounters and amazes us.

158. What then are those facts which we learn, not from Revelation, not from any theological premiss, but from direct and undeniable experience? On the one hand all men see, and must see, with the greatest clearness, the obligation of obeying their Moral Faculty; many will promptly admit, that their earthly happiness is best promoted by such obedience; every Theist in the world confesses, that his *eternal* happiness is simply dependent on it. And yet all mankind with one consent, it is hardly too much to say, have agreed to live for this world, instead of living for duty and for God. We have seen how undeniable it is, that the heathens possessed the elementary idea of moral obligation. We have seen (n. 68, p. 141) how immediate is the inference, that if there *be* such a thing, it should be the one guide of life. And yet we see with equal clearness, that no one of them on record, remaining a heathen, has ever so much as aimed at

enthroning moral obligation in its one legitimate place, the place of supreme and absolute authority. Indeed had any one of them attempted to do so, I am persuaded that his renunciation of heathenism, and belief in his Creator's Existence, must have immediately followed.*

But why dwell on the case of heathen, when the phenomena of the Christian world are even more amazing? Here again I am not at all assuming the *truth* of Revelation; but only the *fact*, that certain multitudes of men firmly *believe* it to be true. Take the case then of some Catholic country, and what do we find? The whole nation is firmly convinced, that this life is but a span; that an eternity of bliss or misery depends on their conduct here; that every moment therefore is worse than wasted, which is not devoted to growth in perfection. This is the belief of *all;* and what is the practise of the great majority? It is difficult to know which would be greater, their horror of a man who should *not* believe it, or their disgust at any one, living in the world, who *should* practise it. Take the case of any layman, who should merely exhibit in practice what all his fellow-believers admit in theory; who should shew, that to him national greatness, or intellectual power, or ancient family, or acquired wealth, is worthless as the seaweed, except so far as they affect (for good or evil) the advance of sanctity: — how will he be regarded by the great majority of his fellow-laymen? on the whole, with wonder and something like disgust. What is the time, or what the country, however exclusively Catholic, in which the immense majority of men have not pursued objects of this world, — their own temporal support or advancement, or their country's temporal aggrandizement, or the interests of their political party, — with far greater zeal and far greater interest, than the sanctification, whether of themselves or of others? What is this deep mystery? what is this broad gulf which seems, as if by some fated

---

* The case of the heathen is to be considered at length — by the light of Theology, Experience, and Reason, — in our theological work, 'de actibus humanis.'

necessity, always and everywhere to exhibit itself, between what man *can* do and *ought* to do—between this on the one hand, and what they *choose* to do on the other hand?

159. I really do not think that Revelation has increased this difficulty, though certainly it has not lessened it. I have already viewed it, as it is shewn simply by the light of experience : that you may see how it stands viewed by the light of Revelation, I will ask you three questions. (1.) Theology teaches us, that all men have the full moral power of arriving at belief in the One True God,—of consistently avoiding mortal sin,—and, *through* that belief and avoidance, of attaining Eternal Salvation. I ask—is there one single heathen on record, who, unassisted by Theistic missionaries, has *exercised* this moral power which is possessed by all? (2.) Theology tells us, that all Catholics at least have the full moral power, to make their own perfection the one main work and occupation of their lives. Now—in regard to that constituent part of the Church to which I have the honour to belong, I mean the laity,—I will ask this question. I will not ask, how large a proportion of us make this the *chief* occupation of our lives, but how many make it *any* part? How great a proportion is there, of laymen living in the world, who give themselves up, say even once in the week, to such occupations as the following? I mean — the carefully examining ourselves, the carefully considering our habitual course of life, in order to discover our latent faults; the careful consideration, the diligent asking of advice at the hand of spiritual guides, as to the best means of correcting those faults; the further examining ourselves, as to our diligence in applying such remedies. In regard to our worldly occupations, we all know what is meant by steadily applying ourselves to their pursuit; we know what is meant, by a man really devoting himself to a merchant's calling, or a lawyer's, or a politician's, or a tradesman's. What I am asking is, how great is the proportion of us laymen, who really devote ourselves to our *Christian* calling? who really make

an *occupation* of such inward exercises, in the same sense in which we make an occupation of our worldly trade or profession? I say, even in the same *sense*, however less in *degree?* We all agree absolutely in theory, that the divine occupation is immeasurably more important than the secular ; do we not agree almost as absolutely in practice, by *neglecting* the former and pursuing the latter? by neglecting that which we hold to be infinitely important, because of our deep interest in those, which we know to be utterly valueless in comparison?

My third question shall be this. Theology tells us, that the whole world has full moral power of being good; I ask, why is it that, in Scripture and ascetical writers, it is assumed, quite as a first principle, that the world is of course bad?

160. It would be simply absurd, if I professed to say one word by way of attempting to *solve* this difficulty. But there is a relevant psychological fact to which, on various grounds, I must solicit your very particular attention. It is this:—our nature is *very strongly biassed in the wrong direction;* it is very far less powerful towards the practice of good, than towards the reckless and unbridled pursuit of pleasure. In so great a degree is this true, that simple quiescence, simple abstinence from effort and struggle towards *good*, will by itself absolutely ensure a constant progress towards what is evil. He who shall abandon himself, without special pains and effort, to float down the current of his Propensions, will most infallibly advance by steady steps from bad to worse; and (unless he change his course) he will assuredly close with a most miserable end.

This fact is of course no solution of the above difficulty: for the question at once recurs,—since men know very well that, without special struggle, they get worse and worse,—and since, by help of prayer and grace, all have the fullest moral power to put forth such struggle,—why does so great a majority fail of doing so? The fact, just stated, fully explains undoubtedly, why it is that, without special struggle, men fall from bad to worse; but it does not even *tend* to explain, why such struggle *is not in fact more universally put forth*. However, for its own sake it deserves our most careful attention; and it will be found (I think) to throw a flood of light, on some of the (otherwise) darkest points of Theology. Let us consider it then with some care, as an observed psychological fact.

161. The first phenomenon, to which I beg your attention, is this. Our will itself is far weaker, in its aim at virtue, than in its aim at pleasure. Let us bring two different cases into juxtaposition. A devoted and enterprising officer, wholly destitute however of all pious principle, goes through a military campaign. His sufferings, both in great matters and small, are severe; his dangers constant; he encounters the whole, with unflinching courage and unbending resolution. What are his sustaining influences? Such as these:—the desire of his countrymen's applause;—ardent attachment to his country;—desire of his own esteem;—and other similar motives. He undergoes perhaps an excruciating operation, without a groan: why? because it would lower his self-respect, it would keenly wound his pride, if he, a brave soldier, could be overcome by pain. In the same army serves a good and zealous missionary priest; enduring the same sufferings; exposed to the same dangers; called to constant and most trying exertion, for the service of God: and he also perhaps undergoes a severe operation. Now I ask, what is this priest's experience? What is his sustaining power? It is *prayer*. Let him give up the practice of prayer, how great will be his power of working for God? Literally, or almost literally, none at all. By help of prayer no doubt, his will may be far more firmly fixed on God, than any worldly man's on his worldly objects: but let him cease from prayer, he almost ceases from God's service. Nay I will ask this :—have any of us the moral power, of so much as enduring, without resentment, one passing insult from a companion,—unless we address ourselves to God and call prayer to our aid?

Now it is sometimes assigned, as a reason for this

c c

contrast, that *visible* objects so press upon our attention; and that the *invisible* has (from its very nature)
so much less power of influencing the will. But you
will find, on consideration, that both soldier and priest
have to *overcome* the visible by thinking of the *invisible*.
The frequent perils, the constant privations, the agoniz-
ing pain, all these surely are *visible* and *palpable* inducements to cowardice; they are so in one case no
less than in the other. On the other hand, on what
does the soldier fix his thoughts, to support him under
these most visible trials? His distant country;—
applause of his absent countrymen;—sense of his own
dignity;—how can these be called *visible* objects? The
godless soldier, I repeat, no less than the pious priest,
contends against the visible by thinking of the invisible.

Nor again can it be said, that the soldier is more
firmly convinced than the priest, as to the reality and
value of his objects. Which of these two, do you suppose, is the firmer? A soldier's conviction that France
or England deserves his love;—that his countrymen's
applause will crown his efforts;—that his own dignity is
great and elevated;—or the priest's firm faith, that God
is an Object worthy of being loved and that God's
approbation is to be most dearly prized.

Another explanation is sometimes attempted, by
those who are unwilling to believe the doctrine for
which I am arguing. They say, that Concupiscence is
an adversary of tremendous power; and that in pursuing
virtue a man is exposed constantly to those powerful
assaults of Concupiscence, from which, in pursuing
worldly objects, he is altogether free. We have not
yet considered precisely the meaning of this word 'Concupiscence;' but we may say generally, that it signifies
the assemblage of those solicitations, which are put forth
by the Sensitive Appetite, against the course of virtue
and the service of God. And this being Concupiscence,
I maintain that the attempt to explain, by means of Concupiscence, those phenomena to which I have directed
your attention, is to the full as untenable, as are those
other explanations which we have already refuted.

Those who dwell so much on the power of Concupiscence, seem most strangely to forget the great power, exercised by the Sensitive Appetite, *in behalf of virtue*. To give merely one instance of what I mean;— they seem to forget altogether the sweetness of sensible devotion (see n. 130, p. 257). To fix our ideas, I will direct your attention to one phenomenon, which is common enough in the interior life. We must all have experienced at times something of this kind. We are perhaps in a state of happy recollectedness; dwelling on the thought of that Love which is entertained towards us, by our Creator, our Redeemer, our Heavenly Mother. We may even *reflect* upon our state; we may *say* to ourselves, ' How incomparably sweeter and happier are these true pleasures, than are the polluted waters of pride and vainglory, at which we so often slake our thirst.' And yet we feel, at the very same time, that (by a kind of spiritual gravitation) we are ever tending *from* the former *to* the latter; tending *from* that, which we *practically feel* to be happier; and tending *to* that, which we practically feel as *less* happy. The fact then of this tendency cannot possibly be attributed to the agency of our Sensitive Appetite. Our Sensitive Appetite is now not only not *opposed* to virtue, but soliciting most powerfully in its *favour;* and yet our *Will* is ever tending downwards. We feel most intimately, that, without prolonged and sustained effort, the dreaded descent is practically inevitable.

162. Such then is the present constitution of our nature. Our Will, in pursuit of *pleasure,* is firm, stable, consistent; in pursuit of *virtue* (except so far as we bring prayer to its support) is most weak, most wayward and capricious. On its weakness we have sufficiently enlarged; it was the *first* phenomenon, to which I asked your attention. But consider also a *second* phenomenon, its waywardness and capriciousness. What is our frequent experience? Such as this. ' Can I be the *same man,* who but yesterday had ' so clear a vision of divine things? who made such ' successful resistance to temptation? who elicited such

' noble acts ?   To-day, on the contrary, I seem moved
' by every breath of emotion;—enslaved to the most
' ignoble tendencies ;—helpless and resourceless in the
' direction of virtue.'

Perhaps indeed, if we were able to examine carefully all the facts, we should ordinarily find, that this
contrast depends on the greater or less degree of completeness, with which we have exercised ourselves
through the day in the spirit of *prayer;* the greater or
less degree of humility and self-distrust, with which
we have placed our sanctification in our Creator's
hands.   There cannot be a more vital doctrine than
this;—the intimate connection of our growth in sanctity,
with our distrust in ourselves, our confidence in God,
our constancy in implicit prayer : and it will occupy a
most prominent place in our theological course.   But
this doctrine does not essentially affect the fact, to
which I am now directing your attention ; for as a matter
of experience, how vast is the difference between one
day and another, as to my *facility* of *giving myself* to
prayer.   We seem never to acquire a stable *habit* of
prayer ; any permanent or reliable facility for its performance.   To-day it is quite easy to me, that I repose
my whole trust in God : while to-morrow the preserving
a spirit of prayer through the day, is like rolling a
stone up a hill ; such constant struggle and effort does
it require.

In reply to this whole statement, (1) of the will's
weakness, and (2) its capriciousness, in the practice of
good,—an objection of the following kind has been
sometimes put forth ; though surely it is a most hasty
and ill-considered objection.   It has been said, that the
will may be *naturally* indeed very weak towards good;
but that when raised to the *super*-natural order it is
strong and vigorous.   It is difficult to imagine what
can be meant by such an allegation.   Look at the
missionary priest, who has served us for our illustration ; the priest who accompanies the army on a
military campaign.   His will is most certainly raised
to the supernatural order, if there be any man in the

world whose will is thus raised. Yet it was in regard to him that we decided, as of a thing palpable to experience, that without prayer his strength for good is as nothing.

163. The third and last phenomenon which I will adduce, as illustrating the present proclivity of our nature to evil, regards, not the Will but the Sensitive Appetite. The Propension of the Flesh, I mean that which tempts us against the Sixth Commandment, differs in various most important respects from all others. A very little consideration will sufficiently shew this. Suppose it is a fast-day : who ever heard of the notion that the mere *sight* of meat,— much more that the mere *reading* about it,— is so proximate an occasion of sin as to be in itself mortal? Or (to avoid objections which may be raised against this particular instance) suppose I were a Cistercian, and meat were always unlawful to me :— who in such a case ever heard of a notion like that above imagined? Yet we all know the frightful peril involved, in allowing ourselves to gaze on evil objects, or even to read about them, in matters of *impurity*. Or let me suppose the case of a Christian, who was once in the habit of stealing, and by help of his thefts leading a comfortable and luxurious life; but who has now reformed, and belongs to some strict order. Who ever heard that the *contemplation* of wealth,— the mere *looking* at fine equipages, grand appointments, handsome houses, — produces the almost inevitable effect, of reviving the passion ' delectatio' in regard to the old mortal sin? Yet in the matter of impurity such would be the case. Nay, take that very Propension, which of all is far the nearest to the one which we are considering ;— take the desire of *revenge*, as it exists in an Italian or Spaniard. To a revengeful man, even when reformed, the sight of his *enemy* might doubtless be a great occasion of sin : but surely no one will deny, that such a man may read the account of murders in *general*, and may enter too into every detail and particular of some individual murder where the parties concerned are quite unknown to him,— without so

much as a passing temptation to his old sin. How totally opposite is our nature, in regard to impurity! Indeed spiritual writers universally recognize this fact. As one instance of such recognition, they will never *permit* any such detailed consideration of past sins under this head, as they *most earnestly recommend* in regard to all *other* sins of whatever kind.

164. From this review, I cannot but draw an inference. Reason shews most clearly, that our nature was formed for virtue; but I think Reason alone would also make the opinion extremely probable, that this same nature of ours has received some wrench, some jar, some disorganization; that it does not in fact wear that very shape, those very proportions, in which it was originally formed. The singular weakness and capriciousness of our Will in the direction of virtue, would by itself strongly recommend this opinion to our acceptance. But the third phenomenon above mentioned seems to give even stronger grounds for its support: for this particular Propension seems to have received quite a morbid intensity; an intensity greatly exceeding what we may suppose to have been God's original design.

And if we may be allowed for a moment to enter on the ground of Revelation, it is difficult not to connect all this with the dogma of Original Sin. The third phenomenon above stated is indeed most remarkable, in connection with that dogma. It is through this particular Propension, that Original Sin is propagated. Our Nature then bears upon it, as we may say, the *stamp*, of that ignominy and degradation in which we are involved by coming into the world; in that the Propension, *whereby* we come into the world, has been thus morbidly exaggerated and perverted.

We shall see however in our theological course, that there is no question, on which theologians go into a greater variety of opinions, than on this. That our Nature has *in itself* suffered at all from the Fall;—that we have lost anything except certain *preternatural* gifts; —this is very far indeed from an universally admitted proposition.   And those theologians, who think that it *has* suffered, differ from each other in no slight degree, as to the particulars in which that suffering exists. The psychological phenomena then, to which I have now drawn your attention, will, at a later period, give us very considerable help, in our theological treatment of this question.

Section VII.

On Certain Philosophical Terms.

165. This last Section of the present Chapter will consist of two parts, totally distinct from each other. It is important that you should understand the meaning of certain philosophical terms, which occur in ordinary theological works; and this seems the most convenient place for explaining them.

The first of these terms will be the word 'Nature;' a term which we have already frequently used, although we have not yet specially considered its precise meaning. No one can say this is an insignificant word, in reference to our own purpose; since the very name we give to our present course is, 'on Nature and Grace.' Indeed to attempt any really complete discussion of this word, would bring us across some of the most difficult philosophical questions which exist. But perhaps we may find it possible to steer clear of such questions, while yet giving a practical explanation of the term, which will be sufficient for our own exigencies.

It is conceivable that God might have so made me, that there should be no kind of regularity or conformity, in the processes and operations of my mind and my body. To-day I can hardly with great effort crawl along the ground; to-morrow (without any intrinsic change in my body) I might find myself flying in the air. To-day the fire warms my hands, to-morrow it nips and freezes them. To-day I derive pleasure from the thought of being liked and approved; to-morrow it gives me pleasure on the contrary, to think that I am hated both by God and man. Had God so made me, I should have had no 'nature;' to say that I have a 'nature,' implies the contradictory to any such supposition as that just made. So far then, it might appear that my ' nature' means simply, 'the assemblage of those fixed laws, according to which God appoints, that the various operations and modifications of my mind and body shall proceed.'

But a little consideration will shew, that as yet our notion is far from sufficient. To fix our ideas,—take the case of my warming my hands at the fire. Plainly it is no sufficient account of the matter to say, that every time I put my hands to the fire, God, by a kind of compact, confers on them the sensation of warmth. This would be to deny the agency of second causes altogether; and such indeed is the opinion of those, who are called in philosophy the Occasionalists. But no Catholic maintains anything like this. No: God has given to the fire, once for all, a *permanent quality;* and He has given to my hand, once for all, a *permanent quality;* in virtue of which two qualities, the warmth ensues. No doubt God, Who gave this permanent quality, may when He pleases suspend its operation; no doubt He must co-operate every moment, when it is called forth into action: still He did, once for all, give that permanent quality; and His subsequent interference in the matter has merely been, to *preserve* what He has once given. I am not professing to *prove* these various statements; I am assuming them from ordinary philosophical treatises. My purpose is merely, by means of them, to explain this term 'nature.' And we are now much nearer at least to our desired point; for my 'nature' would seem to be, 'the assemblage of those permanent qualities, which God has made intrinsic to me.' It is in virtue of *my* nature on the one hand, and *the fire's* nature on the other, that my hand grows warm.

You will object;—'an *acquired habit* is a permanent quality, intrinsic to me.' This objection will make clearer my original statement. Certainly an acquired habit is a permanent quality intrinsic to me; and how close is the connexion between habit and nature, is universally proverbial. But an acquired habit is not a quality which *God* has made intrinsic to me : it is not God, but my own acts, which have been the immediate cause of this quality. My *'nature'* then, is the assemblage of those qualities which God has made intrinsic to me, without any co-operation of mine ; but my *acquired habits* are permanent qualities, which have become intrinsic to me *through my own acts*. On the other hand, my *power* of engendering habits by means of acts,—this power *is* part of my 'nature:' God Himself has implanted this power ; it is a permanent quality, which God has made intrinsic to my soul.

Let us examine this interpretation of the word 'nature,' which I believe to be the true one, by bringing it to bear on various recognized theological propositions. The following statement will include four such propositions. (1) All Catholic theologians agree, that Adam was preserved from Concupiscence, *not* by any part of his 'nature,' but by a series of Divine Acts *supplementary* to that nature. (2) All agree, that he lost no part of his nature by the fall ; neither (3) did he receive (as the Calvinists suppose) some evil addition to his nature. (4) Some Catholic theologians however are of opinion, and I follow them, that his nature received some *wrench* or *disorganization*, making it far weaker towards good.

Now to interpret these four propositions, according to our explanation of the term 'nature.' (1) How was Adam saved from Concupiscence ? By this, that on every single occasion when God saw that temptation would arise, He interposed an act of His Power, to suppress the otherwise inevitable emotion. (2) But suppose God had endowed Adam's soul with some *intrinsic permanent quality*, in virtue of which temptation could not assail him,—then that very thing would have been true, which theologians say is *not* true ; viz. that Adam, by sinning, lost an integral part of his nature. (3) On the other hand, had Adam on his fall received from God some intrinsic permanent quality, which he did not before possess, and in virtue of which evil had a power over him such as it had not in the state of Innocence,—then Calvin's statement would have been true, that there was an evil addition to his nature. But (4) a different supposition is conceivable: viz. that those intrinsic permanent qualities, which assist him in pursuing good, should be weakened; and that those which assist him in *departing* from God's service, should be strengthened: that his intrinsic power *e. g.* of pursuing ' bonum honestum' should be made less; and his intrinsic power of seeking ' delectabile,' without reference to ' honestum,' should be made greater. Those theologians, who should adopt this supposition, would say, that the Fall, without making any evil *addition* to his nature, yet threw it into a state of moral disadvantage and disorganization.

A further objection may be made to this whole statement, which will again make my meaning clearer. It may be said, that, on this view, Habitual Grace would be part of my ' nature;' for surely it is a permanent quality, implanted by God in my soul. I reply, that Habitual Grace is no doubt a permanent quality, made by God *inherent* in my soul; but not therefore *intrinsic* to it. Let me explain this difference by one or two illustrations.

It is no permanent quality, intrinsic to my body, that it shall be warm: yet there is a permanent quality intrinsic to my body, and another intrinsic to the fire, by virtue of which two qualities, my body, when in contact with the fire, becomes warm. Now suppose God, without in any way altering the intrinsic constitution of my body, yet decreed that the effect of the fire should follow me about wherever I went. Well— I should enjoy a permanent gift of warmth; that warmth would be *inherent* in my body; yet it would not be *intrinsic* to it. Take any moment, when I am thus comfortably warm. My body does not possess any quality, which is the full *cause* of that warmth. That warmth is *partially* caused, of course, by an intrinsic quality of my body; viz. its capability of receiving warmth, from fire or other hot substance:

but *another* cause also concurs ; viz. the power of God, *miraculously supplying the effect of fire in its absence.*

Or take another case. Balaam's ass once spoke. This speech was not in any sense due to any intrinsic quality ; there was nothing in the beast's organs, which was even a partial cause of speech ; but God simply used them, as His instrument for a miraculous operation. He might have repeated this miracle through the animal's whole life ; in other words, given him a permanent gift of speech. Still, if he effected no intrinsic change in the animal's organs,—if those organs remained precisely in the same state with those of other asses,—then *this* one would no more possess the intrinsic quality of speech, than *they* do. In any instant, when this ass was speaking, the cause of that speech would not be any intrinsic quality whatever appertaining to his organs, but simply God's miraculous operation.

There is a controversy agitated in the Catholic schools, as to the sacraments, which will afford us another apposite illustration of our point. We considered just now, you remember, two alternatives as conceivable, in regard to the warmth which I derive from putting my hands to the fire. First it might merely have been, that by a kind of pact God made my hands warm, as often as I did so ; the other that He might have given (as in fact He has) an *intrinsic permanent quality*, both to fire and hands. Now take the case of an infant *e. g.* being baptized, and so receiving Habitual Grace. Here, in like manner, two alternatives are imaginable ; and each is defended by various theologians. It *may* be true, that God has promised that, by a kind of pact, He will always infuse Habitual Grace, whenever Baptism is duly administered to a child. But it may *also* be true, that the sacrament, duly administered, possesses a certain *intrinsic quality*, which of its own nature infuses Habitual Grace. Those who hold this, express it by saying, ' sacramenta *physicè* conferunt gratiam ;' intimating very plainly the close connection between the word 'nature' and the idea 'intrinsic quality.'

Thus it is (I conceive) that we may apprehend, what Revelation calls on us to hold, in regard to Habitual Grace. It is a *permanent*, an *inherent*, quality; but it is not *intrinsic*. The *constitution* of the soul is not changed in any one respect, by the infusion of Habitual Grace; but God miraculously supports the two in union.

It is readily imaginable, as we have seen, that God, without in any way altering the intrinsic constitution of my body, yet might miraculously preserve the created quality of warmth, in constant union with it : and on such an hypothesis, warmth would be *inherent*, but not *intrinsic*. Just so, we believe, on the authority of Revelation, that God, without in any way altering the intrinsic constitution of my soul, miraculously preserves the created quality of Habitual Grace, in constant union with it. Habitual Grace therefore is *inherent* in the justified man's soul, but not *intrinsic*.

I need hardly add, that this is to be received simply on faith; and that we have no kind of definite *idea* corresponding to our *words.** We have already seen, that on the nature of the soul *itself*, as distinct from its *operations*, we are absolutely and blindly ignorant; and we can of course have no clearer notion of a *miracle* wrought in the soul, than we have of the soul itself.

166. Hitherto we have spoken of 'my own individual nature.' We are now to rise into the idea, of 'one nature common to me with many others.' You

* The reader may here be inclined to retort, that I have spoken of it (p. 190) 'as one of the very worst habits which can possibly come upon a philosophical student,' that he should 'use words without precise corresponding ideas.' But I have said '*unconsciously* use words without,' &c. Let any one ponder on man's deep ignorance, and on his incapacity of apprehending the Invisible world, and he must readily admit, that we often have to use words, which express no corresponding ideas of our *own;* though (as we firmly believe) they *do* express unknown realities. But it is all-important, that when we thus use words, we should *not* do it '*unconsciously.*' The whole subject here referred to—a most deeply important one,— is most appropriately treated in the theological treatise, 'de Deo Uno et Trino.'

and I have *the same* nature; a rabbit and I have *different* natures : what is meant by this ?

Some scholastics seem to have held, that there is some *real thing*, called human nature, actually existing in all men, and handed down from father to son. This strange notion is now (I believe) universally exploded; but it has been succeeded by another even more strange. Many modern speculators maintain, that the distinction of species is purely an effect of *human reason*. 'I con-'veniently *classify* men under one head, and rabbits 'under another ; just as, with equal propriety, I might 'conveniently classify white animals under one head, 'and black under another. God has no more made 'any true distinction between men and rabbits, than 'between white animals and black.' This is really so absurd, that it would be an insult to common sense if I attempted its refutation. But the question recurs :— what is precisely *meant*, when I say that you and I are of the same nature ; a rabbit and I are of different natures? I suppose the true answer is somewhat as follows. (1.) Compare the permanent qualities made by God intrinsic to you, with those made by Him intrinsic to me : there is quite immeasurably more similarity than discrepancy. Compare those given to me with those given to a rabbit, and the reverse holds. (2.) But I have a further conviction than this. I have a conviction that, by means of experimenting on myself, I may discover an indefinite number of further qualities, which have been hitherto unsuspected. And I have also a conviction that, if I find them in myself, I have the fullest reason for holding that they exist also in you ; though within certain limits of possible variation. I recognize in myself, Love of Approbation, Love of Justice, Love of Acquisition : and I infer, without doubt, that my *fellow-men* have *the same ;* though they may have them in very different proportions, whether as compared with me, or as compared with each other. If you ask, what are the *limits* within which variation is possible, you are treading on those most difficult philosophical questions, from which I desire to keep clear. Nor am I professing at all to consider the *grounds* of my conviction, that you and I are of the same nature, a rabbit and I of different natures; because I am not considering the *grounds*, but the *meaning*, of that statement. The broad fact is plainly as follows.

God has created, not merely *individuals*, but certain great *families* of sentient beings. Each family, moreover, is so united, that (1) all its members agree with each other in possessing an indefinite number of permanent intrinsic qualities, directly implanted by God; and that (2) there is no such quality given by God to any one, which has not its counterpart in every other. In saying this, we save of course individual exceptions — monsters and the like — and speak generally and broadly. Revelation adds to the completeness of this view, by declaring that each species or family comes from a common pair of parents. This fact however is by no means necessary to *the idea itself* of a common nature; as a moment's consideration will shew.

167. There is another string of philosophical terms, with which this will be a convenient opportunity of making you acquainted. I mean those which relate to Aristotle's classification of mental phenomena, as taken from him by the great scholastic writers. No one, I imagine, now adheres to this strange theory; but it is necessary that we should *understand* those terms which express it, because of their frequent occurrence in theological works. The following then is some most general and superficial account of the Aristotelic theory.

Ask Aristotle or St. Thomas, how we obtain a knowledge of the external world, and they will answer as follows. ' From every external thing there flies off ' a ' Species Sensibilis;' bearing to the thing itself the ' same kind of relation, which the *impression* of a seal ' bears to its original. Flies off whither? It takes its ' residence, in that faculty of ours which we call the ' ' Phantasia.' No sooner does the ' Species Sensibilis '

' thus arrive, than the 'Intellectus Agens' is at work,
' transmuting it into a 'Species Intelligibilis;' and this
' 'Species' resides in the 'Intellectus Possibilis.'   All
' *emotions* arise from the 'Species Sensibilis;' but all
' volitions from the 'Species Intelligibilis.'   Hence the
' 'Phantasia' bears the same relation to the Sensitive
' Appetite, which the 'Intellectus Possibilis' bears to
' the Will.   The 'Phantasia,' and Sensitive Appetite
' make up the lower part of the soul, which is common
' to us with the brutes: the 'Intellectus' and 'Voluntas'
' make up the higher part ; which is peculiar to man-
' kind, among the visible creation.   Each part of the
' soul then has its own mode of aiming at an object;
' or its own 'Appetitus :' the lower part, the 'Appe-
' titus Sensitivus ;' the higher part, the 'Appetitus
' Rationalis,' or 'Appetitus Intellectivus,' or 'Voluntas.'
' These three latter expressions all stand for precisely
' the same idea.

' Both the 'Appetitus Sensitivus,' and 'Rationalis,'
' exert themselves in the conscious acts of a sentient
' being.   Thus, man aims by 'Appetitus Rationalis' at a
' certain 'bonum honestum;' and a cow, by 'Appetitus
' Sensitivus,' longs for some nice fresh grass, which is
' just out of her reach.   But there may be a *tendency*,
' which does not shew itself in any conscious act, of
' which even an inanimate object may be capable: this
' is called 'Appetitus Innatus.'   So a stone has an
' 'Appetitus Innatus,' drawing it towards the earth.'

Such is the philosophical theory, which underlies an
immense number of theological propositions, put forth
by scholastic writers.   You will wish to know, how
these propositions may become intelligible to us; how
we may *translate them* (as it were) from the Aristotelic
philosophy into our own.   Two principal rules will
perhaps suffice.

(1.) We drop altogether the distinction between
'Phantasia' and 'Intellectus,' or 'Species Sensibilis'
and 'Species Intelligibilis.'   Every operation, attributed
by Scholastics to the 'Phantasia,' *we* ascribe to the
'Intellect.'

(2.) We drop altogether the 'Intellectus Agens;' and recognize no 'Intellect,' except that called by scholastics the 'Intellectus Possibilis.'

You will find that this Aristotelic philosophy is very far more prominent and pervasive in St. Thomas' Theology, than in that of the great post-Tridentine scholastics; which alone would suffice to make the latter far easier reading.

CHAPTER III.

ON SELF-CHARITY.

168. You are no doubt aware generally, of the great controversy carried on (some two centuries ago) between Bossuet and Fénélon, on man's desire of happiness. It is difficult to imagine opinions more fundamentally opposed.

Bossuet maintained, that every single act, done by every single man, from the dawn of reason, is directed to one, and one only, absolute end;—his own happiness: that his one animating motive, in everything, great or small, which he does or wishes, is simply and exclusively the desire of felicity. Fénélon on the contrary held, that those who have reached the highest state of perfection are quite indifferent to their own felicity for its own sake; that they desire Heavenly Bliss for themselves, in no other sense than that in which they desire it for others; and that the one reason of this desire, is their wish that God's Glory may be the more promoted. This doctrine was most deservedly condemned by the Holy See, as ' temerarious, scandalous, evil-sounding, offensive to pious ears, pernicious in practice, and erroneous.' But I confess, that Bossuet's extremely opposite thesis seems to me quite as plainly and undeniably mistaken as Fénélon's.* It will be our business therefore, in considering both these extremes, to draw out (as best we may) a philosophical statement, which shall be consistent with itself, with Reason, and

* I mean, of course, so far as reason is concerned. The Church has actually condemned Fénélon ; and for believing therefore *his* system erroneous, we have grounds far stronger than an individual's reason.

with the observed facts of human nature. It will be part of our theological course to shew, that the statement, thus recommended by Reason, is also the one which consistently harmonizes the various utterances of Revelation.

It was impossible to treat this subject in either of the preceding Chapters, for this reason. The first Chapter was wholly metaphysical ; the second, wholly psychological : but our present question necessitates consideration both of Metaphysics *and* Psychology. Bossuet's statement is purely psychological, and so therefore must our answer to it be. Fénélon's statement is mainly metaphysical; viz., that the not desiring felicity for its own sake, is ' objectively preferable' (see n. 57, p. 124) to the desiring it. Just then as our answer to Bossuet must be solely psychological, our answer to Fénélon must be mainly metaphysical : and the chapter will therefore naturally divide itself into two Sections, directed severally against the two respective writers whom I am opposing.

Of these two Sections, the psychological must come first. Bossuet maintains, that we are physically necessitated to aim at felicity in every act. This allegation directly crosses our path, and must be disposed of in the first instance. If we are *physically necessitated* thus to seek felicity, it would be absurd enough to enquire, how far we are *morally obliged* to do so. It would be like asking, how far we are under the *moral obligation* of keeping our bodies on the earth, instead of flying up with them into the moon.

Section I.

On Man's Desire of Felicity.

169. We are now then to consider Bossuet's thesis: viz. that the desire of our own happiness is, by the necessity of our nature, our one motive of action. In connection with which statement, let us consider such familiar facts of everyday life as the following. An unhappy man groans, day after day, hour after hour, under the weight of some evil habit, from which he will not shake himself free. He feels most deeply, to his very heart of hearts, that his whole happiness, here and hereafter, depends on his emancipation: he never feels this *more* deeply, than at the very moments when he *does* give way. What becomes then of Bossuet's thesis? Certainly this wretched sufferer would be delighted beyond words, if he could really believe any such thesis; if he could really believe that there is no necessity for him even to struggle or exert himself, but that his firm conviction of Eternal Life being at stake, will *necessitate* his pursuing the course of virtue.

Take another instance. Is there one of you here, who has the slightest doubt, that to lead a life of faultless perfection, is the one thing which would most conduce to your future happiness? Do we find ourselves on that account *leading* such a life? And that indeed quite as a matter of course; — without any kind of struggle; — by physical necessity?

It is really difficult to imagine, what can have led any sane person to put forth a theory, which stands out in such broad contradiction with the most familiar and obvious facts. You may well doubt indeed, whether so great a man as Bossuet can possibly have done so; but such a doubt would be dissipated, in proportion as you should study his writings on the Quietist controversy. It is impossible of course to put before you, in any brief compass, the cumulative evidence which would thus be obtained; but I will adduce two quotations, which can leave no room for question. The first shall be from his work ' Schola in tuto;' in which, more than in any other, he aims at expressing his doctrine with scholastic precision. He prefaces this work, with a formal statement of the various propositions which he undertakes to prove; and the sixth of these propositions stands thus :

" Neque quisquam diffitetur, quin omnes homines, *quidquid agunt, quidquid volunt, quidquid cogitant,* quod ad vitam humanam alicujus momenti esse videatur, *id omne ad Beatitudinem* explicitè, vel implicitè, sive virtualiter, *referant.* Citiùs *animam auferas,* quàm ut cuiquam homini hanc mentem, hunc sensum, hanc animi præparationem eripias."

The only possible doubt which can exist, as to his meaning in this proposition, will turn on the word ' Beatitude;' it may be questioned whether he can really take it as simply synonymous with ' happiness.' There is no such doubt however about the French word ' heureux;' and our second quotation therefore shall be from one of Bossuet's French works :

" C'est non seulement qu'on veut être heureux, mais encore *qu'on ne veut que cela,* et qu'on *veut tout pour cela.*"

This at least is plain enough. And he adds, further on in the page :

" Il demeure toujours véritable . . . . . qu'on ne peut se désintéresser, jusqu'au point de perdre, *dans un seul acte quel qu'il soit,* la volonté d'être heureux ; *pour laquelle on veut toutes choses.*" *

He is claiming throughout undoubtedly the authority of St. Augustin as on his side; but how far he does so truly and legitimately, is a separate question which we are not here considering. What I am here observing, as to the above quotations, is this; that throughout he translates the word ' beatus' by the French word

* Réponse à Quatre Lettres, n. 9.

' heureux.' His statement then is most clear and intelligible; viz., that we desire *nothing whatever* as an *absolute* end (see n. 110, p. 233), except only happiness. ' All ' other ends,' according to Bossuet, ' are relative and ' intermediate ; *the one* absolute end is felicity. We ' can never aim at virtue, because of its virtuousness ; ' we can never aim at pleasure, because of its imme- ' diate pleasurableness ; we desire neither virtue nor ' present pleasure, except merely as means to perma- ' nent felicity. Look at that miserable man, enmeshed ' in a sinful habit, who consents to temptation, under ' a deep sense of the injury which he inflicts on his ' own happiness by doing so ; his one motive for ' sinning, is the *desire* of that happiness, in regard ' to which he knows and most deeply feels, that *his sin* ' *will impair it*. Look at that ecclesiastical student, ' who commits a deliberate imperfection, while distinctly ' remembering that his eternal happiness would be ' better promoted by refraining from such commission ; ' it is his *desire of happiness*, which influences him, ' knowingly and consciously to do that, which will ' infallibly *lessen* such happiness.' Argument seems almost impertinent, when directed against a thesis, so manifestly, so monstrously, at variance with facts. Yet it will be better to examine it, somewhat more accurately than we have yet done.

170. There are three different senses, in which this Felicity-thesis may imaginably be maintained. First it may be asserted, that we always act at every moment in that direction, which we *speculatively believe* most conducive to our permanent and ultimate happiness. According to this version of the thesis, the avaricious man speculatively believes the acquisition of money to be his greatest possible happiness; and the sensualist speculatively believes, that his sum of happiness, here and hereafter, will on the whole be augmented, by committing the various sins forbidden by the Sixth Commandment. Vasquez replies very obviously, that, according to this version, every *sinner* must be a *heretic;* nay, we may add, every one who commits *deliberate*

imperfection must be a heretic. Nor need it be added, that Experience is as diametrically opposed to this version as is sound Theology. In this most extravagant of all shapes, no one of course ever dreamed of advocating the thesis which we are opposing. Whatever Bossuet meant,—and it is difficult to imagine what he *did* mean,—he never can have intended this.

(2.) A more modified version of the Felicity-thesis may run as follows. 'A speculative opinion is most ' different from a practical impression. We by no ' means maintain, that man always pursues, what he ' speculatively believes most conducive to his happiness; ' but what at the moment *practically impresses him* as ' thus conducive. When temptation assails him, the ' tempting object, from its proximity and from the ' violence of his present emotion, *practically* over- ' shadows that, which, though immeasurably more in- ' tense, yet is future and distant. At the moment, of ' sinning then, his *practical impression* is, that he thus ' obtains his greatest happiness.'

Yet a moment's consideration will shew, that this allegation is no less undeniably opposed to Experience, than is the former. Is it not the commonest phenomenon in the world, as we lately stated, that men yield to temptation, with a keen feeling of remorse, and with the strongest practical impression that they are thus injuring their real happiness? When they gratify *e. g.* the Propension of the Flesh, while at the same moment their Propension of Duty and Self-charity inflict on them a severe pang,— I say it is their *practical impression* at the very moment of sinning, and not merely their speculative opinion, that they are sacrificing permanent happiness to present pleasure.

Experience then is most violently opposed to this second version of the Felicity-thesis. But sound Theology is no less opposed to it; for it utterly overthrows the doctrine of Liberty. At this moment I am assailed by some temptation; and my practical impression either is, or is not, that I shall promote my permanent happiness by succumbing. If it is *not*, then (according to this thesis) I háve no *power* to succumb ; if it *is, then* I have no power to *abstain* from succumbing. You will reply perhaps, that I may set to work to *change* this practical impression; but such a reply merely puts the difficulty one step further back. Is it my practical impression, that I shall promote my permanent happiness *by* thus setting to work? If so, according to Bossuet, I am *necessitated* thus to act. Is the reverse my practical impression? then, according to Bossuet, I am *unable* so to act.

Now the doctrine of Liberty is established by Reason, as well as declared by Revelation. We see therefore that Revelation, Reason, Experience, stand all in the most direct and undeniable opposition to this Felicity-thesis, even in the most plausible shape which it can possibly assume.

(3.) At last perhaps nothing more is meant, than that man always pursues present pleasure. If by this it be meant that this is always his *one* end, we have already refuted the statement by anticipation: for we have shewn that man can pursue future pleasure, no less than present; and that he can also pursue ' bonum honestum.' (See nn. 118, 9, p. 243, 5.) According to this version of the thesis indeed, no single virtuous act is physically possible. (See n. 56, p. 123.)

If on the other hand it be only intended to say, that at every moment *some part* of the Will's energy is directed to present pleasure,—I am inclined indeed to regard so universal a statement as mistaken (see n. 118, p. 245); but the whole matter is of the smallest possible importance. There can be no doubt that, in the vast majority of instants through the day, the will *is* aiming in some degree at present pleasure; that pleasure is *one* of the various ends, which actuate and impel it: and if any one thinks that this is the case universally and without exception, I am not aware of any kind of evil result, which would follow from such an opinion. I need not however say, how widely removed is such a statement, from the thesis against which we are arguing; the thesis, viz. not that the will aims *partially*, but that it aims *exclusively*, at happiness; and that from the constitution of our nature it *can* aim at nothing else.

In real truth, the only difficulty I find in dealing with this thesis, is the difficulty of understanding how any sane man can possibly have maintained it.

171. But indeed it seems to me a complete mistake, to maintain that there is *any* one end of all human action. It is not merely a mistake, I say, to maintain that *happiness* is such an end, but that there is *any* such. On the contrary, it has been shewn (I think) in nn. 118, 119, p. 243–6, that there are just as many absolute ends of human action, as there are 'bona honesta' and 'delectabilia' within human cognizance.

To this an obvious reply will immediately be made. ' In saying this, you are running counter to the ' unanimous voice of theologians; for they all agree in ' asserting, that there is but one absolute end of human ' action, viz. Beatitude. You may raise questions, no ' doubt, as to what is *meant* by ' Beatitude;' we can by ' no means take for granted that it is identical with ' 'happiness;' but that Beatitude (whatever is meant by ' the term) is the one absolute end of human action, is ' the assertion undoubtedly and undoubtingly made by ' the great body of theologians.'

I reply (1) that one most eminent school of theologians, viz. the Scotists, have invariably *denied* the statement altogether, that Beatitude is the real end of all human action; and in the ante-Tridentine period, the Scotists were one of the *two* great schools which divided Theology between them. I reply (2) that, among post-Tridentine theologians, the most eminent of those who adopt the statement in *words*, have *explained* it, in a sense absolutely identical with the proposition which I have been maintaining. I will first make good this latter allegation.

Lugo, so far as I am aware, in no part of his works makes any such statement, as that Beatitude is the absolute end of all human action; or that men in every act aim at Beatitude. Vasquez however, Suarez, Viva, and others, do make that statement; and now let us see in what *sense* they make it. The following from Vasquez will shew *his* interpretation of the phrase:—

" Potissima in præsenti controversiâ difficultas est, in assignandâ ratione, ob quam dicatur quis omnia bona, quæ appetit, appetere propter ultimum finem: omnes enim scholastici, excepto Scoto, in eo conveniunt, ut dicant omnia bona, quæ appetuntur, appeti propter ultimum finem : nomine autem ultimi finis intelligimus rationem optimi finis, qui dicitur esse Beatitudo nostra, sive in hâc re sive in aliâ eam esse dicamus. Scotus tamen (in 4 distinctione 49. quæstione 10 §. ' ex his sequitur,') negat omnia bona, quæ appetimus, appeti à nobis propter ultimum finem. Id verò probat primùm, 'quia potest quis appetere aliquod bonum singulare, *ratione bonitatis ipsius singularis, nihil cogitando de Beatitudine;* ergò potest aliquid appetere, quod non appetat propter Beatitudinem: nemo enim potest appetere aliquid propter aliquem finem, si de fine non cogitavit. Deinde potest quis appetere aliquid, quod verè sciat esse *contra veram Beatitudinem;* ut occidere seipsum : et fidelis homo *appetit peccatum mortale, quod certò credit esse contra veram Beatitudinem.* Ergò non omnia quæ appetit homo, appetit propter Beatitudinem.'

"Communis autem et vera sententia est, omnia bona, quæ à nobis appetuntur, *aliquo modo* appeti propter Beatitudinem. Ita docent Sanctus Thomas in hoc articulo, Cajetanus, Conradus, et recentiores Thomistæ ibidem, et idem Cajetanus 1 parte, quæstione 82. articulo 2. dub. 2. dist. 38. quæstione 4. numero 5. Imò verò recentiores Thomistæ nonnulli affirmant, Scoti sententiam, non solùm esse contra sanctum Thomam, sed etiam contra Aristotelem 1. Ethicorum capite 1. 4. & 7 ; Ciceronem libro 1. & 2. de Finibus ; et Augustinum 19. de civitate Dei, capite 1 & 2. Existimant enim recentiores illi Thomistæ, ultimum finem à Doctoribus ita definiri, ut sit, in quem omnia referuntur, hoc est, propter quem omnia appetuntur. Verum prædicti Doctores, locis allegatis, non ita definiunt ultimum finem, quasi omnia in ipsum *actu referantur ;* sed ut talis sit, in quem *omnia referri possint,* quòd sit optimum humanæ vitæ. An verò, quidquid appetitur, *appetatur propter hunc finem,* non definiunt ; tametsi August. alio in loco, quem inferiùs citabimus, hanc communem sententiam, et optimo sensu, *quem nos etiam inferiùs adducemus,* explicatam, planè tradiderit. . . . .

"His suppositis, duo sunt modi defendendi et confirmandi prædictam sententiam, quam contra Scotum diximus veriorem esse. Prior est Caietani in hoc articulo, ad primum Scoti : qui docet, omnia, quæ nos appetimus, ideò appetere propter Beatitudinem et ultimum finem, quia præcessit quædam voluntas Beatitudinis et ultimi finis, quæ ita dicitur habitu manere, ut ratione illius omnes nostræ actiones in eum finem referantur. In quâ sententiâ fuisse videtur Sanctus Thomas in hoc articulo ad. 3 & 1. parte quæstione 60. articulo 2 ; cui etiam fundamento innitens, de priori voluntate circa finem quæ præcesserit, docet quæstione 2. de virtutibus articulo 1. ad secundum, opera existentis in gratiâ esse meritoria vitæ æternæ, ex priori voluntate charitatis. Eandem rationem, et modum explicandi prædictam sententiam, videtur amplexus Durand. in 2. distinctione 38. quæstione illâ 4. numero 8. et Conrad. in hoc articulo in principio, et circa solutionem 3 : quamvis ipse alium etiam modum et rationem hujus sententiæ assignat. Convenit etiam Capreol. in primo dist. 2. q. 3. art. 1. circa primam conclusionem. " Verum hic modus explicandi hanc communem sententiam *firmum fundamentum non habet*. Primùm quidem, quia nemo probabili aliquo fundamento affirmare potest, in omnibus, qui liberè operantur, semper præcessisse voluntatem expressam ultimi finis, qui est Beatitudo nostra; ergo nullus probabili ratione adductus affirmare potest, omnia, quæ nos appetimus, ideò appetere propter ultimum finem, quia præcessit voluntas quædam ultimi finis. Deinde etiamsi præcessisset aliquando talis voluntas ultimi finis, nihilominus ea non sufficeret, ut cætera opera virtute ipsius in eundem finem referrentur. Etenim, ut optimè notarunt Bonaventura (in 2. distinctione 41. articulo primo quæstione tertiâ in corpore, et ad ultimum,) et Ricardus (ibidem articulo primo, quæstione 2.) ut ex aliquâ voluntate finis, quæ præcessit, dicantur aliqua opera sequentia in eundem finem referri, *necesse est talem voluntatem aliquo modo connecti cum sequentibus operibus*, et opera cum tali voluntate. Nam si prior voluntas omninò interrupta sit, nec cum sequentibus operibus connexa, *nullâ ratione ad ipsa opera videtur pertinere ;* ac proinde neque opera sequentia dici possunt ex tali voluntate in finem ordinari : cujus doctrinæ veritas, quam iterum repetemus (disputatione 32. capite 2. et disputatione 75. capite 2.) confirmari potest tribus modis. . . . . . .

" Jam verò, etiamsi concederemus voluntatem ultimi finis in omnibus hominibus priorem esse cæteris voluntatibus, vel quia initio vitæ præcessit, vel quia quovis die vel horâ eam resumimus, nullo tamen fundamento probabili dicere possumus, *ex hâc voluntate derivari in nobis reliquas omnes voluntates*, proximè aut remotè : ut experimento compertum est ; *neque enim singula nostra negotia ex hâc voluntate Beatitudinis universè inchoamus et prosequimur*. Ergò prædicti Doctores non rectè probant, quæcumque appetimus appetere propter Beatitudinem et ultimum finem, ratione præcedentis voluntatis circa talem finem.

" Communis igitur sententia—quæ asserit omnia, quæ appetimus, *dici aliquo modo* appeti propter ultimum finem, qui est Beatitudo,—alio faciliori modo explicari potest, *quem quidem Scotus non negaret :* ut enim colligitur ex rationibus ejus, solum negare voluit, omnia appeti propter ultimum finem, nempe propter Beatitudinem expressè apprehensam : *quod sanè verissimum est.* Facilior igitur modus explicandi prædictam communem sententiam est, quem tradiderunt Durandus et Conradus locis citatis, et videtur sequi Ferrarien (3 contra gent. cap. 17.) colligiturque ex Sancto Thoma (in hoc articulo 6. in primâ ratione); nempe ideò nos dici appetere omnia propter ultimum finem, hoc est, propter Beatitudinem universè consideratam, quia *omnia quæ appetimus, solùm appetimus sub ratione boni :* omnia autem, hoc ipso quòd bona sunt, *suâpte naturâ ad Beatitudinem videntur ordinata.* Hoc autem ità est intelligendum, non quia omnia, quæ appetimus, naturâ suâ sint ordinata ad consequendam veram Beatitudinem ; cùm multa potiùs sint omnino contraria et inepta : sed quia *in omnibus bonis participatione quâdam includitur affectus Beatitudinis.* Nam affectus Beatitudinis est, habere omne bonum et carere omni malo, sive hoc sive illo modo id fiat ; et quia desiderio cujusque rei, quam appetimus, desideramus habere aliquod bonum, et carere aliquo malo, et ita requiem aliquam invenire, quæ est veluti pars quædam Beatitudinis in universum consideratæ, — ideò dicimur omnia appetere propter Beatitudinem, etiam appetendo id quod peccatum est. . . . . . .

   " Ex quâ doctrinâ, et vero sensu hujus sententiæ, constat, quàm parùm roboris habeant rationes duæ Scoti, quæ in primo capite allatæ sunt, ad probandum non omnia, quæ nos appetimus, appetere propter Beatitudinem.   Nam prior ratio solùm probat, nos non velle omnia quæ appetimus, propter ultimum finem (Beatitudinem scilicet in universum), ratione voluntatis præcedentis, quâ omnia futura nostra opera retulerimus in talem finem : *hoc autem nos libenter fatemur ;* atque talem voluntatem, etiamsi præcessisset, ad hoc minimè sufficere capite primo demonstravimus : sed dicimus aliâ ratione nos velle omnia propter ultimum finem, quam superius in hoc capite explicuimus.   Posterior verò ratio Scoti solùm probat, multa eorum, quæ diligimus et appetimus, nihil conferre ad consequendam re ipsâ Beatitudinem in universum ; et ita *rectè probat, nos non appetere, tanquam medium ad Beatitudinis consequutionem, omnia quæ appetimus ;* et præsertim ea, quæ tali consequutioni adversari omninò cognoscimus : hoc tamen non obstat, quò minùs dicamur omnia appetere propter Beatitudinem universè consideratam, eâ ratione, quâ paulo antea in hoc capite id explicavimus, nempe ratione participationis et assimilationis *cujusdam.*"— *In* 1, 2, *Disput.* 6, c. 1 and c. 2.

   Here then we have Vasquez's doctrine ; which may be briefly expressed as follows : *   'By Beatitude is

---

   * Consider his words : ' habere aliquod bonum et carere aliquo malo, est veluti *pars quædam* Beatitudinis in universum consideratæ.'

' meant the sum of every possible bonum. Hence, in
' every act, I am in a very true sense aiming at Beati-
' tude : for I am aiming at *some* bonum or other; and
' consequently at *some* part or other of complete Beati-
' tude.'

So Viva :

" II. Quæritur 2. An quicquid homo vult, præter Beatitudinem
seu finem ultimum, necessariò velit propter illam?

" Resp. cum Vasquez, disp. 6, cap. 2. Salas, Martinonio, quòd
homo, quicquid vult præter Beatitudinem, appetat propter illam
solùm interpretativè. Ratio est, quia non appetimus bona particularia propter Beatitudinem *formaliter et expressè*, ut constat *ex-
perientiâ.* Neque *virtualiter*, ita ut ex intentione finis ultimi
præteritâ procedant omnes intentiones finium particularium; *multa
enim amamus, quin præcesserit amor ultimi finis*, vel, si præcesserit,
*non perseverat virtualiter, dum particularia bona amamus, ita ut
influat ac determinet ad istorum amorem.* Nec demùm habitualiter; tum quia non est necesse, quòd præcesserit intentio ultimi
finis ad amorem bonorum particularium; tum quia etiamsi præcesserit, potuit tamen, per voluntatem oppositam, ejus habitualis per-
severantia interrumpi : nam qui per peccatum deserit amorem
ultimi finis, non dicitur deinde alia bona appetere ex intentione
ultimi finis habitualiter perseverante; cùm ea sit interrupta per
peccatum. Quare quicquid homo appetit, præter Beatitudinem,
solùm interpretativè appetit propter illam, confusè saltem, et abs-
tracto cognitam; quatenùs quisquis particulare aliquid bonum
vult, aut malum fugit, ita *censetur* erga illud affectus, ut bonum
totale, ad quod particulare ordinatur, esset voliturus, si offerretur."
—Pars ii., d. 2, q. 4, n. 2.

And Suarez,—

" *UTRÙM OMNES ACTIONES HOMINIS SINT PROPTER ULTIMUM FINEM
SIMPLICITER, SALTEM EX INCLINATIONE.*

" Ratio dubitandi est, quia vel est sermo de fine ultimo
formali ; aut de fine ultimo materiali, seu de re illâ, ad quam homo
natura suâ tendit, ut ad ultimum finem : neutro autem modo
videtur homo operari semper propter ultimum finem. De primo
patet, quià, ut supra dixi sectione 1, num. 6, intentio finis ultimi
formalis non sufficit ad electiones faciendas; atque adeò nec ad
operandum propter finem, ex propriâ intentione ipsius hominis
operantis : ergò nec etiam naturalis proportio ad hunc finem
formalem sufficit, ut homo in omni actu suo dicatur operari
propter ultimum finem hunc, ex inclinatione naturæ; quia *non
omnia, quæ amat, sunt media ad hunc finem.* Altera pars probatur :
quia finis ultimus, ad quem homo naturâ suâ tendit, est Deus ;

sed non omnia, quæ homo operatur, tendunt in Deum; ut patet
maximè de actibus malis, seu peccatis: ergò,
    "Hæc quæstio facillimè expediri potest, suppositis his, quæ
suprà dicta sunt, in disput. 2. section 4. de variis modis operandi
propter finem: nam hic modus, de quo nunc agimus, non requirit
propriam intentionem ipsius operantis, vel præsentem, vel præteritam;
sed solùm interpretativam, quæ censetur contineri in ipso objecto
proximo humanæ operationis seu voluntatis, quatenùs illud *naturâ
suâ tendit in aliud,* vel tanquam medium ad finem, vel *tanquam
pars ad totum.*   Unde dicendum est primò, hominem in omnibus
actibus suis, tam bonis quàm malis, operari aliquo modo propter
ultimum finem formalem; ex naturali connexione cujuscumque
objecti voluntatis cum tali fine.   Ita est intelligendus D. Thom.
1. 2. q. 1. a. 6. ut clariùs idem explicuit in 4. dist. 49. quæst. 1.
artic. 3. quæstiunc. 4. ubi cæteri Theologi idem sentiunt; præter eos,
qui existimant voluntatem posse ferri in malum sub ratione mali,
quod improbabile est, ut nunc suppono.   Et colligitur eadem con-
clusio ex Arist. (1, Ethicorum capite 4 et 7. et 1. Rhetor. cap. 5,)
et est frequens apud Augustin. (10. Confess. cap. 20 et 21. e lib. 11.
de Trinit. cap. 6. lib. 19. de Civit. capite 1, et lib. de Epicureis et
Stoicis.) 'Nam qui et bonus est,' inquit, 'ideò bonus est, ut beatus
sit; et qui malus est, malus non esset, nisi inde beatum se posse
esse speraret.'   Secundò, ratio est clara; quia homo *naturaliter
appetit complementum omnis boni;* in omni autem voluntate suâ
appetit saltem partem, seu inchoationem aliquam, hujus boni: ergò
implicitè et interpretativè appetit quidquid appetit, quatenùs *confert
aliquo modo ad suum completum bonum;* et hoc est amare illud
interpretativè propter ultimum finem formalem.   Confirmatur, et
explicatur: quia licèt *non præcedat in homine intentio elicita hujus
finis,* præcedit tamen naturalis propensio in illum; et ab hoc
procedunt omnes actus circa particularia bona: ergò saltem
impetu naturæ omnes tendunt in hujusmodi finem.   In quibus
rationibus intelligitur, hoc non solùm procedere in actionibus
liberis, sed etiam in omni appetitu cujuscumque boni.   Intelligitur etiam, hanc habitudinem particularium finium seu objec-
torum ad ultimum finem formalem, non tam esse medii ad finem
propriè loquendo, quàm *partis ad totum; secundùm veritatem, aut
saltem secundùm apparentiam et similitudinem:* ut rectè D. Th.
explicuit.   Nam quando homo appetit, v. gr. voluptatem, aliquo
modo eam existimat *partem sui completi boni;* quia licèt talis
voluptas non semper sit illa, quæ verè pertinet ad perfectionem
felicitatis humanæ, habet tamen *quandam similitudinem cum illâ.*"
—*De ultimo Fine,* disp. 3, sec. 6, nn. 1 and 2.

Oviedo, a Jesuit theologian of no very great
eminence, has happened to express the same doctrine

with extreme clearness; professing simply to follow Vasquez :—

" Hâc præmissâ explicatione Beatitudinis in communi, assero, ex eo homines omnia objecta prosequi propter Beatitudinem in communi, quia ea prosequuntur *formaliter ut bona;* sive eorum bonitas in re vera sit, sive tantùm apparens : et dum fugiunt objecta, ea fugiunt quia mala, quod est prosequi ipsorum carentiam. Unde homo, in quocumque actu, aut prosequitur bonum aut carentiam mali : *quod est prosequi partem Beatitudinis; cùm Beatitudo sita sit in cumulo omnium bonorum et carentiâ omnium malorum,* quæ secum afferunt quietem et tranquillitatem animi, et satietatem appetitûs, quam semper affectat homo in suis actibus, et inveniendam existimat in objectis quæ prosequitur. Ideò in quocumque, saltem *partem Beatitudinis sibi præfigit;* falsò tamen, dum aliquid extra Deum appetit, quia solus Deus animum Deo capacem potest replere et satiare. Appetit insuper homo partem illam Beatitudinis, dum hoc bonum appetit seu carentiam hujus mali, sub illâ ratione, sub quâ omnia quæcumque alia, quibus integra Beatitudo constituitur, ad Beatitudinem pertinent; unde in illo objecto, quod est tantùm partialis Beatitudo, seu ut pars Beatitudinis apprehenditur, *appetit homo rationem illam formalem,* ex vi cujus alia objecta, simul cum isto, Beatitudinem adæquatam constituunt; nempe rationem boni et fugam mali, in quibus appetitus quiescit, et quibus satiatur; sub quâ, ad Beatitudinem sive veram sive fictam, pertinet quidquid illam constituit."— *De Beatitudine,* Contr. i. Punct. 2, n. 11.

Yet it must not be supposed that *all* theologians, who are not Scotists, even adopt the *expression* which we have been considering. For instance, Becanus, a Jesuit whose name as a scholastic stands very high, asserts, in so many words, that we *have* the power ' *nolendi* Beatitudinem in *communi.*' This is the passage :

" Dices, ' Nemo potest nolle Beatitudinem in communi : ergò nec Beatitudinem supernaturalem in particulari, quæ consistit in Visione Beatificâ; cùm sit par ratio.' Respondeo. Verum est, quando Beatitudo apprehenditur secundùm se, sine ullâ aliâ circumstantiâ : falsum, quando apprehenditur, ut difficilis et ardua ad acquirendum. Sed contra : ' Nemo potest nolle bonum in communi, quâcunque factâ suppositione : Ergo etiam non potest nolle Beatitudinem in communi, in simili casu. Antecedens patet, quia omnis nolitio fundatur in volitione; et omnis volitio est alicujus boni.' Respondeo : Negatur consequentia; quia non est eadem ratio de *bono* in communi, et de *Beatitudine* in communi. Nam bonum in communi includitur in omni bono particulari; ac proinde nemo potest velle bonum aliquod particulare, quin simul velit bonum in communi. At *Beatitudo in communi non includitur in omni bono particulari;* quia significat bonum integrum et consummatum, quod non invenitur in omni bono particulari. Unde potest quis velle bonum aliquod particulare, quod repugnet Beatitudini in communi; et consequenter *potest nolle Beatitudinem in communi.*"—*De Beat.* cap. i. quæst. xi. n. 4.

Sporer again, certainly one of the most eminent writers on Moral Theology, thus expresses himself :—

" Hanc libertatem habet homo pro hoc statu, quoad omnia prorsùs objecta; tam ipsum ultimum finem, quàm media quæcumque. Quia nimirum nullum omnino objectum, in hâc vitâ, tam necessariò apparet prosequendum; ut omissio actûs circa illud non etiam aliquam rationem boni habeat. Quin *ipsam etiam Beatitudinem, in hâc vitâ, nec libet nec expedit semper actu appetere.*"— *De Actibus Humanis,* n. 7.

And these words of Bellarmine, which I have already quoted in a different connection, to say the least, breathe a spirit greatly at variance with the statement, that men are always aiming at Beatitude :—

" Est *incredibilis quædam negligentia* in iis, quæ ad beatè vivendum, tum in hâc vitâ, tum etiam post mortem, pertinent."— *De Amiss. Grat.* lib. vi. cap. 10.

You will have observed Vasquez' language, in regard to Scotus. He says expressly, that Scotus would freely hold his (Vasquez') *doctrine;* and he implies therefore, that the difference is merely one of *words.* In regard to that question of words, for myself I most earnestly follow Scotus: I cannot but consider that great confusion and misunderstanding is likely to ensue, so long as the statement which we have been considering is generally admitted into Theology. According to the same mode of speech, as it seems to me, I might say, that the one motive which influences every day-labourer in England to pursue his vocation, is his desire of realizing a million of money. According to our opponents, it may be properly said that man in every act aims at Beatitude, because in every act he aims at some bonum or other, and every bonum is a *part* of Beatitude. I reply, that, according to the same mode of expression, every day-labourer is aiming at the possession of a million of money : because he is aiming at the possession of some small sum; and every small sum is *part* of a million pounds.

All those theologians whom I have cited, you see, plainly hold what I hold; viz. that, instead of there being any one absolute end of human action, there are as many distinct ends, as there are distinct bona within human cognizance. No one can doubt then, that any Catholic, who considers this to be the view indicated by genuine psychological investigation, has the fullest liberty to embrace it. Nor would this liberty be one whit less, even though it were true that St. Thomas or St. Augustine is differently minded.

You may ask me however, what I consider to *be* St. Thomas' doctrine on the subject. In the first place it would seem perfectly clear, that with him 'Beatitude' is by no means synonymous with 'happiness,'—if we consider only what he says in one single article, 1, 2, q. 4, a. 2. In that article he decides, that the Vision of God is a more principal part of Beatitude, than is the delight which follows on that Vision. Our eternal *happiness* on the other hand consists, beyond all possible question, in that delight itself, and in nothing else. Hence our eternal happiness, according to St. Thomas, is not even the principal part of our Eternal Beatitude.

In the second place however, I cannot persuade myself that St. Thomas' meaning is accurately represented by Vasquez and Viva. I hold their doctrine as most certainly *true;* but I cannot persuade myself, that it is St. Thomas' doctrine. What St. Thomas' doctrine is, it is not very easy to discover; and though I do incline to a certain definite opinion on the subject, it is by no means worth while to state and defend that opinion. I have admitted that I cannot claim St. Thomas' authority, for that doctrine on the subject which appears to me true; and the question therefore

E E

what St. Thomas' precise opinion was, becomes a question of merely historical interest.

You may further ask, how far is Bossuet justified in citing St. Augustine as on his side? Both Vasquez and Oviedo maintain, and I think with reason, that when St. Augustine declares that man is ever aiming at Beatitude, he understands by that phrase no more, than the doctrine which Vasquez himself understands by it; a doctrine altogether consistent with the proposition which we have throughout maintained. If you care to examine the matter for yourselves, I would refer you to the entire passages of those theologians, from which I have taken the preceding extracts. You will there find (1) St. Augustine's statement; (2) their interpretation of that statement; and (3) their reasons (in my opinion very cogent ones) for *affixing* that interpretation.

Section II.

On the Claims of Self-Charity.

172. Since then man is no way *necessitated* (far indeed from it) to be ever aiming at his own happiness, it becomes a very practical question, how far he is *morally obliged* so to do. I will only attempt here to state the broad and general principles, which appear to me true in relation to this subject; leaving to our theological course their development and application.

173. First Principle. It is metaphysically impossible, that any act or series of actions, which is morally obligatory, shall be otherwise than conducive to my happiness on the whole; taking in the entire sum of my existence. I consider that this is both an intuitive and also an inferential truth.

(1.) It is an intuitive truth. There can be no better test of a legitimate moral intuition (as we found in Chap. I. Sect. 6) than this,—that all those who have given their Moral Faculty any considerable cultivation, agree in recognizing it as such. Now let any one, thus qualified, imagine for a moment that a duty were proposed to his performance, and at the same time that he were informed, on indisputable authority, that the sum of his happiness would be promoted by violating that duty. Surely such a supposition speaks for itself. He would consider himself, in such a case, to be under two contradictory obligations; or in other words he would intue, that such an imaginary case is metaphysically impossible.

(2.) The same truth is known to us, by way of *inference* from the Existence of a Holy Creator and Moral Governor of the World. It is evidently implied, in the very idea of such a Moral Governor, that the path

of virtue and of real permanent happiness shall in
every single case be made identical; that no one shall
obtain increase of happiness, simply from disobeying
his Creator's Command.

The Christian Revelation on the whole, as is most
evident, confirms this principle which Reason declares;
it tells us, that to every good act God has awarded
recompense, and to every bad act punishment. At the
same time there are certain facts, which, on the surface
at least, seem inconsistent with this principle. As one
instance of what I mean, take such a case as the following, which is often mentioned by theologians. A
Christian, in mortal sin, is under the moral obligation,
e. g. of confessing the Faith and undergoing mar-
tyrdom. It would appear on the surface, that, by com-
plying with this obligation, he irreparably *injures* his
own permanent happiness; for he loses those years,
which he might have devoted to repentance and good
works. I merely mention such cases here, to shew
that I have not forgotten them; for a solution of the
difficulty which they involve, we must wait for our
theological course.

174. Second Principle. It is metaphysically impossible, that one act or series of acts, shall be more
morally worthy than another, without being also more
conducive to the agent's happiness on the whole. This,
like the former, I consider to be both an intuitive
and also an inferential truth. It may be established, on
grounds precisely similar to those on which we rested
our first principle; it may be met by an objection precisely similar; and in this, as in the former case, we
defer our consideration of that objection to our theological course.

175. Third principle. Self-charity is a virtuous end
of action (nn. 54–56). Let us consider what is involved
in this statement. We have seen *e. g.* (n. 54) that
Justice is a 'virtuous end of action.' Let us see what
various propositions this implies; and let us also see how
the same propositions hold in regard to Self-charity.

(1) An act, motived by the virtuousness of Justice,

is itself virtuous; and the more so, in proportion as the will is fixed on that virtuousness with greater firmness and efficacity (see nn. 56 and 58). This holds in every respect of Self-charity. Suppose I am tempted by some immediate sinful gratification : and suppose I resist that temptation, on no other grounds than this;—viz., the virtuousness of preferring my permanent and integral happiness to the passing pleasures of a moment. In proportion as we have cultivated our Moral Faculty, we shall intue, with the greater keenness and irresistibleness, that this act is virtuous; and the more virtuous, in proportion as my will is fixed on that virtuousness with the greater firmness and efficacity.

(2.) Cæteris paribus, A is a more virtuous man than B in proportion as he has acquired the habit of Justice in a greater degree; or (in other words) as he possesses more strongly the prevalent intention (see n. 114, p. 237) of acting justly. It is very evident that in like manner, cæteris paribus, A is a more virtuous man than B, in proportion as he has acquired the habit of *Self-charity* in a greater degree; or (in other words) in proportion as he possesses more strongly the prevalent intention, of acting in accordance with his own permanent happiness. We shall see however, in the course of our theological discussion, that in the case of Self-charity we may go much further than in the case of Justice; and that the qualification ' cæteris paribus ' is unnecessary. We shall see that *simply and absolutely*, in proportion as any one grows in virtue, his prevalent intention of promoting his own permanent happiness will constantly increase.

(3.) Lastly, if I commit an unjust act, *e. g.*, refuse to return a deposit,—my act is sinful, as in various other ways, so also in this, that it is contrary to Justice. Even were it not sinful under other heads, the simple fact of its being contrary to Justice would suffice to make it so. In like manner here. If I commit any sin whatever, such an act, as it possesses various ' malitiæ,' so possesses also this, that it is opposed to Self-charity; ' contra obligationem,' as theologians say, ' procurandæ propriæ salutis;' or 'caritatis erga meipsum.' Even if (per impossibile) it were not sinful on other grounds, this alone would suffice to make it sinful.

These are the three principal truths included in the statement, that Self-charity is a 'virtuous end of action.'

176. Fourth principle. It often happens, that I avoid sin from the motive of promoting my own happiness, while yet my will is not at all directed to the *virtuousness* of that motive. I may be tempted, *e. g.*, to some sin of sensuality: and the thought of Hell-fire may protect me against the temptation, simply from *this* fact; viz., that the practical impression of that future suffering preponderates (even in the way of simple emotion) over the practical impression of present pleasure. Under these circumstances, the temptation in fact ceases; and the act of will, whereby I resolve not to commit the contemplated sin, is motived, not by the virtuousness, but by the (negative) pleasurableness, of escaping so awful a doom. 'Surely,' it may be said, 'such an act is most commendable, although not motived at all by the *virtuousness* of Self-charity.'

It is impossible certainly that an act can be virtuous, of which pleasurableness is the absolute end. In regard however to the act in question, we may say in the first place that it is at all events *indifferent;* free from the very slightest admixture of evil. This will be abundantly proved in our theological course, when we come to consider what are the characteristics of an evil act.

We may add further (and this will be our second remark on the subject) that this act, in itself indifferent, is invariably accompanied by another, which is always virtuous, and commonly virtuous in a very high degree. This virtuous act, in the particular case which we have taken as our instance, may be thus analysed: 'I 'fix my mind earnestly on the thought of Hell-fire, '—that I may escape from this temptation,—that I 'may the better conform my Will to God's, Who is so 'worthy of love;' or 'that I may obey the commands 'of my Holy Creator;' or 'that I may promote my own 'permanent happiness;' or the like. Such acts as these then vary indefinitely from each other, as to the precise motive which influences them; but in the *substance* (as distinct from the *end*) they agree.   In all such acts, the Will compels the Intellect to ponder, *e. g.*, on the awfulness of Hell-torments, so intently and resolutely, that the needed practical impression is produced, and the temptation vanishes.   And such an act is always present in the case supposed : because, when some present pleasure is offered, it is only by *means* of an effort, nay, in general of very considerable effort, (as daily experience shews) that we can bring the thought of future anguish to bear on the present pleasure, and neutralize its impression.   Acts of this kind will be specially considered in our theological course, under their recognized appellation, ' actus extrinsecè imperantes.'

Such then I consider to be the true philosophical principles, on which our theological treatment of Self-charity must throughout be based.

CHAPTER IV.

177. This is the last philosophical subject, which it will be necessary to consider in this introductory book. And in this, as in other cases, our intention is by no means to probe it to its depths; but to say only what is absolutely necessary, for the purposes of that part of Theology, which we are afterwards to treat. There are several questions, of great intricacy and difficulty, connected with the various kinds of certainty; but we shall be able (I trust) altogether to avoid these, without injuring at all the scientific completeness of our work.

Things may be certain in *themselves*, or certain *to us*.* The former kind of certainty may be called 'objective,' the latter 'subjective;' and the latter is that with which we shall commence. Things are considered certain to us, if these two conditions concur: (1) that we have in fact no doubt about them; (2) that we have fully sufficient *reason* to be thus without doubt.†

178. Subjective certainty is either (1) experimental or (2) theoretical. By experimental certainty, I mean our conviction that our various judgments of experience

---

* "Est autem duplex certitudo: *Una* objecti, id est, rei cognitæ, vel creditæ; *Altera* subjecti, id est hominis cognoscentis, vel credentis. Prior certitudo est immutabilitas rei, quæ re verâ aliter se habere non potest, quàm creditur, vel cognoscitur: quâ notione dicimus, certum esse, Deum esse bonum, peccatum esse malum. Posterior certitudo est firmitas quædam *assensûs nostri* ad rem, quæ cognoscenda vel credenda proponitur: de quâ certitudine loquimur, cùm dicimus: 'Hoc mihi est certum:' 'ego de hâc re certus sum:' 'hoc habeo pro comperto:' id est, 'ita firmiter adhæreo huic sententiæ, ut prorsùs de illius veritate non dubitem.'"—Bellarmine, *De Justificatione*, lib. iii. cap. 2, n. 2.

† "Qui *certò* credunt ea quæ *falsa* sunt, non tam *certi*, quàm *persuasi*, dici debent."—Bellarm. *De Just.* lib. iii. cap. 2, n. 5.

(see n. 1, p. 5) are correct. I feel at this moment the sensation which we call cold, or I experience the phenomenon which we call anger. That I really *do* have this feeling,—that I really *do* experience this phenomenon,—is to me a matter of 'experimental' certainty. Every other kind of subjective certainty we may call 'theoretical.'

179. The first and most important kind of 'theoretical' certainty, may be called 'fundamental:' it is our conviction that we may *trust our faculties;* that we may confidently form certain 'intuitive' judgments. See n. 6, p. 14.

180. The second kind of theoretical certainty is called 'metaphysical.' It exists, whenever, on sufficient grounds, we recognize any truth as necessary. See n. 13, p. 24. I am metaphysically certain, that a rectilineal figure of three sides has three angles; that the base angles of an isosceles triangle are equal to each other; that in a right-angled triangle the square of the hypothenuse equals the sum of the square of the sides; that there is such an attribute as moral evil, appertaining to certain actions; that Veracity and Humility are virtuous ends of action; that generosity is morally better than selfishness; that a Holy Creator exists, Infinite in all Perfections; that obedience to Him is our highest duty; &c. &c.

181. The third kind of theoretical certainty, is called 'physical.' It is that which arises necessarily, from my knowledge of this or that definite and assignable natural property, or assemblage of natural properties. See n. 165, p. 392–7. It is physically certain to me, that, unless a miracle be wrought, no human beings are able to remain supported in mid-air; that, unless a miracle is wrought, an explosion will take place, whenever fire is brought into contact with dry gunpowder; that, unless a miracle be wrought, the expectation of severe pain is itself painful; that, unless a miracle be wrought, a proud man, who receives some galling insult, will experience violent emotions of anger; &c. &c.

Two different ways of expressing ourselves, are here

possible. We may express ourselves thus: ‘It is phy-
‘ sically certain that no human being can remain in
‘ mid-air; that the expectation of pain is itself painful;’
&c. &c. Or we may express ourselves, as I have done:
‘ It is physically certain that, *unless a miracle is wrought*,
‘ these results will ensue.’ I prefer this latter mode of
expression; because otherwise physical certainty would
not be *absolute*, but only hypothetical, certainty.

182. But there are very many things, of which I am
absolutely certain, which cannot be ranked under any
of these heads. Thus I am absolutely certain that the
city of Rome exists; quite as certain as I am that fire,
put to dry gunpowder, will produce an explosion. Yet
I have never seen Rome; nor if it were alleged that all
the witnesses who testify its existence had combined to
deceive me, could it be said that this allegation is
opposed to any definite and assignable natural properties. In like manner, I am absolutely certain, that a
stout and lazy man, reasonably well off and not miserly,
will not go ten miles in two hours for the sake of a half-
crown wager. And yet no *physical* property would be
violated if he did so; he has perfect physical power to
achieve the bodily feat in question; and if he were pursued all the way by a man with a drawn sword, trying
to kill him, he probably would achieve it.

It is a characteristic of moral certainty, that it is
constituted by a gradual increase of those conditions,
which constitute probability. If three independent
witnesses assure me of Rome’s existence, the fact
becomes probable to me; if ten, very probable; if fifty,
almost certain: but long before you reach that number
and variety of informants who in fact combine their
testimony, absolute certainty has been reached. So
again, that such a man as above described will not go
four miles in two hours for such a wager, is very probable; that he will not go six, almost certain; that he
will not go anything like ten, is quite absolutely certain.
The phrase ‘morally certain’ is sometimes used indeed
in a *less* strict sense, to express that which is in *the very
greatest degree probable*, though not quite absolutely

certain. But this sense of the word is wholly distinct from our use of it in this Chapter; and indeed (to prevent confusion) I shall never myself use the phrase in any such sense.*

183. So much on subjective certainty, or things certain to us: but there is also an *objective* certainty; there are things certain *in themselves.* Here indeed an obvious difficulty may be interposed. 'Of course very ' many things are certain in themselves: for of *every* ' *thing* which ever happened or ever will happen, we ' may truly say, that it *certainly* happened,—that it ' *certainly* will happen.' Such certainty is 'à posteriori;' and the remark is undoubtedly true. But there are many things 'objectively' certain 'à priori;' and it is of these things that it is important to speak.

Truths are ' objectively certain à priori,' when there are grounds for certainly knowing them, quite independently of any *direct* knowledge, that they have existed or will exist. And yet it may happen very frequently indeed, that these truths are not certain *to us:* because we have not the means of knowing these grounds; or have not the faculties, enabling us to deduce from them their legitimate inference. Thus, there is a very large number of mathematical truths, *objectively* certain; to the *Angels* perhaps *subjectively*

---

* "Evidentia Metaphysica est, quando clarè apparet, rem nullo modo posse aliter se habere : v. g. duo et duo esse quatuor; nihil posse simul esse, et non esse ; et alia similia. Evidentia autem Physica est, quando constat clarè, rem, licèt metaphysicè possit aliter se habere, non tamen physicè, seu *attentâ virtute causarum physicarum et naturalium;* v. g. ignem applicatum subjecto capaci calefacere ; sub accidentibus panis dari panis substantiam ; et similia. Denique Evidentia Moralis dicitur, quando, licèt metaphysicè non repugnet contrarium, neque etiam physicè, hoc est, attentâ virtute causarum naturalium,—apparet tamen clarè talis et tanta difficultas, ut ratione illius *numquam contrarium ponatur, vel ponendum credatur, in aliquo casu.* Et ideò dicimus esse Evidentiam Moralem apud nos, de *existentiâ regionis Indicæ,* quam nunquam vidimus : quia licèt, attentâ virtute causarum naturalium, non repugnet physicè, quod omnes, qui nobis testificati sunt de Indiâ mentiri voluerint ; hoc tamen ipsum est adeò difficile, ut non credamus id unquam eventurum, ut tot tamque diversi testes convenerint ad volendum nos decipere ; et cum tantâ uniformitate et constantiâ nobis eadem, diversis etiam temporibus et locis, testificentur, absque ullâ discrepantiâ : et idcirco dicimus, nos habere Moralem Evidentiam, et plusquàm fidem humanam, de Indicâ regione; quod sufficit, ut intellectus convincatur, nec possit, nisi per summam dementiam et obstinationem, dissentire."—LUGO, *De Fide,* Disp. 2, n. 40.

certain ; but which no *man* has ever yet proved or even thought of.

Objective à priori certainty is either ' metaphysical,' ' physical,' or ' moral :' a division which altogether corresponds, to the division of 'subjective certainty.' All necessary truths, whether we recognize them as such or not, are ' metaphysically' certain à priori. Every truth is 'physically' certain à priori, which results from definite and assignable laws of nature; and there are, I need not say, multitudes of such truths, whereof we have no suspicion. The law of gravitation, *e. g.* was physically certain à priori in Homer's time no less than in our's; it has become *subjectively* certain only within the last centuries. Every truth which is ' objectively certain à priori,' and yet neither metaphysically nor physically certain, is 'morally certain à priori.'

184. If any truth is certain à priori, its contradictory is ' impossible :' and there are therefore the same kinds of 'impossibility,' which there are of objective à priori certainty. Thus it is metaphysically impossible, that there can be a triangle, whose united angles shall exceed two right angles; or that a rational creature can, without sin, refuse obedience to his Holy Creator. It is physically impossible, that, unless a miracle be wrought, a stout man can walk on a bridge made of ordinary paper; or a proud man receive a galling insult, without experiencing emotions of rage. It is morally impossible, that a stout lazy man, reasonably well off and not miserly, shall go ten miles in two hours, for the sake of a half-crown wager.*

We have said as much on this subject of certainty and impossibility, as is requisite for our subsequent Theology. At the same time I am well aware, how extremely superficial our remarks have been, if they are considered as any approach to a full philosophical treatment of the whole matter.

* " Ad hoc enim ut aliquid sit moraliter impossibile, duo requiruntur ; nec unum sine altero sufficit : scilicet quòd illud nunquam fuerit, vel futurum sit, imò nec videatur futurum sub conditione, in hâc vel aliâ simili hypothesi ; et præterea, quòd hoc ipsum oriatur ex summâ difficultate, quam oporteret vincere ad ponendum illud."—LUGO, *De Incarnatione,* disp. 2, n. 14.

APPENDIX

THE FIRST CHAPTER.

On the Relation between God and Necessary Truth.

185. I BEGAN the first Chapter of this Book, with the intention of avoiding this subject; as being of an exclusively philosophical interest. See n. 13, p. 26 ; n. 21, p. 53 ; n. 22, p. 56 ; and n. 75, p. 152. As I proceeded however, my view of the case changed. The principles maintained in the first Chapter, especially in the second and third Sections, seem to me of the most extreme importance ; insomuch that unless they are both thoroughly accepted and most clearly apprehended, great part of the theological edifice will be utterly destitute of any secure foundation. And yet there is one difficulty, which indisposes various thinkers to accept those principles, which it is quite impossible to solve, without carefully investigating the relation which exists between God and necessary truth. I may add also, that in one or two passages, which occur in the earlier part of the first Chapter, I was obliged to express myself very awkwardly and confusedly, precisely *because* of my then intended omission.

We *assume* then the Existence of God : we will first consider the relation between that God and mathematical truth ; and we will then apply to moral truth, the principles which we shall have established.

186. It may be *assumed* of course, that mathema-

tical truth *is* necessary. Every rectilineal figure of three sides has *necessarily* three angles : the base angles of an isosceles triangle are *necessarily* equal to each other. If this truth were called in question, it must follow that no one of our faculties can be trusted. (See n. 6, p. 14.) Every one of ordinarily cultivated mind intues, that the mathematical axioms are necessary; and intues, that the validity of the reasoning process is necessary also. From these two propositions then we *infer*, that all those *other* truths are necessary, which are deduced *from* those axioms *by* that reasoning process.

187. Now let us consider two negative propositions, which are implied by this word ' necessary,' in regard to mathematical truth.

(1.) Necessary truths are not derived from *God's Command*. No one will say, that a rectilineal three-sided figure has three angles rather than four, for *this* reason ; viz. because God has so *commanded*. In saying that the axiom in question is *necessary*, I imply the negation of this very statement, that its truth arises from God's Command. Nor is there any kind of difficulty, in holding that verities *may* exist independently of God's Command. Consider those very fundamental verities, God's Self-Existence and Indestructibility : what could be more monstrous than to say, that they originate in a Divine command?

(2.) There is a second negative proposition, implied by the word ' necessary,' which a moment's thought will shew to be equally undeniable with the former. Necessary truths do not derive their verity, from the fact that *God necessarily intues them*. Rather the very opposite is the fact : God necessarily intues them, *because* they are necessary truths. Who would say *e. g.* that God is necessarily Self-Existent, *because* He intues Himself to be so ? On the contrary of course : He intues Himself to be so, *because* He *is* so. In like manner He necessarily intues the base angles of an isosceles triangle to be necessarily equal, because they *are* necessarily equal ; He necessarily intues that

the three angles of every triangle together necessarily
equal two right angles, or that the square of the hypothenuse necessarily equals the sum of the squares of
the sides, because in each instance the truth *is* so.

It is indeed (as is manifest) the very excellence of
God's Intellect, that it is necessarily determined by
Truth; or in other words His Intellectual Perception
depends on Truth, not Truth upon His Intellectual Perception.

What Vasquez says of moral truth, is applicable
to all necessary truth of whatever kind. ' Ante omnem
' Dei Voluntatem et Imperium, immò etiam ante omne
' *Judicium*,' this truth must be conceived as existing;
' præcedens, secundùm rationem, omne Judicium Divini
' Intellectûs.' (See n. 30, p. 81). It follows therefore,
that through all Eternity God is constantly and necessarily gazing on the vast mass of necessary mathè-
matical truth.

188. But now is the assertion endurable, that God
is gazing through all Eternity on some mass of necessary truth, *external* to and *independent* of Himself?
on truth, *co-eternal* with Himself, and yet *distinct* from
Himself? on truth, *equally necessary* with Himself, and
yet *not* Himself? Surely not : and thus we are led to
the conclusion stated in n. 22 (p. 55). We infer, that
mathematical truth is *not* distinct from God Himself;
that (in some way wholly incomprehensible to us) it
is identified with Him; that, in gazing on it, He is not
gazing on something external to Himself, but merely
penetrating and comprehending the depths of His Own
Nature. That this fact is totally mysterious, I of
course fully admit; though really not more so, than is
every proposition which concerns the Incomprehensible
Creator. It is totally mysterious : but there is no
difficulty whatever (so far as I am aware) in the way
of our receiving it.

189. The sum of the matter then is this. It could
lead to nothing less than complete and total scepticism,
if the least doubt were thrown on the proposition, that
mathematical truth is necessary ; but if it *be* necessary,

then it exists without the slightest dependence on any exercise of the Divine Intellect or Will. On the other hand, to say that anything *can* thus necessarily exist, which is not *identical* with God, this is to put forth a statement, the difficulty of which is at all events extremely great, and appears to me altogether insurmountable. Hence we are brought, by the very exigency of the case, to that one hypothesis, which avoids all difficulties, and harmonizes all data; that hypothesis, which admits all that reason testifies, on the absolute independence possessed by necessary truth; while it even deepens and intensifies our apprehension, of God's Greatness and Incommunicable Necessity.*

190. Let us now apply these principles to moral truth. It has been shewn most abundantly (I trust) in the First Chapter, that such propositions as the following are necessary, in the very same sense in which mathematical propositions are necessary. 'The commands of a Holy Creator are of moral obligation.' 'A Holy Creator cannot command us to cherish the spirit of pride or vindictiveness.' 'Justice and Benevolence are virtuous ends of action.' 'The conduct of one who aims at perfection is (so far) morally preferable to that of one who does not so aim.' To deny the necessity of moral truth, would no less inevitably lead to complete scepticism, than to deny the necessity of mathematical truth.

191. Let us consider then, in the case of moral truth, as we have already done in the case of mathematical, certain negative propositions, which are implied by this word ' necessary.'

(1.) Necessary truths are not derived from God's command. The truth, *e. g.* that Justice and Bene-

---

* It may be objected, that I here express myself with much more confidence on the certainty of this hypothesis, than I did in the first Chapter. See n. 22 (p. 55), where I only speak of it as a theory to which I *most strongly incline*. The fact is, that I had actually written a sentence expressing confident belief in its truth; but I erased it for the following reason. I did not intend at that time to enter into the grounds on which the theory rests; and as I am aware of comparatively little producible Catholic authority in its behalf, I thought it was not right to express such complete conviction in its favour, as I really felt.

volence are virtuous ends of action, is not in any way derived from the circumstance that God commands them: on the contrary;—He commands them, because they are virtuous ends of action. So again, that other truth,—' the Commands of a Holy Creator are of moral obligation,'—is not derived from any Command of God: on the contrary, it is that very truth, which *gives* to the various Commands of God their legitimate authority over our conduct. No more however need be said, on a matter so fully argued in the Third Section.

(2.) Neither are necessary moral truths derived, from the fact that God necessarily intues them; on the contrary, God necessarily intues them, *because* they are necessary truths. God necessarily intues that Justice and Benevolence are virtuous ends of action, because they necessarily *are* so.

(3.) There is a third negative proposition, which is of importance in the case of moral truth, though it would be unmeaning in the case of mathematical. On this third negative proposition therefore, we must speak somewhat more at length.

It is sometimes said then, that pride, and lying, and vindictiveness, are necessarily evil, because God necessarily detests them. But the very opposite is undoubtedly true. This third negative proposition is in fact altogether analogous to our second. We have already seen, that these qualities are not necessarily evil *because* God necessarily intues them to be so; but the very contrary: God necessarily *intues* them to be so, because they *are* so. Precisely similar is the case here. These qualities are not necessarily evil, because God necessarily detests them; but the exact contrary: God necessarily detests them, *because* they are necessarily evil. It is the very excellence of God's Intellect, as we have seen, that it is necessarily determined by what is true; and in precisely the same manner, it is the very excellence of His Will, that it is necessarily determined by what is good. It is not that the object is good, *because* God's Will is necessarily determined

F F

PHILOSOPHICAL INTRODUCTION.

to it; but the very reverse: His Will is necessarily determined to it, *because* it is good.*

192. We see then that these various moral propositions are necessary, altogether independently of any Act whatever, elicited by the Divine Intellect or the Divine Will. To quote again Vasquez' words;—' Ante

* Since however it is of extreme importance to make this point perfectly clear, I will run the risk of wearying my reader, rather than of falling short in necessary proof. Those of my readers who are already convinced, may easily save their time and trouble by simply omitting to read the present note. In n. 22 (p. 57) I make the following remark. Five arguments had been brought forward by me in n. 20, against those who maintain that the term ' morally evil' is synonymous with the term ' forbidden by my Creator;' and in the passage referred to I observed, that these arguments are available with precisely equal force, against those who maintain, that the term ' morally evil' is synonymous with the term ' necessarily *detested* by my Creator.' Such was my statement; and I now proceed to enforce it at somewhat greater length. I implied indeed that the first of these five arguments is not so obviously applicable as the other four; but a very little modification will make it so, as will be immediately seen. I will beg my readers then to refresh their memory of the various arguments adduced in n. 20 (pp. 43–53), that they may the more readily see how easily the same arguments are available in the case before us.

All mankind agree that certain acts,—contrary *e. g.* to the virtues of Justice, Veracity, and Benevolence,—are morally evil. Our opponents maintain, that by this is merely meant ' necessarily detested by the Creator.' This is the allegation, against which our arguments are to be directed.

(1.) ' Our Creator necessarily detests what is morally evil.' Certainly this is no *tautologous* proposition (see p. 44), but one of the most real and important propositions in the whole world; it is the very foundation of our whole belief in God's Sanctity. Yet on our opponent's view it is simply tautologous. According to him, the term ' morally evil' simply *means* ' necessarily detested by our Creator:' hence, according to him, the above proposition will be no other than this;—' Our Creator necessarily detests what He necessarily detests.'

(2.) On our opponent's view, the proposition ' our Creator is Holy' is literally destroyed and emptied of all meaning. The whole second argument may here be read, as it stands from p. 46 to p. 48: only instead of '*forbidden* by our Creator' here we must say ' *detested* by our Creator.'

(3.) We can easily *imagine*, that certain rational beings had been created by a demon, who *detests* Benevolence, Humanity, and Purity. Would these qualities then be *morally evil* in such beings? See the third argument from page 48 to p. 50.

(4.) I have no means of knowing that my Creator *does* detest injustice, mendacity, and malevolence, unless I first know that these qualities are intrinsically evil, *apart* from His detestation. See the fourth argument from page 50 to p. 52.

(5.) God is *necessitated* to detest malevolence, impurity, and the rest. But this would be a very great imperfection, unless they were intrinsically evil, *independently* of His detestation. See the fifth argument from page 52 to page 53. See also pp. 57 and 8.

' omne (Dei) Imperium, ante omnem Voluntatem, immò
' ante omne *Judicium*, est regula quædam harum ac-
' tionum, quæ suâpte naturâ constat.' (See n. 30, p. 81.)
193. We have seen that God is necessarily gazing
on mathematical truth through all Eternity; and the
same is now established in regard to moral truth
also. In accordance with His attribute ' Verus in
cognoscendo,' He intues the whole Natural Rule, in
its widest sense, and of course with the most unfailing
accuracy. (See n. 74, p. 150.) Nay indeed we may
go immeasurably further than this. He intues what
would be morally evil, what *would* be of obligation,
what *would* be preferable, *under every possible circumstance*, in which any rational creature could be placed.
The whole mass of moral truth then is as vast and
apparently inexhaustible, as the whole mass of mathematical truth. Let us call this vast body of truth by
the general name the ' Moral Rule:' The ' Natural
Rule' being that comparatively small part of the
' Moral Rule,' which applies to mankind; to us, with
that nature, and under these circumstances, in which
God has thought fit to place us.

But now moral truth gives scope to another Attribute altogether of God, as well as the attribute
'Verus in cognoscendo:' it gives scope to the Attribute ' Sanctus.' In virtue of that Attribute, God necessarily detests, that which is intrinsically evil; and
necessarily prefers, that which is intrinsically preferable. Again, on the supposition of His *freely* creating
rational persons, and *freely* placing them under certain
circumstances, He *necessarily* commands them, to do
that which is of intrinsic obligation; He *necessarily*
prohibits, that which is intrinsically evil; He *necessarily* counsels, that which is intrinsically preferable.
(See n. 86, p. 188–90.)

But here again, as in the case of mathematical truth,
we make one final enquiry. Is the assertion endurable,
that God is gazing from all Eternity on some body of
necessary truth, external to, and independent of, Himself? Nay, that He is regulating necessarily His whole

conduct by a Rule, which is co-eternal with Himself, and yet distinct? which is equally necessary with Himself, and yet *not* Himself?

It is quite *incredible*. This great mass of necessary moral truth, whereof the Natural Rule is but a small portion, is not distinct from God Himself; but in some way, wholly incomprehensible to us, it is identified with Him. In gazing on it, in regulating necessarily His conduct by its dictates, He gazes on nothing external to Himself; He constitutes nothing, external to Himself, as the authoritative rule of His actions; He is but penetrating and comprehending the depths of His own Nature.

It must not be understood from this, that the Natural Rule is simply the Natural Law. Very far indeed from it. The Natural Law flows from the Divine *Will;* but the Natural Rule, and the Moral Rule of which it is a part, is altogether *independent* of the Divine Will, and is its necessary Rule of Action. The Natural Law *follows* God's resolve, to create rational persons, of such a nature, and to be placed under such circumstances; but the *Moral Rule*, in order of nature, *precedes* all this.

194. Here we see the force of an expression, which is very often used by Catholic writers. It is often said, that if God revealed false doctrine, *e.g.* or commanded mendacity, He would falsify or contradict His Own Nature. The Moral Rule, we have seen, is identical with His Own Nature: to contradict that Rule, would be to contradict Himself.

195. This conclusion, that the Natural Rule is identical with God, is based on the same grounds, which establish the parallel conclusion in the case of mathematical truth: in this case, as in that, such a conclusion is the only possible mode of avoiding objections, otherwise insuperable. But there are reasons in this case, of quite a different kind, which *also* press most strongly towards the same conclusion. Those various intuitions, which point to the Natural Rule, point also to that Rule as *identified with some Superior*

Being. I recognize that Rule, as an authority which legitimately claims my most abject and unreserved submission; which possesses by right an absolutely paramount and indefeasible claim on my allegiance. Is it possible to think that such an authority as this is a mere abstraction? Who can suppose it? Surely, in intuing such an authority, we intue a *Personal Being* : and so the unanimous testimony of mankind proclaims. Indeed, among all the various ways whereby men are drawn to a knowledge of their Creator, there is probably none so universally efficacious, as that which leads them to Him, through their obeying the Moral Voice within them.*

196. We are thus able to give a far more satisfactory explanation, than is otherwise possible, of a recognized Catholic phrase: ' bona opera naturâ suâ *tendunt* ad Deum.' It is always said by theologians, that an act, done for the sake of abstract ' bonum honestum,' *in its own nature* tends to God. On our view this is most intelligible. In intuing abstract ' bonum honestum,' we are all in real truth intuing God, though we know it not. (See n. 22, p. 55.)

197. Finally it may be asked, ' is this Moral Rule the same thing with that ' Eternal Law' of which theologians speak? for Perrone (see p. 111) seems to think that it is so.' No general answer however, I think, can be given to this question; for the senses are most various, in which that phrase ' the Eternal Law' is used. If St. Thomas' sense be the one taken, (see 1, 2, q. 91, a. 1) plainly the ' Eternal Law' is totally different from that ' Moral Rule ' of which we have been speaking.

198. I may make a concluding remark, on a matter totally different and purely verbal. It may be asked, whether it is suitable to use the word 'intuition,' as I have throughout done; as applying equally to ' true ' and ' false ' intuitions. ' Is not the word,' you may ask, ' always so used, as to imply the *truth* of that which is ' intued ' ?' It seems to me more conformable with

* See the second part of the quotation from Father Newman in the note at p. 143.

analogy, to use the word as I have used it.   We speak of true or false *reasoning;* why not of true or false intuitions?   There are two principal functions of the Intellect; to intue and to reason : (see Tapparelli quoted in note to p. 19).   If, when the second of the two is performed amiss, we yet *call* the process ' reasoning,'—when the first of the two is performed amiss, it should equally be called ' intuition.'

199. And I will take this opportunity of supplying an accidental omission.   In n. 85 (p. 188) we made this remark.   Suppose that, independently of God's Preference, act A is subjectively better than act B, but that God intimates to me His preference ' hìc et nunc ' for act B : in this case act B becomes to an indefinite extent intrinsecally better.   I should have cited a passage from Lugo, corroborative of this view; which passage I here subjoin :

" Si Deus consuleret hìc et nunc complecti objectum ex se minùs perfectum, v. g. matrimonium omissâ virginitate ;—vel si consuleret actum minùs intensum omisso intensiori ;— tunc nulla esset imperfectio electio matrimonii vel elicere actum minùs intensum : immò *esset major perfectio;* quia excessus, quem virginitas vel actus intensus habebunt ex se, abundè compensatur et superatur, per *circumstantiam* consilii vel majoris beneplaciti Divini, quod esset in opposito." — *De Incarnatione,* d. 26, n. 131.

London :—Printed by G. BARCLAY. Castle St. Leicester Sq.

CPSIA information can be obtained
at www.ICGtesting.com
Printed in the USA
BVHW081616220819
556561BV00018B/3929/P